CONTENT AREA READING

AN INDIVIDUALIZED APPROACH

MARY M. DUPUIS
EUNICE N. ASKOV

The Pennsylvania State University

Prentice-Hall, Inc., Englewood Cliffs, New Jersey 07632

Library of Congress Cataloging in Publication Data

Dupuis, Mary M.
    Content area reading.

    Includes bibliographies and index.
    1. Reading comprehension–Study and teaching–Teacher
training.   2. Individualized reading instruction–
Teacher training.   3. Study, Method of–Handbooks,
manuals, etc.   4. Teachers–In-service training.
I. Askov, Eunice Nicholson.   II. Title.
LB1050.45.D86   428.4'07'1   81-19172
ISBN 0-13-171363-9   AACR2

Printed in the United States of America

10   9   8   7   6   5   4   3   2   1

Editorial/production supervision: Maureen Connelly
Cover design: Karolina Harris
Manufacturing buyer: Edmund W. Leone

ISBN 0-13-171363-9

Prentice-Hall International, Inc., *London*
Prentice-Hall of Australia Pty. Limited, *Sydney*
Prentice-Hall of Canada, Ltd., *Toronto*
Prentice-Hall of India Private Limited, *New Delhi*
Prentice-Hall of Japan, Inc., *Tokyo*
Prentice-Hall of Southeast Asia Pte. Ltd., *Singapore*
Whitehall Books Limited, *Wellington, New Zealand*

To
    Betsy,
        David,
            Pam,
                and others like them

Contents

Preface

This book is designed for teachers of content subjects, preservice or inservice. Any teacher who deals with science, mathematics, social studies, literature, health, home economics, and other subjects will find useful teaching techniques within it. Actual teacher-tested examples of the techniques included in the book cover grades 4–12.

The major goal of the book is to help teachers feel comfortable planning and teaching reading skills necessary to understand their content material. Many content teachers feel helpless and inadequately prepared to deal with reading and their own students. This book will help them feel competent to teach reading in their subject and, therefore, more comfortable doing it.

In order to gain this confidence and competence, teachers must develop knowledge about reading and positive attitudes toward teaching reading in their own classrooms. A unique feature of this book is the assessment of both knowledge of reading and attitude toward teaching reading. These assessments are part of the Preview, to give pretest information, and part of the Conclusion, to give posttest information. The tests are self-scoring, so that readers may assess their own change in knowledge and attitude, independent of course requirements, tests, and grades. The reader's own sense of increased competence and confidence is the most important result of this assessment.

The educational philosophy underlying this book centers on *individualization*. Each student, in any grade and subject, deserves to be treated as an individual. This is especially important in reading, since reading ability varies widely within classes. Realistically, the secondary teacher with large numbers of students will aim for individual attention but will practice it in classes by grouping students differently within classes for different teaching goals. *Grouping* thus becomes the practical application of the principle of individualization.

A second facet of the book's goal is that teachers learn to integrate the teaching of reading into their content instruction. Viewed from this angle, *integration* keeps content goals as primary. Reading goals are derived by analyzing content goals, teaching style, and available resources to derive those reading skills necessary to learn the content material under discussion. The content teacher does *not* become a reading teacher. Reading is viewed as a means to the end of content reading, not as an end in itself.

Readers of this book can determine for themselves how much to tackle at any one time. The book will serve, as it has in its two previous versions, as the text for a regular two- or three-credit college course in content area reading, taught over a regular semester. It can also serve as a manual for long-term inservice programs, taking place over an academic year or more. It will also work well as a reference book for teachers throughout their teaching careers. Techniques which can't be tried during the initial course or program, often because of time constraints, can be reviewed and tried later (even several years later). Learning to teach reading in content subjects is a long-term process. Active, professional teachers find it never ending as they continually reflect on their students' needs and their own capabilities.

As with all professional materials, we hope to affect students in the schools by helping their teachers understand them better and plan more effectively for their learning. The three students the book focuses on—Betsy, David and Pam—are prototypes of the students all teachers find in their classes. We dedicate this book to Betsy, Pam and David and the thousands of students like them.

Acknowledgments

The authors wish to acknowledge the invaluable assistance of many people in developing this book. Our thanks:

To Drs. Sandra L. Snyder, Gillian M. Craig, Joyce W. Lee, and Andrea Lee from the original development and field-testing of the materials, to the revision and extension of them. Their creativity and support have been beyond thanking.

To the many teachers and students whose work is included here, and acknowledged by name where it appears.

To the instructors in the Content Area Reading Program state-wide network, who taught from this book in preliminary forms, for their valuable feedback and ideas.

To Pat Simmet, Michelle Rishel, and Bonnie Schaedel, for fast and efficient service at the typewriter when deadlines were past.

To Joe Prewitt, for his insight and contribution to our work with bilingual students.

To our husbands and families, for their patience and understanding.

Preview

WHAT THIS BOOK IS ABOUT

Premise of This Book

1. Teachers of content subjects can become competent and confident in teaching reading skills as an integral part of their content teaching. The integration of content objectives with those of reading necessitates careful assessment of student ability and long range planning for instruction by the classroom teacher. Teachers' sensitivity to students' individual differences can be developed so that teachers will appreciate the necessity for providing individual and small group experiences for all students. The goal is to improve teachers' attitudes toward the importance of teaching reading, their feeling of confidence in their own ability to do it, and their command of some techniques for doing it, geared to each one's subject area.

2. Diagnostic teaching, using diagnosed student needs as the basis for instruction, is the most effective way to approach reading in content areas—and other kinds of teaching, as well.

The First Step

Throughout the book, we will ask you to assess your students' level of knowledge and skill before you start teaching them. That means we must also assess *your* present level on two of the issues mentioned here: (1) your present level of knowledge of reading skills, and (2) your present attitude toward teaching reading in your content classroom.

Following are two assessment tools which have been used with preservice and inservice teachers. They represent both our affective and cognitive goals for the reader of this book. The assessments will allow you to see what you need to know in order to teach your students effectively and attend to their needs. The attitude assessment will help you see how you presently feel about the problems students have with reading and your responsibility to help them read better in your class. So assess yourself by answering the questions as well as you can right now. Be as honest as you can. We expect that you are not familiar with many of the concepts described here; we also expect that much of the terminology will be new. However, you may find that you know more than you thought. After you score your own tests, you can compare your scores with others who have taken them.

KNOWLEDGE OF CONTENT AREA READING

E. N. Askov, M. M. Dupuis, J. McLaughlin

These multiple choice questions are designed to test your knowledge of basic materials and methods for teaching reading in various content areas.

Answer each question by marking the letter of the best choice in the space to the left of the number. Please answer each item. Mark answer *e* if you really do not know the answer and prefer not to guess. We are more interested in what you know than in a lucky guess.

_____ **1.** The primary task of the content area teacher with respect to diagnostic teaching of reading is to
a) foster the transfer of basic reading skills to content area materials.
b) develop positive attitudes toward content subjects.
c) provide phonics instruction to those students who need it.
d) assess student performance in relation to graph norms.
e) I honestly don't know.

_____ **2.** Study skills are *best* described as those skills concerned with
a) understanding the main idea.
b) recognizing relationships and sequences of events.
c) labeling concepts.
d) locating and interpreting information.
e) I honestly don't know.

_____ **3.** A structured overview or advance organizer can be effective in developing vocabulary skills mainly because it requires the student to
a) illustrate a concept in order to demonstrate understanding of vocabulary words.
b) rely on the conceptual organization of the material to clarify the meanings of new words.
c) rewrite the selection in his/her own words, thereby reinforcing knowledge of new words.
d) develop his/her own list of "key words" or "key ideas."
e) I honestly don't know.

_____ **4.** Criterion-referenced evaluation procedures provide information related to
a) achievement of general curriculum goals.
b) achievement with respect to established community or national norms.
c) achievement of specific instructional objectives.

    d) achievement with respect to individual ability levels.

    e) I honestly don't know.

_____ **5.** The learning center technique provides a means of adapting material to a student's particular learning style in that the technique

    a) allows for a variety of learning strategies.

    b) is based primarily on student planning.

    c) places emphasis on the student's interpersonal relationships.

    d) focuses only on practical skill development.

    e) I honestly don't know.

_____ **6.** Which of the following is *not* a major component of readability?

    a) comparison with the average reading level in the class.

    b) reader's interest in the subject.

    c) reader's background information.

    d) aids to reading found in a textbook.

    e) I honestly don't know.

_____ **7.** Which of the following strategies would be more effective than the others for instruction in specific skills, ideas, or concepts?

    a) informal reading inventory.

    b) SQ3R.

    c) library reference center.

    d) learning activity package.

    e) I honestly don't know.

_____ **8.** "Readability" is most often measured in terms of

    a) the average number of syllables and sentences in a given passage.

    b) the general reading ability of the student.

    c) the potential use of a book for independent reading.

    d) the number of specific oral reading errors occurring in a given passage.

    e) I honestly don't know.

_____ **9.** Which of the following statements corresponds to the psycholinguistic definition of reading?

    a) Reading involves the recognition of words through letter-by-letter processing.

    b) Cultural backgrounds influence reading comprehension in a negative way.

    c) A student needs to be able to use language efficiently to read well.

    d) The reader must recognize each word in a sentence before comprehension can take place.

    e) I honestly don't know.

_____ **10.** A "change agent" can best be described as an individual who

    a) tends to be more tolerant of ambiguities than more authoritarian individuals.

    b) provides teachers with skills necessary for dealing effectively with administrators.

c) introduces change from the outside of a typically "closed" system.

d) understands group relationships and the dynamics involved in facilitating change.

e) I honestly don't know.

_____ **11.** Vocabulary skills, in content area reading, are *best* described as those reading skills concerned with

a) reading for significant detail.

b) concept labeling.

c) spelling rules.

d) word analogies.

e) I honestly don't know.

_____ **12.** Which of the following techniques places the *least* emphasis on student self-direction and self-pacing?

a) directed reading activity.

b) learning centers.

c) individualized reading.

d) learning activity package.

e) I honestly don't know.

_____ **13.** Which of the following is *not* a potential source of diagnostic information relative to reading in the content areas?

a) group reading inventory.

b) standardized reading tests.

c) cumulative records.

d) cloze procedure.

e) I honestly don't know.

_____ **14.** Which two methods would be most useful for determining the suitability of content materials for specific students?

a) informal reading inventory and directed reading activity.

b) language experience and learning activity package.

c) cloze technique and informal reading inventory.

d) directed reading activity and learning activity package.

e) I honestly don't know.

_____ **15.** Which of the following decisions should be made first for diagnostic teaching by grouping?

a) specify teaching goals for each student.

b) group students by interest, need, and ability.

c) select instructional materials.

d) identify relevant characteristics of each student.

e) I honestly don't know.

_____ **16.** The learning center approach is *most* valuable for which of the following reasons?

a) It allows the student to direct his/her own learning, within guidelines set by the teacher.

b) It allows for a wide range of linguistic differences within the class.

c) It provides reading material based on the student's own language.

d) It provides a built-in means of assessing general reading ability.
e) I honestly don't know.

_____ **17.** Which of the following is the *most* critical factor for a teacher or change agent to consider when attempting to introduce change in school situations?
a) classroom structures.
b) other teachers' values and needs.
c) authority of the change agent.
d) societal and organizational systems.
e) I honestly don't know.

_____ **18.** Which of the following statements is most related to the concept of language "registers"?
a) Students with poor language habits tend to do poorly in analytical subjects like math and science.
b) Lack of early experiences with communication results in poor language development.
c) Speech consists of various forms which are appropriate to different social situations.
d) Students will tend to model the incorrect language forms of family and peers.
e) I honestly don't know.

_____ **19.** A group reading inventory for a content area consists of which of the following?
a) a list of questions related to the students' interest in the content area.
b) a random sampling of topics from the table of contents of a content area text.
c) a text passage in which every fifth word has been deleted.
d) a representative section of a textbook, chosen to assess skills necessary for using the text.
e) I honestly don't know.

_____ **20.** A self-directed behavior rating scale can be used to distinguish between
a) independent and dependent learners.
b) authoritarian and passive learners.
c) adaptive and nonadaptive learners.
d) motivated and unmotivated learners.
e) I honestly don't know.

_____ **21.** At the inferential level of reading comprehension, the student will
a) recognize and recall the main idea and sequence of a passage.
b) make critical judgments about the reading material.
c) predict outcomes and understand figurative language.
d) identify emotionally with characters or events.
e) I honestly don't know.

_____ **22.** The results of a group reading inventory can best be used to
a) assess achievement in a content area.

b) assess student interest in reading.
c) provide materials which allow for a diversity of learning styles.
d) provide a basis for the formation of temporary skills groups.
e) I honestly don't know.

_____ **23.** According to Havelock, by stating that a school is an "open system," one is referring to the fact that it is characterized by
a) a combination of diagnostic, prescriptive, and evaluative components.
b) a wide variety of community and school-related instructional resources.
c) a number of internal and external variables acting upon one another.
d) direct involvement by elements of a local community.
e) I honestly don't know

_____ **24.** In selecting media components, based on Dale's "Cone of Experience," which of the following categories would represent the highest level of abstraction?
a) exhibits.
b) contrived experiences.
c) study trips.
d) verbal symbols.
e) I honestly don't know.

_____ **25.** Which of the following is an example of an "enabling" teacher statement?
a) Please tell the class your reason for saying that.
b) No, that's not what I had in mind; try again.
c) The real reason the flame went out was that it didn't have enough oxygen.
d) If you had observed more carefully, you would have heard three objects bump against the sides.
e) I honestly don't know.

_____ **26.** It is important for teachers to study and understand a variety of language styles mainly because
a) most students have initial difficulty with standard forms.
b) socio-cultural background is an important factor in reading comprehension.
c) language difficulties are often related to the use of improper styles.
d) students can be helped to extend and practice their individual styles.
e) I honestly don't know.

_____ **27.** The directed reading activity approach can be distinguished from the language experience approach in its focus on
a) student selected materials which promote skill development.
b) an understanding of meanings along with word recognition.
c) teacher questions before reading to foster comprehension after reading.

d) comprehension skills beyond recognition and recall.
e) I honestly don't know.

_____ **28.** Of the following alternatives, a student who achieves at the "instructional level" on an informal reading measure could best be served by
a) activities focusing on isolated skill development.
b) teacher guidance through a directed reading activity approach.
c) longer reading selections with an emphasis on higher levels of comprehension.
d) alternative reading materials suitable to his/her lower reading level.
e) I honestly don't know.

_____ **29.** Which of the following is *not* likely to be a barrier to change?
a) group participation in decision making.
b) administrative objectives.
c) uncertainty.
d) fear of obsolescence.
e) I honestly don't know.

_____ **30.** In the past, readability levels for content area textbooks were usually found to be _____ the grade level designations provided by the publishers.
a) about the same as
b) slightly lower than
c) somewhat higher than
d) exactly the same as
e) I honestly don't know.

_____ **31.** The following questions would most likely represent what level of questioning? (1) What do you think happened just before Mr. Swartz entered the storeroom? (2) Can you suggest a moral for this story? (3) What preparation is necessary in order to build this model following the directions in your book?
a) appreciative.
b) evaluative.
c) inferential.
d) literal.
e) I honestly don't know.

_____ **32.** Which three language styles are most likely to be found within a school situation (among students and teachers)?
a) frozen, intimate, and casual.
b) consultative, frozen, and intimate.
c) frozen, consultative, and casual.
d) formal, consultative, and casual.
e) I honestly don't know.

_____ **33.** The cloze procedure can best be used by the content area teacher to draw conclusions concerning a student's
a) general reading ability.
b) ability to read specific text material.

c) attitude toward a particular content area.
d) ability to be self-directed.
e) I honestly don't know.

_____ **34.** The language experience approach, when used in the content area classroom, provides a means of
a) developing a visual and tactile approach for students who need such experiences.
b) clarifying concepts through a graphic representation of language.
c) developing reading material based on the student's own language.
d) organizing the classroom according to specific language skill needs.
e) I honestly don't know.

STATEMENTS SURVEY: TEACHING READING IN CONTENT AREAS

Joyce W. Lee, Carlotta Joyner Young, Eunice N. Askov, Mary M. Dupuis

Instructions

The following are statements about instructional procedures of content area teachers. The intent of this survey is to determine how you feel about these procedures in relation to your own teaching situation or prospective teaching situation.

Read each statement and rate it according to your experience in your classroom or what you think would be true when you teach. Please note that the general term *teachers* which appears in each statement is meant to include all teachers in the content areas such as in English, foreign language, social studies, science, math, home economics, health, vocational subjects, art, music and reading.

You are to rate each statement on the following scale which appears below each item; the scale appears for each item. Mark an X above your choice on the scale.

Strongly Disagree	Slightly Disagree	Not Sure	Slightly Agree	Strongly Agree

Here is how to use the scale:

If you "strongly disagree" with the statement, put an X in the space above Strongly Disagree; if you "slightly disagree" with the statement, put an X in the space above that statement, and so on.

1. It is important that teachers be competent in assessing the general reading levels of students.

Strongly Disagree	Slightly Disagree	Not Sure	Slightly Agree	Strongly Agree

2. It is inappropriate for teachers to devote class instruction time to vocabulary development.

Strongly Disagree	Slightly Disagree	Not Sure	Slightly Agree	Strongly Agree

3. All teachers should be able to provide alternative means by which students can obtain information they may be unable to read.

Strongly Disagree	Slightly Disagree	Not Sure	Slightly Agree	Strongly Agree

4. It is inappropriate for teachers to assess students' specific comprehension skills such as making inferences, following sequence, detecting bias or recognizing main ideas.

Strongly Disagree	Slightly Disagree	Not Sure	Slightly Agree	Strongly Agree

5. It is important that teachers provide a variety of materials which cover similar content but which represent a wide range of readability.

Strongly Disagree	Slightly Disagree	Not Sure	Slightly Agree	Strongly Agree

6. It is important that teachers be able to identify those students who are having trouble figuring out unfamiliar words.

Strongly Disagree	Slightly Disagree	Not Sure	Slightly Agree	Strongly Agree

7. It is not important for teachers to conduct guided or directed reading lessons for students unable to read the text on their own.

Strongly Disagree	Slightly Disagree	Not Sure	Slightly Agree	Strongly Agree

8. It is not necessary for teachers to develop and use diagnostic instruments for assessing mastery of skills needed in their subject area(s).

Strongly Disagree	Slightly Disagree	Not Sure	Slightly Agree	Strongly Agree

9. Teachers should include questions at various comprehension levels in class discussions, worksheets, study guides and tests.

Strongly Disagree	Slightly Disagree	Not Sure	Slightly Agree	Strongly Agree

10. It is not important for teachers to be able to develop and use instruments for diagnosing mastery of reading skills.

Strongly Disagree	Slightly Disagree	Not Sure	Slightly Agree	Strongly Agree

11. Teachers should not spend class instruction time teaching students study skills.

Strongly Disagree	Slightly Disagree	Not Sure	Slightly Agree	Strongly Agree

12. It is desirable that teachers determine for which students a reading selection is or is not appropriate.

Strongly Disagree	Slightly Disagree	Not Sure	Slightly Agree	Strongly Agree

13. Teachers should teach those reading skills needed in their subject area(s).

Strongly Disagree	Slightly Disagree	Not Sure	Slightly Agree	Strongly Agree

14. Only reading teachers should provide materials written at various reading levels for groups of students with differing reading abilities.

Strongly Disagree	Slightly Disagree	Not Sure	Slightly Agree	Strongly Agree

15. Teachers should know how to assess mastery of the comprehension skills needed in their subject area(s).

Strongly Disagree	Slightly Disagree	Not Sure	Slightly Agree	Strongly Agree

16. Only reading teachers should be concerned with diagnosing vocabulary development of students beyond the elementary school level.

Strongly Disagree	Slightly Disagree	Not Sure	Slightly Agree	Strongly Agree

17. It is necessary that teachers be able to identify those reading skills specifically needed in their subject areas.

Strongly Disagree	Slightly Disagree	Not Sure	Slightly Agree	Strongly Agree

△**18.** Content teachers should not need to develop skill in assessing student strengths and weaknesses in various study skills.

| Strongly | Slightly | Not Sure | Slightly | Strongly |
| Disagree | Disagree | | Agree | Agree |

△**19.** It is not desirable for teachers to conduct small group lessons in specific reading skills.

| Strongly | Slightly | Not Sure | Slightly | Strongly |
| Disagree | Disagree | | Agree | Agree |

◯**20.** It is appropriate for teachers to identify those students who are experiencing reading difficulties because of language differences such as a dialect or second language.

| Strongly | Slightly | Not Sure | Slightly | Strongly |
| Disagree | Disagree | | Agree | Agree |

Score your own assessments now.

The answers to the *Knowledge Test* are given in Appendix C. You get 1 point for each correct answer.

Your score is _____ of a possible 34.

Discussion of these items will occur during the rest of the book.

Score your Statements Survey on a scale of 1–5 for each item:

On items with circles around them ◯1 :   Strongly Agree   = 5
                                        Strongly Disagree = 1

On items with triangles around them △2 :   Strongly Agree   = 1
                                          Strongly Disagree = 5

Add up your score (somewhere between 20 and 100).

Your score is _____ .

You will want to figure out how your score stands in relation to others who have taken these assessments. Here are the figures for preservice and inservice teachers who worked through a course with content similar to that presented in this book:

| | Before course | | After course | |
	skills	attitude	skills	attitude
Preservice teachers	13	86	24	90
Inservice teachers	15	86	25	91
Your scores	_____	_____	_____	_____

How do your scores compare to the other teachers' scores before training in content area reading? The preservice and inservice teachers represented by these mean scores (averages) came from many different content areas: English, social studies, science, math, home economics, health, industrial arts, foreign languages. They also taught at many different grade levels. When you have completed this book, you'll take these assessments again. And, again, compare your posttest (after training) scores to these teachers. This change is the most important thing: it demonstrates how much you have learned. It will also demonstrate how your attitude has changed.

How This Book is Organized

This book is organized to make it easy for you to learn the material in each chapter and section. To assist your efforts, we have provided an *Overview* at the beginning of each of the eight Parts. The Parts each have an important task in the development of your competence to teach reading in your content area. The sequence of parts is determined largely by the steps in the planning model introduced in Chapter 2. This planning model provides you with a systematic step-by-step approach to planning instruction.

Each chapter begins with a *Preview*, a short statement of the purpose and content of the chapter. The Preview will give you an idea of what to look for in the chapter.

An additional aid for you is the *Summary* at the end of each chapter. You may find it useful to read it first, *before* you read the chapter, as a kind of advance organizer (more on that later!).

A final—and very important—aid is the list of activities at the end of each chapter. This book is practical, full of teacher-tested techniques for integrating reading into your teaching. Therefore, it is important for you to develop some of these techniques and try your hand at using them in your classroom, if you can.

The activities are designed to permit those of you who are preservice teachers to gain experience in developing tests and exercises while inservice teachers can also administer or teach the test or exercise. The section entitled *Learn to Do It!* is for preservice and inservice teachers; *Do It!* is designed for inservice teachers. You are encouraged to complete activities using texts from the content area and grade in which you are or will be teaching so you can develop competence and confidence with the materials and skills you will be dealing with in the future.

Watch for Betsy, Pam and David as you read the book. These three real students are introduced in Chapter 2, then followed throughout the book. They represent common problems with reading among students in our schools.

Now it's time to get started. Part I provides you with *Some Important Background*.

PART I
SOME IMPORTANT BACKGROUND

OVERVIEW

Content area reading is a complex topic which combines reading concerns with the cognitive content of subject area classes. Chapter One, "What is Content Area Reading?" defines reading. It also discusses reading and cognitive development, demonstrating the relationship between reading in content classes and the conceptual material taught there. Bloom's Taxonomy of the Cognitive Domain is the hierarchy used to demonstrate the connection, with Barrett's Taxonomy of Reading Comprehension the example for reading. The taxonomies show similarities in structure and development. The results suggest ways to integrate content and reading instruction in the same classroom. The definition of reading as comprehension—getting meaning from printed material—is discussed, as well as the purposes for reading given by most readers.

"Individualizing Teaching in Content Area Reading," Chapter Two, introduces David, Betsy and Pam, three students you'll be seeing throughout the book. It also introduces the Decision Model for Diagnostic Teaching by Grouping. The Decision Model encourages teaching reading in the content classroom by a diagnostic-prescriptive approach. It is the organizing principle for the rest of the book, using the step-by-step methods exemplified by the model.

Chapter 1
What Is Content Area Reading?

Content teachers teach content: information, thinking processes, skills for handling or seeking information, concepts and ways to work with them. Most of the time, the content comes clothed in words, usually printed words. In most classes, content teachers use reading as the major means of studying the content to be learned.

Content teachers also teach students, those live bodies who are sometimes annoying, sometimes delightful. Teaching in *any* area means working with students of all shapes, sizes and colors. In fact, teachers know they are successful only when their students learn. This book is about helping students learn.

The readers of this book are teachers or prospective teachers of many different subjects—English, social studies, science, math, home economics—any subject taught from grade four through high school. They have developed considerable expertise in the *content* of their subject: what to teach. This book asks them to concentrate now on the *process* of teaching: how to teach.

The focus is their need to know how well their students can handle the materials they must read. What alternatives are there in choosing materials? How can teachers make it more likely that their students will learn what they want them to learn? Before these questions can be answered directly, we must discuss what reading is and why some students have more difficulty than others in learning content subjects.

A Little Background

The problem of reading instruction, and its place in content area teaching, continues to be a subject of debate among educators. Kingston (1964) points out that while interest in the reading problems of students beyond the elementary level has resulted in increased concern for the reading tasks faced by these students in mastering the content in subject areas such as English, social studies, science and math, not much guidance or assistance has been generated by research for the teacher who must cope with these problems. Early (1973) suggests that the status of reading instruction in secondary schools has changed very little in the past thirty years, pointing out that the current demands for the whole faculty to teach reading in the content areas are the same as those found in the literature as far back as 1942. She notes that only limited progress has been made in extending reading instruction beyond the elementary grades. For example, in a chapter in the 26th Yearbook of the Society for the Study of Education (1937), entitled "Reading in the Various Fields of the Curriculum," Snedaker and Horn propose to discuss the "responsibilities of all teachers for the effective direction of the reading pertinent to their curriculum fields" and further, to present "methods and means for developing [these] reading habits" (p. 133). Schleich (1971) notes that in a school-wide testing program conducted prior to an inservice project in reading instruction, mean scores on a standardized reading test at each successive grade from nine to twelve showed a significant downward trend for the same group of students, suggesting that these students did not adequately continue to develop higher level reading skills as they moved through high school. Rubin (1974) suggests that one of the most salient factors leading students to drop out of high school is lack of the reading skills necessary for success in content subjects. Singer (1972) reports that, particularly among minority students, reading deficiencies can create sufficient frustration in secondary students of average intelligence that many drop out rather than face the embarrassing consequences of continued failure or low achievement in content subjects.

The National Assessment of Educational Progress provides an overview of reading achievement across the country. Three assessments of reading have been completed—one in 1970–71, the second in 1975–76, and the third in 1979–80. Three school-age levels were tested: nine-year-olds (roughly fourth grade); thirteen-year-olds (eighth grade); and seventeen-year-olds (twelfth grade). Different tests were used at each level, so no comparisons among grade levels can be made. However, results show that 65 percent of the nine-year-olds successfully completed the reading assessment, 61 percent of the thirteen-year-olds, and 72 percent of the seventeen-year-olds. This suggests that teachers of fourth, eighth, and twelfth-grade students may face classes in which 30 to 40 percent of the students cannot handle the basic skills of literal and inferential comprehension and the use of basic references.

An additional concern arising from these data is that there is little change in the thirteen- and seventeen-year-olds' scores from 1971 to 1980. The hopeful sign is that nine-year-olds improved from 1971 to 1980 in their overall reading ability, as measured by this assessment.

Reading experts suggest that these data, as all data that purport to be national in scope, be interpreted cautiously. Cultural differences and special (or exceptional) students are not carefully accounted for. However, the reading achievement level of students remains an open question. Almost certainly, teachers of all subjects will face students who are unable to read, even on a basic level, and many who cannot read with higher level skills, e.g., inferential comprehension (Tierney and Lapp, 1979; Ward, 1981).

Reading and Cognitive Development

Most content reading concerns fall in the *cognitive* domain. Content teachers plan to encourage their students' cognitive development—that is their major goal. Cognitive ability can be developed through many sources. Students can *listen* to lectures, audiotapes or records. They can *listen* to and *view* videotapes, movies, slide-tapes, filmstrips. They can *view* pictures, graphs, diagrams or three-dimensional objects like globes and models. But *reading* has traditionally been the most important source of information in the learning situation. The textbook is frequently the major source of knowledge in content classes. Even when supplementary materials are used, these materials often involve reading as the process necessary to gain information. The history teacher may require students to read the text's treatment of the American Revolution. Or s/he may suggest that the students supplement the text with additional sources. These sources may be primary sources—Thomas Paine, Thomas Jefferson, and others—or other sources written about the war at lower reading levels or with other points of view. However the choice is made, these sources of cognitive information require reading.

Cognitive development may be viewed as a hierarchy (Bloom *et al.* 1956; Gagné and Briggs 1974). Such a hierarchy moves from lower to higher level processes, all aimed at the students' cognitive processing. Using Bloom's hierarchy as an example, reading can be involved in each level. The student can move from knowledge, the factual level, through application (such as giving examples), analysis and synthesis, to evaluation of the knowledge without moving from a single written source. Reading comprehension will be discussed later in terms of levels parallel to Bloom's. It is worth noting that comprehension on Bloom's cognitive scale (Level 2) does not mean the same thing as reading comprehension, although there are similarities. Bloom's "comprehension" means understanding, being able to restate something in one's own words. Reading comprehension has a broader meaning, subsuming all of reading into the process of understanding at many cognitive levels. In this book, *comprehension* will henceforth refer to this broader meaning related to reading. However, the possible confusion in meaning underlines the essentially cognitive nature of much reading; it is a process of gaining understanding from printed material.

Researchers have recently viewed reading as a series of *schemata*, or structures of knowledge. In this theory, the important element in reading is the reader's ability to fit the new information in a reading selection to his/her existing schemata, or prior knowledge. Readers need to have two types of schema. First, they need to understand the structure of texts, such as language structures, organization of reading selections, and the larger organization of chapters and whole books. This knowledge will allow readers to anticipate where information can be found in a reading and how it will fit together into a coherent whole (Kintsch 1978).

A second schema is the reader's goal and his/her purposes for reading. That is, the reader's expectancy for the content of the reading. The reader's prior knowledge of the subject area provides him/her with the framework, or knowledge structure, to which s/he can attach the new information (Otto and White 1982).

Seen in this view, reading becomes the interaction of reader and text (Kintsch and VanDyk 1978; Rosenblatt 1976). The reader must be able to comprehend, or understand, the text by making appropriate inferences and finding in his/her memory the appropriate connections to things s/he already knows. This schema theory of reading places heavy emphasis on the cognitive aspects of reading.

Affective Components of Reading

Reading has an affective component, as well. Krathwohl, *et al.* (1964), define the affective domain of learning as a value structure, a set of attitudes. Student attitudes toward reading are always important, but never more than in the upper grade levels.

Student attitudes toward reading, as toward learning and school, are developed early in life. Parents and community are important in determining how students feel about reading: is it important? how does time spent reading compare to time spent watching TV? By junior high school, students are also affected by their peers' attitudes toward reading and learning. Some students can read but won't. Willingness to read, eagerness to learn new things, enthusiasm for school (and the negative versions of these statements) are all affective concerns. The student who can read, but won't, is the reading equivalent of the old saying about leading a horse to water. If a student refuses to read, to learn, or to care about school, the best plans and organization by a teacher will not result in student learning. This problem is sometimes called "motivation." Developing student interest and enthusiasm—or motivation—is a critical responsibility of teachers.

Student interest in reading is reported to decline during junior high school. It may be that student attitude plays a role in this achievement decline (Schleich 1971). However, student interest and attitude can be improved by teacher concern and effort. Specific techniques for increasing motivation will be described in detail in Part III. No teacher can afford to ignore student motivation and the entire affective domain.

Reading and the Psychomotor Domain

The third domain of learning is the psychomotor, involving the interaction of mind and body, coordination, muscular control, and the like. Harrow's psychomotor hierarchy (1972) moves from Reflex Movements to Basic Fundamental skills, basic muscle control, to Perceptual Abilities, including visual acuity and visual discrimination. At a higher level, Skilled Movements occur when a fluent reader reads, integrating all the physical processes necessary to convey the symbols to the brain.

One analogy to reading is the process of driving a car. Remember learning to drive a car with a manual transmission? The hardest thing to learn is the eye-hand, both-feet coordination involved in starting off in first gear. The new driver jerks, starts, stops, stalls the car as s/he tries to let out the clutch at the same time s/he presses down on the accelerator. After practice, this same driver starts off without even thinking consciously.

A beginning reader goes through many similar stages, consciously attending to all the details in the process. By the time s/he becomes a fluent reader, this process has become unconscious and feels natural. Laberge and Samuels (1974) call this achieving *automaticity*, when the process has become automatic. However, a reader who has never gone beyond the beginning stages over several years finds reading a tiring and tiresome process, and s/he may well feel that the results aren't worth all the effort.

Reading requires certain specific physical processes. Visual acuity and discrimination are essential. Acuity, the ability to see clearly, means focusing on the letters. Acuity problems may require larger print or correction with glasses. Teachers may falsely assume that all vision problems are identified in elementary school. However, a significant number of students develop visual acuity problems as adolescents. Therefore all teachers should be aware of warning signs—squinting, rubbing the eyes, watering eyes—as clues to emerging vision problems.

Visual discrimination or perception may also cause problems with reading. Students must discriminate between letters by shape (as in *b* vs. *d*) and by size (*C* vs.

c). Students with severe problems in perception may be called learning disabled (LD) or dyslexic. Such students need specialized treatment, but they may well remain in the regular classroom for much of their schooling. We will discuss techniques for working with exceptional students like this in Chapter 21.

Reading requires that the eyes move efficiently across the letters and words. Readers of the English language are required to move their eyes from left to right and from the top to the bottom of a page. Readers of Hebrew read right to left. Chinese writing requires readers to read from top to bottom. However readers read, their eyes move in regular patterns. These visual signals move directly to the brain for processing, using both the linguistic (language) and cognitive (thinking) parts of the brain. Any interruption in the signals or the processing will hamper the comprehension of the reader. The coordination of all these physical and mental processes, like driving a car, becomes natural to most people, but this doesn't make the process any less complex or amazing.

The psychomotor domain may seem to be less susceptible to teachers' control than the cognitive and affective. Teachers can't organize lessons to improve students' visual acuity. However, they can be alert for clues to physical problems and alert students and parents to them. They can take physical problems into account in planning activities. They can work with resource teachers in teaching children with special needs.

Definitions of Reading

Viewing reading as including cognitive, affective and psychomotor learning suggests a particular definition of reading. Some definitions of reading focus on decoding, a lower level process of calling out words or sounds. Decoding is a necessary process, but it is not sufficient. Reading must extend into the higher levels on all three hierarchies in order for teachers to be satisfied that a reader is *fluent*, the usual term for a mature reader.

Recent research in reading by psycholinguists has identified three stages of performance in the reader's process:

1. perception of characters, or visual operations,
2. perception of syntax, or sensitivity to grammar, and
3. direct perception of the meanings of words (Kolers, in Smith 1973, p. 30).

Smith defines these stages as mutually exclusive. That is, when a reader is doing one of them, s/he can't do either of the others. A fluent reader reads for stage 3—direct meanings of words. S/he reads only enough of the words to get the meaning. Fluent readers *don't* read every word. However, when any reader is reading something unfamiliar or difficult to read, s/he must move down to stage 2 and read the material word for word. S/he may even need to move down to stage 1 and sound out the word or identify it letter for letter. Whenever a reader moves to lower stages of reading, s/he loses speed and efficiency in reading. Reading becomes more time consuming and burdensome, less satisfying to the reader. For the many students who have *never* moved beyond stage 1 or 2, reading is a difficult and unrewarding process. Looking at reading as a three-stage process of getting meaning makes it easier to identify particular students' problems (Smith 1971).

As early as 1906, a prophetic reading researcher, Edmund B. Huey, stated that "it is well to place the emphasis [in reading] strongly where it really belongs, on reading as *thought getting*" (p. 350). Later, William S. Gray (1937, p.26) reinforced this position:

> The reader not only recognizes the essential facts or ideas presented, but also reflects on their significance, evaluates them critically, discovers relationships between them, and clarifies his understanding of the ideas apprehended (p. 5).

The same levels, the same sense of hierarchy in the fluent reader's approach to reading, are present in Gray's work, as in Bloom's and others who have suggested hierarchial sequences.

Recent writers in the field of reading echo the same definition. Harold Herber sees reading as "a thinking process which includes decoding of symbols, interpreting the meanings of the symbols, and applying the ideas derived from the symbols" (Herber 1978, p.9). The idea of reading levels and an emphasis on reading as thinking, are still with us. Herber's view of reading in content learning is that it is essentially a cognitive process, but with concern for the affective domain, as well.

An important aspect of defining reading is identifying the reader's purpose, that is, what schema s/he has with which to connect the reading. Stauffer (1969) suggests that knowing his/her purpose in reading is the reader's first responsibility. Purposes for reading may be classified as functional, career-based, or recreational.

Functional reading includes most school reading. The reader reads for a practical reason—to answer questions, to find specific information, to identify the steps in a process—which the teacher should define clearly for the student. A functional reading assignment in biology could be: "Read chapter three on one-celled animals and answer the questions at the end of the chapter." While the purpose given here is functional, it is general and emphasizes the wrong goal, answering questions, rather than a more appropriate goal, understanding one-celled animals. A more effective assignment, then, on the same reading, for the same functional purpose, is: "Read chapter three on one-celled animals. List three animals described in the chapter, giving at least two characteristics for each one." The teacher should set the purpose for reading as s/he makes assignments. It is to the reader's advantage if the teacher sets the purpose as specifically as possible and emphasizes what the reader is to learn from the reading.

Functional reading can range from low-level coping skills to high-level evaluations. Coping skills include reading for everyday living; reading the driver's manual to prepare for the driver's license examination; reading the newspaper; reading job applications. Higher-level reading purposes include reading to compare the writing style of two different novelists; reading to prepare for a debate over air pollution controls; reading to compare three alternative ways to conduct a chemistry experiment. Thus, functional reading is not a negative term, nor is it limited to the lowest cognitive levels. It involves a necessary purpose for reading which will be useful throughout the reader's life. Although functional reading is a major purpose of school reading, its use is not restricted to school. Everyone needs to read functionally throughout life.

Career-based reading involves a specific purpose, aimed at preparing the reader for a career. The reading required for specific jobs tends to focus on material specific to that job and to use language with meanings specific to the job. This language or vocabulary is sometimes called *jargon*. As the reader becomes more familiar with the job's jargon, so that s/he uses it naturally and unconsciously, s/he can read material which is unintelligible to the uninitiated. A good example of this is the student who wants to be a mechanic and devours car magazines. S/he can discuss carburetors and exhaust systems in great detail. History and English teachers may well be aghast, since his/her functional reading level in their classes is quite low. Generally, reading purposes—or motivation—are stronger for career-based reading. The reader feels the need to learn about new products, new processes, new information.

The amount of career-based reading done by students varies greatly. Some students identify careers early and focus a great deal of school time on those careers, while other students remain unclear about career goals and, thus, must work from more general purposes. In general, firm career choices are not expected by elementary or junior high school students. Such choices become more likely as students advance in grades. It is still true that many students will complete high school without identifying any career choice.

Recreational reading is the third major general purpose for reading. Recreational reading means reading for enjoyment, for the pure fun of it. English and reading teachers often list this as their major purpose, and helping students read for fun as a major instructional goal. The contradiction in this is that by requiring reading, for example of *Huckleberry Finn*, an English teacher is providing the student's purpose: the reading is now functional, not recreational.

Recreational reading means *self-selected* reading—that is, reading selected by the reader because s/he wants to read it. Since reading requires practice, it is important for readers to read in order to improve their skills and increase their fluency. This is the rationale for *self-selected sustained silent reading*, a technique which can occur in any class—or anywhere else, for that matter. In its usual form, SSR involves setting aside a few minutes—fifteen or thirty—at a regular time for everyone to read self-selected material. This can be a magazine, book, or newspaper, and it may include everyone—teachers, custodian, secretary and students. A single class can do it or an entire school. This technique can help to develop fluent reading through practice, and it can help students believe that reading can be fun. The fact remains, however, that most school reading is not recreational, despite teachers' best intentions.

It is worth pointing out that functional reading can be interesting rather than boring, lively rather than dull, personal rather than impersonal. When teachers select reading materials, they can consider these affective concerns as a way to increase student interest. More detailed suggestions for developing student interest will follow in Part III.

The Nature of Content Area Reading

Given the definition of reading as primarily a thinking and cognitive process, but also affective and psychomotor, and given the purposes for reading outlined here, we must place this general discussion in a more specific focus.

Look at some examples of content reading:

1. *Mathematics.*   This is a section on fractions from a seventh grade general mathematics book designed for average students:

You have compared several pairs of fractions with equal denominators and different numerators. In all cases the fraction with the larger numerator was the larger fraction.

This is always true: for fractions with equal denominators, the one with the larger numerator is the larger fraction. Clearly, when the whole is divided into a given number of parts, the more parts there are, the bigger the fraction.

You have also compared pairs of fractions with equal numerators but different denominators. In all cases the fraction with the smaller denominator was the larger fraction. This is always true: for fractions with equal numerators, the fraction with the smaller denominator is the larger fraction. This is because, when the whole is divided into more and more equal parts, each part gets smaller and smaller. A given number of the smaller parts is less than the same number of the larger parts.

(From Haber-Schaim, Skvarcius, and Hatch, *Mathematics 1*. Englewood Cliffs, N.J.: Prentice-Hall, Inc., 1980), pp. 122–123.

2. *Chemistry.* Now try a section from an introductory chemistry course:

An experimental procedure for determining molecular weights (the relative masses of molecules) has been outlined. Notice that in using this procedure, we made two arbitrary choices. First, oxygen was selected as the standard gas; and second, a molecular weight of 32.00 was assigned to it. After we made these choices, we could determine the molecular weight of any other gas.

An interesting question now arises: what unit should be assigned to molecular weight values? In choosing a unit, it is convenient to select a unit appropriate to the usual dimensions of the item being weighted. For example, we use grams to measure out laboratory reagents, tons to express the weight of ocean liners, and pounds to buy hamburger meat. Because an individual molecule is so small, we need a very small, new unit to express the mass of a single molecule. We unknowingly defined this new unit when we selected the oxygen molecule as a standard and assigned it a value of 32.00. This new unit, the *unified atomic mass unit* (u), is so small that 32.00 U are present in the mass of a single oxygen molecule.

(From Parry, R. W., P. M. Dietz, R. L. Tellefsen, L. E. Steiner, *Chemistry, Experimental Foundations*. Englewood Cliffs, N.J.: Prentice-Hall, Inc., 1975, p. 33.)

3. *Government.* This selection is from the first chapter of a book designed for required senior high government courses:

What Do Governments Do? You have been examining reasons why people form governments, reasons that reflect people's expectations of what governments will do for them. Remember that a government is established by men and women who want the government to create certain conditions for a group. The Iroquois, the Pilgrims, the framers of the Constitution, the citizens of Kimberling City—all formed governments to do specific things for them that they could not accomplish without government.

When you begin to think about what governments do for people, many different kinds of activities may come to your mind, like collecting taxes, building schools, and passing laws. If you include private governments, you'll probably think about ways in which the officers and rules of groups such as clubs, churches, and student governments guide the activities of those groups.

All these functions of government can be grouped into several major classifications. Not all governments perform all these functions. However, these are basic areas in which many governments act.

1. Governments can provide representation.

2. Governments can provide order and security.

3. Governments can provide services.

4. Governments can manage relations with other governments.

(From J. Gillespie and S. Lazarus, *American Government: Comparing Political Experiences* (Englewood Cliffs, N.J.: Prentice-Hall, Inc., 1979), p. 28.

4. *English.*   Communication and group problem-solving are the topics of this book for secondary English:

What is a Problem? A Solution? Logic?

You may define a *problem* as any unsatisfactory or undesirable condition that needs to be corrected. That undesirable condition is placing a hardship on someone or something—a person, persons, or the company. Problems in business might range from job discrimination to loss of profits, from cafeteria food to lack of proper supplies.

A *solution* is anything that remedies the unsatisfactory or undesirable condition without causing an even greater difficulty. The hardship caused is relieved: cafeteria food is improved; adequate boxes are provided for shipping, and so on. Often a solution may not be permanent or even conclusive; it may be just the best remedy for the time. At any rate, when you solve a problem, you do relieve the unwanted situation to the benefit of most people concerned.

(From C.J. Howard, R.F. Tracz, and C. Thomas, *Contact: A Textbook in Applied Communications*, 3rd ed. (Englewood Cliffs, N.J.: Prentice-Hall, Inc., 1979), p.138.

5. *Computer Programming and Data Processing.* This technical field is now part of most high school and vocational programs. This selection is from an introductory text:

Information Revolution

Computer products and services make up the fastest-growing major industry in the world. Computer sales have grown from an estimated $339 million in 1955 to figures which exceeded $60 billion per year for the years in the early to mid-1980s. Clearly the computer has become the information machine of our age—a machine which has actually created knowledge or information industries. As media theorist Marshall McLuhan has suggested, the computer has become the central nervous system of our society. The computer has certainly expanded man's general capacity to manage the information existing in our complex world. Yet it almost becomes a dichotomy similar to the unanswerable chicken question: Which came first, the chicken or the egg? Which came first, the information, or the computer to handle the information? It might be easiest to say that certain societal pressures created a need for more efficient methods of handling data, and once the computer was devised to lend structure and organization to existing information, it was found that the computer could be used to synthesize that information in ways creating new information. Therefore, the computer, which was originally designed to organize information, has actually evolved into a machine used as a source of information itself.

(From J. Frates and W. Moldrup, *Introduction to the Computer: An Integrated Approach* (Englewood Cliffs, N.J.: Prentice-Hall, Inc., 1980), p. 9.

These selections from content textbooks have several things in common. First, they are all *expository* writing: that is, writing which explains something. *Narrative* writing, or telling things in a time frame, in chronological order, is the form most often used in elementary reading texts. Hence, reading these content selections, and the books they come from, takes different reading skills from the typical elementary reading text. In other words, the schema for reading a content area textbook is vastly different from that required in reading a story in a basal reader.

Second, these books assume that students want to know what is being discussed. The books are not full of enticements to read. They say things in a straightforward, efficient manner. Their goals are clear: cognitive learning.

Third, these books assume background knowledge. Even introductory books assume certain information in the area is already known, especially information related to important background concepts underlying the content field.

Fourth, new terminology is introduced and used in context immediately. Readers must use the new words as soon as they are mentioned. They must be able not only to decode or say these words, but also to understand the meanings of the words and related concepts.

These and many other characteristics of content texts will be discussed throughout this book, but the conclusion is inescapable—content reading is *not* the same as reading narrative materials. Teachers and readers alike need to become alert to the differences and to understand the characteristics of content textbook writing.

Most junior and senior high school students have mastered the basic decoding skills of reading. If they haven't, they should be receiving remedial reading instruction. However, low-functioning readers will still be in content classes. Even if they have learned to decode, many students have difficulty moving to higher comprehension and cognitive levels.

Content teachers have the responsibility for diagnosing students' ability to handle the skills necessary for a subject area. Then the teacher must decide what is most needed to teach those students who are deficient in particular skills. In other words, instruction must be based on students' diagnosed needs. For example, one of the things social studies teachers need to know is how well their students can read and interpret maps. Biology and math teachers may have no concern for students' map skills, but they do rely on students' ability to read tables and graphs. All teachers are concerned with students' learning new vocabulary. However, English teachers often prefer that students identify word meanings through context, while chemistry teachers require precise definitions. So teachers must identify the reading skills necessary to learn their content material and must diagnose and prescribe appropriate reading instruction for their students. Diagnostic-prescriptive teaching of reading is the emphasis of this book.

A Taxonomy of Reading Comprehension

We accept the definition of reading as a process of getting meaning from printed material. That is, reading for content area purposes is a process of *comprehension.* Comprehension is the reason teachers read and the reason teachers ask students to read.

Barrett (1972) developed a useful way of showing the relationship between reading comprehension and the cognitive and affective taxonomies discussed earlier. Barrett's *Taxonomy of Reading Comprehension* gives four levels of comprehension: Literal, Inferential, Evaluation, and Appreciation. Here is Barrett's definition of these levels and some specific tasks that readers perform at various levels.

TAXONOMY OF READING COMPREHENSION (BARRETT, 1972)

1.0 *Literal Recognition or Recall.* Literal comprehension requires the recognition or recall of ideas, information, and happenings that are explicitly stated in the materials read. *Recognition Tasks*, which frequently take the form of purposes for reading, require the student to locate or identify explicit statements in the reading selection itself or in exercises that use the explicit content of the reading selection. *Recall tasks* demand the student to produce from memory explicit statements from a selection; such tasks are often in the form of questions teachers pose to students after a reading is completed. Two additional comments seem warranted with regard to literal comprehension tasks. First, although literal comprehension tasks can be overused, their importance cannot be denied, since a student's ability to deal with such tasks is fundamental to his ability to deal with other types of comprehension tasks. Second, all literal comprehension tasks are not necessarily of equal difficulty. For example, the recognition or recall of a single fact or incident may be somewhat easier than the recognition or recall of a number of facts or incidents, while a more difficult task than either of these two may be the recognition or recall of a number of events or incidents and the sequence of their occurrence. Also related to this concern is the hypothesis that a recall task is usually more difficult than a recognition task, when the two tasks deal with the same content and are of the same nature. Some examples[1] of literal comprehension tasks are:

    1.1 *Recognition or Recall of Details.* The student is required to locate or identify or to call up from memory such facts as the names of characters, the time a story took place, the setting of a story, or an incident described in a story, when such facts are explicitly stated in the selection.

    1.2 *Recognition or Recall of Main Ideas.* The student is asked to locate or identify or to produce from memory an explicit statement in or from a selection which is the main idea of a paragraph or a larger portion of the selection.

    1.3 *Recognition or Recall of Sequence.* The student is required to locate or identify or to call up from memory the order of incidents or actions explicitly stated in the selection.

    1.4 *Recognition or Recall of Comparisons.* The student is requested to locate or identify or to produce from memory likenesses and differences among characters, times in history, or places that are explicitly compared by an author.

    1.5 *Recognition or Recall of Cause and Effect Relationships.* The student in this instance may be required to locate or identify or to produce from memory reasons for certain incidents, events, or characters' actions explicitly stated in the selection.

    1.6 *Recognition or Recall of Character Traits.* The student is requested to identify or locate or to call up from memory statements about a character which help to point up the type of person he was when such statements were made by the author of the selection.

2.0 *Inference.* Inferential comprehension is demonstrated by the student when he uses a synthesis of the literal content of a selection, his personal knowledge, his intuition and his imagination as a basis for conjectures or hypotheses. Conjectures or hypotheses derived in this manner may be along convergent or divergent lines, depending on the nature of the task and the reading materials involved. For example, inferential tasks

---

[1] Although the examples in each of the categories are logically ordered from easy to difficult, it is recognized that such a finite hierarchy has not been validated. Therefore, the user of the Taxonomy should view the examples as some of the tasks that might be used to help students produce comprehension products that relate to the type of comprehension described in each of the four major categories of the Taxonomy.

related to narrative selections may permit more divergent or creative conjectures because of the open-ended possibilities provided by such writing. On the other hand, expository selections, because of their content, may call for convergent hypotheses more often than not. In either instance, students may or may not be called upon to indicate the rationale underlying their hypotheses or conjectures, although such a requirement would seem to be more appropriate for convergent rather than divergent hypotheses. Generally, then, inferential comprehension is elicited by purposes for reading, and by teachers' questions which demand thinking and imagination which are stimulated by, but go beyond, the printed page. Examples of inferential tasks related to reading are:

2.1 *Inferring Supporting Details.* In this instance, the student is asked to conjecture about additional facts the author might have included in the selection which would have made it more informative, interesting or appealing.

2.2 *Inferring the Main Idea.* The student is required to provide the main idea, general significance, theme, or moral which is not explicitly stated in the selection.

2.3 *Inferring Sequence.* The student, in this case, may be requested to conjecture as to what action or incident might have taken place between two explicitly stated actions or incidents; he may be asked to hypothesize about what would happen next; or he may be asked to hypothesize about the beginning of a story if the author had not started where he did.

2.4 *Inferring Comparisons.* The student is required to infer likenesses and differences in characters, times, or places. Such inferential comparisons revolve around ideas such as: "here and there," "then and now," "he and he," "he and she," and "she and she."

2.5 *Inferring Cause and Effect Relationships.* The student is required to hypothesize about the motives of characters and their interactions with others and with time and place. He may also be required to conjecture as to what caused the author to include certain ideas, words, characterizations, and actions in this writing.

2.6 *Inferring Character Traits.* In this case, the student may be asked to hypothesize about the nature of characters on the basis of explicit clues presented in the selection.

2.7 *Predicting Outcomes.* The student is requested to read an initial portion of a selection, and on the basis of this reading to conjecture about the outcome of the selection.

2.8 *Inferring about Figurative Language.* The student, in this instance, is asked to infer literal meanings from the author's figurative use of language.

3.0 *Evaluation.* Evaluation is demonstrated by a student when he makes judgments about the content of a reading selection by comparing it with external criteria, e.g., information provided by the teacher on the subject, authorities on the subject, or by accredited written sources on the subject; or with internal criteria, e.g., the reader's experiences, knowledge, or values related to the subject under consideration. In essence, evaluation requires students to make judgments about the content of their reading, judgments that have to do with its accuracy, acceptability, worth, desirability, completeness, suitability, timeliness, quality, truthfulness, or probability of occurrence. Examples of evaluation tasks related to reading are:

3.1 *Judgments of Reality or Fantasy.* The student is requested to determine whether incidents, events, or characters in a selection could have existed or occurred in real life on the basis of his experience.

3.2 *Judgments of Fact or Opinion.* In this case the student is asked to decide whether the author is presenting information which can be supported with objective data or whether the author is attempting to sway the reader's thinking through the use of subjective content that has overtones of propaganda.

3.3 *Judgments of Adequacy or Validity.* Tasks of this type call for the reader to judge whether the author's treatment of a subject is accurate and complete when compared to other sources on the subject. In this instance, then, the reader is called upon to compare written sources of information with an eye toward their agreements or disagreements, their completeness or incompleteness, and their thoroughness or superficiality in dealing with a subject.

3.4 *Judgments of Appropriateness.* Evaluation tasks of this type require the student to determine whether certain selections or parts of selections are relevant and can contribute to resolving an issue or a problem. For example, a student may be requested to judge the part of a selection which most appropriately describes a character. Or he may be called upon to determine which references will make significant contributions to a report he is preparing.

3.5 *Judgments of Worth, Desirability, or Acceptability.* In this instance, the student may be requested to pass judgments on the suitability of a character's action in a particular incident or episode. Was the character right or wrong, good or bad, or somewhere in between? Tasks of this nature call for opinions based on the values the reader has acquired through his personal experiences.

4.0 *Appreciation.* Appreciation has to do with students' awareness of the literary techniques, forms, styles, and structures employed by authors to stimulate emotional responses in their readers. Obviously, tasks which fall into this category will require varying degrees of inference and evaluation, but their primary focus must be on heightening students' sensitivity to the ways authors achieve an emotional as well as an intellectual impact on their readers. More specifically, appreciation involves cognizance of and visceral response to: (a) the artistry involved in developing stimulating plots, themes, settings, incidents, and characters, and (b) the artistry involved in selecting and using stimulating language, in general. Examples of tasks that involve appreciation are:

4.1 *Emotional Response to Plot or Theme.* Tasks of this type are based on the assumption that the plot or the theme of a given selection has stimulated and sustained a feeling of fascination, excitement, curiosity, boredom, sentimentality, tenderness, love, fear, hate, happiness, cheerfulness, or sadness. Provided this assumption is met, the students may be requested to determine what the author did in the process of developing the plot or theme that elicited a given emotional response.

4.2 *Identification with Characters and Incidents.* Some appreciation tasks should require students to become aware of the literary techniques and devices which prompt them to sympathize or empathize with a particular character, or to reject him, for that matter. Other tasks should require students to consider the placement, nature, and structure of events or incidents which cause them to project themselves into the action.

4.3 *Reactions to the Author's Use of Language.* In this instance, the student is required to recognize and respond to the author's craftsmanship as reflected in his selection of and use of words. Such tasks may deal with the connotations and denotations of selected words and the influence they have on a reader's feelings. In addition, students should at times note figures of speech, e.g., similes and metaphors, and the effect their use has on the reader.

4.4 *Imagery.* Tasks of this nature require the reader to recognize and react to the author's artistic ability to "paint word pictures." In other words, students should become sensitive to the techniques an author uses in order to enable them to see, smell, taste, hear, or feel things through reading.

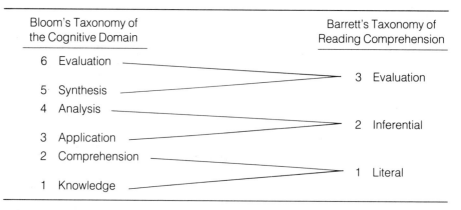

Bloom's Taxonomy of the Cognitive Domain	Barrett's Taxonomy of Reading Comprehension
6 Evaluation	
	3 Evaluation
5 Synthesis	
4 Analysis	
	2 Inferential
3 Application	
2 Comprehension	
	1 Literal
1 Knowledge	

FIGURE 1–1. The Cognitive Taxonomy and Comprehension Levels

The first three of Barrett's levels of comprehension are closely related to Bloom's cognitive levels. Figure 1–1 shows that relationship.

Another way of looking at Barrett's comprehension levels is considered in Figure 1–2. The triangle shape is purposeful, to show that a great deal of reading, as a great deal of learning, is necessary at the literal level. However, literal comprehension is only the base for higher levels of reading and thinking at the Inferential and Evaluation levels. Somewhere in the Inferential level, and at the Evaluation level, comprehension ceases to be convergent and becomes divergent. Convergent comprehension includes all questions and discussion in which there is a single correct answer which readers (students) must discover. Divergent comprehension at higher levels encourages multiple answers to questions, usually assuming that readers can justify or support their answers effectively.

Barrett's fourth level of comprehension, Appreciation, fits well with Krathwohl's taxonomy of the Affective Domain. Appreciation deals with readers' emotional response to reading, their response to the values included in the reading.

Comprehension levels will be used throughout this book, beginning with diagnosis in the next section and continuing through instructional procedures, reading skill analysis, and evaluation.

Comprehension remains the most important concern for teachers. Students must comprehend their reading and be able to work with the ideas and concepts gained from reading in the content classroom.

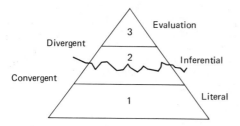

FIGURE 1–2 Comprehension Levels in Context

Summary

This chapter is a question: What is content area reading? The answer is that content area reading includes all three domains of learning, cognitive, affective and psychomotor. However, content teachers are most concerned with cognitive learning. Reading is defined as the process of understanding (or comprehending) the text, a highly cognitive process. The affective domain includes students' attitudes toward reading and school. The psychomotor domain includes the physical processes related to reading and the interaction between mind and body.

Three purposes for reading are most important: functional reading, or reading for practical purposes; career-based reading, or reading to learn about and keep current in a career; and recreational reading, or reading for enjoyment.

Content area reading materials have several characteristics in common. They are expository; they are cognitively oriented; they require background knowledge; and they use new terminology immediately.

Barrett's *Taxonomy of Reading Comprehension* provides a useful hierarchy of comprehension levels parallel to Bloom's cognitive hierarchy. Levels of comprehension are useful to content teachers in many areas of teaching, from diagnosis to skill development.

Chapter Activities: Using What You've Read

Learn to Do It!

1. You have completed the pre-test on attitude and skill and you have just completed Chapter 1. How do you feel about teaching reading in your own classroom right now? Make some notes and keep them for future reference.

2. Analyze your reading for the past week. How much of it was functional? _____

    career based? _____ recreational? _____

3. Look at the text that you are using or could use for one of your classes. Study the "comprehension" questions the authors developed and group them into Barrett's levels. How many questions are on the evaluative and appreciative levels? How many are literal? inferential?

4. Using Barrett's Taxonomy (pp. 25–27) develop one question on each broad level for either (a) a reading in a text in your content area or (b) one of the content selections (pp. 21–23). Try to develop questions also at each of the subsets of the broader category, but recognize that this is not always possible.

Do It!

1. You were introduced to the terms instructional, independent and frustration level readers. Using only anecdotal evidence or test scores you already have, assign each member of one of the classes you teach into one of the reading levels. You will have an opportunity later to check your assumptions.

2. Analyze the reading you assigned to your classes last week. How much of it was

    functional? _____ career based? _____ recreational? _____

3. Use the questions you wrote for 3 (above) with a class. Which level of questions did students find easiest to answer? hardest?

References

Barrett, T. C., "Taxonomy of Reading Comprehension," *Reading 360 Monograph.* Lexington, Mass.: Ginn, 1972.

Bloom, B. S., ed., *Taxonomy of Educational Objectives, Handbook I: Cognitive Domain.* New York: David McKay, 1956.

Dupuis, M. M., E. N. Askov, and J. W. Lee, "Changing Attitudes Toward Content Area Reading," *Journal of Educational Research,* 73: 2, November–December, 1979, 66–74.

Early, M. J., "Taking Stock: Secondary School Reading in the 70's," *Journal of Reading,* 16 (1973), 364–73.

Gagné, R. M., and L. J. Briggs, *Principles of Instructional Design.* New York: Holt, Rinehart & Winston, 1974.

Gray, W. S., "The Nature and Types of Reading," *The Teaching of Reading: A Second Report.* 36th Yearbook of the National Society for the Study of Education, Part I. Bloomington, Ill.: Public School, 1937.

Harrow, A. J., *A Taxonomy of the Psychomotor Domain.* New York: David McKay, 1972.

Herber, H. L., *Teaching Reading in Content Areas* (2nd ed). Englewood Cliffs, N.J.: Prentice-Hall, 1978.

Huey, E. B., *The Psychology and Pedagogy of Reading.* Cambridge: M.I.T. Press, 1968 (first published, 1908).

Kingston, A. J., "What Do We Mean by Reading in the Content Areas?" *Journal of Developmental Reading,* 7 (1964), 146–48.

Kintsch, W., and T. VanDijk, "Toward a Model of Text Comprehension and Production," *Psychological Review,* 85 (1978), 363–84.

Krathwohl, D. R., *et al. Taxonomy of Educational Objectives, Handbook II: Affective Domain.* New York: David McKay, 1964.

LaBerge, D., and S. Samuels, "Toward a Theory of Automatic Information Processing in Memory," *Cognitive Psychology,* 6 (1974), 293–323.

Otto, W., and S. White, eds., *Understanding Expository Text.* Academic Press, 1982.

Rosenblatt, L. M. *Literature as Exploration* (3rd ed.). New York: Noble and Noble Publishers, Inc., 1976.

Rubin, D., "Inner-City High School Teachers as Teachers of Reading: a Possible Solution to the Drop-out Problem," *Journal of Negro Education,* 43 (1974), 337–47.

Schleich, M., "Groundwork for Better Reading in Content Areas," *Journal of Reading,* 15 (1971), 119–26.

Singer, H., "Reading Content Specialists for the Junior High School Level," in *Investigations Relating to Mature Reading*, ed. F. P. Green. 21st Yearbook, National Reading Conference, 1972, 283–91.

SMITH, F., *Understanding Reading.* New York: Holt, Rinehart & Winston, 1971.

———, *Psycholinguistics and Reading* (2nd ed.) New York: Holt, Rinehart & Winston, 1978.

SNEDAKER, M., and E. HORN, "Reading in the Various Fields of the Curriculum," in *Part One: the Teaching of Reading,* ed. C. M. Whipple. 36th Yearbook, National Society for the Study of Education. Chicago: University of Chicago Press, 1937, 133–82.

STAUFFER, R. G., *Directing Reading Maturity as a Cognitive Process.* New York: Harper & Row, 1969.

TIERNEY, R., and D. LAPP, *National Assessment of Educational Progress in Reading.* Newark, Del.: International Reading Assn., 1979.

WARD, B. J., ed. *NAEP Newsletter,* 14:1, Spring 1981.

Chapter 2
Individualized Teaching in Content Area Reading

Preview

Individualized instruction begins with a clear understanding of the students in the class, what they need to know and how well they currently function. The assessment of current levels of functioning is known as diagnosis. Diagnosis is not a concept which is discussed frequently by content teachers. It usually is understood as diagnosis of students' cognitive level or their mastery of content material. Diagnosis of reading level may be seen as the responsibility of the reading teacher, or for secondary teachers, the oft-maligned elementary teachers. However, this book asserts that

1. Informal diagnosis of reading levels is the responsibility of the content teacher;
2. Content teachers can develop, administer, and evaluate informal diagnostic instruments;
3. Students should be taught with materials and methods which fit their abilities in reading and in content knowledge; and
4. Content teachers can use diagnostic information, teach the necessary reading skills, and not neglect their content responsibilities.

Students in Content Classes

Students in content classes are diverse in background, learning ability, interests, and many other things, including reading ability. Much of this book describes specific types of students and specific teaching techniques useful with them. To make the procedures and techniques easy to apply to the "real world," we have identified three students who are typical of students any teacher may have. Throughout the book, these students will be used as examples of how suggested activities or techniques might work with them.

The first student is David, an engaging and enthusiastic fifth-grade boy.

David enjoys reading to his younger sister, Karen, who is in second grade. *(Photo by Joseph Bodkin)*

David is from a suburban family with one younger sister. His parents both work. Both are college educated. David likes animals. He has several pets and assumes responsibility at home for taking care of them. David is a Cub Scout and a member of his church's youth group. He plays Little League baseball, basketball, hockey and whatever sport is in season.

David is what is called *an instructional level reader*. This means that he is reading at a level appropriate for his grade, and much of the material designed for his subjects and grade will be suitable for him.

David's reading interests are beginning to diversify. Now that reading has become more fluent for David, he is beginning to feel confident in his ability to try new kinds of reading material. He has been reading animal stories for some time. Recently he has begun to read science fiction like *The Lion, the Witch and the*

Wardrobe. David likes sports and reads the sports page of the daily paper. He has as yet little interest in the other parts of the paper or in magazines. However, his sports interest could lead to greater reading in that area in the near future.

The second student is Betsy, a red-headed eighth grader, thirteen years old. Betsy lives on a farm with her parents, both high school graduates, who run the farm. She has two older siblings, a brother and sister. Betsy is active in 4-H work, raising dairy cows and showing them at the county fair. She is active in her church youth group and takes part in school activities.

Betsy is interested in school, but she has difficulty reading. Her reading has been assessed as *frustration level* with grade level materials, which suggests that much of the material designed for her grade level is too difficult for her to read.

Betsy reads material on her own, despite her difficulty with classroom reading. She enjoys books about animals, like *The Black Stallion, Big Red* (whose leading character is an Irish setter), and *The Incredible Journey,* the story of three animals who traveled many miles searching for their family. Betsy skims the newspaper daily, reading the parts she likes, and skims dairy and farm magazines that come to her parents.

Pam is the third student, a junior in high school. She lives in a city of 250,000, a relatively urban area. She lives with her parents, both high school graduates with some college work. Her father works in a factory, while her mother is a secretary in a

Betsy keeps careful records of her Jersey cows' milk production for her 4-H club. She has won many ribbons showing her dairy cows. *(Photo by Joseph Bodkin)*

Pam enjoys playing the piano for relaxation and as a way of extending her love of music. *(Photo by Joseph Bodkin)*

corporate office. She has four brothers and sisters. Pam is happy with her circle of friends, though she is not always interested in school. She does plan, however, to go to college, probably at the local community college. She has been assessed as an *independent level* reader, one who can easily read most materials in her grade and subject without much instruction from the teacher.

Pam's reading habits are well developed. She especially enjoys historical fiction and biographies of what she calls "interesting people." She has recently read Michener's *Chesapeake* and Costain's *The Magnificent Century.* Pam reads the local paper daily. She especially enjoys the local news and reports of activities of the community and church groups to which she and her parents belong. Pam's family subscribes to few magazines, so she goes to the school library to read *National Geographic, Time,* and *Reader's Digest.* Pam reads voraciously, choosing to read whatever interests her, regardless of difficulty level.

These three levels of reading skills—instructional, frustration, and independent —will be discussed in detail in Chapter 4. The responses of these three students to various activities and techniques will be highlighted throughout the book. However they are defined, all teachers can expect to have some of these three types of students in their classes. Two major questions remain for the rest of this book:

How do teachers know what kinds of students are in their classes?

How can teachers teach content materials to these different kinds of students?

Needed Diagnostic Information

Content teachers need to know a great deal about the reading skill levels of their students. First, teachers must analyze the objectives and materials on which their courses are based to determine which skills students must be able to use in order to be successful in their classes. then they must determine from earlier teachers, curriculum guides, and student records which skills the students have already been taught. Questions to be answered include: Which of these skills have the students mastered? Can students transfer skills learned in reading class (or any other class) to the content material in this class?

A great many skills are introduced in the elementary grades in the context of reading class; for example, word attack skills using roots and affixes (prefixes and suffixes) to find the meaning of unfamiliar words. The task of the content teacher is to teach consciously for the necessary transfer of these basic vocabulary skills, reinforcing and expanding the skills for particular use in the given content area.

Consider this possibility: students enter seventh grade having some familiarity with roots and with inflectional affixes and some basic derivational affixes. (Inflectional affixes include plurals, verb number and tense markers. Derivational affixes change the word's meaning or part of speech.) The junior high school science teacher asks students to begin using specifically scientific affixes and the Greek and Latin roots so common in scientific language. Diagnostic questions include:

1. Can students identify and apply inflectional affixes in non-scientific words, like car*s*, walk*ed?*
2. Can students recognize the component parts of basic scientific terms?
   Think of *pollution, photosynthesis,* and *sulfate.*
3. Can students build new words from groups of roots and derivational affixes and identify probable meanings? Can they move from microscop*e*, to microscop*ic*, to microscop*y?*

After the basic skill is transferred and reinforced, the science teacher can introduce more elaborate root and affix work, combining basic sound pattern rules (again, familiar from elementary school) and the word-building process. The complexity of the process of vocabulary building is important for content teachers to see; vocabulary skills are discussed in detail in Chapter 12.

This set of vocabulary skills, synthesizing several basic known skills in the approach to unfamiliar words, represents the second major diagnostic problem for content teachers. Once they have determined students' mastery of skills taught earlier, content teachers must assess their mastery of developing skills, ones not assumed to have been mastered earlier. For such skills as these, students need direct instruction, not merely transfer and reinforcement. These skills need sequential work, carefully planned and systematically introduced. Examples of developing skills include higher level problem-solving and searching skills; drawing abstract conclusions, like determining the "theme" of literature; and appreciating figurative language.

A third diagnostic problem for content teachers at all grade levels is to match the reading level of texts and other pieces of reading to the reading abilities of the students. This match requires that content teachers be able to assess the difficulty of texts. It also requires that they be able to assess the reading levels of their students. With this information, teachers can find reading materials appropriate for the students or, if that is not possible, they can adjust their teaching and the students' uses of the material to account for differences.

Content teachers can develop the skills necessary to incorporate the teaching of reading into their special content. The long-range goal is the synthesis of necessary reading skill instruction with regular content instruction. Selection of content goals is the primary consideration, with the students' mastery of these content goals the critical outcome. However, since such mastery will not occur without adequate reading skills, these content goals must be coupled with reading skill instruction. This requires both the application of diagnostic information and integration of reading objectives with those in the content area.

The Decision Model for Diagnostic Teaching by Grouping

The key concept in this approach for content teachers is the Decision Model for Diagnostic Teaching (Cartwright, Cartwright and Yssledyke 1973). This model, based on analysis of each student's potential, requires professional decisions at specific points in the planning of each teaching situation. The original decision model, designed for teachers of exceptional students in regular classes, works well in any class in which individualized attention can be given to a student, or in the individualized atmosphere of a learning center.

Realistically, individual attention to each student is not possible for secondary content teachers, faced with 150 or so students each day, for discrete periods of time, with little flexibility in space. A more reasonable model for such teachers is an adaptation of Decision Model for Diagnostic Teaching by Grouping given in Figure 2–1. The adapted model also assists teachers in forming groups for social as well as cognitive reasons. However, it is based on the same principle, a step-by-step planning sequence for a teacher to follow throughout the teaching-learning process.

Step one is a careful assessment of each student to *identify relevant characteristics,* in this case of his/her reading ability, using informal assessment of reading skills by content teachers using their own materials. Teachers can develop group informal reading inventories (Shepherd 1978; Thelen 1976; Earle 1976; Lunstrom and Taylor 1978) and cloze techniques (Dupuis 1976; Riley 1973) and use classroom observation techniques. They must assess students' prior knowledge of the content so that they begin instruction "where the student is." They can assess students' self-direction level to determine which students can best learn through independent activities. Many teachers have done this, but for too many, this valuable diagnostic information is gathered, then never used. Other teachers do not gather diagnostic information since they do not know how to use it. The rest of the model shows teachers how to act on this information.

Step two asks teachers to *specify teaching goals* for each student. This requires writing objectives which speak to student learning, both in content area and in reading skills (Dupuis 1973). The objective prescribed for each student may differ in which reading skill is being learned, or in what medium is the source of content information (for example, book, videotape, microfilm, magazine article, or audiotape). The objective may allow choice in the method of demonstrating knowledge (such as oral or written response, creative project or research paper), or in the route to gaining the skill or information (for example, classwork, learning centers or learning packets).

It seems reasonable that these student objectives be considered in groups or clusters rather than individually. That is, objectives can be grouped together in clusters of three or four which are somehow similar; the reading skill is the same, or the topic is the same, or the process is the same. These clusters are found to be useful

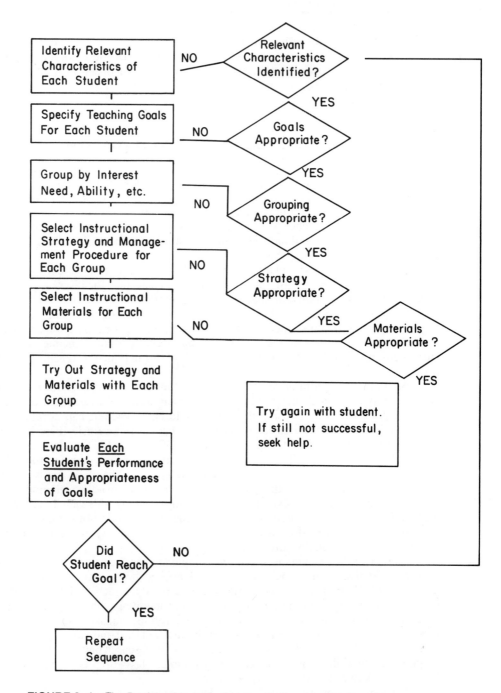

FIGURE 2–1 The Decision Model for Diagnostic Teaching by Grouping

for several students, hence a group of students working on the same cluster of objectives.

Step three of the model is the process of grouping. The teacher makes the professional decision that certain objectives for certain students can be achieved in a group. These groups can be based on skill strengths or weaknesses, interests, extent of background knowledge, special abilities; or a group of students can be matched to particular alternative reading materials. Such groups differ from typical homogeneous groupings because they are reevaluated after each sequence. They can be changed at any time, either when weaknesses have been corrected or when interests have changed; whenever the need for the group no longer exists.

Step four of the model directs the teacher, perhaps with the students, to choose which instructional strategy to use—that is, lecture, guided discovery, inquiry, small group discussion, independent laboratory work, research in the library, or learning packets. Each of those strategies uses different skills and requires different kinds and amount of reading. Each allows the teacher to direct students to use their strong skills and/or to build up their weaknesses. The classroom management procedure is dictated by the instructional choices. Will the class be in one large group? Small groups? Independent study in the classroom? Somewhere else? The teacher remains responsible for knowing what each student or group is doing. The teacher must direct or guide students carefully, allowing appropriate degrees of decision making by students. Content teachers can move gradually into grouping patterns other than the single large group, although this change may happen slowly and in small increments. As teachers become comfortable in different situations, as they know they can manage the class, they can try additional patterns.

Step five of the model may seem out of place—selecting instructional materials. For many teachers, this is the first step—the adopted textbook is the material. The Decision Model suggests that teachers put the horse and cart in the proper order, and make the materials serve the goals and procedures which the teacher has selected. The text may still be the appropriate material. However, vast numbers of alternative materials are available. Teachers must become familiar with many different materials in their content area, assessing each in terms of its suitability in reading level, skills, and content material. An additional procedure at this step is learning to adapt texts for use by students who cannot otherwise use them by developing study guides (Thomas and Robinson 1973), and reasoning guides (Herber 1978), and even by rewriting the critical parts of the content material.

Step six directs the teacher to try out these plans with each group. Inservice teachers can try out the techniques in their classes as they read this book. Preservice teachers can use field experience or simulation exercises to get similar results. Feedback from student to teacher is *step seven*—evaluation. At this point, the model shifts its emphasis from the groups formed after step two back to the individual student. Each student's individual performance must be assessed to determine where s/he met the designated objectives. This means, of course, that students in the same class may be reaching different objectives. While the content objectives may be the same for all of them, the reading skill objectives may well differ.

The decisions to be made during the evaluation are included in diamond shape on the model. If the student reached the goal set, then the sequence can be repeated. If s/he did not reach the goal, the teacher looks for the reason why. At which step did the teacher's planning go awry? Suitable revision should allow the student to succeed on the next attempt. It is at this point that the grouping changes if the needs of the group have changed. Indeed, based on a new set of goals for each student, the grouping patterns will necessarily change frequently. Thus, the instructional pattern described here will not lock a student into a "track" or any kind of continuing group. The teacher's professional judgment will be used after each instructional sequence to be sure that the groups are serving the best interests of each student.

Different instructional sequences can be planned, using the Decision Model, from a single class period to a full year. Practical considerations suggest that content teachers work in *units* of instruction, two to six weeks in length, so that such a process is manageable. *Units* are instructional plans developed by teachers using curriculum guides or other general guidelines. Hilda Taba (1962) gives the most concise description of the unit-building process. She says developing units is the answer to many classroom organization problems, "the organization of content and the organization of learning experience" (p. 291). According to Taba, a unit has sequence and helps provide cumulative learning. A unit is integrative; it helps students to create "a unity of knowledge" (p. 299). A unit has focus, and provides variety in modes of learning. Units and related instructional techniques are discussed fully later in this book, as are techniques related to each step on the Decision Model.

Use of the Decision Model provides a number of positive results. First, teachers will have immediate information available to use in establishing who has mastered the unit objectives and who hasn't. Students who are unsuccessful can be given immediate attention so they can stay with the class. These data also assist in determining student grades.

A second positive result is that teachers can identify reading skills and content topics in a reasonable order, developing objectives which can be integrated into a cohesive whole. Student knowledge, reading level and interest can be taken into account, so that it is more likely that students can achieve success.

A third result is that teachers can look over plans for a teaching unit and balance out the amount of reading, the number of papers to be written and graded, and the outside projects—a benefit to both teachers and students. Variety in teaching strategy and different grouping patterns can be built in both for ease in student learning and for economy of instructional time.

Finally, the Decision Model helps teachers plan for exceptional children, using alternative grouping and instructional plans to build on their strengths and minimize their weaknesses. Specific objectives from Individualized Educational Programs (IEPs) can be accommodated in the unit and grouping plans.

Summary

Diagnostic teaching in content area reading means careful assessment of student ability in each teacher's class. Teachers need to know their students' ability to read the necessary materials, their background knowledge, and the methods by which students learn most easily.

The Decision Model for Diagnostic Teaching by Grouping is a practical way for teachers to plan and carry out diagnostic teaching. The seven steps in the planning model make it possible for teachers to plan and evaluate their teaching, from a single lesson plan to a six-week unit.

Now it is time to deal with specific techniques in Step I, diagnosis, and Step III, grouping, on the Planning Model. The next part of the book deals with answers to questions like these:

What are the relevant characteristics of students? In reading? In content material? In attitude? In interest? How can students be grouped to learn most effectively?

Chapter Activities: Using What You've Read

Learn to Do It!

Develop a list of objectives for one unit you want to teach to determine what reading skills students must be able to use to be successful.

Do It!

Development of more formal diagnosis comes in a later chapter. For one class you teach or may teach, determine what reading skills the students already have by (a) talking to previous teachers, (b) looking at curriculum guides and (c) reviewing student records.

References

CARTWRIGHT, G. P., C. A. CARTWRIGHT, and J. E. YSSLEDYKE, "Two Decision Models: Identification and Diagnostic Teaching of Handicapped Children in the Regular Classroom," *Psychology in the Schools,* 10 (1973), 4–11.

DUPUIS, M. M., "The Cloze Procedure: Can It Be Used with Literature?" *Reading Improvement,* 13 (1976), 199–203.

————, "The Cloze Procedure as a Predictor of Comprehension in Literature," *Journal of Educational Research,* 74: 1, 1980, 27–33.

DUPUIS, V. L. "A Design for Accountability in Curriculum Evaluation," *The New Campus,* 26 (1973), 11–16.

EARLE, R. A., *Teaching Reading and Mathematics.* Newark, Del.: International Reading Association, 1976.

HERBER, H. L., *Teaching Reading in Content Areas* (2nd ed.) Englewood Cliffs, N.J.: Prentice-Hall, 1978.

JOYCE, B., and M. WEIL, *Models of Teaching* (2nd ed.) Englewood Cliffs, N.J.: Prentice-Hall, 1980.

LUNSTRUM, J. P., and B. L. TAYLOR, *Teaching Reading in the Social Studies.* Newark, Del.: International Reading Association, 1978.

RILEY, P. M., *The Cloze Procedure—a Selected Annotated Bibliography.* Lae, New Guinea: PNG University of Technology, 1973.

SHEPHERD, D. L., *Comprehensive High School Reading Methods* (2nd ed.) Columbus, Ohio: Merrill, 1978.

TABA, H., *Curriculum Development: Theory and Practice.* New York: Harcourt, Brace & World, 1962.

THELEN, J., *Improving Reading in Science.* Newark, Del.: International Reading Association, 1976.

THOMAS, E. L., and H. A. ROBINSON, *Improving Reading in Every Class: A Sourcebook for Teachers.* Boston: Allyn & Bacon, 1976.

PART II
DIAGNOSIS AND GROUPING IN CONTENT AREA READING

OVERVIEW

A necessary preliminary step to prescribing appropriate instruction is diagnosis of students' abilities to handle reading demands as well as content requirements. The Decision Model for Diagnostic Teaching includes diagnosis as its first step: identifying *relevant* characteristics of students. One might ask how a content teacher who teaches in a departmentalized situation can take time to group students and provide differential instruction. Many content teachers initially feel that they have neither the time nor the resources to implement differential instruction in content area classes. They are well aware, however, that many of their students are unable to handle the reading demands of their classes.

In all content areas—social studies, science, home economics, music are examples—differences in the ability to handle content demands are obvious. One student might have background in a particular content area, such as industrial arts, through the influence of a family member. Another might excel in social studies, having traveled widely in varying countries. The need to individualize instruction in content is clear.

Just as teachers cannot assume that students have equal background in the content field, they also cannot assume that the reading abilities of their students are equal. Some students, even those who may have been adequate readers in elementary school using a basal reader, have difficulty reading content area textbooks due to the specialized vocabulary, difficult concepts, and factual material not written in a narrative style.

Therefore, diagnosis of abilities, in relation to both content requirements and reading demands, is a necessary preliminary step before instruction. The focus in this section is on the reading skill requirements in most content area studies. Content teachers will also need to gather diagnostic information concerning previous background in the particular content subject.

SOURCES OF DIAGNOSTIC INFORMATION

Information about students' reading abilities is available from a variety of sources. Previous teachers may pass on information about particular students' reading abilities. The librarian may also be able to provide information about students' use of library resources, if library use is required in the content study. A questionnaire may be given to the student to determine self-perception of reading abilities. Conversations with parents during a back-to-school night might provide helpful information useful in planning instruction.

Cumulative record folders usually contain reports of testing in reading and other areas done throughout a student's school career. These scores usually represent the results of the survey level of testing which is conducted primarily for the purpose of screening. Norms are provided so that individual and group scores may be compared to those obtained by students of the same age or grade placement.

Teachers should consider all sources in gathering diagnostic information. They should consider not only reading abilities but also other factors such as linguistic differences and motivation. The focus of the next chapter, however, is upon using formal measures to determine reading achievement and content mastery.

Chapter 3
Formal Testing

Preview

Because formal testing is commonly carried out at all grade levels in the schools, we will discuss the two major types of formal testing, presenting the uses as well as strengths and weaknesses of each. The next chapter focuses on informal teacher-made tests.

Formal Tests

Norm-referenced tests are the most common type of formal testing. Their intent is to compare the achievement of a local group or individuals to a national sample of students of the same age or grade. Because their function is to make comparisons, they are carefully standardized; that is, testing conditions are specified in the test manual. Tests are aimed so that all students take the tests with the same limitations. They are often administered at the beginning or end of the school year, or in some cases at both times of every year.

Some school districts, however, have decreased the amount of norm-referenced testing—testing only fall or spring every two or three years—in favor of another type of formal testing, criterion-referenced testing. In criterion-referenced testing, students are compared *not* to age or grade mates but to themselves in terms of a set of objectives. Appropriate objectives are stated in behavioral terms, with the conditions for testing specified as well as the mastery level expected (see Gronlund, 1981). Then items are written to determine whether or not each student can perform the behavior(s) specified in the objective at the predetermined level of acceptable performance. If so, the student is said to have *mastered* the objective, thereby not needing further work related to that objective.

Some school districts have developed their own criterion-referenced tests for reading and language arts. For example, one objective at the upper elementary level for reading in a local curriculum (State College, PA, Area School District, 1976) is as follows:

> After reading an essay on a series of articles, etc., the students will summarize the main ideas.

A sample item from those which measure mastery of this objective (79 percent is required for mastery level) follows:

READ THE DIRECTIONS AND ANSWER THE QUESTIONS

Directions: Read each selection. Read the three statements under each selection. Choose the statement which best explains the *main* idea of the selection. Mark your choice in the correct space on your answer sheet.

Jody tore himself from the fascination of his father's performance and moved to his end of the pond. He cast badly for a time, tangling his line and laying his bob in the most unlikely places; over-reaching the narrow pond and enmeshing the hook in the tough saw-grass. Then something of harmony came to him. He felt his arm swing in a satisfying arc. His wrist flexed at the proper moment. He laid the bob exactly where he had meant to, at the edge of a patch of switch-grass.

a. With practice Jody learned how to cast perfectly.

b. Jody was fascinated by his father's expert casting.

c. Jody tangled his fishing line and caught the hook in the tough saw-grass.

While these two types of formal tests are very different in intent, they do share the advantages and disadvantages of being formal tests. In other words, because they are formal tests, item pools have been carefully written. The tests should have been field-tested to establish test *validity* and *reliability*. *Validity* concerns whether a test measures what it purports to measure; it is usually estimated by measuring whether a new test gets the same result as an established test of the same ability. If similar results are obtained each time the same group is tested under the same conditions, the test is said to have adequate *reliability* because the results are reproducible. A technical bulletin should be available to present substantiating data for claims of validity and reliability.

Another advantage of formal testing is uniformity. Test administration manuals should clearly specify testing conditions, such as time required and materials needed. Tests administered by one teacher should produce comparable results if administered to the same group by anyone else. At the secondary level, it is often convenient to do mass testing in one location, such as the cafeteria, to minimize disruption of the school schedule.

Some disadvantages of formal testing are that formal tests sometimes produce anxiety, preventing students from performing at maximum levels. Performance on a particular day may not be typical of usual performance levels. Some students who are not highly motivated may be overwhelmed by the formal nature of the test and may randomly guess or not perform up to capabilities. One must be sure that the local group is similar to the norming group; if not, comparisons cannot be made and standard scores (such as grade equivalents) cannot be used. Students who do not speak English as native speakers may not even understand the test directions, which may be read only a specified number of times. Poor readers may not be able to read well enough to take the test in written form. Machine scoring, while convenient for the teacher, makes error analysis difficult or impossible.

With that general background, let us consider the uses as well as strengths and weaknesses of each type of formal testing in content classes.

NORM-REFERENCED TESTS

Norm-referenced tests are widely available for measuring not only reading level but also levels of functioning in the various content areas. If the test norms are appropriate for the individuals being tested, the scores can indicate general reading ability or extent of knowledge of a content field. However, a single score in reading—or even a separate score for vocabulary and comprehension—doesn't provide diagnostic information about the students' strengths and weaknesses in reading. Without knowing which items are missed, the teacher cannot look for a pattern of errors. Without this diagnostic information, the test scores do not provide much help in planning instruction. These scores, however, do indicate a general level of functioning in reading, although they often tend to overestimate the level at which a student can actually function in the classroom.

These tests are not appropriate for special learners, such as mentally retarded or learning disabled students, since they cannot be compared to their age or grade mates. Poor readers, who might perform adequately on a test of science or social studies content if tested orally, also cannot read well or fast enough to score appropriately. They score poorly on all types of standardized tests—whether for reading or a content area—because of their inability to read the test items within specified time limits.

For students who can adequately read a content area test, such as social studies or mathematical reasoning, the test results do provide the content teacher with an indication of background in the content area. Knowledge of the major concepts of the field is assessed as well as some important factual knowledge. The content teacher can see how individuals and the local group compare to national groups that supposedly represent typical levels of functioning.

Care must be taken, however, to be sure that the content area tests measure what the local curriculum teaches. The same concepts, vocabulary, and main ideas should be taught as well as tested in order for the test to be a valid measure of what students are learning.

The reading demands of the curriculum and tests should also be compatible. A content teacher who emphasizes learning the main ideas and concepts would not want to pick a test that emphasizes retention of factual knowledge. Unless a test is carefully studied by the content teacher, s/he may not realize why her/his students do not perform well on norm-referenced tests. The mismatch between the type of reading expected in class and on a norm-referenced test could lower students' scores. Again, the test would not provide a valid measure of students' learning in a content area.

A suggestion for analyzing the compatibility of a norm-referenced test with the curriculum is for the teachers of a given content area to create a matrix similar to that presented below using a hypothetical science example.

Curriculum Objectives	Test Items	*Test Items not included in Curriculum Objectives
1. To be able to explain the process of photosynthesis and the effects of that process on living things. (main ideas)	#5, 6, (main ideas) #7 (detail)*	#15, 24, 29

*Test items incompatible with curriculum objectives.

One way to improve poor norm-referenced test scores, if the tests are not selected by teachers and cannot be changed, is to use such a chart in planning instruction. We are not suggesting that specific test items be taught, but that the important vocabulary, concepts, and knowledge found on the test be included in the curriculum. If students are also taught how to read items similar to the types of test items found in the test, scores should improve.

In summary, norm-referenced tests may be useful in indicating general levels of functioning in a content area and in reading. Care must be taken to insure that the tests used fit the objectives of the instructional curriculum. Care must also be taken to insure that the test norms are appropriate for the local group. Such tests should not be given to special learners and severely disabled readers; they should be assessed orally on tests measuring knowledge of a content field.

CRITERION-REFERENCED TESTS

Criterion-referenced tests which measure the attainment of a specific objective may be either formal or informal. Formal criterion-referenced tests, such as part of the *Wisconsin Design for Reading Skill Development* (Otto and Askov 1972), should provide evidence of established validity and reliability. Informal criterion-referenced measures are discussed in the next chapter, dealing with informal testing.

Because the intent of criterion-referenced tests is only to measure whether or not an individual has reached a predetermined proficiency level—specified as the "mastery level"—items should be approximately of equal difficulty on a given criterion-referenced test. On a norm-referenced test, however, items become increasingly more difficult as the student progresses through the test because the intent is to place the individual on a continuum that compares him/her to comparable age or grade mates.

In selecting a criterion-referenced test, teachers must exercise care to insure that the test objectives are compatible with the curriculum objectives. Compatibility is easier to establish here than with norm-referenced tests, since most formal criterion-referenced tests specify the objectives measured in behavioral terms. It is, therefore, relatively simple to determine whether the same or similar objectives are being measured.

Criterion-referenced tests are useful in planning instruction because they indicate the skills that have and have not been mastered. Groups of students who have not mastered particular skills can be pulled together for instruction. Criterion-referenced tests must not, however, be used simplistically; mastery attained at one point in time will not necessarily be retained if opportunities are not provided for application and practice. Therefore, objectives should be written to achieve a spiraling effect so that skills are reviewed at each successively higher level with greater complexity and difficulty. For example, in learning the study skill of using a scale bar on a map, students should initially be asked to find the distance on the map where one inch equals one unit of measurement, say one mile. At a higher level one inch may represent two or three miles. At a still higher level, after students have mastered these easier skills, they might have to calculate the distance represented by two-and-one-half inches. Articulation among teachers at the various grade levels is necessary to be sure that appropriate skills are being taught at each level.

Some more complex comprehension skills may not be amenable to criterion-referenced measurement since mastery or non-mastery may depend on the text material presented in the testing situation. Some authorities argue that the reading process cannot be fragmented into discrete skills, while others say that specific skill instruction is used for certain aspects of reading instruction. (See Guthrie 1977 for a discussion of the issues.) We concur with the latter point of view—that some reading skills can be taught and are therefore amenable to criterion-referenced measurement. In fact, use of this type of diagnostic-prescriptive model on a large scale has produced significant achievement gains (Kamm 1978).

In the following chapters on informal testing and on reading skills we will suggest the skills that seem to us worthy of instruction. If they are to be taught, teachers can assess mastery of the skills through criterion-referenced measurement.

Summary

Formal testing may include norm-referenced and criterion-referenced tests. While formal tests have the advantage of professional and technical development, they may not match the local curriculum. The local group also may not be similar to the national norming group, making comparisons of local scores and those obtained by the national norming group invalid. Informal testing designed by local teachers, on the other hand, can be tailored to the local curriculum.

Chapter Activities: Using What You've Read

Learn to Do It!

1. Are Scholastic Aptitude Tests/College Boards norm-referenced or criterion-referenced? Are most college class tests norm-referenced or criterion-referenced? What arguments can you see for the choice of a norm- or criterion-referenced test in either case?

2. If you were a test developer having created a test to measure reading competence in English for speakers of other languages, describe how you would establish the (a) validity and (b) reliability of your test.

Do It!

Look at the curriculum objectives for a discrete section of your curriculum and at the formal reading test used by your school (SAT, CTBS, etc.) and develop a matrix similar to the one on p. 48 to analyze the compatibility of the test with the curriculum.

References

GRONLUND, N. E., *Measurement and Evaluation in Teaching* (4th ed.), New York: Macmillan, 1981.

GUTHRIE, J. T., ed., *Cognition, Curriculum and Comprehension*. Newark, Del.: International Reading Association, 1977.

KAMM, K., "A Five-Year Study of the Effects of a Skill-Centered Approach to the Teaching of Reading," *Journal of Educational Research* (1978), 104–12.

OTTO, W., and E. ASKOV, *The Wisconsin Design for Reading Skill Development; Rationale and Guidelines,* Minneapolis: National Computer Systems, 1972.

STATE COLLEGE AREA SCHOOL DISTRICT, *Elementary Language Arts Criterion-Referenced Test, Advanced Intermediate Reading Story*. State College, Pa.: State College Area School District, 1976.

Chapter 4
Informal Testing

Preview

Because standardized norm-referenced tests do not provide diagnostic information, in spite of their established validity and reliability, teachers ought to develop informal assessments in making a diagnosis of individual and group strengths, weaknesses, and reading levels.

Informal Testing

Diagnosis of reading ability in content subjects is twofold. First, diagnosis of general reading abilities must be carried out to determine whether students can use content curriculum materials. It is not at all unusual in a seventh-grade social studies classroom, for example, for some students to function in reading ability at a third-grade level while others are functioning at upper high school levels.

Second, proficiency in specific reading and study skills may vary widely depending on past experiences, prior instruction, and general ability level. Although proficiency in specific study skills is certainly related to general reading ability, it is possible for poor readers to have achieved mastery of specific reading and study skills through opportunities outside the classroom. Both general reading ability in content materials and the ability to apply specific reading and study skills should be assessed by the content teacher.

THE CRITERION-REFERENCED GROUP READING INVENTORY

The group informal reading inventory, as presented elsewhere (Shepherd 1978), has proved to be a useful diagnostic tool in content area reading to determine general reading ability as well as specific strengths and weaknesses in reading and study skills. As an adaptation of the informal reading inventory, the group informal reading inventory may be administered to a large group. The original informal reading inventory, used extensively by elementary teachers and reading specialists, asks an individual student to read orally a series of paragraphs graded in difficulty and answer comprehension and vocabulary questions. On a group informal reading inventory, students are asked to read silently a selection from the content textbook to determine their reading level in relation to the textbook itself. If several textbooks of varying difficulty levels are available, then a selection should be taken from each to determine which is most appropriate for each student.

Shepherd (1978) identifies some common skills that should be assessed regardless of content area, such as using parts of the book, including the use of the table of contents, index, and glossary. Vocabulary skills, such as identifying word meanings in context, dividing words into syllables, and picking out frequently used roots and affixes, can also be included in all content area assessments. Comprehension skills are assesssed through reading a particular selection from the textbook. Scanning to locate specific information and skimming to get a general overview may be assessed, in addition to reading rate.

Teachers may also consider the graphic skills that are unique to their content areas. For example, social studies teachers might include assessment of map reading skills while science teachers might assess the interpretation of tables and graphs. Home economics teachers, on the other hand, might focus on students' abilities to read charts and diagrams.

The difficulty with the group informal reading inventory, as described by Shepherd and others (for example, Burmeister 1978; Singer and Donlan 1980), is the lack of sufficient items to provide a reliable measure of skill attainment. Therefore, we propose that content teachers create *criterion-referenced* group reading inventories.

DEVELOPING A CRITERION-REFERENCED
GROUP READING INVENTORY

The process of developing a criterion-referenced group reading inventory includes the steps given here:

1. The content teacher selects a section of the textbook or other reading materials used for instruction, usually from the middle of the book, four to six pages in length. The section should be relatively self-contained, not largely dependent on prior reading, and reaching some sort of closure at the conclusion of the section. Comprehension should be assessed using Barrett's *Taxonomy of Reading Comprehension* (1972). Literal questions (ten to twelve) which emphasize recall of the main ideas and important details should be written. As nearly as possible, an equal number of inferential questions, requiring students to "read between the lines," should also be written. Care should be taken to make the comprehension questions dependent on having read the text material. In other words, a student shouldn't be able to answer the questions through background knowledge. (See Barrett's *Taxonomy* in Chapter 1 for further distinctions between literal and inferential comprehension.) The student's ability to determine the meanings of vocabulary words should be assessed with words from the selection; usually ten to twelve items are needed.

2. The content teacher decides which skills are important in using the chosen content textbook or other reading material. For example, a social studies teacher might select additional vocabulary skills, main ideas and sequential comprehension skills, and several map reading skills. Behavioral objectives might be formulated to define the parameters of the skill. Ideally, this process should be done in collaboration with other teachers of the same content area so that skills may be taught and reviewed at successively higher levels with increasingly more complex and difficult materials. Approximately four to six skills are selected for assessment.

3. Items are written to measure attainment of each skill. Answers can be obtained only through using the textbook. Usually ten to twelve items per skill are needed. Mastery level, or the percent required to indicate attainment of the skill, is set for each skill. Usually 80 percent is considered sufficient; however, the figure may be adjusted upward if mastery at a higher level is considered important in using the content area textbook or if the students are particularly capable. One hundred percent is not recommended due to inevitable test error.

One teacher created the following criterion-referenced group reading inventory for a seventh-grade life science class.

GROUP READING INVENTORY *

Life Science, Englewood Cliffs, N.J.:
Prentice-Hall, Inc., 1980

General Directions: This is a survey to help me evaluate skills you will be using in this course. This is not a test to see what facts you know and you will not be given a grade. Read each question carefully and give the best answer you can find.

I. Reading Skills—Comprehension

This part of the Reading Inventory will help me see how much you understand of the material you will be reading during this course. Turn to page 227 of your Science book to the section called "Plant Structures." Begin reading at that point on page 227 and continue to read over to but *not including* "Flowers and Cones" on page 235. When you are finished reading, raise your hand so that I may record the time it took you to read this section. (Don't hurry; read at your usual speed for this type of material.) After I have noted your time, then answer the questions. You may now turn to page 227 and begin reading.

Directions to students: On the lines in each of the following sentences, write the word that best completes the sentence. Notice that one of the sentences asks for two words but the remainder of the sentences only require one-word answers.

1. The seed plant has _____ main parts.

2. Roots, stems, and _____ provide the day-to-day needs of the plant.

3. _____ anchor the plant in the soil.

* Prepared by Rodger L. Smith, Mifflin Co., Pa., School District.

4. There are _____ main types of roots.

5. _____ help to support the plant and display the leaves and flowers.

6. Most plants have stems that are _____ .

7. Many plants have green stems. Green stems contain _____ .

8. With few exceptions, _____ _____ occurs in the leaves of seed plants.   (Two words)

9. Most leaves are flat and _____ .

10. Most leaves have _____ parts.

Directions to students: Answer the following questions about the material you have read.

11. If a seed plant lost its reproductive parts, it would not die; however, what would happen to future generations of seed plants? _____

_____

12. Some of the large cacti may contain enough water in their stems to supply their needs for several years. Why is this a good adaptation in a desert environment? _____

_____

13. Bulbs contain both stems and leaves. Onions are examples of bulbs that you can eat. What would happen when you put an onion in a pot of moist soil? _____

_____

14. What would happen to a plant if its leaves were not arranged in a spiral around the stem and why? _____

_____

15. Why might it be an advantage for cacti to have thin spines instead of broad leaves? ___

_____

16. In measuring one rye plant, biologists found that the roots measured 608 km in length! Since a rye plant has an underground root system, how were the biologists able to measure the root system? _____

_____

17. Plants you may have heard or read about are air plants, such as orchids. These do not have roots that anchor them in the soil. How do you suppose these plants get the minerals they need to grow? _____

_____

18. What time of year is best for observing the branching pattern of a tree and why? _____

_____

19. What might happen to a seed plant that lost the root cap and why? _____

_____

II. Reading Skills—Vocabulary

This part of the Inventory will show me how well you understand the meaning of words by using context clues. "Context clues" means getting the meaning of new words by using the words around them.

Directions to students: On the lines in front of each of the following sentences write the letter of the phrase that best matches the ***italicized*** word or words in the sentence.

_____ **1.** The *epidermal cells* protect the root cells from being injured as the root grows.
   A. cells that transport food to the plant stem
   B. cells that cover the root cap
   C. cells that photosynthesize sunlight

_____ **2.** It is through the *root hairs* that the plant absorbs water and minerals
   A. cells that take in food for the plant
   B. cells that cover the root cap
   C. cells that transport food to the plant stem

_____ **3.** Some kinds of plants have one large root called the *taproot.*
   A. a root that taps water from the ground
   B. a type of plant that has one big root
   C. a type of plant that has many roots growing under the ground

_____ **4.** Roots that are slender and are all nearly equal in size are called *fibrous roots.*
   A. a plant with one main root
   B. a plant with only two roots
   C. a plant with many roots

_____ **5.** Some plants have *tendrils* that wrap around plant stems or other objects for support.
   A. slender projections from the stem that are used to help a vine stand up
   B. slender projections from the stem that are used to absorb water
   C. slender projections from the stem that are used to catch insects

_____ **6.** Some plants have stems called *stolons* that creep over the ground.
   A. stems used to gather food for the plant
   B. stems used to reproduce new plants and roots
   C. stems used to move up walls and other vertical objects

_____ **7.** One kind of an underground stem is called a *rhizome.*
   A. the leaves of a plant that help it grow
   B. the part of the plant cell that is underground
   C. a stem that does not grow above the ground

_____ **8.** Large swollen structures at the end of underground stems are called *tubers.*
   A. big growths at the base of a plant stalk
   B. big growths at the very tip of a root cap
   C. big growths at the end of underground stems

_____ **9.** The *stalk* attaches the leaf to the plant stem.
   A. a part of the root system
   B. a part of the stem
   C. a part of the leaf

_____ **10.** The *blade* is the flat, thin portion of the leaf.
   A. a part of the stalk of a leaf
   B. a part of the stem of a plant
   C. a part of the leaf of a plant

*Note—To avoid testing fatigue, the remainder of the Inventory should be given as separate tests on different days.

Group Reading Inventory   NAME _____

III. Knowing where to look   DATE _____

This part of the Reading Inventory will tell me how familiar you are with the different parts of your book.

Directions to students: On the line in front of each of the following phrases write "T" if the information could be found in the table of contents. Write "G" if it could be found in the glossary and "I" if the information could be found in the index.

T— table of contents
G—glossary
I— index

_____ **1.** What page Unit One starts on.

_____ **2.** Definition of *crustaceous*.

_____ **3.** Page number on the topic of rocky mountain spotted fever.

_____ **4.** How many chapters does Unit 5 contain?

_____ **5.** How many syllables does the word *multicellular* have?

_____ **6.** Page numbers that deal with the reproduction of plants.

_____ **7.** How do you pronounce *antennae*?

_____ **8.** How many units does the book contain?

_____ **9.** How many meanings are used in our textbook for the word *conjugation*?

_____ **10.** How many pages long is chapter seven?

_____ **11.** Where could you find a pronunciation key?

_____ **12.** A respelling of the word *spiracles*.

_____ **13.** Key words used as examples of the respelling symbol /zh/.

Group Reading Inventory   NAME _____

IV. Vocabulary Skills—prefix meaning   DATE _____

This part of the Reading Inventory will tell me how well you can figure out the meanings of words when you know what the prefixes of the words mean.

Directions to students: Study the chart below. Then put together the meaning of the prefixes bio, de, geo, and in-, to match each word with its meaning.

Prefix	Meaning	Example
bio	life, of living things	biology
de	to break down or remove	deregulate
geo	earth; of the earth	geochemistry
in	no, not, without	incomplete

*Write the letter of the meaning from List II that matches each word given in List I. The words in parenthesis (   ) are given to help you.

<table>
<tr><td>

LIST I

_____ **1.** biochemistry

_____ **2.** decomposer

_____ **3.** geology

_____ **4.** inorganic

_____ **5.** invertebrates (backbone)

_____ **6.** bioluminescent (light)

_____ **7.** desalination (salt)

_____ **8.** geothermal (temperature)

_____ **9.** involuntary

</td><td>

LIST II

A. not living
B. having the ability to produce light
C. study of chemical make-up of living things
D. heat energy from the earth's crust
E. not under conscious control
F. organism that breaks down dead matter
G. animals without backbones
H. process that removes salt
I.   study of the earth
J. to remove the backbone of

</td></tr>
</table>

Group Reading Inventory   NAME _____

V. Using Visual Aids   DATE _____

Each of the following exercises was designed to show me how well you can use the pictures and diagrams in your Science book.

Directions to students: Read each of the following questions and follow the directions given. Then answer the questions that are asked. You may look at the picture or diagram for as long as you like.

1. Turn to page 170 and look at figure 5–13. Which is the largest biome found on the North American continent? (biome—a major division of the earth having distinct climate and

vegetation. _____

_____

In which biome do we live primarily? _____

2. Turn to page 216 and look at figure 7–9. What is the third stage of mitosis called?

_____

3. Turn to page 221 and look at figure 7–15. Several organs join together to form a(n)

_____ . (complete the sentence)

4. Turn to page 237 and look at figure 8–17. What parts of the flower make up the stamen?

_____

5. Turn to page 253 and look at figure 9–1. What is another name for your hipbone? _____

_____

6. Turn to page 258 and look at figure 9–8. In what layer of skin is the oil gland found?

_____

7. Turn to page 296 and look at figure 10–4. What is the chemical symbol for Mercury?

_____

8. Turn to page 307 and look at figure 10–10. What are the deficiency symptoms that result

from a lack of vitamin C? _____

_____

9. Turn to page 348 and look at figure 12–12. In what ways is water returned to the

atmosphere? _____

_____

Group Reading Inventory   NAME _____

VI. Getting the Main Idea   DATE _____

This section of the Reading Inventory will tell me how well you can get the main idea from paragraphs that you may be reading in your Science book.

Directions to students: Read the following paragraph, noting the underlined sentence.

There are more species (about 700,000) of insects than of all other animals combined. Imagine, it has been estimated that the total weight of all the ants on the earth is greater than the total weight of all the other land-dwelling animals combined!

*The sentence that has been underlined can be called the *main idea* of the paragraph. It tells us what the paragraph is about. The remainder of the paragraph supports the main idea or helps further explain what the paragraph is about. Any idea or sentence that supports the main idea is called a *supporting detail.* Now, read the next paragraph.

There is a greater variation in body forms and habits among the insects than among any other group. But there are also several common features that are shared by all insects. An insect body has three parts: head, thorax, and abdomen. Most insects have one pair of antennae on the head. They all have three pairs of legs attached to the thorax. Some insects are wingless, but most have two pairs of wings. (An exception is flies that have only one pair of wings.) Now that you know these basic characteristics, see if you can name five insects.

*As you can see, the main idea of a paragraph is not always contained in the first sentence. Below, in outline form, I have rewritten the paragraph using only short sentences and phrases.

I. Main Idea—Common features of all insects
   A. supporting detail—body has three parts:
      1. head
      2. thorax
      3. abdomen
   B. supporting detail—most have one antennae
   C. supporting detail—all have three pairs of legs
   D. supporting detail—most have two pairs of wings

      * Now read the next paragraph.

Almost all insects are land-dwellers. Some may live in fresh water, but none are considered marine, or sea-dwelling.

      * See if you can complete the outline below by writing the supporting detail on the appropriate blank.

II. Main Idea—Almost all insects are land-dwellers.

    A. supporting detail— _____

    _____

      * You should have answered something similar to—some may live in fresh water, but none considered sea-dwelling. Now read the next paragraph. The main idea and some of the supporting details have been identified for you. Please complete the outline by filling in the remaining supporting details.

Insects breathe through spiracles. These are holes along the sides of the thorax and abdomen. These holes lead into air tubes called trachea. The tubes have many branches that extend into the body tissues. Oxygen is taken into the body through the spiracles and reaches every cell of the body through the trachea.

III. Main Idea—How insects breathe
   A. supporting detail—breathe through spiracles

   B. supporting detail—(1)_____

   C. supporting detail—air tubes called (2)_____

   D. supporting detail—(3)_____

      * Now read the next paragraph and try to complete the outline by yourself.

For young insects to become adults, they must change from one stage of development to another. The changes may result in forms that look very different from one another. This changing is called metamorphosis. Most kinds of insects have four stages in their metamorphosis: egg, larva, pupa, and adult. Some insects go through all four stages in a few days. Others require years to complete their metamorphosis. The insect may change both in appearance and habits in each stage. A caterpillar, for example, is the larval stage of a butterfly.

IV. Main Idea—(4)_____

    A. supporting detail—(5)_____

B. supporting detail—four stages of development

1. (6) _____

2. (7) _____

3. (8) _____

4. (9) _____

C. supporting detail—(10) _____

D. supporting detail—(11) _____

* When you have finished, turn your paper in to me.

USING A CRITERION-REFERENCED GROUP READING INVENTORY

Usually the inventory is administered at the beginning of the school year to enable the content teacher to pick appropriate reading materials for assigned use. It can also be administered again at the end of the school year to assess growth in skill development. Time limits should not be set so that students are encouraged to do their best work. The following steps are recommended in administering the inventory.

1. Students are asked to read the preselected four to six pages of the content textbook or other reading material silently. They should be given any background as needed to understand the selection, but new vocabulary should not be introduced. Rate of reading may be noted by asking students to raise their hands as they finish reading; time should be noted by the teacher on the grouping chart (included in the discussion of grouping, Chapter 7) which may later be converted to words read per minute.

2. When students have completed their reading, they should be given the criterion-referenced group reading inventory. First, they should answer the literal and inferential comprehension questions over the selection they have just read. Vocabulary questions dealing with words in context should also be presented immediately after reading the material. Students may refer to the reading selection if necessary in answering the questions. At another time, if the teacher wishes, memory or recall comprehension may be checked by having students close their books before answering comprehension questions.

3. Next, or at a later time, students answer the skills portion of the test. During this portion the textbook must be used in answering items. The papers are collected upon completion.

The scoring procedure for the inventories is as follows:

1. Calculate the number correct of each of the following: literal comprehension questions, inferential comprehension questions, and vocabulary meanings derived from the context. Enter these figures on the grouping chart.

2. Calculate the total *percent* correct of the literal, inferential, and vocabulary questions combined and enter it on the grouping chart.

Using the same criteria presented elsewhere, (Shepherd 1978; Burmeister 1978; Singer and Donlan 1980), scores above 90 percent indicate that the reading materials are at the independent level (which students can use on their own). Scores between 70 to 90 percent correct indicate an appropriate instructional range (students can use the materials with some teacher guidance), and scores below 65 percent correct indicate that reading material is at the frustration level, too difficult for use in instruction. If the material is appropriate, students should score at the instructional level (70 to 90 percent correct). Scores between 65% and 70% are questionable, since the difference between frustration level and instructional level is important. Therefore, teachers should assess these students further in those skills in which they demonstrated difficulty.[1]

3. Calculate the number of items correct of each skill that was assessed. Enter each on the grouping chart. From the grouping chart the teacher can see the general reading level of the students as well as strengths and weaknesses in skill acquisition. If most students in a class score at the independent level, the teacher should find supplementary study materials. If most students score at the frustration level, the teacher should attempt to find alternative reading materials written at an easier level. If these are unavailable or limited, the teacher needs to consider techniques for adapting or rewriting the textbook or use of study guides to help students focus on the important elements in the textbook.

CLOZE PROCEDURE

Another informal teacher-developed technique for determining students' reading level is the cloze procedure. While readability formulas, as discussed in Chapter 16, may be general estimates of textbook difficulty, they do not account for the individual student's background knowledge in a content area, language abilities, interest level, ability to draw inferences, and so forth. The teacher who uses students' standardized reading test scores to match students to reading material will have some success. However, a standardized test score in reading does not indicate the student's knowledge and prior experience in a particular content area. Since comprehension is greatly influenced by a student's prior knowledge and experience, the criterion-referenced group reading inventory and cloze procedure may permit a teacher to match students to reading materials more accurately.

The term *cloze* relates to the concept of closure. Fluent readers do not read every word; our eyes make fixations or stops along a line of print to take in one or two words. The mature reader comprehends by reading a sampling of the words rather than laboriously reading every word (Smith 1978). With the cloze procedure, words at regularly spaced intervals (for example, every fifth word) are omitted. The student

[1] Shepherd (1978) advises that the total percentages, by which general reading level in relation to the textbook is determined, should be calculated on the basis of *all* items in the group informal reading inventory. We believe that general reading ability in relation to the textbook materials is best determined through assessment of literal and inferential comprehension and vocabulary in context. Skill mastery should be considered separately, we believe, because students may or may not have mastered certain study skills due to previous exposure rather than due to general suitability of the textbook materials.

uses the surrounding context to supply the missing words. The use of the cloze procedure to estimate reading levels has been well established (Klare 1965; Bormuth 1967). If a passage from the content area textbook is used, then the teacher can determine a student's reading level in relation to that material.

Teachers select a passage of approximately 250 words from the content textbook or other required reading materials. The first sentence is left intact, with no omissions. Beginning with the second sentence, every fifth word is deleted from the passage so that a total of fifty deletions is attained. After a sample cloze exercise to introduce students to the activity, students are instructed to fill in the deleted words in the passage.

Betsy is shown in the picture taking a cloze test using a passage from her social studies textbook. Because she was able to fill in only 30 percent of the blanks correctly in the selected material, her teacher concluded that the social studies textbook represents frustration level reading for Betsy. She should not use the textbook without adaptation or special help.

The same teacher who constructed the criterion-referenced group reading inventory on the seventh grade life science book also created a cloze test on the same book to determine reading levels quickly in relation to the textbook and to form tentative groupings within the class.

Betsy works on the cloze test for her social studies class. *(Photo by Joseph Bodkin)*

CLOZE TEST *

Life Science, Englewood Cliffs, N.J.:
Prentice-Hall, Inc., 1980, pp. 437–438.

Readability (according to Fry Graph): Approximately 7th grade level
p. 11   142 syllables   6.8 sentences
p. 241   142 syllables   7.8 sentences
p. 434   161 syllables   7.5 sentences
Average: 148.3 syllables   7.3 sentences

Directions to students: You are to fill in the blanks in the following selection with the word that has been left out. Try to supply the exact word the author used. Only one word has been deleted from each blank. You will have as much time as necessary to complete this exercise.

In the early 1800's the French biologist, Jean Lamarck, proposed his theory of evolution, or gradual change in organisms. Lamarck's theory was based (1)_____ the idea that organisms (2)_____ change to fit into (3)_____ environment. He believed that (4)_____ organism can acquire certain (5)_____ that will better adapt (6)_____ to the environment and (7)_____ these acquired traits can (8)_____ passed on to the (9)_____.

For example, Lamarck believed (10)_____ all giraffes developed long (11)_____ because they needed to (12)_____ for food in trees. (13)_____ a giraffe kept stretching (14)_____ neck, the neck would (15)_____ longer. The offspring, then, (16)_____ inherit this acquired trait (17)_____ be born with a (18)_____ neck. The offspring would (19)_____ slightly different from its (20)_____ but would be better (21)_____ to the environment. Lamarck (22)_____ that in this way, long-necked (23)_____ gradually evolved.

Likewise, Lamarck (24)_____ that if certain parts (25)_____ the body were not (26)_____, these parts would eventually (27)_____ The offspring, then, would (28)_____ born without these parts.

Lamarck's (29)_____ has never been proven (30)_____ be true. In fact, (31)_____ is highly criticized by (32)_____ people. One reason for (33)_____ his theory incorrect is (34)_____ present-day knowledge of genes (35)_____ hereditary factors. For body (36)_____ to change and to (37)_____ these changes passed on (38)_____ offspring, the genes of (39)_____ organism must change. Even (40)_____ the giraffes could stretch (41)_____ necks to become longer (42)_____ like people who lift (43)_____

and develop their muscles, (44) _____ genes would not be (45) _____ .
And the genes determine (46) _____ an organism's offspring will
(47) _____ like. Why won't a (48) _____ with well-developed
muscles produce (49) _____ child with well-developed muscles?

In (50) _____ mid-1800's Charles Darwin proposed a different theory of
evolution. He developed his theory as a result of observations he made during a voyage
around the world.

ANSWERS:

1. on	26. used
2. can	27. disappear
3. their	28. be
4. an	29. theory
5. traits	30. to
6. it	31. it
7. that	32. many
8. be	33. believing
9. offspring	34. the
10. that	35. as
11. necks	36. parts
12. reach	37. have
13. if	38. to
14. its	39. an
15. get	40. if
16. would	41. their
17. and	42. much
18. long	43. weights
19. be	44. their
20. parents	45. changed
21. adapted	46. what
22. believed	47. look
23. giraffes	48. person
24. believed	49. a
25. of	50. the

*Prepared by Rodger L. Smith, Mifflin Co., Pa., School District.

In scoring a cloze test, the teacher must decide whether only the exact word that was deleted is to be accepted as correct or whether a synonym is also acceptable. If the student must supply the exact words, then the instructional range is usually considered to be 44 to 57 percent correct (Bormuth 1968). Students scoring in this range can comprehend the material if given teacher guidance before, during and after reading. Scores below that range may indicate that the material is too difficult. That is, the reading material is at the frustration level for students scoring below the minimum cutoff score. Scores above that range indicate the independent reading level, and more challenging supplementary materials are needed. If the teacher chooses to accept synonyms for the deleted word, then scores of approximately 50 percent correct (as a minimum level) would indicate suitability of the material for instruction (Dupuis 1980). Acceptance of synonyms makes scoring more difficult since each choice must be considered for acceptability. While acceptance of only the exact word speeds up the process of scoring, it does go against principles of flexibility and variety in word choice.

Although diagnostic information about skill attainment is not obtained as obviously by use of the cloze procedure as with a criterion-referenced group reading inventory, an observant content teacher can draw some conclusions about students' language skills. If, for example, a student inserts a verb where a noun belongs, or if a sentence no longer makes sense, then the student probably is not deriving meaning from the reading selection.

Since cloze tests are so easily constructed and scored, teachers can create them for all reading materials to insure that students are using appropriate materials. For example, if several resources are available on the same topic, a cloze test using a passage from each resource could indicate which students should be reading which resource.

Thus, reading level in relation to content materials may be determined by both the criterion-referenced group reading inventory and the cloze procedure. Skill attainment, however, is best measured by the criterion-referenced group reading inventory since the student is required to use content materials in the application of the skills.

LIMITATIONS OF INFORMAL TESTING

Although standardized norm-referenced tests do not yield diagnostic information, they do have the virtues of usually being valid and reliable. Validity and reliability are problems inherent in informal testing. In norm-referenced tests, items are typically reviewed by content experts to be sure that they adequately sample the material. Most tests have also been field-tested with large numbers of students to insure that the results are reproducible. With teacher-made informal tests, however, one does not know whether students miss an item because they have not grasped what it is measuring or whether it is a poorly written item. Likewise, the test may not emphasize what is covered in instruction (that is, be valid), or the results may not be reproducible (that is, reliable).

Several steps may be taken to overcome the shortcomings of informal teacher-made tests. First, teachers may systematically review their objectives for instruction and write items to measure attainment of those objectives. In other words, they may create a criterion-referenced test which measures whether or not students have mastered a particular objective stated in behavioral terms. Mastery level (for example, 80 percent correct) should be determined by what is a realistic level of performance to be expected.

Next, the items should be reviewed for appropriateness in measuring the objective; this can be done by other teachers of the same content area. Wesman (1971) suggests aspects of objective tests that are appropriate to consider.

GUIDING QUESTIONS FOR WRITING OBJECTIVE-TEST ITEMS*

1. Is the item expressed clearly?
2. Do the words used have precise meanings?
3. Are complex or awkward word arrangements avoided?

*Adapted from A. G. Wesman, "Writing the Test Item," in R. L. Thorndike, ed., *Educational Measurement.* Washington, D.C.: American Council on Education, 1971. Used by permission.

4. If qualifying statements would improve an item, are they included?
5. Are nonfunctional words omitted?
6. Is unnecessary specificity avoided? (names, dates, etc.)
7. Are the items as accurate as possible?
8. Is the difficulty of the item appropriate for the group?
9. Are irrelevant clues to correct responses avoided?
10. Are stereotyped phrases avoided in the items or the correct responses?
11. Are irrelevant sources of difficulty avoided?

Sometimes one aspect of an objective is inadvertently given disproportionate weight, or perhaps the wording of distractor choices for particular multiple choice items may be confusing. Colleagues can often identify these problems when looking at the items objectively.

After the test has been used with a group of students, the responses to particular items should be studied closely. Items missed by students who achieve high total scores should receive special study. If the same items seem to be difficult for the high scorers, it may be that the wording is ambiguous or the choices are confusing. Local norms can be created by collecting data over a period of time. In other words, a student's performance may be compared to those who have taken the same teacher-made test during the last few years.

Finally, the accuracy of the test as a predictor of success in reading content materials should be considered. At the end of the school year the results of the informal teacher-made test, given at the beginning of the school year, may be compared to each student's final course grade and to the teacher's assessment of his/her ability to handle the content reading materials. If high test scores were obtained by students who proved to be successful in the course, test validity has been demonstrated. If the test indicated reading weaknesses in an otherwise strong student, and these weaknesses were overcome through instruction, then the test's diagnostic value has been established.

In spite of the limitations of informal assessments, they provide the best indications of strengths and weaknesses in reading and study skills as applied in particular content areas. Therefore, teachers can usually rely on them to supplement information from standardized achievement tests.

Summary

Informal teacher-made tests, while they may have difficulties in terms of validity and reliability, can focus more directly on assessment of what is actually being taught than standardized tests. The criterion-referenced group reading inventory estimates each student's reading level as well as indicates strengths and weaknesses in related reading and study skills. The cloze procedure provides a quick estimate of reading level. Both informal assessments estimate reading levels in relation to particular reading materials, such as the content textbook, rather than general reading passages as in standardized reading tests.

Chapter Activities: Using What You've Read

Learn to Do It!

1. Develop a cloze test on a passage you are using or may use.
2. Develop a criterion-referenced test for a unit or chapter of a text. Use questions for writing objective test items.
3. Using the steps beginning on p. 51, develop a group informal reading inventory for a text you will/may use in the future.

Do It!

1. Administer the cloze test to one class and record the test scores.
2. Administer the criterion-referenced test to a classroom or a small group of students.
3. Administer the informal reading inventory to a class, following the scoring procedures on p. 60.

References

BARRETT, T. C., "Taxonomy of Reading Comprehension," *Reading 360 Monograph.* Lexington, Mass.: Ginn, 1972.

BORMUTH, J. R., "Comparable Cloze and Multiple-choice Comprehension Test Scores," *Journal of Reading,* 10 (1967), 291–99.

————, "The Cloze Readability Procedure," *Elementary English,* 45, no. 4 (1968), 429–36.

BURMEISTER, L. E., *Reading Strategies for Middle and Secondary School Teachers* (2nd ed.) Reading, Mass.: Addison-Wesley, 1978.

DUPUIS, M. M., "The Cloze Procedure as a Predictor of Comprehension in Literature," *Journal of Educational Research,* 74, no. 1 (1980), 27–33.

KLARE, G. R., "The Cloze Procedure—a Survey of Research." In E. L. Thurston and L. E. Hafner, eds., *The Philosophical and Sociological Bases of Reading.* Fourteen Yearbook of the National Reading Conference, 1965, 113–50.

SHEPHERD, D. L., *Comprehensive High School Reading Methods* (2nd ed.) Columbus, Ohio: Merrill, 1978.

SINGER, H., and D. DONLAN, *Reading and Learning from Text.* Boston: Little, Brown, 1980.

SMITH, F., *Understanding Reading* (2nd ed.) New York: Holt, Rinehart and Winston, 1978.

THORNDIKE, R. L., ed., *Educational Measurement.* Washington, D.C.: American Council on Education, 1971.

Chapter 5
Cultural and Linguistic Differences in Students

Preview

The culture students bring to school with them—what difference does it make? What about their language? This chapter concerns both the culture and language of students and what teachers need to consider about students' language. Considering the differences in *dialect* and *register,* two important concepts in this chapter, teachers can assess their students' language and plan their instruction to deal with language differences. This chapter focuses on three examples of linguistic differences: students who speak black English, students who speak rural white English, and Puerto Rican bilingual students.

Cultural and linguistic differences among students are concerns which teachers have long discussed. These concerns have become more visible in recent years, in light of the federal court ruling known as the *Lau* decision (Teachner, 1977). This decision holds that students whose native language is not English are entitled to receive an education appropriate to their linguistic proficiency. This decision has many ramifications, not all of them known at this time. At minimum, the *Lau* decision and federal legislation regarding bilingual education suggest that content teachers must understand the issues involved and be sensitive to the teaching of non-English speaking children in their classes.

The issue of language differences in schools was extended legally to include black English speakers by a recent Ann Arbor, Michigan, court decision. The Ann Arbor case found that students who spoke a dialect different from standard English, in this case black English, were not receiving equal educational opportunity because their teachers did not adjust their teaching to take these language differences into account (*English Journal,* September 1980). Again, the full impact of this decision is not clear. However, it has required, as a minimum, that teachers come to understand the significant dialects spoken by students in the schools, so that they can provide instruction appropriate to the students in their classes. This chapter provides background information for content teachers on identifying and assessing students' cultures and language.

Culture and Student Differences

One area of difference among students is the culture and language they bring with them to school. By and large, neither culture nor its component, language, can be materially changed by the teacher independently. Thus, our concern is primarily coming to understand the culture the students live within and the language they speak and hear.

As Edward Hall suggests, a teacher's first problem is to understand the culture of the community in which s/he is teaching:

> Each culture is not only an integrated whole but has its own rules for learning. These are reinforced by different patterns of over-all organization. An important part of understanding a different culture is learning how things are organized and how one goes about learning them in *that* culture. (1977:131).

The teacher's job becomes one of discovering how a person learns something in that culture so that s/he can understand how a student has learned how to learn all his/her life, usually without being conscious of it.

One way many cultures, or subcultures, in this country learn to learn is by oral transmission. That is, people pass on the local news, history and opinions on topics of importance by talking with each other. This talking may occur at the general store, the local fire hall, a church meeting, or any other gathering place. Astute observation by a teacher who is new to the community can help him/her identify where the word is passed and who is influential in passing it.

These influential members of the culture are the models for students as they move toward adulthood and full membership in the culture. Adolescents pass through a period of initiation into adulthood by rites established in their culture. These rites may be formal, such as religious rites of confirmation and bar or bat mitsvah, which lead to full adult membership in the church. The rites may be legal, such as the legal age to drive, drink, marry and do other things presumably reserved to adults. In a very real sense, graduating from high school (or leaving it another way) is a rite of passage. After that event, a person is presumed to be independent, self-sufficient; able to marry, raise children, hold a job; and responsible for him or herself.

Teachers become significant models for many students. This has led to expectations, historically and even today, that teachers will behave in ways that are culturally acceptable in the community. It may be worth considering the extent to which teachers serve as models for students, especially in areas related to reading and language. A teacher's oral language reflects his/her own cultural background. How similar or different s/he is from the students and the community is worth noting.

The community's attitude toward education in general includes the value of education as perceived by the community. Is it important to do well in school? To aspire to schooling beyond high school? Is schooling seen as primarily of functional value? Or is schooling a liberating process of developing students' talents? Is it academic or vocational?

It is important to identify the value of reading and "book learning." Oral cultures, those whose history and news are transmitted orally, may see little value in having students read well. They may not value reading literature, favoring practical reading materials only. They may also see little value in writing. These cultural values can be identified by asking such questions as these: What do the adults in the community read? What is the public library like and who uses it? Do these adults write much? Letters? Reports at work? Other kinds of writing? It is safe to assume that if students don't see models of reading and writing at home, they will be less inclined to do it themselves. Here, again, teachers can serve as models of wide reading and effective writing, if such models are not available at home. Teachers can also seek out and use other influential people in the community who see reading and writing as important—the clergy, businesspeople, government officials and the like.

Overall, the important issue regarding culture and the school is that culture provides the framework in which the school must operate to touch the lives of its students.

Language—Some Basic Components

What is Language?

Language is the basis for a great many human activities. Reading and writing require language; speaking and listening require language. Since reading is based on language, it seems important to define the basic ingredients.

Language is a system of sounds used by a group of people to communicate and carry on their normal activities. Nelson Francis, a linguist, defines language as "an arbitrary system of articulated sounds made use of by a group of humans as a means of carrying on the affairs of their society" (1958:13). This definition contains a number of important principles.

The first important principle is that language is *oral*. It is primarily in speech that humans use language. Listening and speaking are the earliest language processes a child learns. Every human society has oral language. A small minority of languages can be written down, and hence read. Most Native American (Indian) languages have no written form, but each language is complete in itself and is passed down from one generation to another.

A second important principle is that language is *arbitrary*. The symbols used are determined by the society using them and these arbitrary symbols can be changed by the decision of those who speak them. These *symbols* are important, too, because the words which make up a language only represent the things they stand for. That is, the word *chair* is not the real, physical object; it stands for the object. So all words and other symbols in a language are representations of the real world. These symbols change from language to language; within a language they change from dialect to dialect, and also over time.

A third principle is that language has *system*. Every language has an organized process for communicating through sound and word patterns. Such features as sound patterns, word endings, and word order are part of the system in English. The term "system" suggests that the patterns which occur are not random or chance. These patterns recur and mean something to the users of the language.

Principle four is that language is a series of *habits* which children learn and internalize at an early age. Such habits include using the system of one's native language, learning the accepted word order, word endings, and sound patterns. Many of these habits are learned from a child's immediate environment—his parents and other family members. Like other habits, language is not easy to change, especially as one grows older.

The final principle in the definition of language is that its purpose is *communication*. Language is useful only if it allows one person to communicate with another. This may mean speaking to someone who listens, or writing for someone to read. The listener and reader are communicating as much as the speaker and writer. But it does not seem useful for one to speak if no one is listening, or writing if no one will read. Some artists might argue that they write only for themselves, but most artists are writing to communicate with other people.

The three basic components of language are sound, syntax and semantics. *Sound* patterns include the way sounds fit together to make meaningful units, or words. Sound patterns are both oral and written, but written patterns are given a different name—spelling. The sound-to-symbol relationships in learning to read are called *phonics*. That is, learning to make orally the sound written on a page is called learning phonics. We assume that upper elementary and secondary students can do this, that they can sound out an unfamiliar word when they see one. The assumption may be erroneous. More on this when we discuss vocabulary.

Syntax is really a familiar topic but it is probably known by another term— grammar. Syntax refers to the way words fit together, usually into sentences. Word order, identity of phrases and clauses, and organization of sentence patterns are concerns in syntax.

Semantics refers to the meanings of words. Words change meaning depending on who is using them. Or, as Humpty Dumpty says in *Alice in Wonderland,* "When I use a word—it means just what I choose it to mean—neither more nor less" (Carroll, p. 247). We will ask, as Alice does, "whether you can make words mean so many different things." In fact, we know that words change in meaning from one social group to another, from one historical period to another and from one geographical area to another.

Linguistic Differences in Students

When teachers talk about differences in the language students bring to school, they generally are referring to the distinction between *standard* and *nonstandard* English. Standard English is that English spoken by the majority of Americans. In its most obvious form, it is the English of the news broadcaster who is trained so that his/her language reveals no geographic or social distinctions. All other varieties of English are then labeled nonstandard.

The nonstandard forms of English which most people speak are often identified as *dialects,* usually applied to a form of language persisting in a locality or among a specific group. Dialects have specific differences from the standard form in sound patterns, syntax and semantics. Dialects have a system which is regular, following all the rules of any language. For example, some black speakers regularly delete the verb *be* from their speech. Standard English "He is going" becomes black English "He goin'." Speakers who use this form use it at all times, not as a "mistake."

Nearly all content area reading materials are written in standard English. Therefore, the dialect students bring to school appears to be important. Questions like these are useful:

> Does the student have a single dialect or can s/he speak, read, understand, and write in more than one dialect?
>
> If s/he reads standard English, does s/he respond to that reading in standard English or in his/her dialect?
>
> Does s/he do the same thing in speaking and writing?

Register—Social Styles in Language

A different but equally useful method for describing language is to view it as a series of *registers*. Registers deal with social levels rather than geographic distinctions.

Registers, or styles, may be loosely defined as varieties of language appropriate to some given social situation. Everyone uses different language styles in different situations. It is part of communicative competence to be able to change the language used for a particular audience. We don't speak the same way to the boss as we do to a four-year-old. Martin Joos (1961) defines five registers —frozen, formal, consultative, casual and intimate.

Frozen—A style for writing. It is frozen in the sense that it is not subject to change by interaction with the Addressee, and so it is permanent—it may become "literature."

Formal—A style of pre-involvement; a style in which, for instance, introductions take place. It has formal phrases ("May I introduce . . .") in which the Addressor is not committing himself to more than a distant relationship.

Consultative—The style for coming to terms with strangers. The Addressor supplies background information—not assuming he will be understood without it; and the Addressee participates continuously.

Casual Insiders, people within a particular social group—friends, colleagues, acquaintances—don't have to supply information to one another in the way they do to strangers. The casual style is marked by ellipsis (omission) of words, syllables. "Can I help you?" is consultative. "C'n I help you?" is casual. It is also marked by slang.

Intimate—Usually between two people, between whom so much information is shared that what Joos called "jargon" is used (i.e., words with a special meaning for the two) and parts of sentences only may be employed.

Examples of these registers would include:

Frozen—I shall withdraw to seek repose

Formal—I believe it is time to retire

Consultative—I think I'll go to bed

Casual—It's time for me to turn in

Intimate—I think I'll hit the sack

The message is the same, but the register conveys the tone, the relationship between the speakers and their social status.

Within a school situation teachers are likely to find only three registers, more probably two—the formal register put on for formal presentations and speeches, and the casual, used in the largest percentage of school time. The consultative may appear in written form. To have a large percentage of time in the casual mode is a fairly recent development. At one time there was a clear distinction between school language and street or home language. Now street language, usually the casual register, seems to have moved into the classroom.

THREE STUDIES IN LANGUAGE AND CULTURE

Cultural and linguistic differences are a part of each of us. Many groups in this country retain specific cultural identities and unique languages. Thus, it is not possible to describe all the different sorts of cultures a teacher may face. We have chosen to focus on three separate groups, for several reasons. First, they represent fairly large groups in our society and in the schools. Second, they have a concern for their own culture and language and a determination to retain them. Finally, they have been fairly well described in the professional literature. These three subcultures are black communities, rural white communities and Hispanic communities.

BLACK LANGUAGE AND THE BLACK COMMUNITY

Is There a Black English Dialect?

Much research conducted in the late 1960s and early 1970s by Labov, Shuy, Baratz, and others found that there is a distinct black English dialect.

There is some feeling that, in fact, black speakers' English differs little from that of standard English speakers. Certainly it is not true to say all blacks speak black dialect, just as it is not true to say all whites speak standard dialect. Shuy lists only three linguistic forms which would distinguish a northern black from a northern white speaker and require special attention for cross-cultural material (Baratz and Shuy 1969).

Variable	Standard English	Black English
negation	doesn't have	ain't got no
past conditional	He asks if I ate	He asks did I eat
negative + be	When I am there he isn't afraid	When I there he don't be afraid

Does Black English Hinder the Learning Process?

Is black English inferior to standard English or is it merely different from standard English? This is part of the "deficit or difference" debate that raged hotly in the 1960s. Educators like Englemann and Jensen felt that black English speakers were definitely inferior in intellect as a result of their language, or inferior in language development as a result of their intellect (Williams 1970).

Labov (1972), on the other hand, showed that black English is equal to, but different from, standard English. The concept of verbal deprivation has no basis in social reality. In fact, Labov felt black children in the urban ghettos receive a great deal of verbal stimulation, hear more well-formed sentences than middle class children and participate fully in a highly verbal culture. They have the same basic vocabulary, possess the same capacity for conceptual learning, and use the same logic as anyone else who learns to speak and understand English.

Labov's stand has more credence today than that of Jensen and Englemann. As Charlotte Brooks (in Laffey and Shuy 1973) points out, linguists say that all languages and dialects are of equal merit and that good language is simply language which produces the desired effect with the least trouble for the user.

Most research has shown that most black dialect speakers are not seriously hampered in reading standard English. From an early age black English speakers are exposed to standard English. Most television, movie and radio programs are still in standard English, although there has been a group of black English programs like "Good Times" and "The Jeffersons." With exposure to actual standard English, students learn to comprehend it adequately enough to enjoy the story, even though they may not choose to use the language themselves. With at least five years of exposure to school English and having read books written in standard English from the beginning of their reading, by junior high school age most black English speakers can comprehend written and spoken standard English adequately.

Attitude

If it is agreed that black English need not interfere with the learning process, what are the disadvantages to black English speakers? The most important one is attitude. Standard English speakers tend to look down on black English speakers as being less intellectually capable. This applies to teachers, particularly to white teachers, but as Taylor (in Laffey and Shuy 1973) showed, to middle-class black teachers, too. The Ann Arbor, Michigan decision mentioned earlier is aimed primarily at this factor.

Teachers react adversely to children who speak black English on the basis of their speech. It is extremely important that this reaction be faced by teachers themselves. It may well be that black English has more effect on the education of children than it does directly on the children's ability to either communicate or understand (Cazden, in DeStefano 1973).

If teachers feel negatively about the language their students bring to school, it is difficult for them to work objectively with these students to do anything other than try to turn disadvantaged black children into middle-class children so they can fit the curriculum, and to teach standard English as a replacement dialect rather than an alternate dialect.

Prejudice against black English speakers occurs outside the classroom as well. The largest percentage of unemployment is among young blacks, and this is due in part to their language. These children need to learn standard English because it is essential for vocational, social and academic success. As long as the school curriculum is based on the ability to speak standard English, it is necessary for academic success. Stated another way, black children need to learn standard English so they can be successful whenever they have to function in the dominant middle-class culture.

RURAL WHITE CULTURES

The cultural group being described here is the large group of white rural people who live throughout the eastern United States, especially in the hilly areas. According to Horn (1970), the people who live in general farming and self-sufficient rural areas are characterized by fierce independence, traditionalism and fatalism. These rural people face danger with seldom-paralleled bravery, but fear being separated from family and community. They conceive goals in terms of relationships within the community, not material goals. Napier (1972) states that rural areas are characterized by low-density population, homogeneous and informal social groupings, integrated roles and a traditional orientation. Other researchers found that children reared in rural areas exhibit a tendency to be more fearful, more shy, more suspicious and more self-deprecating than urban children.

One Pennsylvania valley is a good example of such a community. Farming is the major industry in the valley, though a percentage of the men, and a much larger percentage of the women, drive into nearby towns to work. The population is sparse and tightly knit, the older established families having been there for over two hundred years. However, the community is by no means isolated from outside influences since all areas get at least one television channel.

Does this valley have a rural dialect as such? Probably not a distinct, clearly defined dialect, but because of their culture, and to some degree their inwardness and isolation, they tend to lack a wide range of registers. This is true in many communities today, but it is more noticeable in a rural situation. There seem to be few register shifts—everyone from the principal to the youngest student is addressed in much the same way in public. This may be a part of the closeness of the community; no one is superior to the next person, so no one needs to be "talked up to" or "talked down to."

Read this short transcript of an eighth-grade boy's statement about fishing, a favorite pastime in his Pennsylvania valley home.

> I fish down here at Penn's Creek. They'll be stockin' it here next month, I think, whenever the ice thaws out. Do you know where the Contress road is down here? Well, you go down that there until you get down to the stop sign and then you'll be able to see the creek right there. My uncle lives right along it, along the creek. I go fishin' down there by his house. That's where you go in to pay for fishin'. They got a board up there; if you fit under that it's half price and then I can't fit under the board and so then I'll have to pay $3.50 and my dad has to pay $3.50. You're allowed to keep four fish. They got blue gill, eel, and catfish, trout. What it is is just a private pond like. They got a great big pond and they divide it up in sections and put different fish in different places.

> Well, my sister thought she caught an eel 32 inches long. That was down here at the Coburn part of the tunnel. So my mom she was with us. She don't like it to go fishin', but we were camping and stuff so we went down there and my sister was fishin' and my mom seen it. She pulled it up out of the water and my mom seen it and it was a black snake so she hurried up and ran into the truck and then Kathy she gave the rod to my dad because my dad he knew how to bring eels in and so he brought that in and we took pictures of it and stuff.

This boy's use of language is consistent and typical of the rural area he lives in. His dialect includes using the past participles instead of the simple past ("my mom seen it") with some irregular verbs. He also used the double subject ("my mom she," "Kathy she," "my dad he"). These features, and others in this speech, are common in rural areas. The specifics of the dialect in central Pennsylvania differ somewhat from those of rural Kentucky, Tennessee, or Georgia, but there are many common characteristics.

White rural children have the same need to learn to read and write standard English that black children have—to be successful in the dominant middle-class culture. However, these children face an additional dilemma. If teachers are successful in encouraging these rural children to aspire to college and careers requiring further education, they must often leave home for college and for the careers they seek. In this culture, close family ties are important. Hence, leaving home is not a valued goal for parents or children, and encouraging such aspirations is not always looked upon positively within the community.

HISPANIC COMMUNITIES*

A third group of linguistically different people are the Hispanic Americans. This group is comprised of 20 million Chicanos (Mexican-American), Puerto Ricans, Cubans, Mexicans, and Central and South Americans (Valverde 1978). The total Hispanic population on the mainland is calculated at 12,079,000.

The Hispanic population is on the verge of becoming an influential force in shaping the character of American education. Pifer (1979) and Valverde (1978) suggest three basic reasons for this potential power. First, the American citizenry of Hispanic ancestry, especially the school-age population, is increasing faster than any other ethnic minority. Second, more and more the prevailing practice of ethnic and racial groups is to take pride in holding onto their culture. Third, just as there are characteristics common to the various Hispanic groups, there are other characteristics which reveal their rich diversity.

The federal government has designed a program to assist Hispanic children in school called bilingual education. Bilingual education is an instructional tool that has developed over the past fifteen years to help students whose first language is not English overcome their linguistic and academic difficulties and perform as well as their English-speaking peers in school (Pifer 1979). We will deal in this section primarily with the Puerto Rican student as an example of Hispanic students.

The Puerto Ricans

The nature of the mainland United States educational system and the cultural background and training that typical American teachers bring to the classroom often create conflicts for the recently migrated Puerto Rican student. The extent of such conflict and its effect upon the student's adjustment and academic success vary widely depending on self-awareness, the ability of parents to help with the adjustment, the knowledge and understanding of teachers and counselors, and the extent of the student's embodiment of traditional rural Puerto Rican cultural values.

Migrations, from the mainland to the island and back to the mainland, have had serious repercussions on the personality of the Puerto Rican student (Kavestky 1978; Ramos-Perea 1978). It should be remembered that the decision to migrate was made by the parents, and the students themselves had no say in it. Therefore, they are not voluntary migrants. They may experience homesickness and the feeling of not belonging. Puerto Rican migrant students often have to undergo the migration process more than once. Each move is characterized not only by a feeling of loss, but also by a transformation in the roles of family members.

Migration as an isolated event does not change the behavior of the Puerto Rican student. Some researchers in the New York area (Mizio 1974; Vazquez de Rodriguez 1971) and in New England (Leach 1971; Martinez 1972) have studied the cultural patterns of the Puerto Rican family. They concur that the Puerto Rican family contrasts to that of most Americans. The Puerto Rican family is an extended family where intimate relationships with the kinship system are of high value and a source of pride and security (Mizio 1974). In contrast, the sociolegal system of the mainland addresses itself to the nuclear family.

*This section prepared by Dr. Joseph Prewitt Diáz, Assistant Professor of Education and of Bilingual Education and Puerto Rican Studies, The Pennsylvania State University.

The conflicts which arise in in-school behavior on the mainland are often the result of adjusting family structure from an extended family pattern to a nuclear family pattern. On the mainland the support system is no longer found within the family, but has to be sought elsewhere. When Puerto Rican migrant students need to modify their behavior to adjust to the school environment on the mainland, the teacher can expect some conflict to arise.

The intolerance of the school system due to the lack of knowledge of the student's cultural frame of reference (Montalvo 1974) fosters a negative feeling in the student toward school. On the other hand, a consistent failure in expressing cultural values has an inhibiting effect on the Puerto Rican migrant children (Thomas 1969). Thus, these conflicts result in blocking the road to success. Students lose the desire to achieve, and their fear of failure increases.

The intellectual capacity of Puerto Rican migrant students seems to be initially impaired by their inability to adapt to accepted classroom behavior on the mainland. Consequently, many students are placed in the lower academic tracks and older students are referred to vocational subjects. This is based upon an argument that the migrant Puerto Rican students lack the necessary skills to survive in higher education (Vazquez de Rodriquez 1971).

The interactions of the student with the adults and peers in his/her household provide the first source of language development and cultural identity. Subsequently, when the student enters the school system on the mainland, these experiences are modified. The Puerto Rican migrant students are placed in a position in which they must decide between the two languages and the two cultures, English and Spanish (Montalvo 1974). It is at this point that the home culture and in-school behavior enter into conflict. Researchers, such as Schumann (1978), discuss different variables which affect the second language acquisition of young children. Some of the variables deal specifically with personality factors, others with the socialization process.

Teacher expectations are another important aspect of in-school behaviors. The Pygmalion theory, as described in *Pygmalion in the Classroom* (Rosenthal & Jacobson 1968), suggests that students will behave according to teachers' expectations for their behavior. Hence, it is important that the teachers of Hispanic students hold reasonable academic expectations based on the students' ability to learn rather than on their second language proficiency or other superficial factors.

The linguistic differences between Spanish and English, as in any other second language situation, are too complex to be discussed in great detail here. However, content teachers must consider the option of providing instruction and reading materials either in the native language or in English, at the level the student can understand. A Puerto Rican student who can read Spanish may be able to read a text *in Spanish* at his/her grade level, but that does not necessarily mean that s/he is able to read an English text at the same level. An Hispanic student who can read neither Spanish nor English at or near grade level is at an even greater disadvantage. Important diagnostic information for teachers of these students is the knowledge of how well the students can read in *both* Spanish and English. If they read well in Spanish but not in English, the teacher may elect to use Spanish texts for the content information. If they read only in English, however poorly, teachers must find English materials at appropriate reading levels. The question of materials and methods used with Hispanic students will be discussed in more detail in Chapter 22.

The Role of the Teacher

What is the role of the teacher in dealing with speakers of different dialects? First the teacher must realize that their English is not inferior to standard English. But students need to learn standard English in order to understand and be understood outside of their own domain, so that when they speak or write, their thoughts and feelings are communicated widely. We are not suggesting here that a student's dialect be replaced. That would be a pointless, and hopeless, job. A dialect is a sign of belonging, a part of group membership, and to take it from students is to deprive them of their own culture, their own roots. Rather, students should be taught a second dialect, an alternate dialect, to be used for certain purposes, in certain situations.

What we as teachers need to undertake is helping students develop a *variety of registers*. The nature of language is strictly functional; its purpose is to promote communication. Whatever forms of language facilitate clear, concise and accurate communication may be defined as "good language"; whatever forms of language fail to communicate clearly or lead to ambiguity may for practical purposes be defined as "bad language." In one situation, one register, for example the casual, communicates well; in another, the consultative may be more appropriate.

Language, Culture, and the Teaching of Reading

Does the language a student uses affect his/her ability to read? Yes and no. The closer the tie between a student's own language and the words s/he reads in print, the easier s/he will find the reading to be. This is true at all ages and stages of reading. Even within the same basic dialect, a student who uses only a casual register may find difficulty in reading texts which are in the main written in a formal or at least consultative register, to use Joos' terminology. This is all the more true by junior high school age, when content area textbooks usually have a high vocabulary load of words that students are not used to, and are written in a linguistic style with which students are not familiar.

What can the teacher do? Simplistically, there are two possibilities: (a) teach the students the formal language of content area textbooks; or (b) rewrite the texts in casual language. Perhaps the best solution lies between the two. Teachers who are aware of the lack of match between their students' own language and the language style they are expected to read are likely to make efforts to help students cope. This is no easy one-shot task, but with a concerted effort it is possible for a school to teach its students the formal language to be found in reading. The same formal language is also the expected norm in the students' written work. And for a more immediate answer, teachers can help their students "translate" the formal language into something they can comprehend themselves. Helping students restate textbook material into their own language, perhaps through a modified Language Experience Approach, could provide links between the two registers. More on the Language Experience Approach in Chapter 9. These links help students move toward the formal level to the point that they can read formal language and process it for understanding without going through the cumbersome translation.

Summary

Teachers need to be aware of their students' cultural and linguistic background. They should be able to use this background to help students learn the necessary content. Any dialects found in the students' language should be identified. An additional concern is what registers are used by the students out of school and in school. Teachers need to assess the registers they use in teaching and the demands they make on students. Many different language and ethnic groups are part of American schools. Black English speakers, rural white English speakers, and Puerto Rican Hispanic speakers are used as examples here. Teachers' assessment of the groups in their classes enables them to use students' strengths in planning instruction while they encourage students to try to overcome weaknesses. Increasing student work with oral activities and greater sensitivity to potential reading problems are two suggestions for teachers.

Chapter Activities: Using What You've Read

Learn to Do It!

1. Undertake an analysis of the language in your community. Where did the people who settled in this area come from? How did they come? What changes in population have taken place since the original settlement? Make your own linguistic map, like the Detroit map on page 40 of Shuy (1967).

2. Undertake an analysis of local place names. What do they tell you about the language background of your area?

3. Notice representation of dialects in various works of literature. (*Discovering American Dialects* by Roger Shuy, NCTE, 1967, would be a useful guide in all these exercises. It could be used with grade six and above.)

Do It!

1. Undertake an analysis of the speech of your local community. Your students can take notes regarding the speech habits of members of the community, describing the type of person observed, age, probable occupation and employment, the place and occasion of observation and characteristics of his speech. Specific attention can be given to the presence or absence of in-group terms or occupational jargon, the general level of familiarity or formality, the relationship of word choices and sentence structure to the tone and purpose of the communication, the use of nonstandard or variant inflections, pronoun forms, etc. Further ideas for this kind of usage survey can be found in Pooley (1974).

2. Look at other "languages"—for example, CB—in both their structural properties and social functions. CB dialect can be used to model the aspect of language we may want to teach, including grammar, vocabulary, speech sounds, jargon, code switching, punctuation, content and even the discrimination and dislike which exist between some speakers.

   a. Set up a CB in the classroom. Let students listen and then discuss what they heard, how they went about deciphering it (contextual clues, etc.) and how they felt listening to an unfamiliar dialect.

   b. Put together a glossary of CB.

   c. Work on a contrast chart of CB and Standard English. Harvey Daniels, "The

Windy City Crocodile," has many more ideas in "Breaker, Break, Broke: Citizens Band in the Classroom," *English Journal,* December 1976, pp. 52–7.

References

BARATZ, J. C., and R. M. SHUY, *Teaching Black Children to Read.* Washington, D.C.: Center for Applied Linguistics, 1969.

CARROLL, L., *Alice's Adventures in Wonderland.* New York: Collier Books, 1962.

DANIELS, H., "Breaker, Break, Broke: Citizens Band in the Classroom." *English Journal,* 65:4 (December 1976), 52–7.

DESTEFANO, J. S., *Language, Society and Education: A Profile of Black English.* Worthington, O.: Charles A. Jones, 1973.

FRANCIS, W. N., *The Structure of American English.* New York: Ronald Press Co., 1958.

HALL, E., *Beyond Culture.* Garden City, N.Y.: Anchor Books, 1977.

HORN, T., *Reading for the Disadvantaged.* New York: Harcourt, Brace & World, 1970.

JOOS, M., *The Five Clocks.* New York: Harcourt, Brace and Co., 1961.

KAVESTKY, J., "The Return Migrant Student: Questions and Answers." *El Sol,* XXII, Num. 2 (April 1978), 11–17.

LABOV, W., *Language in the Inner City: Studies in the Black Vernacular.* Philadelphia: University of Pennsylvania Press, 1972.

LAFFEY, J. L., and R. W. SHUY, *Language Differences: Do They Interfere?* Newark, Del.: International Reading Association, 1973.

LEACH, J., "Cultural Factors Affecting the Adjustment of Puerto Rican Children to Schooling in Hartford, Connecticut," Ph.D. dissertation, University of Connecticut, 1971.

MARTINEZ, A., "An Analysis of Factors that Create the Educational Problems of the Puerto Rican Students in New England." Boston: Puente, 1972.

MONTALVO, B., "Home-School Conflict and the Puerto Rican Child," *Social Casework,* 55, February 1974.

MIZIO, E., "Impact of External Systems on the Puerto Rican Family," *Social Casework,* 55, February 1974.

NAPIER, T., *Rural and urban differences: Myth or reality.* ED 085, 145, 1974.

"Our Readers Write," *English Journal,* September 1980, 69:6, pp. 68–74.

PIFER, A., "Bilingual Education and the Hispanic Challenge," Annual Report, Carnegie Corp. of New York, 1979.

POOLEY, R. C., *The Teaching of English Usage* (2nd ed.). Urbana, Ill.: National Council of Teachers of English, 1974.

PREWITT DIAZ, J. O., "Culture and the Education of Puerto Rican Students," *El Observador,* III, no. 7–17, Hartford, Conn. (1978a).

———, "Atletismo Sirve de Estimulo Intellectual," *El Observador,* III, no. 6, 4 (April 1978b).

———, "Choosing the Language for Initial Reading Instruction in Bilingual Education," *Educacion,* Department de Instrucion Publica de Puerto Rico, 47 (May 1980), 55–59.

RAMOS-PEREA, I., "Migrant Adjustment to the School Setting," *El Sol,* Vol. XXII, No. 2, April 1978, pp. 25–30.

ROSENTHAL, R., & L. JACOBSON, *Pygmalion in the Classroom.* New York: Holt, Rinehart, & Winston, 1968.

SCHUMANN, J. H., "Social and Psychological Factors in Second Language Acquisition." In J. C. Richards (Ed.), *Understanding Second and Foreign Language Learning.* Rowley, Mass.: Newbury House, 1978.

SHUY, R., *Discovering American Dialects.* Urbana, Ill.: National Council of Teachers of English, 1967.

TEACHNER, R. V., "Bilingualism and Bilingual-Bicultural Education." *Hispania,* March 1977, 60, p. 116.

THOMAS, SISTER M., *Puerto Rican Culture.* Paper read at the New York State Bar Association: Family Hour section, January 29, 1969.

VALVERDE, H., "Bilingual Education for Latinos." Washington, D.C.: Association for Supervision and Curriculum Development, 1978.

VAZQUEZ DE RODRIGUEZ, L., "Needs and Aspirations of the Puerto Rican People," *Social Welfare Forum.* New York: Columbia University Press, 1971.

WILLIAMS, F., ed. *Language and Poverty: Perspectives on a Theme.* Chicago: Markham Publishing Co., 1970.

Chapter 6
Assessing Student Attitudes and Interests

Preview

At the beginning of this book, we assessed your attitude toward teaching reading in your content area. We stated then that we were concerned about your willingness to involve yourself in teaching necessary reading skills to your students. This concern centers on your attitude. Our assumption was (and is) that we can present a lot of information to you in this book, but if your attitude is negative, you will learn little from the experience. The same thing is true with your *students'* attitude toward reading. This chapter deals with ways you can assess your students' attitudes and interests so you can plan activities of maximum interest to them.

Attitudes and Reading

"Attitudes toward reading seem to influence how much and how well children read." (Alexander and Filler 1976, p. v). This statement, by researchers in reading and attitudes, says simply why we must be concerned with student attitudes. Attitudes, for our purposes, include "a system of feelings related to reading which causes the learner to approach or avoid a reading situation." (Alexander and Filler 1976, p. 1). In Chapter 1, we discussed the affective domain of learning. It is this, the affective domain, which contains attitudes. Within our affective concerns, we care about student attitudes toward school and education in general. This concern may be related to a student's cultural background, as we discussed in Chapter 5.

In addition to his/her attitude toward education, we care about the student's attitude toward the subject. For example, in science, does s/he have positive memories of science from past years? Does s/he enjoy scientific procedures? Does s/he watch TV programs related to science? Teachers can develop a list of questions related to their own subject area. They will want to know how their students feel about their content area.

However, this book is about *reading* in content areas. This chapter deals primarily with attitudes toward reading, and with those attitudes in students beginning with grade 4. Timing and age are important in attitudes. Students who have mastered basic reading skills are more likely to feel good about reading in general. They are more likely to read material that teachers ask them to read. Students who have not yet mastered basic reading skills are more likely to feel that reading is unpleasant, something to be avoided. These students may simply not read what teachers ask them to read.

Several important educational variables are related to attitudes. Self-concept, a student's perception of self and his/her worth, is related to reading attitude. Students with low self-concepts frequently expect to fail and usually live up to their own expectations. A student who has done poorly in reading in earlier grades will likely expect to fail in later years, a self-fulfilling prophecy.

School achievement is often related to attitude. Frequently, students who succeed in school or in particular subjects demonstrate better attitudes.

Parental example and involvement in students' reading and school activities seem to correlate with positive student attitudes. Parents who read a lot, talk about reading with their children, and have reading materials around seem to help their children develop better attitudes toward reading.

Another variable related to reading attitude is the teacher and the classroom climate created by that teacher. A positive atmosphere "is one in which learners are accepting of one another and in which a group spirit prevails" (Alexander and Filler 1976, p. 10). Peer attitudes and actions in the classroom, as well as the teacher's behavior and talk, are important. The "Pygmalion" theory of Rosenthal and Jacobson (1968) is applicable here. Teachers' expectation levels will likely be met. Teachers who expect their students to be uninterested and nonreading will probably find them to be that way. Thus, teacher enthusiasm and positive thinking are important in developing and continuing positive student attitudes.

Other variables have often been related to attitudes: sex, socioeconomic level, and intelligence. Recent research has suggested that the traditional wisdom in these areas may not be accurate. Girls have been assumed to have more positive attitudes toward reading than boys. However, recent studies do not support this (Greenberg *et al.* 1965; Ransbury 1973). The same caveat applies to socioeconomic level. It is inappropriate to assume that students from lower socioeconomic levels have less positive attitudes than those from higher socioeconomic levels (Filler 1973; Heimberger 1970). Intelligence as a factor in reading attitude works the same way. Reading achievement correlates highly with intelligence, but reading attitude does not (Hansen 1969; Groff 1962). On these three factors, sex, socioeconomic level, and intelligence, the teacher is well advised to make no negative assumptions.

"Not making assumptions" may be translated into two kinds of action. First, teachers who don't make assumptions don't label a class the "dummies" and expect them not to read homework assignments or take part in class. The same teachers don't label another class "my good class" and assume they will always read and take part in class. These teachers treat all students as potential learners with equal value to themselves, the class, and the world at large.

Second, teachers who don't make assumptions try to find out in each class just who does care about reading and who doesn't. This vital information must come from the students themselves. Attitudes may change during adolescence, and attitude data is less reliable than achievement data. Therefore, previous attitude assessments are less useful and it is more necessary than ever for teachers to develop their own data for their own students.

As a summary of this section, it is true that some students at any grade level and in any subject have positive attitudes toward reading and some do not. In middle and junior high schools, it may be fashionable among peers to talk down reading and study. However, the careful teacher will collect individual data from students to ascertain attitudes in that class at that time.

A special case.   Junior high school teachers (and others) report a special type of reader. This reader is one who "Can Read, But Won't." The "Can Read, But Won't" reader has average or above average achievement in reading and other areas. S/he simply doesn't want to read. Sometimes it's hard to identify this student from a student who has real reading difficulties, because s/he hands in blank test papers. Sometimes this student responds well to materials in areas of high interest to him/her. Sometimes the school's reading teacher can find ways to work with him/her. A very small number of these students have serious psychological problems requiring a counselor and outside help. A student who may be a "Can Read, But Won't" reader needs some special attention from the teacher and referral to other specialists for more help.

STUDENT INTERESTS

We traditionally separate attitude from interest in education although the two are closely related and both are part of the affective domain. Interests change fairly frequently as students grow up, especially during adolescence, so that records of student interest easily become out of date. Interests can change from June to September! Thus a careful teacher wants up-to-date information on student interests to assist in selecting alternative materials, projects and enrichment activities.

Student interests are usually defined as what they like or don't like; what they want to read and what they avoid reading. Carlsen (1980) has suggested that the topics or types of books students most often choose are grouped by ages—early adolescence (age eleven to fourteen), middle (age fifteen to sixteen) and late (age seventeen to eighteen) adolescence. However, even Carlsen's categories leave much room for individual variation. Figure 6–1 gives the subject areas given as most often of interest to these age groups.

A careful review of these types of reading suggests that many are especially appealing to a particular age group but may remain appealing to some students for

FIGURE 6–1   Reading Interests of Adolescents

Early (11 to 14)	Middle (15 to 16)	Late (17 to 18)
animal stories	nonfiction adventure	search for personal values
adventure stories	biography and auto-	social significance
mystery stories	biography	strange and unusual
supernatural tales	historical novels	human experience
sports stories	mystical romance	transition to adulthood
growing up around the world	stories of adolescent life	
home and family life stories		
slapstick humor		
settings in the past		
science fiction		

long periods of time. Interest in mystery stories, for example, may begin at an early age with the Hardy Boys. Some students read a few and go on to other things. A few may retain an interest in mysteries, so that they move on to Sherlock Holmes, Agatha Christie and Erle Stanley Gardner.

Teachers need to be aware of student reading interests in general. However, they are most interested in student interest related to their subject area. Social studies teachers may review this chart and decide that an American History unit for grade 10 or 11 will need enrichment reading including historical novels, biographies and autobiographies of people studied in the unit, and first-person nonfiction accounts of the events studied. A biology teacher whose students are in the transition from early to middle adolescence (grades 9 and 10) will look for enrichment reading in many areas: animal stories for students still in the early stage, biographies of biologists and nonfiction accounts of biological discoveries for those who have moved to the middle period. Science fiction is valuable on this list, too.

Many good book lists are available for teachers to use as references. The school librarian is an excellent resource for books on particular topics at particular levels. Carlsen (1980) and Fader (1976) are good sources, as are *Books for You* (1976), a senior high list, and *Your Reading: A Booklist for Junior High Students* (1975), published by the National Council of Teachers of English. Other titles from NCTE and the International Reading Association are available. All are updated regularly to reflect new titles in the field. Professional journals are sources in other content areas.

ASSESSMENT PROCEDURES FOR ATTITUDE AND INTEREST

Assessing attitude and interest is a tricky process, primarily because the major source of information is the student. There are three major forms of assessment we can use: the teacher can assess a student, a student can assess another student, or a student can assess him/herself. All three of these are subjective, can be unreliable, can be faked, and are generally "soft" data. However, students are generally interested in finding out what they believe and what they like. Thus, a teacher who prepares students well for such an assessment, and who has a positive rapport with the students, can feel reasonably confident in the results obtained. Multiple measures of the same kind will demonstrate the reliability of the assessment, but many teachers feel they don't have time to give the same assessment two or three times. (For further suggestions on how to counteract the possible problems in assessment procedure, see Gronlund 1981; pp. 427–78).

Teachers can assess student attitude and interest by direct observation. This can range from a barely conscious assessment that "Jack isn't interested" (that is, he isn't paying attention in class) to more structured methods. The widely used forms of teacher assessment include:

1. Anecdotal Record— a statement of what the student did or said, time and situation. These anecdotes are useful if the same behavior occurs over and over— and is recorded carefully.
2. Rating Scales—the teacher rates the student on an item using a 3 to 5 point scale.
3. Checklists—the teacher uses a list of acceptable or unacceptable behaviors and checks off their occurrences.

4. Interview—the teacher asks a set of questions of the student and makes observations of his/her reactions. This combines both teacher observation and student self-assessment.

Students may be asked to rate other students, using rating scales and checklists, on such items as their contributions to a group discussion, their common interest in certain topics, or their involvement in a group project.

Assessments which ask students to provide information on their own attitudes and interests are most commonly of four types, ranging from more subjective and unstructured to more structured and objective.

More subjective More unstructured			More objective More structured
1 —————————	2 —————————	3 —————————	4
Open-ended	Paired choice	Summated (Likert)	Semantic differential (Osgood)

Open-ended assessments ask students to fill in or complete statements or to answer questions:

What do you read most?

or   Reading is ————————————————— .

I like to read ————————————————— .

Such items reveal students' thoughts fairly well. However, answers are hard to quantify and compare among a class.

Paired choice assessments ask students to choose between a given set of items:

Would you rather:
play or read
do a science lab or read
watch TV or read

This approach is more structured than the open-ended items. However, students sometimes feel frustrated because they don't like the choices—they like both choices or they dislike both of them.

Summated items, developed most notably by Likert (1967), ask students to agree or disagree with statements. A four or five-point scale is used most frequently:

a. strongly agree
b. agree
c. don't care
d. disagree
e. strongly disagree

Students must choose which level of response they feel. Answer C allows students to avoid choosing, since they can opt not to respond and still answer the question. This can be avoided by forcing the choice, omitting C and offering only four possible choices.

Statements in a Likert scale, to which one of these responses is necessary, might look like these:

I like to read magazines.

Most textbooks bore me.

Semantic Differential. Osgood *et al.* (1967) developed the semantic differential technique to provide both structure and depth to the assessment of attitude. A single word or statement, sometimes several sentences, is used to establish the topic or issue to be rated. Under that are given a set of bipolar adjectives (good-bad, strong-weak) and a five, seven, or nine-point scale. The student rates the topic or issue on each set of adjectives:

How do you feel about reading the newspaper?

| good | | X | | | | | | bad |

| useful | | | | X | | | | useless |

How do you feel about going to the library?

| happy | | | | | | | | sad |

| unimportant | | | | | | | | important |

These techniques should be used carefully, so that the results are reasonably reliable and useful in classroom planning.

It is clear by now, no doubt, that the attitude instrument used as a preview to this book is a *summated* scale using Likert procedures. Review that instrument now, if you need to, to become familiar with a complete attitude scale. Several good examples of scales on attitudes toward reading can be found in Fader (1976). Following is an example of a Reading Questionnaire developed by a high-school English teacher.* This questionnaire contrasts student reading preferences in school and out of school. The author developed his questions so that he could discuss the results with the entire class and with individual students. In the class he taught, reading stories was compared with watching movies and TV, so the answers were directly related to the curriculum; one of the advantages of teacher-made assessments is that they can be immediately related to class content. He also adjusted the item types so that sometimes students could choose "other" and specify an answer different from the choices given—another advantage of teacher-made assessments.

Self-Direction

Since we have a central concern in this book for individualizing instruction, we have a special interest in another affective area—a student's perception of his/her own ability to work independently, his/her sense of *self-direction*. Many of the student-

*David Petkosh, English Dept. Chairman, Manheim Central High School, Manheim, Pa.

READING QUESTIONNAIRE

Check the answer which best describes what is true for you.

1. Outside of classwork, what kind of reading do you do most?

_____ A. newspapers

_____ B. magazines

_____ C. novels

_____ D. short stories

_____ E. non-fiction (biography, personal accounts, diet-plans, etc.)

_____ F. other _____

2. When you have adequate time and money, what kind of reading do you enjoy most?

_____ A. newspapers

_____ B. magazines

_____ C. novels

_____ D. short stories

_____ E. non-fiction

_____ F. other _____

3. When do you read "non-classwork" literature most often?

_____ A. study halls

_____ B. library

_____ C. evenings at home

_____ D. weekends

_____ E. summer or vacation

4. When you read leisure material or classwork, do you ordinarily read

_____ A. in absolute silence?

_____ B. with music playing?

_____ C. with the TV on

_____ D. other _____

5. When you read leisure material (only), do you ordinarily read for

_____ A. 15 minutes at a time?

_____ B. 30 minutes at a time?

_____ C. 1 hour at a time?

_____ D. more? _____ (how long?)

6. When you read classwork (only), do you ordinarily read for

_____ A. 15 minutes at a time?

_____ B. 30 minutes at a time?

_____ C. 1 hour at a time?

_____ D. more? _____ (how long?)

7. How many books of your own do you have?

_____ A. none

_____ B. 1–5

_____ C. 6–10

_____ D. 11–20

_____ E. more than 20

8. If you were stranded on an island alone with one object, would you prefer

_____ A. a book?

_____ B. a game?

_____ C. a pocket calculator?

_____ D. a diary and a pencil?

_____ E. some method of playing music?

9. Do you feel more at ease

_____ A. reading?

_____ B. writing?

10. Do you enjoy reading for leisure or pleasure sometimes?

_____ A. Yes

_____ B. No

11. Do you ordinarily finish what you begin to read eventually?

_____ A. Yes

_____ B. No

12. Do you ordinarily read what you think your parents would approve?

_____ A. Yes

_____ B. No

13. Do your parents give you complete control over what you read?

_____ A. Yes

_____ B. No

14. When you read for pleasure, do you read as closely and carefully as you do (or should) for classwork?

_____ A. Yes

_____ B. No

15. Have you ever reread a book for pleasure?

_____ A. Yes

_____ B. No

16. Do you prefer TV and movie stories to reading stories?

_____ A. Yes

_____ B. No

17. Is it possible for a book to be "better" than a TV or movie adaptation?

_____ A. Yes

_____ B. No

18. Are books ever a topic of your conversation with others (in the way movies are)?

_____ A. Yes

_____ B. No

19. If you were desperate for something enjoyable to read (not to look at), could you find one good book in our school library?

_____ A. Yes

_____ B. No

20. If a friend were in the hospital, in prison, or held captive, could you think of two thoroughly entertaining books to send to him/her?

_____ A. Yes

_____ B. No

If you can, name two below.

_____   _____

Name: _____

Sex: _____

Grade: _____

Class: _____

directed techniques included in Chapter 11 are designed for students to operate under some level of self-direction. In order to counsel students appropriately, teachers need to know to what extent students are self-directed when they enter the class.

Self-direction involves a student's ability to operate in the learning process relatively independently; for example, to read and follow directions without outside help. A student who can do this can take a recipe in home economics and make it alone; s/he can follow a lab procedure in science, work math problems from a model, carry out library research, and do many other kinds of classwork with minimum assistance from a teacher or other students. Carrying out these processes involves three components: reading, content background, and self-direction. We talked earlier about assessing reading and content background. We need now to assess students' self-direction level.

Figure 6–2 is a Self-Directed Behavior Rating Scale (Wood 1973) which can help students assess their preferred level of self-direction and teacher assistance. Students can score their own answers (the range is 8 to 40). Students who score 8 to 16 are quite teacher dependent in the areas assessed. Those who score 32 to 40 are quite self-directed. Those who score in the middle need some help to become self-directing.

FIGURE 6–2   Self-Directed Behavior Rating Scale

1. *Amount of Teacher Direction:*

I totally depend on the teacher for directing my work. I have to be told what to do.		I like the teacher to direct me part of the time, but I take the lead with some activities.		I work independently using the teacher only when needed for special assistance.
1	2	3	4	5

2. *Seeking Answers Independently:*

I rely on the teacher and textbook as a total source for answers to my questions.		I look for answers to questions, using the teacher, other students, and outside information sources.		I independently seek answers to questions without teacher assistance.
1	2	3	4	5

3. *Using Class Time:*

I waste class time frequently rather than doing assigned tasks.		I usually use class time to do assigned tasks.		I spend class time working on assigned tasks with little, if any, wasted time.
1	2	3	4	5

4. *Planning a Work Schedule:*

I do not develop a plan for my work. I lack organization and have poor study habits.		I develop a systematic plan for attacking most learning activities, primarily when I'm told to do so.		I independently set up an efficient plan for completing my work.
1	2	3	4	5

5. *Using Study Skills:*

I lack basic study skills. I have trouble using those that I know.	I use basic study skills when I'm told to do so.	I use basic study skills as a natural part of my work routine.

1	2	3	4	5

6. *Using Self-Teaching Curriculum Packages:*

I am unable to use independent learning materials or packages without my teacher's constant assistance.	I follow independent learning materials or packages with limited assistance from my teacher.	I am able to use independent learning materials or packages by myself.

1	2	3	4	5

7. *Adapting Curriculum:*

I never skip an activity or assignment regardless of whether it is needed or not. I may skip activities I know I need.	I skip some activities or assignments that deal with things I already know.	I skip activities or assignments that deal with things I already know, and sometimes I plan my own activities.

1	2	3	4	5

8. *Pace of Learning:*

I don't work as fast as I can.	In most cases, I work as fast as I can.	I always work as fast as I can.

1	2	3	4	5

Once the assessment is complete, the teacher must decide whether to group students in terms of their present level of self-direction or whether to try to move students toward more self-direction. The difference in this judgment is in the planning done for those students on Steps 3, 4, and 5 of the Decision Model. Look at some examples. A student is assessed as teacher-dependent (score of 13 on the scale). If the teacher wants to accommodate this, s/he plans highly structured, teacher-directed activities for the student. On the other hand, if the teacher wants to begin moving the student to more self-direction, s/he gives the student small independent assignments which s/he can complete independently, but in a short time. The teacher may group this dependent student with two or three self-directed students, so s/he can model his/her behavior on theirs and receive support while s/he is trying to work independently.

Look at the matrix given as Figure 6-3. When planning a unit or lesson, the teacher can look at the variables on the scale and identify how the steps in the planning process interact with the variables in self-direction.

A specific example may be helpful. By looking at "amount of teacher direction," we can trace how differences on this variable might affect the instructional components.

Instructional Objectives (Cell A): If a teacher wants students to become more self-directed, s/he might write objectives to develop the student's ability to operate independently, to seek answers to questions without help, to use class time effectively, to develop a plan for completing a research paper.

FIGURE 6–3 Instructional Implications of the Self-Directed Behavior Rating Scale

	Instructional Components				
Individual Differences	A. Instructional Objectives	B. Content	C. Learning Experiences	D. Materials	E. Evaluation Techniques
1. Amount of Teacher Direction					
2. Seeking Answers Independently					
3. Using Class Time					
4. Planning a Work Schedule					
5. Using Study Skills					
6. Using Self-Teaching Curriculum Packages					
7. Adapting Curriculum					
8. Pace of Learning					

Content (Cell B): The content of a unit could be affected. Some unit objectives could focus on how to use the card catalogue or Reader's Guide to Periodical Literature to locate materials; this would provide the student with additional tools s/he could use to find answers independently.

Learning Experiences (Cell C): In this cell, the teacher has two choices: "either design learning experiences to help students become less dependent (change) or adjust (adapt) his teaching plans to the degree of direction needed by a student," (Wood, 1973, p. 29). This might include suggesting to the student where related books and other materials can be found or, getting the books and giving them to the student. What is important with either the "change" or "adapt" approach is not to prescribe learning experiences which demand too much or too little self-dependence.

Materials (Cell D): For a student with a high need for direction, audio-visual and print materials should be designed to be used easily. If the student is given a reading assignment, step-by-step directions need to be provided, or someone, either the teacher or another student, should be available to guide him/her through the task. Materials should be chosen both for their accuracy and relevance to the instructional objectives, and for the ease with which students can determine what they are expected to do.

Evaluation Techniques (Cell E):   When a student is dependent, test instructions must be clear and written in simple language. A self-directed student may thrive on independent testing on his/her own time, with no need for assistance. (Wood, 1973).

Self-direction is a characteristic of students' personalities. As such, it is not quickly and easily changed. Students have developed patterns of dependence or self-direction over long periods of time. These patterns may well be reinforced by family and community, so changing them in the school alone is difficult. Hence, teachers who hope to change their students' self-direction levels, as with other attitudes, should allow plenty of time for the change to take place. Assessing self-direction in September and again in May can show change, but it is not likely that change will occur in a few weeks.

It is important to note, too, that intelligence and school achievement are not necessarily correlated with self-direction. Some bright and successful students are highly teacher-dependent. Conversely, some students with low achievement and reading levels can exhibit high self-direction. As with other attitude variables, self-direction should be assessed independently. Pam, our independent level student, is a good example of this problem. Pam reads very well, but she is not particularly self-directed. She is shy and prefers to do her work quietly, following the teacher's instructions. However, her social studies teacher has decided to work toward greater self-direction in Pam. He has developed a short independent activity for Pam to complete on her own in the library, with the librarian's assistance. The librarian represents a support for Pam in her independent work, if she needs help. Such a well-planned effort to encourage greater self-direction is based on appropriate assessment.

The conclusion of this discussion of attitude and interest simply confirms that reading is a part of school and life which is very much affected by attitude. The best teaching plans are of no avail if the students refuse to consider the topic. Understanding students' attitudes toward reading and the content area is the responsibility of every teacher.

Summary

Assessing attitudes and interest is a complex and subjective but necessary task for teachers. Of major concern is the students' attitude toward reading. Other concerns include their attitude toward the specific content area or toward school in general. Different assessment techniques are given.

Student interest also needs to be assessed. Lessons and activities which are in student interest areas will be better received by students. Teachers need to plan activities, alternative readings and other materials to meet student interests whenever possible.

References

ALEXANDER, J. C. and R. C. FILLER, *Attitudes and Reading.* Newark, Del.: International Reading Association, 1976.

CARLSON, G. R., *Books and the Teenage Reader* (2nd. rev. ed.). New York: Harper and Row, 1980.

DONELSON, K., ed., *Books for You: A Booklist for Senior High Students.* Urbana, Ill.: National Council of Teachers of English, 1976.

FADER, D., *The New Hooked on Books.* New York: Berkley, 1976.

FILLER, R. C., "Effects of Socioeconomic Status on Attitudes Toward Reading," Unpublished master's thesis, University of Tennessee, 1973.

GREENBERG, J. W., and others, "Achievement of Children from a Deprived Environment Toward Achievement Related Concepts," *Journal of Educational Research,* 59 (October 1965), 57–61.

GROFF, P. J., "Children's Attitudes Toward Reading and Their Critical-Type Materials." *Journal of Educational Research,* 55 (April 1962), 313–14.

GRONLUND, N. E., *Measurement and Evaluation in Teaching* (4th ed.). New York: Macmillan, 1981.

HANSEN, H. S., "The Impact of the Home Literacy Environment on Reading Attitude," *Elementary English,* 46 (January 1969), 17–24.

HEIMBERGER, M. J., *Sartain Reading Attitudes Inventory* (April 1970). ERIC, ED. 045 291.

LIKERT, R., *The Human Organization: Its Management and Value.* New York: McGraw-Hill, 1967.

OSGOOD, C. E., G. J. SUCI, and P. H. TANNENBAUM, *The Measurement of Meaning.* Chicago: University of Illinois Press, 1967, pp. 25–30.

RANSBURY, M. K., "An Assessment of Reading Attitudes," *Journal of Reading,* 17 (October 1973), 25–28.

ROSENTHAL, R., and L. F. JACOBSON, "Teacher Expectations for the Disadvantaged," *Scientific American,* 218 (April 1968), 19–23.

WALKER, J. L., ed., *Your Reading: A Booklist for Junior High Students.* Urbana, Ill.: National Council of Teachers of English, 1975.

WOOD, F. H., "Individual Differences Count," *NASSP Bulletin,* 57 (January, 1973), pp. 23–31.

Chapter 7
Grouping in
the Content Classroom

Preview

Information from diagnostic instruments is useful only if it provides the basis for planning instruction. The Decision Model for Diagnostic Teaching by Grouping (presented in Chapter 2) shows that groups should be formed using the information from diagnostic testing as well as other sources. These groups should accommodate differences not only in reading abilities but also in prior background, knowledge, language abilities, and interests.

Why Group?

Some content teachers typically do not group their students. One reason given is that with as many as five to seven different classes per day, a teacher can't find time to group. We believe that, with the diagnostic tools and instructional techniques presented in this book, grouping should not be an overwhelming task. Consider the alternative of *not* grouping. Students who vary widely not only in their knowledge of the content field, language background and interests, but also in their reading abilities are forced to use the same learning materials and move at the same pace through instruction.

Some content teachers worry that they will lose control if students are permitted to work in groups. It is true that group work has to be carefully planned. Students can learn to operate well in small groups. However, groups must understand their tasks and be given guidance as needed. Teachers who have successfully used grouping often have fewer discipline problems in their classes because students are not frustrated or bored with inappropriate materials and instruction.

Think back to your own experiences in junior and senior high school. Chances are that the most interesting classes were those in which you were permitted—indeed expected—to take responsibility for your own learning. The least interesting classes may well have been those in which students were treated as a whole group and given very little opportunity for independent learning. Accommodation of individual differences is even more important today, with mandated mainstreaming of special learners into content area classes.

The intent of this chapter is to show how grouping may be accomplished on the basis of general reading ability as well as strengths and weaknesses in reading and study skills. Other types of groups are also suggested.

GROUPING BY READING LEVELS

Since the group reading inventory yields three reading levels—independent (those scoring above 90 percent correct), instructional (those scoring from 70 to 90 percent correct), and frustration (those scoring below 65 percent correct)—these divisions form logical groupings for working with assigned reading materials. The cloze test also yields these three levels—independent, those scoring above 57 percent correct; instructional, those scoring between 44 to 57 percent correct; and frustration, those scoring below 44 percent correct.

Figure 7–1, for example, shows a sample of a grouping chart which organizes the information obtained by diagnostic testing with a criterion referenced group reading inventory. Look at Jane's scores in the example. The reading material is appropriate for Jane—in other words, it is written at her instructional level. (Her score of 83 percent correct, found in the shaded column, is clearly within the instructional range of 70 to 90 percent correct on literal and inferential comprehension and vocabulary in context combined.) She is, however, weak in three skill areas. George, on the other hand, has mastered the skill areas of reading maps, tables, and graphs, but he is generally weak in reading. The materials are at George's frustration level and should not be used with him without adaptation.

The teacher may ask the *independent* readers to read longer sections at a time, perhaps using a study guide to insure comprehension. The study guide—or teacher's questions after reading—can focus primarily on higher levels of questioning rather than primarily on the literal level of comprehension. The independent group may also be assigned further work to gain greater depth in the topic which could be shared later with the rest of the class. Additional study might involve library research, explorations in the community, or projects created after independent research. While this group can operate more independently than the others, the teacher must be sure to guide these students in their work, focusing on higher level comprehension and study skills. Through sharing their research, this group can enrich the study of the other reading groups.

The *instructional* group should be guided in their reading through the directed reading activity approach as described in Chapter 9. Before an assignment is made, the teacher provides background for the students, first creating interest in the topic of study, introducing new vocabulary in the context used in the reading selection, and filling in concepts or understandings that would help students grasp the reading material. Guide questions are given to direct students' reading so that they know what is important for them to gain from the selection. After they have read the selection, the teacher discusses the answers to the guide questions in addition to other questions at various levels of comprehension. An alternative is to direct students' silent reading through the use of a study guide. The study guide for instructional level readers would need to focus more on the literal level of comprehension initially than does the guide for independent readers. The teacher's questions after reading, however, should also focus on higher levels of comprehension.

Names	Literal Comprehension (10)	Inferential Comprehension (10)	Vocabulary in Context (10)	Total Comp. and Vocab. (percent)	Vocab. Word Parts (10)	Table of Contents and Index (10)	Map Reading (10)	Rdg. Tables and Graphs (10)	Time	Reading Rate # words ÷ # minutes
Jane	11	(9)	10	83	10	11	(8)	(7)	9 min	250
George	(8)	(6)	(7)	58	(6)	(9)	10	11	12 min.	190

Number in Each Group

Note: Numbers in parenthesis indicate the number correct on the test necessary to attain 80% correct. (All subtests contain 12 items.) Numbers in the chart represent the number of items correctly answered. Circled numbers represent scores below 80% correct, indicating that mastery was not attained.

FIGURE 7–1 Grouping Chart Format

The *frustration* level readers should not be asked to read the assigned reading material unless special guidance is available. If alternative reading material on the topic of study, written at an easier level, is not available, several options exist. These are described in detail in Chapter 19. One alternative, for example, is a detailed study guide which would direct students to skip some portions of the textbook, to read headings, opening and summary paragraphs, and to study graphic materials. Care must be taken to make the study guide simple enough that it can be used by disabled readers.

Probably the best strategy in using the three groups is to seek variety. Sometimes the teacher may work with the frustration level readers; sometimes an independent reader can lead a discussion with the frustration level group; sometimes peer tutoring can occur in pairs; sometimes portions of the textbook can be rewritten; a listening station may contain a tape of the essential portions of the textbook.

Variety in grouping plans may also prevent the stereotypes of the "smart," "average," and "dumb" groups. Use of other grouping plans also avoids this problem.

GROUPING BY SKILL NEEDS

The criterion-referenced group reading inventory also yields information about the skill mastery of each student. From studying the number of correct items in the vocabulary section, for example, the teacher knows which students need additional work in that area in order to use the assigned reading materials effectively. Often skill groupings, particularly in the study skills, may include students from all three reading levels. In the example presented in Figure 7–1, both Jane from the instructional level group and George from the frustration level group demonstrated a weakness in inferential comprehension. The group stays together only as long as the various members have not mastered the skill being taught. Therefore, grouping by skill needs is yet another type of grouping that prevents a stigma from being attached to group membership by reading levels. Group membership should be changed as soon as the particular skill has been mastered, usually lasting no longer than several weeks. Groups are then re-formed for new skill needs.

One junior high school teacher, using a criterion-referenced group reading inventory in his American history class, formed the groups in the adjacent charts:

GROUPING
Criterion-Referenced Group Reading Inventory*

	Informal Reading Inventory Scores					
Name	I Parts of Book	II Resources	III Charts & Graphs	IV Vocab- ulary	V Main Idea	VI Compre- hension
Possible Correct	7	5	5	5	2	5
Adrian	7	4	5	2	1	0
Faye	5	3	5	3	3	3
Michele	7	5	4	5	2	4
Sharon	6	3	4	2	1	1
Jackie	6	2	2	4	0	2
Mike	5	4	3	3	1	1
Carol	7	5	5	5	2	2
Vickie	6	2	2	2	1	2
Wendy H.	6	2	3	2	1	2
Marie	6	2	4	1	1	1

*Prepared by Bob Sealy, Penns Valley Junior-Senior High School, Spring Mills, Pa.

Deanne	7	5	5	5	2	5
Kathleen	7	5	5	5	2	4
William	7	5	5	5	2	5
Jeffrey	6	2	3	2	2	0
Cynthia	6	1	3	1	0	0
Robert	3	3	3	2	1	1
Roger	4	4	4	2	1	1
Tina	3	2	2	1	1	0
Martin	7	4	5	5	2	4
Donna	5	3	5	1	0	3
Thomas	7	5	4	5	2	4
Wendy	7	5	5	4	2	4
Cindy	6	2	3	3	1	1

GROUPING BY SKILLS

Parts of Book
Faye	Jeffrey
Sharon	Cynthia
Jackie	Robert
Mike	Roger
Vickie	Tina
Wendy H.	Donna
Marie	Cindy

Use of Resources
Adrian	Jeffrey
Faye	Cynthia
Sharon	Robert
Jackie	Roger
Mike	Tina
Vickie	Martin
Wendy H.	Donna
Marie	Cindy

Use of Charts and Graphs
Michele	Jeffrey
Sharon	Cynthia
Jackie	Robert
Mike	Roger
Vickie	Tina
Wendy H.	Thomas
Marie	Cindy

Vocabulary
Adrian	Jeffrey
Faye	Cynthia
Sharon	Robert
Jackie	Roger
Mike	Tina
Vickie	Donna
Wendy H.	Wendy
Marie	Cindy

Main Ideas
Adrian	Marie
Faye	Cynthia
Sharon	Robert
Jackie	Roger
Mike	Tina
Vickie	Donna
Wendy H.	Cindy

Literal and Inferential Comprehension
Adrian	Jeffrey
Faye	Cynthia
Michele	Robert
Sharon	Roger
Jackie	Tina
Mike	Martin
Carol	Donna
Vickie	Thomas
Wendy H.	Wendy
Marie	Cindy
Kathleen	

Since most of this teacher's class displayed weaknesses in literal and inferential comprehension, the teacher plans to devote time in class to discussions of assigned materials. He may need to review or teach comprehension skills, such as getting the main idea. The skills should be taught and applied using the textbook. Study guides may also be useful to help students read assigned materials at home. Structured overviews as well as prereading guide questions may be helpful in introducing new units of work. These techniques and others for improving comprehension of written materials are presented in later chapters.

OTHER TYPES OF GROUPINGS

Interests

Students may be grouped by interests, such as various sports, to do math problems. For example, word problems pertaining to football, baseball, basketball, tennis, and running may be created to emphasize the skill being taught, such as fractions. Students work the problems pertaining to their chosen sport. Grouping by interests tends to enhance interest and motivation in the content area study.

Students may also be given choices in studying certain aspects of a unit, such as transportation, customs or tools of the pioneers. Members of each study group can be given reading material appropriate to their reading levels. Within the same group an independent level reader may be reading a rather technical textbook while a member of the frustration level group may be reading a pamphlet or viewing a filmstrip in order to make a contribution to the topic chosen for study by the group. Independent readers may also be able to provide leadership to the group, helping the group to function effectively.

Knowledge and Experience

Students may also be grouped by prior background, such as experiences with certain tools, before working in the industrial arts class. For example, students who, through previous experiences, have worked with a lathe would not need basic instruction in using one in a construction project. Students who have traveled extensively might be grouped together—or perhaps interspersed within groups in a social studies class. Through hobbies, students may have extensive knowledge related to a content area. An interest in astronomy, for example, that had led to extensive independent study provides background for a physical science class.

David, for example, has had an interest in animals for some time. He became particularly interested in turtles when he found Myrtle, a wood turtle, in a stream. He and two others who were interested in reptiles extended their knowledge through independent research as part of their wildlife unit in science. He is sharing the posters and other materials created as a result of his research with the other group members.

The first step in individualizing instruction in the content areas is the formation of various types of groups for different purposes. More information on various instructional designs to accommodate individual differences is given in Part III.

David has prepared a poster describing turtles to use as he shares his turtle, Myrtle, with the group. *(Photo by Joseph Bodkin)*

Language Abilities

Teachers who have students of different language backgrounds within the same class usually try to group across language groups to promote socialization among groups. We do not recommend grouping by ethnic groups because one goal of education is integration of diverse groups.

Students for whom English is not a native language should be mixed with native English speakers as much as possible. On occasion, however, grouping Limited English Proficiency (LEP) students together may be necessary. They may need some extra instructional help if they are having difficulty grasping the content due to language problems. Grouping LEP students together in the content classroom should be on a special needs basis only, or perhaps to use special bilingual materials. They should be mixed with native English speakers in other types of groupings as much as possible to enhance their English-speaking abilities.

One junior-high English teacher with students from families of different cultural groups who had settled in the same rural valley grouped students by their elementary school in a study of their "roots" or ancestry. Although she usually grouped across elementary schools to promote socialization, grouping by previous schools meant that students were grouped with others of similar cultural backgrounds. This grouping was appropriate in the study of their ancestry.

GROUPING BY TOWN OF RESIDENCE*

In the book, many references are made to areas in Pennsylvania and the Indian tribes who lived in these areas. As part of our study of this novel, I plan to have my students explore their various backgrounds in connection with their ancestry and the history of their "villages." Students will be grouped according to what town or area they live in. Each group then is responsible for "digging up" information about the history of that town. The emphasis will be on discovering what tribes of Indians prevailed in the area, and any existing links to these tribes in "current" families.

Each student within the group will also devise a family tree tracing his culture and heritage as far as he can. Any similarities found within groups will be noted.

To initiate the activity described above, the class will be divided into five groups. These groups will be comprised of members who live in the same general region of this valley. They will work together in uncovering the background of their home areas. Following are the groups that will be used.

Centre Hall	Spring Mills	Madisonburg	Woodward	Aaronsburg
Dave O.	Ron R.	Jay S.	Charlie R.	Kevin R.
Jim B.	Dittie S.	Brian B.	Mike Z.	Allen V.
Don S.	Ian S.	Peggy R.	Polly W.	Lonnie H.
Steve W.	Scott W.	Ron P.	Dana G.	Kevin M.
Bernice W.	Chuck W.			Karen R.
				Carolyn W.

Summary

Grouping within the content area classroom can individualize instruction. While it is impossible for a content teacher to tailor instruction for each individual, it is realistic to accommodate group needs.

Grouping by reading levels is typical in the elementary school reading program. Grouping by reading levels should continue in the secondary school when different materials are used for the different reading levels.

Groups may become stereotyped if formed only on the basis of reading levels. Grouping by skill needs, interests, prior knowledge and background, and so forth prevents the formation of stereotypes. Variety in groupings also helps maintain interest in content area study.

*Prepared by Candace Marion, Penns Valley Junior-Senior High School, Spring Mills, PA.

Chapter Activities: Using What You've Read

Do It!

1. You developed and administered a cloze test, a criterion-referenced test and/or a group informal reading inventory as Step One on the Decision Model. Use these data to develop a chart like that on pp. 99 and **100** and group your class by need and ability.

2. You also developed a questionnaire to measure interest in reading. Group your students according to their answers on the questionnaire.

PART III
ORGANIZING FOR INSTRUCTION IN CONTENT AREA READING

OVERVIEW

Instructional design can be viewed two ways during the creation of teaching plans. One view is the planning process itself, a systematic way of developing plans, whether for a full year's course of study or for a single lesson plan. The second view is of the content being planned. That is, what form does the year's curriculum take? How are elements within the large curriculum related to each other?

The curriculum under discussion here is frequently determined in large part by forces beyond the control of any particular teacher—state department of education regulations, school district curriculum guides, national curriculum trends and the like. Even though teachers often contribute to decisions about the shape of the course of study, such decisions are made, in the final analysis, by larger groups. Thus, a teacher faced with teaching American history, or Algebra I, or ninth-grade English, is usually working with a given set of expectations about what students will learn (or be exposed to) during a given course. We begin, then, with this "given," a course of study which is usually stated in terms of content to be mastered and, sometimes, affective goals to be worked toward, as well.

The instructional procedures given in this book ask content teachers to build teaching plans which integrate reading skill instruction and practice with the content material that is a regular part of the curriculum. One result of the integration process is that content teachers are confronted with several questions regarding both content and reading instruction: *Why* is this content being taught? And why *now*, in the context of the full course of study? How can this content be presented so that these students can learn it as efficiently as possible?

Chapter 8
The Unit as the
Central Organizer

Preview

Organizing instruction in content teaching and reading is most efficiently done in chunks of instruction called *units*. Look for the steps in planning units and definitions of important components, objectives, evaluation, and culminating activities. You'll need to use the knowledge of *diagnosis, grouping* and *motivation* you learned in Part II. By the end of the chapter, you'll be ready to follow the steps given here and the model unit in the Appendix to build your own unit.

Planning the Unit

The process of organizing for instruction, or planning, is the primary mechanism for integrating content and reading skill. The unit is the most effective way for classroom teachers to organize their instruction, to insure that important content objectives are included, and to build in necessary reading skill instruction, reinforcement, and transfer.

Taba (1962) has clearly described the rationale for units as a focus for the instructional planning process. Her view of unit planning meshes well with the Decision Model, as we discussed in Chapter 2. Unit planning as a central organizer has been discussed since the 1930s. Taba's discussion and more recent interpretations in Joyce and Weil (1980) bring unit planning into contemporary focus. The content teacher who is responsible for a certain chunk of material must be the decision maker on content. A teacher is continually fitting his/her piece of instruction into a statewide curriculum, a districtwide curriculum or a course outline accepted in his/her school. Introductory biological science, American history, eighth-grade English, Algebra I: each of these has a set of limits and definitions. Some, like Algebra I, have a fairly well-defined and agreed-upon content, leaving relatively few decisions to a teacher on what to include or exclude. Eighth-grade

English, on the other hand, is not well-defined nationally; it does not have an "understood" content. Thus, state, district, department, and personal curricula become important as teachers determine what to teach. Unfortunately, the adopted textbook sometimes becomes the curriculum, determining not only the content but also the extent to which any topic is treated and the order in which topics are presented to students (English 1980).

Planning by the *Decision* model requires that the teacher—not the textbook—make the professional decisions on what is taught, to whom, and how. The teacher makes these decisions, given the constraints under which s/he operates, and always putting the students' learning needs at the center of the decision process. Using units allows teachers to plan for three to six weeks of organized instruction on a central topic or theme. The unit will follow accepted curricular outlines for content, allow for use of different instructional strategies and materials, and accommodate different reading levels and needs of students.

The most common length for a unit is three to six weeks. However, any time frame is possible, from one week to a full year. The same organizing and planning processes occur, regardless of length. A teacher's decision on unit length is based on a number of factors. Factors related to students include (1) their attention span, (2) their ability to carry on long-term assignments, and (3) their interest in the topic. Factors related to the teacher and curriculum include (1) the emphasis to be placed on the topic and its importance in the curriculum, (2) the materials and activities which are available, and (3) the teacher's interest.

Each unit should contain the following components:

1. Introduction and rationale. This tells other professionals the unit's central focus (theme, concept, topic), how it is developed, grade level and content area, and other general information.
2. A list of general teaching goals and specific objectives or learning outcomes. Specific objectives dealing with reading skills necessary to master the content material in the unit should be included.
3. A list of student activities leading to mastery of the objectives given. Where possible, several activities for each objective from which the teacher can choose should be included.
4. A list of teaching strategies or modes appropriate for each activity.
5. A list of materials needed for student and teacher, including hardware and software.
6. Evaluation procedures designed for each objective. These procedures should evaluate all activities listed for a given objective, which may require more than one alternative procedure for evaluation.
7. A culminating activity (project, exam, etc.) which serves as a synthesizing process and provides a sense of closure.
8. A Motivation-Readiness activity designed to introduce the unit and prepare students for what will be included.
9. Media other than the written word included in alternative activities, to meet the differing needs of students.
10. Materials to be read by students tested for reading level by the Fry Graph or another method. An effort should be made to find reading materials at several levels for each reading assignment.

In the Appendix is a model of the unit process, a six-week unit on Mexico, its people and culture, titled "Neighbors to the South," * designed for Social Studies, grades 7 to 9. The unit follows the format given here and is labeled so that specific elements can be identified (using the numbers given above). It demonstrates that once primary content objectives are identified, related reading objectives are integral to the learning process. In addition, learning centers and learning packages are placed effectively within the unit and instructional media are used in appropriate teaching situations.

THE UNIT AS THE LARGEST INSTRUCTIONAL PROCEDURE USEFUL IN TEACHER PLANNING

The following steps occur in the process of building a unit.

Step 1. Identifying the Concepts/Content to be Taught

Teachers should review their curriculum or course of study to determine the logical division of content that we call units. These "chunks" of content need to include some larger topic or concept that provides the organizing focus for teacher planning. They may be specified by the curriculum or may be left to the teacher to determine. Teachers should look for concepts or topics which they perceive to be of central value to students either as preparation for further study or as basic knowledge in the subject. Such decisions are primarily content decisions. Concepts should be appropriate for students' cognitive levels, should have some specifiable boundaries and should permit teachers flexibility in the use of teaching strategies and materials.

Step 2. Identify the Relevant Characteristics of Students

This step is diagnosis in action. The information gathered from informal reading inventories, cloze procedures, and other diagnostic tools should be evaluated here. Questions to answer include the following:
a. What is the students' prior knowledge on this topic?
b. What student reading levels and skills must be accommodated?
c. What special student needs must be accounted for?
This analysis will determine, first of all, the kind(s) of pretests needed. It will also determine some necessary activities and materials. Perhaps a pretest in content and one on a particular reading skill are needed. Perhaps a text or other reading source must be checked for suitability in reading level—which means trying it out with students. Perhaps exceptional students will need specific activities and materials not necessary for others (for example, a blind student needing a braille text, or a cerebral palsied student needing special access to lab equipment.)

Step 3. Define the Objectives

Once the central concepts of the unit and the important student characteristics have been determined, it is possible to define the general objectives to be met during the unit (point 2 on the Decision Model for Diagnostic Teaching by Grouping). Integrating reading instruction with the unit requires that the central concepts and general objectives be investigated to determine which reading skills will be most

---

* This unit was developed by Dr. Anne L. Mallery, currently on the Millersville, Pa., State College faculty, and Dr. Andrea Lee, now of Marygrove College, Detroit, Mich.

necessary during the unit. Will new vocabulary be needed? Higher level comprehension skills? Specific study skills? Mastering these reading skills becomes a set of objectives to be met during the unit, along with the content objectives.

"Neighbors to the South," on pages 000, is a good example of these decisions. The unit, designed for junior high school social studies, deals with the culture and people of Mexico. The objectives (pp. 000) include cognitive process objectives (for example, D, F, U) and reading skill objectives (for example E, O, P). According to the objectives, the informational content of the unit is not evaluated in this unit. Rather, the teacher has phrased the objectives according to processes. Hence, the students will be learning about the geography, history, music, art and government of Mexico, but they will be evaluated primarily on their ability to use important learning skills: taking notes, writing reports, making oral reports, using the library, and working effectively in groups. This unit is useful here as an example of one teacher's way of conceptualizing the teaching of social studies and integrating into it instruction in important reading skills.

The list of objectives should be given in the approximate order of teaching, with domains and levels indicated. The model unit has one major terminal goal, with the instructional objectives listed at two levels: General Learning Outcomes (GOs) describing larger conceptual outcomes for the unit, and specific learning outcomes (SLOs), known in other formats as enabling objectives. For information on writing objectives, see Gronlund (1981). These SLOs are the precise objectives evaluated carefully throughout the unit. Notice on the list given that many SLOs contribute to the final evaluation of more than one GO. We are constantly reminded of the complexity of the learning process, so that teaching plans are not neatly divided into mutually exclusive little pieces. Instead, students learn in ways that interrelate one topic with another, one process with another. As always, students learn and do many things in a unit which are not specified in objectives. The listed objectives represent the goals that the teacher has chosen to concentrate on, from a much larger list, and are subject to revision by the teacher whenever s/he sees that they have become inappropriate.

Step 4. Plan to Group Students

Grouping plans are necessarily tentative at this point in planning. It is important, however, to look carefully at the student characteristics and objectives identified and list the kinds of groups which are likely to occur. Will groups occur because of student interest and choices? Because of prior knowledge of the topic? Because of differing reading ability? Because of need to develop a specific reading skill? Check Chapter 7 again for the kinds of grouping patterns that might occur.

Actual grouping of students will occur while the unit is being taught. In order to accommodate the many types of students a teacher may have, it is important to keep grouping flexible and provide as many kinds of groups as possible. Even though we can't teach students in totally individualized ways, we can attend to their needs by using groups carefully within the classroom.

Step 5. Generate a List of Student Activities

These student activities represent ways students may go about mastering the objectives given earlier. Ideally, the unit plan will include a large number of activities for each objective. Since teachers write units to cover many different students and do much of their planning before a specific group of students arrives, the activities list should allow for individualizing the attainment of objectives by grouping students in various ways. Students can be grouped by and activities should be available for different learning styles, different reading levels, different interests and attitudes, different exceptionalities (learning disabled, EMR, visually impaired, etc.)

The model unit provides some examples of the variety in student activities. Some activities are flexible enough for students to be grouped within them. In "Neighbors to the South," the research report is such an activity. Each student will make an oral report and s/he will undertake library and research work. But within that process, s/he may choose the report topic from a large list, based on his/her own interest. The activity involving developing TV commercials is similar. In the fiesta, however, the students have an even wider selection to choose from—creative activity in dance or music, costume, food preparation, and many more. The value of grouping in such situations, beyond the socialization values, is that students are working with other students having similar needs or interests. The nature of these groups and their specific task orientations insure that the groups will not continue indefinitely. Instead, these groups terminate when their purpose is satisfied, when the unit or the specific objective has been completed. More discussion of grouping will occur when we discuss other specific techniques, like learning centers and learning packages.

Step 6. Choosing Teacher Strategies and/or Modes

Teacher strategies are an obvious companion to student activities. As point 4 of the Decision Model suggests, the teacher must choose how s/he will organize the class and the learning situation. Teacher strategies include lecture-recitation, guided discovery, small group work, laboratory experiences, inquiry, independent study and perhaps more. (Joyce and Weil 1980; Eggen, Kauchak and Harder 1979). These strategies can be classified as convergent or divergent, also as teacher-directed or student-directed. These strategies and modes are not mutually exclusive. Each has strengths and weaknesses. Each works with some kinds of students better than others. The Decision Model emphasizes that the use of strategies and modes is a professional decision and perhaps one that teachers need to take more seriously. We believe that variety in teaching strategies and modes, for most children, is an important goal. Therefore, a teacher planning a unit and, ultimately, a year's course should look at the pattern of strategies and modes s/he uses. Teachers should be comfortable with their own teaching strategies, but they must also consider their students' attitudes and other feedback in determining which strategies are working and when these strategies need to be changed. Chapters 9 and 10 look in detail at Teacher-Directed and Student-Directed Activities.

Step 7. Develop a List of Needed Materials and Equipment

As point 5 of the Decision Model directs, the selection of specific materials should be made only after earlier professional decisions have been made. In order for teachers to have flexibility in the specific reading and audiovisual materials to use with different types of students, the list of materials developed at the planning stage should be as complete as possible—readings at different reading levels, according to a readability formula like Fry, readings at different cognitive levels, readings with different organizational patterns (for example, with many pictures and visuals, or in chronological or narrative pattern, or in expository form with diagrams).

In addition, materials need to be identified to make use of various audiovisual processes—films, filmstrips, video and audio cassettes, slides, transparencies and hands-on materials. These AV materials provide variety in instructional presentations. They have other important purposes, too. Children who read poorly can be helped to learn content material by using visuals as pre-reading activities. For example, a set of slides can show the steps in a scientific process before students read about it. A film showing historical or contemporary events makes it easier to understand the written description. AV materials can also be used to teach some kinds of reading skills and to provide direction to small groups of students working in Learning Centers.

A problem in using such AV materials with content teaching and reading is that the particular set useful in a given unit may not be available commercially. Reviewing the way units are developed, it is clear that the particular combination of content and reading skill chosen by one teacher will not necessarily be the same as any other teacher's. However, more and more AV materials are available all the time, so that a search through commercial catalogs is worth making as a part of the planning process. This search and selection process will be described more thoroughly in Part V of this book. Teachers will find, we predict, that they need to plan the time to develop some AV materials that fit their teaching specifically. Hence, parts of Chapters 9 and 10 are spent describing ways of making learning centers, learning packages and media materials for use in teacher-planned units. Here again, it is important to complete the planning process early enough to allow time to develop these materials.

Step 8. Set up Evaluation Procedures for Each Objective

Evaluation is defined very broadly here, as everything from teacher observation, student peer evaluation, tests, and quizzes, through papers, projects and creative products. At the planning stage, teachers can consider multiple options for students in demonstrating their mastery of given objectives.

In the model unit on Mexico, a specific evaluation is given for each SLO (See Appendix A, pp. 323). The evaluation techniques range from simply taking part, or participation by the student, to peer evaluation, as in the videotaping of commercials, to teacher evaluation of student writing and the exam. The goal of the planning process here is to provide different kinds of evaluation during a unit. That way, students can perform in different formats, in some of which they'll do better than in others. Student strengths will be tested as well as their weaknesses. It is also possible to build in choices for students, so that they can decide which of the several ways to demonstrate their competence (for example, written or oral reports). As long as the teacher controls the objectives to be mastered and the methods of mastery, s/he can be sure that s/he samples student skills in important ways. Further discussion of ways to evaluate objectives for students will be discussed in Chapter 23.

Step 9. Develop a Culminating Activity or Product

One of the principles of unit design is to help students organize their learning into appropriate "chunks." This suggests that units or "chunks," have both beginnings and ends. Providing students a sense of closure, completion, ending, is important. The typical form of unit closure is the final exam, something to be dreaded, a kind of negative conclusion. We recommend that unit planners look for alternative ways to end units. Exams are often necessary. The model unit, *Neighbors to the South*, gives one (on day 29). However, it is not such a large part of the unit that it alone determines student success. It does provide evaluation for certain objectives. An additional and alternative culminating activity is the fiesta, planned all during the unit, to take place on the last day. Many of the affective and social objectives are evaluated there—working in groups, creative activities, and the like. This activity is more likely to help students synthesize the various parts of the unit's study of Mexico than is the exam. However, both kinds of culminations are useful in the total teaching-learning situation.

Now is a good time to point out that evaluation of objectives and completion of the culminating activities are not necessarily related to the grading process. Yet we all know that teachers must assign grades to students based on classroom activities. The Mexico unit gives one way (of many) to bridge the gap between evaluation and grading. In this unit (see Appendix A, p. 323), grades are assigned based on points earned from a variety of activities through the unit. One principle important in this unit's grading procedure is that students should be able to show their learning in multiple ways. Simply doing well or poorly on the final exam is not critical to a student's grade. This unit rewards the student for consistent work, accruing points over a fairly long period of time in a variety of activities.

Step 10. A Motivation-Readiness Activity

Motivation and readiness are ongoing, a constant concern for teachers. We recommend that units begin with an activity designed to give students an overview of the content and reading skills to be presented in the unit. You can only plan this activity *after* you see what the whole unit looks like. This activity should pique the interest of the students at the same time that it gives them an overview of important concepts. The Mexico unit includes a slide show about contemporary Mexico, carefully including the major topics to be discussed in the unit (see Objective A). The teacher also collected posters and other visual materials for the classroom walls and bulletin boards. Audio-visual materials are good for motivation and readiness but there are many other ways to do this, such as simulation and hands-on activities, field trips, lab experiments, and games.

The final unit planned by content teachers should include, as a rule of thumb, at least one objective dealing specifically with a reading skill and at least one use of audio-visual media outside of reading. Many units will use several of each. The unit plan should also include copies of worksheets, study guides or other teacher-made materials as they are constructed. Then when the time comes to teach the unit, all of the materials will be available for ordering or duplication.

An advantage of this kind of unit planning is that once it's completed, the unit is always available, for next year's class or for other classes on the same topic. Teachers can add to or revise the unit plan and its materials over several years' time, changing it to fit particular students and gradually making it more and more effective.

Summary

The unit plan is the central organizing concept for teaching. Teachers plan by dividing the curriculum into "chunks" of content, each one usually taking three to six weeks to complete. Each chunk becomes a unit.

Planning a unit involves using the Decision Model to establish goals and objectives to integrate instruction in reading into the content to be taught. Ten steps in the process of planning a unit give a clear picture of how to develop an instructional unit:

Step 1. Identify the Concepts or Content to be Taught.

Step 2. Identify the Relevant Characteristics of Students.

Step 3. Define the Objectives.

Step 4. Plan to Group Students.

Step 5. Generate a List of Student Activities.

Step 6. Choose Teacher Strategies and/or Modes.

Step 7. Develop a List of Needed Materials and Equipment.

Step 8. Set Up Evaluation Procedures for Each Objective.

Step 9. Develop a Culminating Activity or Product.

Step 10. Develop a Motivation-Readiness Activity.

Chapter Activities: Using What You've Read

Learn to Do It!

Develop a unit in your content area, using the steps given here and using *Neighbors to the South* as a model.

Do It!

Teach the unit you develop to your own class. Keep careful notes on what happens, like a pilot project, so you can evaluate the unit when you're finished.

References

EGGEN, P. D., D. P. KAUCHAK, and R. J. HARDER, *Strategies for Teachers*. Englewood Cliffs, N.J.: Prentice-Hall, 1979.

ENGLISH, R., "The Politics of Textbook Adoption," *Phi Delta Kappan*, 62, no. 4 (December 1980), pp. 275–78.

GRONLUND, N E., *Measurement and Evaluation in Teaching* (4th ed.), New York: Macmillan, 1981.

JOYCE, B., and M. WEIL, *Models for Teaching* (2nd ed.) Englewood Cliffs, N.J.: Prentice-Hall, 1980.

TABA, H., *Curriculum Development: Theory and Practice*. New York: Harcourt, Brace & World, 1962.

Chapter 9
Teacher-Directed
Learning Activities

Preview

Within a unit plan, numerous techniques may be used to individualize instruction. Content teachers typically claim that individualization of instruction is not possible when one is teaching perhaps five to seven different classes, each consisting of about thirty students. Admittedly, one-to-one instruction is probably not feasible under such circumstances, and such is not our intent. The content teacher, however, can provide means for helping individuals in a group setting. The classroom can be structured to accommodate the needs of individuals in various ways without actually requiring the teacher to offer individual instruction. These techniques also fit easily into a unit structure, thereby helping the teacher meet individual student needs in both reading and content study. In this chapter we will discuss teacher-directed instruction; in the next chapter we will present techniques for encouraging student-directed learning.

DIRECTED READING ACTIVITY

One approach for increasing comprehension, used frequently in the elementary schools with basal readers, is the Directed Reading Activity (DRA). It is equally useful for content teachers at the secondary level. The DRA is an approach to making reading material more meaningful to students, thereby increasing their comprehension of the material. The DRA technique, as outlined below, should be used whenever the teacher makes a reading assignment. Depending on the students' reading abilities and backgrounds with regard to the subject matter, the DRA may be abbreviated or expanded. It is usually used with a group of students who are reading the same material and ideally at their instructional reading level. Adaptations in the DRA have to be made for students reading at the independent and frustration levels.

DIRECTED READING ACTIVITY OUTLINE

I. Preparation for reading
   A. Building background
      1. Creating interest through relating selection to past experiences
      2. Developing concepts
      3. Introducing new words in context
   B. Establishing purposes for reading
II. Directed reading
   A. Silent reading
   B. Questions and discussion
      1. Literal meaning
      2. Inferential meaning
      3. Evaluation
      4. Appreciation
III. Skill instruction
IV. Enrichment
   A. Extending reading skills (either working on related reading skills or doing further reading on the same subject)
   B. Engaging in writing and creative activities

Pre-reading portions of the DRA (Section I) emphasize arousing student interest in the material to be read. If the material is part of an ongoing unit of study, this step may not be necessary with each reading assignment. Development of new concepts related to content reading is particularly important, much more so than in using a basal reader in which the reading material concerns familiar subjects. Recent research in reading has stressed the background of the reader in determining how much s/he understands. If the student has no prior knowledge to which to link new knowledge, the new knowledge will either be distorted to fit what the student does know, or else rejected. For example, in a social studies class the concept of interdependency of community members is crucial background understanding to the concept of taxation which may be the focus of the textbook discussion. If the students do not understand the concept of interdependency, they will probably not comprehend the textbook information on taxation.

Vocabulary skills, such as roots and affixes, can be reinforced with the introduction of the new vocabulary. Vocabulary development is closely related to concept development, as many of the new words may in fact be concept labels. It is important that students be familiar with specialized terminology in the reading assignment *before* reading so that they will derive as much meaning as possible from what they are reading.

The last step among the pre-reading procedures is to provide students with a purpose for reading. Are they to read for detail, or are they only to skim the material for the main ideas? What types of information are important and will be tested? If you doubt the importance of this step, try reading material that is completely unfamiliar, such as a medical or law textbook. Imagine the difference in your approach to reading if you need to learn only the main ideas as opposed to recall of details. Students likewise need to be directed so that they understand why they are reading the material and what they are expected to learn. "Read pages 200–230 for tonight" is not a sufficient directive. As students learn to vary the purposes of reading, the teacher can encourage them to determine for themselves the purpose of their reading, particularly in reading materials on their own. They should learn that rate is flexible, depending on the purpose for reading as well as the difficulty of the material.

After preparation for reading, silent reading (Section II) may occur in class or as a homework assignment. The teacher needs to consider the students and other demands upon their time in making this decision. Is homework commonly assigned by other teachers? Do the students complete assigned homework? Do they live in homes where school work is valued and encouraged so that a suitable environment for homework exists?

The teacher also needs to consider the nature of the reading material. Highly technical information, perhaps presented in a graph or flowchart, should be read in class where the teacher can help individuals as needed. Comprehension and discussion of some materials are best done immediately after reading, for example, poetry in an English class. Research (Rothkopf 1982) has shown that questions and discussion interspersed in silent reading produce greater comprehension than longer uninterrupted stretches of reading followed by questions and discussion afterwards. Apparently, the teacher's questions guide students in what to look for in reading material. The teacher may find variety helpful, with some silent reading done in class and some at home.

Frequently, content teachers have students read aloud in "round robin" fashion to assure that at least the material is being read. Many problems exist with this method, and it is not recommended practice. Comprehension in silent reading is superior to that during oral reading for the student who is reading. The other students are listening, not reading, and good silent reading habits are not being reinforced. The poor reader suffers great embarrassment when it is his/her turn to read, and other students learn little from the halting performance. Oral reading has its place only when a portion is read aloud to answer a question, illustrate a point, or share literature (which has been prepared ahead of time) with other class members.

Comprehension of the material read may be checked by discussion questions or by student completion of a study guide. Three-level study guides (Herber 1978), guides for the same reading material but written at three comprehension levels, can individualize the use of the reading material. With less capable students the guide may concentrate on literal level questions, the facts and main ideas in the selection. Sometimes the guide may direct poor readers to study only certain sections of a textbook (such as introductory and summary paragraphs or visuals). Readers at the instructional level should have a balance in the types of comprehension questions, sampling various levels of Barrett's *Taxonomy of Reading Comprehension* (1972) presented in Chapter 1. Very capable students should focus on higher level questions and perhaps do supplementary reading or research (for example, to compare different points of view on a subject).

Skill instruction (Section III), such as vocabulary or comprehension skills, may be incorporated as one of the previous steps. Study skills need to be taught to enable students to use their textbooks effectively and efficiently. If students are required to do research, instruction in library skills may be necessary. Skill instruction should grow out of the needs in content area reading and not be offered as isolated instruction.

Enrichment activities (Section IV) may serve as the culmination to a set of related reading assignments, such as a unit of study. Ordinarily enrichment would not be necessary after each reading assignment. Enrichment should be relevant to the content being studied and serve as a reinforcement and extension of skills and content being taught as part of the DRA. For example, as an appropriate enrichment activity after reading about a particular scientific phenonemon, students may conduct a laboratory experiment, following written directions, to see the process in action. The enrichment part of the DRA also aids comprehension since it extends and reinforces what has been learned. Sometimes the appreciation level of comprehension is the focus of an enrichment project. For example, two upper elementary teachers had their students design their own original machines after a study of kinetic energy. These projects gave their students a chance to consolidate their new learnings in original and creative ways. Their understanding of the assigned reading material was not only extended as they tried to apply the new concepts and generalizations to their own creations, but the material was also made more memorable, as students had to use problem solving and creative skills in the appreciation level of comprehension.

The following DRA was created by a reading teacher as an example for a tenth-grade home economics teacher. The roman numerals and letters from the DRA outline given earlier have been added to highlight each step.

DIRECTED READING ACTIVITY*

Henrietta Fleck and Louise Fernandez,
Exploring Family Life, chap. 16, "Cooking the Basics"
(Englewood Cliffs, N.J.: Prentice-Hall, 1977), pp. 138–49.

Since this high school places the students in ability sections, the students in each of the three home economics classes have scored, on the cloze test, at approximately the same level as their classmates. Each of the three sections will deal with the material in a slightly different way.

INDEPENDENT READING LEVEL

These students will read the assigned chapter for homework. Additional reading will take place in the classroom. Projects and follow-up activities will also be done for classwork.

INSTRUCTIONAL READING LEVEL

It is these students with whom this Directed Reading Activity will be specifically used. The reading will take place in class. Concepts and vocabulary will be taught before the reading. Follow-up activities will take the form of classwork and the larger unit project.

FRUSTRATION READING LEVEL

This group will be given reading material that is at their instructional level of ability. Cookbooks, pamphlets, and hands-on types of activities will make up the bulk of their classwork. The text will be used for exploratory graphs, charts, pictures, and recipes. A list of additional resources is provided at the end of the plan.

*Prepared by Sara Mills, Reading Specialist.

Creating Interest

I.A.1   The students will identify this chapter as the logical "next step" in the food and cooking unit of study. The unit will be completed in six weeks. The first two weeks of this unit cover nutrition, wise eating, health, and manners. The second section of the unit begins (in the third week) with a study of weights and measures, cooking terms, and cooking utensils. Actual cooking instruction will begin with the chapter being read in this DRA, "Cooking the Basics."

The unit project will also generate student interest for the reading of this chapter. The unit project will be completed in the final week of the unit. The class will work in groups of four to five. Each group will be responsible for: (a) planning menus for a family of four for one week; (b) making a shopping list (using consumer information, nutrition information, and coupons from a Sunday newspaper); (c) budgeting a certain, specified amount of money; (d) buying the food necessary for one evening meal (to be bought during a field trip to the grocery store) and (e) preparing and serving the meal.

Developing Concepts

I.A.2   A main concept necessary for understanding this reading material is the importance of the food groups in one's diet. Nutrition has already been taught, so that the concept is understood by the students. Specific, daily nutrition needs have not been covered, though. A series of films will be presented for the development of this concept.

Film: *Nutrition—Foods, Fads, Frauds, Facts*—A series—three parts.

Another concept of importance is that of wise cooking behavior. Using appliances and utensils irresponsibly may cause injuries. This concept has already begun to be developed in the previous chapter, "Before You Cook." The teacher will ask for suggestions on safe, effective cooking. The students will state safety rules for kitchen behavior at this point. The rules will be written on a chart, by the students, to be hung on the wall of the kitchen.

Introducing New Words

I.A.3   All of the vocabulary words appear to be phonically regular. The following sentences will be put on the board. Students will define using context clues.

1. The *basics* of cooking must be learned before you can cook gourmet foods.
2. *Fundamental* is a synonym for *basics*.
3. Many say that eating *yogurt* makes people live longer.
4. Using your *ingenuity* will make your cooking more interesting.
5. Boil the juice until it has the *consistency* of a thick syrup.
6. The average time of *incubation* for yogurt is five hours.
7. Plan your meals so that you get a *maximum* amount of nutritional value from them.
8. Please arrive *promptly* for class.
9. Vitamin pills may *supplement* a poor diet.
10. We will make up a variation of that *recipe*.
11. What *adaptations* can be made in your diet for better health?

The words in the sentences will be read aloud as the teacher moves her hand under the sentence. The word is underlined. Using contextual analysis and, if necessary, dictionary skills, the students will write a definition for each vocabulary word. They will also be required to make up new sentences using the words. Definitions and sentences will be turned in to be checked by the teacher.

Establishing Purposes

I.B.1   The students will again identify this chapter as part of the foods and cooking unit. Questions concerning the unit project will be answered. The students will explain the meaning of the chapter title, "Cooking the Basics," and list possible ideas and activities contained in the chapter.

They will also list the "basics" they are already able to cook, and those they would like to be able to cook.

Silent Reading

II.A.   Questions to precede silent reading sections:

pages 138 to 141

Do you think people should drink milk every day? Why, or why not?

What are some foods we eat that contain milk?

How could we make desserts from milk?

pages 142 to 145

What nutrients do we get from vegetables?

What are some ways to fix vegetables?

Why are fruits an important part of a person's diet?

pages 145 to 147

What are the main sources of protein in your diet?

What other sources are available?

pages 147 to 148

Other than bread, what are some foods in this group?

The reading will be done at home by the group reading at the independent level. Those reading at frustration level will use only the recipes. Other ideas will come from pamphlets on nutrition.

The group reading at the instructional level will read the material in class. All sections will cover the material in four class periods.

Class Period I—Milk. Pages 138 to 141.

Class Period II—Fruit and Vegetables. Pages 142 to 145.

Class Period III—Meat and Alternates. Pages 145 to 147.

Class Period IV—Breads and Cereals. Pages 147 to 148.

The students will be sitting with their unit project groups. If a student finishes the reading before other class members, s/he may continue working on research and writing for the unit project.

Questions and Discussions

II.B.   Ask students the following questions after reading each section:

Milk. Pages 138 to 141

1. What are several meanings of "basics" used in this chapter? (literal)
2. What are three ways listed to keep the nutrients in the food you prepare? (literal)
3. List some ways, other than those listed in the book, to include milk in your family's diet. (appreciation)
4. List the ways the book suggests for serving milk. (literal)
5. Is milk actually as important to your diet as the authors imply? (evaluation)
6. What will happen if you shorten or lengthen the incubation time for yogurt? (inferential)
7. List several desserts that are made from milk. (literal)
8. What would be your favorite recipe to try from this chapter? (appreciation)
9. Why is making yogurt like "a science experiment"? (inferential)

Fruit and Vegetables. Pages 142 to 145

1. List the three ways given in the book for keeping the vitamins and minerals in the vegetables you prepare. (literal)
2. Could you make vegetables your favorite food? How? (appreciation)
3. List the nine cooking hints for vegetables. (literal)
4. Look at the list of vegetables. With what other foods might these vegetables be served? (inferential)
5. What is the boiling time for fresh broccoli? For frozen peas? For fresh asparagus? For frozen asparagus? (literal)
6. Which have a longer boiling time, fresh or frozen vegetables? (literal)
7. Why do you cook fresh vegetables longer? (inferential)
8. What would happen if you overcooked vegetables? (inferential)
9. List the six points in preparing salads. (literal)
10. What are your favorite salads? (appreciation)
11. What are some ways you can think of for using fruits in your diet? (inferential)

Meat and Alternates. Pages 145 to 147

1. List some of the meats mentioned. (literal)
2. Explain the use of certain foods eaten together to supplement protein deficiencies. Give an example. (literal)
3. Which of the variations of the Meal-in-a-Skillet Dinner would you like best? (appreciation)
4. Think of some variations of this recipe. (inferential)
5. What are some protein foods in the salad on page 147? (inferential)

Breads and Cereals. Pages 147 to 148

1. List some breads and cereals not listed on page 147. (inferential)
2. What is the nutritional value of foods in this group? (literal)
3. What are some adaptations you could make on the granola recipe? (appreciation)
4. Why would you make these adaptations? (evaluation)
5. What does the book suggest you put on french toast? (literal)
6. Do the suggestions for serving french toast fit the way you have had it? Explain. (evaluation)

III. Skill Instruction

An exercise in notetaking from textbook material would be useful since the passage is well organized by headings and subheadings. Since the students have already read the material at this point, a good opportunity exists to teach them the skill of notetaking using this passage.

Begin with the first section; ask them what is the main idea that the author is trying to convey. If they parrot a sentence from the book, ask them to put it in their own words.

Next ask them if there are any supporting details which are necessary in understanding the main idea of the section. Students sometimes have difficulty sorting out the important from the unimportant details; the test is whether knowing the details helps the students understand the main idea.

The main idea and supporting details may be written on the chalkboard in outline fashion:

I. Main Idea
   A. Supporting detail
   B. Supporting detail

A more informal system is to write a main idea flush with the left margin of the paper and supporting details indented underneath.

After working together on the first section, have students take notes independently on the second section. Afterwards have several students copy their notes on the chalkboard for comparison and discussion.

If the students seem to understand the procedures, have them finish notetaking on the rest of the reading assignment. If not, continue discussion. Collect their notes to check accuracy and provide individual guidance as necessary.

Until the notetaking habit is established, continue to collect their notes or check them in class. Another alternative is to have students check each other's notes.

After an examination, an evaluation of students' own notes to see whether the notes helped them with the exam questions should prove beneficial. If the notes have included points covered on the examination, students will see the value of notetaking. Periodic checking may be necessary to be sure that the habit becomes well established.

IV. Extending Reading Skills

A. The unit project will necessitate the use of various resources for completion. These resources will include cookbooks, pamphlets, consumer magazines, and newspapers.

All three ability levels will be required to complete this project. Resources in the classroom will include material for each level. The students will be expected to use resources in the home as well.

B. The students will submit the project in writing.

The recipes in each section will be made by the students at the conclusion of the reading portion of class time. Students will work in pairs, and each pair will be expected to use its own variation of the recipe.

ADDITIONAL RESOURCES

BARCLAY, M. S., et. al., *Teen Guide to Homemaking*. New York: McGraw-Hill, 1972.

COTE, P., *People, Food, and Service*. Lexington, Mass.: Ginn, 1972.

PECK, L., et al., *Focus on Food*. New York: McGraw-Hill, 1974.

St. Marie, S. S., *Homes Are For People*. New York: John Wiley & Sons, 1973.

Thal, H. M., and M. Holcombe, *Your Family and Its Money*. Atlanta: Houghton Mifflin, 1973.

THE LANGUAGE EXPERIENCE APPROACH IN THE CONTENT AREA CLASSROOM

Another teacher-directed technique for individualizing instruction is the language experience approach. The language experience approach has often been advocated as a technique for teaching beginning reading. As described by Stauffer (1970), Van Allen (1976), Veatch *et al.* (1973), and others, it is based on the premise that students can best learn to read if they see that reading is merely "talk written down." For this reason, the language experience approach has often been considered the natural way to teach young children to read since the reading materials consist of their own language products. The following suggestions are drawn from an article (Askov and Lee 1980) pertaining to the use of the Language Experience Approach in content area classes.

Briefly, the language experience approach consists of the following steps:

1. A stimulus idea or activity, selected by the teacher or student, is discussed spontaneously.
2. The teacher then suggests that students record their ideas on chart paper, chalkboard, or transparency.
3. The students dictate their ideas to the teacher who writes them, usually on a chart, while the students watch.
4. The students read what they have dictated.
5. The chart may be put into more permanent form (perhaps bound into a "book" with other experience stories) or transcribed on a ditto to be reread and shared with others.
6. The story may become the basis for skill development, such as teaching vocabulary skills.

The language experience approach has been used successfully with older students, primarily in remedial settings rather than in content area classrooms. For example, Wilson and Parkey (1970) report its use in a middle school reading program with poor readers. Girdon (1973) used the approach with severely disabled junior high school students while Abbott (1966) applied a modified language experience approach with culturally disadvantaged high school students.

The language experience approach can be used effectively in content area classrooms. All readers, whether disabled or not, can benefit from the procedures. The technique is particularly useful in adapting difficult content materials for those students who are unable to read them successfully.

Some stimulus ideas or activities that might be used in the language experience approach in content area classrooms are pictures, slides, films, filmstrips, experiments, demonstrations, oral reading by the teacher, audio- or videotapes, records, new events, art, and music. The concepts related to the content are brought out during the discussion which follows the stimulus activity.

Some examples of uses of the language experience approach in content area classrooms follow:

English

–The teacher reads aloud a piece of literature (for example, a short story) that would be too difficult for the students to read independently. After a discussion the students dictate a summary. The teacher later transcribes the student-dictated material to a ditto master for use in teaching the skill of writing plot summaries.

–Students dictate letters to friends and relatives who live far away. Through the teacher writing the dictated letters in the proper format, the students are taught the correct form for a letter.

Social Studies

–News events which the students have heard on radio or seen on television are dictated to the teacher during the study of current events. The charts for one day may be bound together to form a daily "newspaper." Those collected over a period of time may be bound together to show how history may be recorded.

–The teacher tapes a chapter of a difficult textbook which the students listen to at a listening center while they follow along in their textbooks. After all have completed the chapter, they dictate the main ideas to the teacher who records them on a chart and then on a ditto master. This rewritten version in effect becomes the students' textbook, written in a version that is readable to the students. Rewritten portions of the textbook (on ditto) may be used the following year with students who are unable to read the textbook.

Science

–The teacher conducts an experiment. The students dictate the steps or procedures followed while the teacher records them on a chart or ditto master. The chart or dittoed sheet serves as the guide when students perform the experiment themselves.

–After viewing a film, the students dictate the main ideas presented. These are placed on a ditto master which aids in reviewing the science concepts presented in the film.

Mathematics

–The teacher presents a problem to some students, using only numbers. The students create a word problem which the numbers might represent. The word problem is dictated and placed on a chart or ditto master for other students to solve. The challenge is to get the same answer as in the original problem.

–As students read a word problem, they dictate the important facts, omitting irrelevant details. The dictation which is placed on a chart helps them understand the process of solving word problems.

Home Economics

–The teacher discusses the procedures for preparing to cook safely in school. The students then dictate these rules, which are written on a chart to serve as a reminder throughout the cooking experiences.

–Similar to the science example above, the teacher may demonstrate procedures (such as for cutting out a pattern) to the class. The students dictate the step-by-step procedures which they are then to follow in working with their own materials.

Industrial Arts

–The teacher reads portions of difficult technical manuals to the students. After these are discussed, the students dictate the directions in a simplified form which are placed on a chart or ditto master to guide students in their use of the machinery.

Foreign Language

–The students dictate a brief dialogue or play, using current vocabulary words. After the dictation is placed on a ditto master, the students reread it for additional practice.

Music or Art

–The teacher plays a record of a musical selection or shows a picture or slide of a work of art. After students discuss the mood created, they dictate their ideas which are written on a ditto master to help them remember the work.

–The teacher plays a melody on the piano. Some students dictate lyrics which would fit the tempo. These are placed on a ditto master and duplicated for all students to sing.

–When students are learning a selection in music class which is related to a folk tale or other story, the classroom teacher may ask the student to dictate the story for a chart; the story is then put into a form of a "script" for choral reading to be used in the next music class for an introduction to the song or in the content classroom for follow-up or reinforcement.

The language experience approach has been particularly successful with frustration level readers, those students who find the textbook too difficult to understand. While all students may participate in the stimulus activity and subsequent discussion, the dictated discussion becomes the "textbook" for the poor readers. If it is placed on a ditto master, this simplified version may become the "textbook" for the poor readers in future years.

REWRITING MATERIALS

The key to effective use of the language experience approach is that materials are written in the students' own language. This means that disabled readers or others with reading problems can read materials at their own levels. Using the language experience approach, the students writes the reading materials for him/herself and other students to read.

What can a teacher do with other difficult materials when the language experience approach is not the appropriate strategy? One possibility is for the teacher to rewrite critical parts of the materials for student use. The process of rewriting sounds simple, but it is time consuming. Therefore, teachers need to be sure that the rewritten materials are of broad usefulness this year and for time to come.

The following is an outline of the rewriting process:

1. Select the materials to be rewritten.
2. Systematically sort out concepts, key words and phrases which must be included in the simplified form. Rewrite sentences to shorten sentences and word length, being sure to include those key words and phrases.

3. Use a readability formula (provided in Chapter 16) to check readability levels before and after writing.

4. Aim for a reading level appropriate for the group reading it. For example, ninth-grade biology students may need sixth-grade reading level as measured by formal or informal testing. Rewritten materials should aim for fifth-grade level, *one grade level below* the students' assessed reading level. This rule of thumb should allow students to read the material with minimal difficulty and maximum comprehension.

5. Check out rewritten material with students and let them help edit it to encourage comprehension.

6. Be sure to use visuals whenever possible—pictures, drawings, tables, graphs, diagrams, figures, and maps.

The following is an example of how a teacher rewrote a tenth-grade home economics textbook to the sixth- and third-grade reading levels. Students functioning at these different reading levels could thus read the same content. The first passage, written at the tenth-grade readability level, is directly from the textbook.

REWRITING THE TEXT*

Henrietta Fleck and Louise Fernandez,
Exploring Family Life
(Englewood Cliffs, N.J.: Prentice-Hall, Inc., 1977), pp. 84 85.

Tenth-Grade Reading Level

CALORIES:

Calories are a unit of measure, like pounds and inches. In nutrition and related sciences, calories express the amount of energy it takes to perform certain tasks. Calories also measure the energy value found in foods.

Needs for Energy

You need energy for three different operations, all taking place at the same time. First, you need energy to run your body processes—to breathe, to circulate blood, and so on. This energy is used no matter what else you do. Second, you need energy for each and every one of your activities. These include walking to school and sitting in class as well as riding a bicycle and playing ball. Third, you need energy in the growing process. It takes calories to lay down muscle tissue and to lengthen your bones. When you have attained your full growth and development, this final need will be satisfied.

Your Calorie Needs

How can you tell how many calories you need each day? The exact amount is difficult to determine, but some guides based on scientific experiments are available. The first need, to supply energy for normal body function, is called basal metabolism. Studies have shown that individuals will vary in the number of calories needed. Generally speaking, it has been found that a large person needs more calories to keep going than a small one, and that boys need more than girls. There are also additional individual influences.

*Prepared by Donna J. Dickstein, Mifflin Co., Pa., School District.

Some studies have shown how many calories are required for various activities. For example, it takes more calories to ride a bicycle than to talk, to go upstairs than to go down, and so on. Studies of this kind are lengthy and expensive, and much more information is required. Table 11–1 shows the recommendations of the Food and Nutrition Board of the National Research Council for caloric needs of young people aged 11 to 14.

Caloric Content of Foods

Almost all foods contain calories. Some contain few, if any. It is the proteins, fats, and carbohydrates that supply calories. Proteins and carbohydrates provide four calories per gram and fats nine calories per gram.

There are several influences on the number of calories in a food. Because fat is concentrated and has more than twice as many calories as protein or carbohydrate, naturally the amount of fat in a food will make a difference-the more fat, the more calories. In contrast, water does not contain any calories, so watery foods like green leafy vegetables or fruit juices are low in calories. What you add to food can increase the number of calories, such as butter or margarine on a slice of bread, mayonnaise on salad, or sour cream on a baked potato.

Table 11–2 shows the calories in some common snacks. Note the wide range in caloric value. Identify other nutrients found in each food. Some have few, if any, that will contribute to your diet. Some items, such as pancakes and waffles, have additions, usually of butter or margarine and syrup or preserves. Are you surprised at the few calories in some of the snacks?

Most American foods have been analyzed so that we can tell approximately how many calories each contains. Although calories are important, other nutrients in foods are also of interest.

Sixth-Grade Reading Level

CALORIES:

Calories are a way to measure, like pounds and grams. In nutrition and other sciences, calories tell how much energy it takes to do tasks. Calories tell how much energy you get from foods, too.

Needs for Energy

You need energy for three things that take place at the same time. First, you need energy to run your body functions—to breathe, to circulate blood, and so on. This energy is used no matter what else you do. Second, you need energy for all of your activities. These include walking to school and sitting in class as well as riding a bicycle and playing ball. Third, you need energy for the growing process. It takes calories to lay down muscle tissue and to lengthen your bones. When you have stopped growing, you will no longer have this need.

Your Calorie Needs

How can you tell how many calories you need each day? You can look at guides to find out. The first need, to run your body functions, is called basal metabolism. Studies have shown that each person has his own calorie needs. It has been found that large people need more calories than small people and boys need more than girls.

Some studies have shown how many calories you need for some activities. For example, it takes more calories to ride a bike than to talk, to go upstairs than down, and so on. More studies of this kind need to be done. Table 11–1 shows the calorie needs of young people aged 11 to 14.

Caloric Content of Foods

Most foods have calories. Some have quite a few. It is the proteins, fats, and carbohydrates that give us calories. Proteins and carbohydrates have four calories per gram and fats nine per gram.

There are a few things which affect the calories in a food. Fat has two times the calories as protein or carbohydrates so that the more fat in a food, the more calories. Water does not have any calories, so foods with lots of water like green leafy vegetables or fruit juices are low in calories. If you add fats like butter or oil to a food you raise the calories of that food.

Table 11–2 shows the calories in some snacks. Some snacks have lots of calories while others have few. Look for the nutrients in each food. Some have few, if any, that will help your diet. Are you surprised at the few calories in some of the snacks?

Most foods have been testsed so that we can tell how many calories each one has. Calories are important but so are the nutrients in foods.

Third-Grade Reading Level

CALORIES:

Calories are a way to measure. In nutrition, calories tell how much energy it takes to do things. They tell how much energy you get from foods, too.

Needs for Energy

You need energy for three things. First, you need energy to do work for your body. Your body works when you breathe and when your blood flows. You do not need to think about this work. Second, you need energy to work and play. You use it to play ball, ride a bike, and sit in class. Third, you need energy to grow. You use the calories you get from food to build strong bones and muscles.

Your Calorie Needs

A calorie guide can tell you how many calories you need to eat each day. You might not need to eat the same things as your friend. If you are big, you might need to eat more calories than if you are small. If you are a boy, you might need to eat more things than if you are a girl.

You use calories to do most things. If you ride a bike you use more calories than if you just talk. You use more when you walk up steps than when you walk down steps. Table 11–1 shows the calories you use to do things.

Caloric Content of Foods

Most foods have calories. Some foods have a lot. Some foods have few. It is the proteins, fats, and carbohydrates in foods that give us calories. These things in our foods tell how many calories there will be. The more fat in a food, the more calories it will have. Water does not have calories at all. Foods with lots of water like greens or fruit juice are low in calories.

Table 11–2 shows the calories in some snacks. Some snacks have lots of calories. Some snacks have few.

Tests have been done on most foods. We can tell the calories in each one. Calories are important but so are the nutrients in foods.

Summary

The techniques presented in this chapter have been teacher-directed. In other words, the teacher prepares and assigns the instructional materials, and evaluates the outcomes of instruction. The teacher's role is an important one. The teacher should consciously guide students through the reading material to be sure that his/her goals and objectives are being carried out in instruction. These goals should be clearly communicated to students so that they know how to read assigned reading materials. The teacher should gradually shift the responsibility from him/herself to the student. Opportunities for greater student responsibility and self-direction are presented in the next chapter.

Chapter Activities: Using What You've Read

Learn to Do It!

1. Develop (a) a Directed Reading Activity (DRA) for a unit or chapter of your textbook (be sure to establish a purpose for the reading) and (b) a plan for using the Language Experience Approach for students reading your text at the frustration level.

2. Find a chapter of a text that you feel handles content well but is written at a level beyond that of your students. Rewrite it at a level one grade below that of your students' assessed reading level.

Do It!

Administer either the DRA or Language Experience lesson you developed. Note students' reaction to and success with these different techniques.

References

ABBOTT, M. K., "An Experience Approach in a Senior High School Reading Lab," in S. W. Webster (ed.), *The Disadvantaged Learner: Knowing, Understanding, Educating*, pp. 533–37. San Francisco: Chandler, 1966.

ASKOV, E. N., and J. W. LEE, "The Language Experience Approach in the Content Area Classroom," *The Journal of Language Experience*, 2, no. 1 (1980), 13–20.

BARRETT, T. C., "Taxonomy of Reading Comprehension," *Reading 360 Monograph*. Lexington, Mass.: Ginn, 1972.

GIRDON, M. B., "Helping the Disabled Reader," *Elementary English*, 50, no. 1 (1973), 103–05.

HERBER, H. L., *Teaching Reading in Content Areas* (2nd ed.) Englewood Cliffs, N.J.: Prentice-Hall, 1978.

ROTHKOPF, E. Z., "Adjunct Aids and the Control of Mathemagenic Activities During Purposeful Reading." In W. Otto and S. White (eds.), *Reading Expository Material*. New York: Academic Press, 1982.

STAUFFER, R. G. *The Language Experience Approach to the Teaching of Reading*. New York: Harper & Row, 1970.

VAN ALLEN, R., *Language Experiences in Communication*. Boston: Houghton-Mifflin, 1976.

VEATCH, J., and others, *Key Words to Reading*. Columbus, Ohio: Merrill, 1973.

WILSON, R. M., and N. PARKEY, "A Modified Reading Program in a Middle School," *Journal of Reading*, 13, no. 6 (1970), 447–52.

Chapter 10
Student-Directed
Learning Activities

Preview

In the last chapter we discussed techniques for accommodating individual differences within teacher-directed instruction. While all instruction is usually planned by a teacher, students may be given more opportunities for self-direction than with the techniques previously described. The teacher designs the following instructional tools, but the students use them more or less independently, depending on their capabilities.

Student-directed instructional techniques are some of the instructional strategies that may be incorporated into the unit plan. Because they provide opportunities for individualization, they may meet the needs of different types of readers and learners.

Student-Directed Activities

Having developed an overall unit design, teachers should select a small group of related objectives which might best be attained by means of alternative instructional strategies. In addition to exploring this possibility, further analysis of diagnostic information on students in terms of interests or skill strengths and weaknesses in specific areas can lead to development of more narrowly-focused instructional components. These learning capsules may deal with a selected group of objectives, be directed toward more specialized treatment of individual or small group skill deficiencies, expand upon skill achievement, or explore interest in a particular area.

LEARNING CENTERS IN CONTENT
AREA READING

Learning centers have been used successfully at all levels of teaching. However, they are not widely used at the secondary level, primarily because secondary teachers are not familiar with the process. Therefore, examples presented here will be from the secondary level. Other books (for example, Greff and Askov 1974) exist to guide teachers in creating learning centers for reading and language arts at the elementary level.

A learning center is a place, a defined space in the classroom to which students go for specific activities. Students may carry out some or all of the activities right at the center or they may select their activities and return to their seats or go elsewhere to complete them. Center activities may be organized for individual work or for small group work. Students may be sent to the center at specific times, scheduled so that only a few are there at one time, or they may go to the center on their own time (after completing certain tasks or in otherwise free time).

Learning centers provide a means of handling the diverse learning styles of students and offer an especially attractive alternative for those needing a more visual or tactile approach to learning. From an organizational standpoint, a classroom using a variety of learning centers maximizes chances that students will find a means of learning a skill or concept which corresponds to their particular learning style. Learning centers allow students to progress at individual rates through carefully sequenced activities. Centers may offer a broad spectrum of optional activities addressing a diverse set of needs or interests.

Structurally, a learning center approach in a classroom makes optimum use of space. Centers may be portable or permanent; elaborate or simple; address one or many concepts; and contain tasks or activities representing one or several levels. Choices are made in the light of professional knowledge and with reference to external constraints, such as space, time, and cost.

There are two basic types of centers: skill centers and interest centers. Centers which focus on the acquisition of necessary skills or knowledge are called skill centers; those exploring ideas, concepts or topics tangential to the core content are termed interest centers. When teachers begin to introduce learning centers into their classrooms, students usually require much direction as to the type of center selected and amount of time to be spent on various activities. As they become more familiar with the center approach, students may be guided toward responsible selection of learning centers and productive use of them. In fact, an important feature of learning centers is the emphasis on helping students become responsible and self-directed.

The following learning centers were designed by three educators* as part of the Content Area Reading Project (Dupuis and Askov 1977). They were constructed of materials that teachers usually have in their schools.

Lost Cities

The following model center demonstrates both what a center is and how it fits into content area reading. The "Lost Cities" learning center is built into the sample unit *Neighbors to the South* for a junior high social studies class. It is given as Objective P, to be introduced on May 21. The learning center includes an introduction on videotape, written and recorded by the teacher and a few students from one of her classes. The videotape starts with slides of Lost Cities of Mexico and the process of discovering them. During this motivational and content-oriented introduction, several words are used which become the examples for the reading skill to follow.

The reading skill is identifying and using roots and affixes (prefixes and suf-

---

* Andrea Lee, Gillian Craig, and Betty Holmboe.

fixes) in the context of social studies. (Words are included such as *archaeology*, *monolith*, *inscription*, and *anthropologist*.) The teacher is assuming that the concept of prefix-root-suffix is not totally new to these seventh and eighth-grade students, but that they need to transfer and reinforce the skill. The videotape shows the teacher manipulating color-coded word parts as she takes words apart and builds new ones. It then shows her introducing cubes with the same color coding, on which are printed the same word parts, so the students can play a game of building new, often nonsense words. The cards and cubes are simple to make—students can do it!—using paper-board, press-on letters, and masking tape. Velcro attaches the word cards to a small board.

Both the word cards and the cubes are also available in the learning center for students to use after the videotape is finished. Also in the center are five different sets of worksheets pertaining to roots and affixes, one on each of the activities covered in the videotape and in the same order.

The physical layout of the center is shown in the photograph. The center can be placed on any table, with all the parts movable to adjacent tables or student desks. Materials for the center include

1. backdrop
2. class set of five vocabulary exercises (with answer keys included)

Students watch the videotape introduction to the Lost Cities Center before beginning the vocabulary skills work in the center. *(Photo by Joseph Bodkin)*

3. folders for completed papers
4. set of word cubes and word parts with board
5. additional reading materials on Lost Cities at various levels of difficulty.

This center aims at (1) requiring the basic work in root and affix vocabulary development, (2) providing extra hands-on activities for students with reading problems (using the word cards and cubes); and (3) providing further reading on the topic of Lost Cities for students interested in it. Only the basic vocabulary work, as prescribed in the objective, is required of all students and even then the student may choose or be assigned to only some of the five exercises. The teacher may, therefore, use diagnostic information on a student's strength or weakness in root-affix work to prescribe specific exercises or to add more work in this skill. Referring to the Decision Model presented in Chapter 2, the teacher may assign individuals or groups of students (step three), based on diagnosis (step one) and the resulting objectives (step two), to undertake activities in the learning center (step four). The evaluation process (step seven) has been identified in advance and the materials (step five) have been developed by the teacher to meet the precise needs of this content and class.

Overall, then, a learning center needs to include a specified general teaching goal, one or more specific objectives or learning outcomes, a list of prerequisite skills or skill levels which students need before attempting the center, the procedures to be used, and the evaluation procedures to determine student success and also to evaluate the center's effectiveness.

That's News to Me

This learning center is a part of an English class, useful to reinforce and extend comprehension skills and work with higher level critical reading skills. The content is learning about the newspaper, its parts and its functions. The center may be laid out on a table as shown in the photograph.

The center is introduced by a short audiotape which directs students on the procedures and the work sheets in the center. The motivation-readiness device is a quick look at six or eight newspapers gathered into the center, ideally including

Two eleventh grade students working at the "That's News to Me" center looking through newspapers as they listen to the tape. *(Photo by Joseph Bodkin)*

That's

1. different kinds of newspapers
2. major sections in a newspaper.

HOW TO WORK THROUGH THIS CENTER. . .

1. Listen to the tape on different kinds of newspapers. It will give you some directions also.

2. You will notice that the center is divided into sections which are color-coded. The sections are some of the different kinds of articles you can find in the paper. Here is the color-coding system:

N E W S

NEWS	red	choose 1 red activity
EDITORIALS	green	choose 1 green activity
FEATURES	yellow	choose 1 yellow activity
SPORTS	blue	choose 1 blue or 1 light blue activity
ENTERTAINMENT	light blue	
CLASSIFIED	purple	choose 1 purple, brown or orange activity
PICTURES	orange	
ADS	brown	

Altogether you will do 5 activities—one News, one Editorial, one Feature, one from Sports or Entertainment, and one from Classifieds, Ads, or Pictures.

To Me

Turn Page...

EVERY activity which you choose MUST be completed on your own paper. You may write one-word answers except where the directions tell you to do something else. Your paper should look like this:

NAME
ACTIVITY COLOR; NUMBER & LETTER

1.
2.
3.   ANSWERS &
4.   CORRECTIONS
5.

draw a line to separate activities

ACTIVITY COLOR; NUMBER & LETTER

1.
2.
3.   ANSWERS &
4.   CORRECTIONS
5.

1. Use your own paper unless you need paper without lines

2. Do NOT write on Activity Cards

3. Put your finished paper in the correct place

4. Extra activities = EXTRA CREDIT

PLEASE PUT ALL MATERIALS BACK IN THE CORRECT PLACES. . .

When you have finished everything (at least 5 activities), list five ways you can use the newspaper which did not occur to you before. If you can think of ways not shown in this center, better yet!

1. _____   4. _____

2. _____   5. _____

3. _____

Finally, describe in a few sentences where you can see reading skills on the LITERAL, INFERENTIAL, EVALUATIVE and APPRECIATIVE levels being developed here. (Refer to Barrett's Taxonomy if necessary.) How could you apply this in your classroom?

(Use the back of this sheet.)

3. When the tape tells you, take a ticket from the pocket marked TICKETS — your ticket will tell you what color activity to do first, second, etc. This is so no section of the center will get too crowded.

4. Choose your activities from the box marked "Reading the Paper." You will notice that each article has a color, a number and a letter.

    — The color tells you what kind of article it is.

    — The number will help you locate the activity or task card and the key.

    — The letter (A or B) tells you the difficulty level.
       A = easier; can be accomplished quickly
       B = harder; will take a longer time

So YELLOW 4A — Would tell you it is a Feature article; that you can find the activity card under yellow-4 in the activity box, or the key under yellow-4 in the key cards; and that it is an easy activity which you can finish in a fairly short time.

TO MEET THE OBJECTIVES OF THIS CENTER, YOU MUST:

1. Listen to and follow instructions on tape.

2. Read and follow instructions on the center display.

3. Complete 5 activities (according to color-coding system on the first page of this booklet):

EVALUATION — Take the key and score your own — where answers are given; your teacher will score the rest. Correct your own mistakes.

↓

TO BE ELIGIBLE FOR

O   OUTSTANDING = at least 3 "B" level activities chosen/completed.

S   SATISFACTORY = at least 2 "B" level activities chosen/completed.

A   ACCEPTABLE = all "A" level activities chosen/completed.

R   RECYCLE = activities not finished; incorrect format; mistakes.

national and local papers, daily and weekly papers. The reading selections are color-coded by the kinds of articles; for example, news in red; sports in blue. Students come to the center in groups and pick up a worksheet and assignment ticket telling them which colors to work with in which order. This eliminates everyone's reading the same articles and avoiding topics they know nothing about.

Reading comprehension is developed by a process much like many comprehension exercises. Each article is accompanied by an assignment card containing questions to be answered after reading, as shown in the photograph. The selections and questions increase in difficulty in each section. Again, the teacher may allow free choice to students in difficulty level or s/he may assign students to levels according to diagnostic information. Following is the worksheet which serves as direction for the center.

MAPerrific

MAPerrific is a center designed for transfer and reinforcement of map reading skills for eighth and ninth-grade students in social studies. MAPerrific begins with an audiotape giving basic information on maps and directions for individualized work in the Magnificent Map exercises available at the center.

The instruction specifies that a group of six to nine students work together at this center through the 40-minute audiotape and accompanying fifteen transparencies (which are placed on the overhead projector by a member of the group). As the tape and transparencies direct, the student works through the study guide, using crayons to color in the maps appropriately. All answers are provided by the tape and

The media technician, a member of the group, shows one of the maps in MAPerrific, while a group listens to the audiotape instructions. *(Photo by Joseph Bodkin)*

transparencies. At the end of the audiotape, directions for the individualized activities are given clearly.

LISTENING CENTERS

Another option for developing skills in the content classroom is through listening centers. These are similar to learning centers except that the students assume less responsibility for directing their own learning. The teacher through the audiotape provides the structure for the learning experience. Content that is too difficult for students to read in their textbook may be presented through a listening center. Betsy, our frustration level reader, is following along in her math textbook as a tape recording directs her to look at specified shapes and diagrams. She receives both visual and auditory versions of the text simultaneously, a technique that is often useful with frustration level readers.

A listening center can also be designed as a skill development center. Listening and notetaking skills are especially appropriate for a listening center. Although all students may engage in the center, they may do so on an individual basis after they have completed other assigned work. The center can be based on an audiotape which guides students through a series of exercises to be worked through as a group or individuals. In one listening center, the concept of notetaking is introduced on an audiotape developed by an English teacher. Students are then directed to turn off the tape recorder to devise their own list of guidelines for notetaking, and these are discussed in the group before the tape is turned on again. Techniques for notetaking are introduced, such as editing notes to make them organized and meaningful for the student, recitation and notetaking from memory, and a review of notes. Students are asked to apply these techniques in a skill practice when they are directed to take

Betsy and a classmate are working at a listening center with geometric shapes following directions on the tape. *(Photo by Joseph Bodkin)*

notes on a lecture on notetaking and then compare their notes. The tape concludes with a review of notetaking procedures.

INSTRUCTIONAL GAMES

Games may be used to reinforce unit concepts and skills. Some games may involve reading, while others may focus on the content area. For example, a sixth-grade teacher,* as part of a nutrition unit, used the following set of games to reinforce the new vocabulary: scrambled words which were to be matched with definitions, a crossword puzzle for the six classes of nutrients, word search (student is to locate key words which are embedded in many random letters), and concentration, to be played on a large game board with word and definition cards. In addition to vocabulary study through games, she had the student decipher the benefits of good nutrition, which were written in code, and answer questions at all comprehension levels about a bread recipe. She also asked the students to develop their own games involving either reading or content skills around the nutrition unit. These games then could be played with other students, providing additional reinforcement. Students monitored their own progress through the set of games on a checklist by checking each game and writing in the date as they completed each game.

LEARNING ACTIVITY PACKAGES

Learning Activity Packages (LAPs) are individualized teaching procedures, carefully planned by the teacher so that students can complete them with minimal teacher involvement. All instructional materials, activities and assignments are included in the LAP. The LAP is not space-oriented as the learning center is, but the two teaching techniques can be used together most effectively. A LAP is usually quite short, designed for as little as 15 minutes or as long as a week. The objectives are spelled out carefully and, as with the learning center, may be part of a larger unit plan.

A LAP may thus serve as one alternative method for learning a specific skill, idea, or concept. As a method which allows students to progress at their own rate through a carefully sequenced set of activities geared toward attainment of selected objectives, a LAP may be a particularly appropriate means of teaching necessary reading skills within a content unit. For while all students in a particular class may need to master content, they may differ widely in their reading levels and skill development. Teachers might construct several LAPs which cover the same content concept but differ markedly in the reading skills which are to be emphasized.

A LAP is designed to teach specific skills to a specific group of students. Objectives are stated clearly, activities sequenced and accompanied by clear directions to facilitate independent progression through the LAP. Checkpoints at various stages of the LAP help teachers to maintain accurate records and monitor student progress. Although many LAPs contain only paper-and-pencil activities, teachers should explore creative options as they select activities for the LAP. Provision for some group activities can also be included as an option. Designing an explanatory

---

*Donna J. Dickstein, Mifflin Co., Pa., School District.

flowchart is important since it serves as a check for teachers as to coherence and congruence of activities, and for students as a graphic portrayal of the LAP sequencing.

Since most teachers have neither taught nor learned through the use of LAPs, it seems appropriate to explain how to develop a LAP by means of a LAP on LAPs.

a LAP

on LAPs

HOW TO WRITE A

LEARNING   ACTIVITY   PACKAGE

Name: _____

Teaching Field: _____

School: _____

Adapted from H. W. McLean and D. L. Killian, *How to Construct Individualized Learning Pacs* ©
H. W. McLean and D. L. Killian, 1973. (Dubuque, Iowa: Kendall/Hunt Publishing Co.)

LAP ON LAPs

A Learning Activity Package (LAP) is one way to learn a concept, idea, or skill. A LAP is
one way teachers can individualize instruction and still retain control over what students are
learning. LAPs are particularly useful in teaching reading skills along with content material.
Students frequently have different needs for instruction in reading skills, but may all need to
learn the same content material. Teachers can construct several different LAPs which teach
the same concept, but focus on different reading skills in each LAP.

As you go through this LAP on LAPs, you will read about various kinds of LAPs—their
format, uses and construction. You'll be referred to more extensive discussions of LAPs and
concepts necessary to write a LAP. And you'll be invited to study samples of LAPs. Then
you'll be ready to construct your own LAP. The following flowchart shows you the order of
your activities in this LAP.

FLOWCHART FOR THIS LAP ON LAP

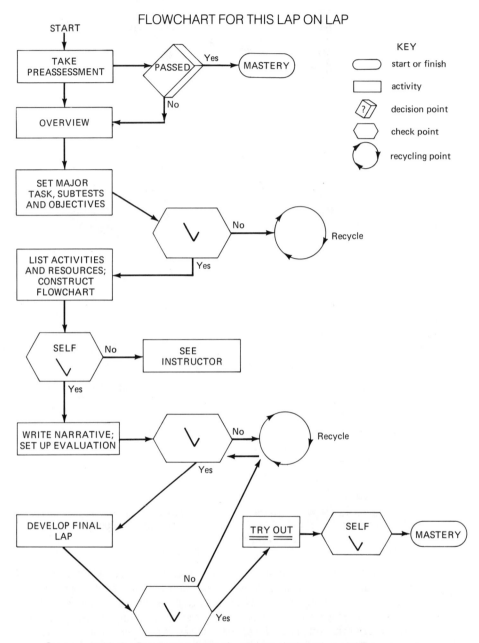

Start now with the Pre-assessment of your knowledge about LAPs.

PRE-ASSESSMENT

Directions: A pre-test is included to determine if you need to complete the following LAP. If you are uncertain about any or most of the terminology, have questions about the reason for the particular sequence of items, or can see you will experience some difficulty in completing most or some of the pre-test, you obviously need to skip the pre-test and complete the LAP. If you find it necessary to read ahead in the LAP in order to answer questions on the pre-test, you should immediately skip the pre-test and begin work on the LAP. The pre-test is a self-screening instrument.

1. From an area you teach, select an appropriate MAJOR TASK (an idea, skill, generalization, attitude) and write it in the following space.

2. Sub-divide the Major Task and write 2 of its SUB-TASKS in the spaces.

    a. _____

    b. _____

3. Write an INSTRUCTIONAL OBJECTIVE for each of the Sub-Tasks just identified. (If you can't do this, go directly to the beginning of the LAP and begin working.)

    a. _____

    b. _____

4. Identify 2 ACTIVITIES and 2 RESOURCES you would use to develop the Instructional Objectives written in #3 above.

    Activities To Do   Resources To Use

    a. _____   a. _____

    b. _____   b. _____

5. On the top of the following page, sketch a FLOWCHART you would use to structure and sequence the Activities and Resources into a learning LAP. (If you don't know about flowcharting, skip this test and begin work on the LAP.)

6. Write 2 QUESTIONS for assessing what has been learned by the student in #1–5 of this test.

    a. _____

    b. _____

(from McLean and Killian, pp. 16 and 17)

Check this pre-assessment with your instructor if you feel you answered the questions correctly. If not, turn the page to begin this LAP now.

Objectives

So you are going to write a LAP! Here are the instructional objectives you will master by the time you finish this LAP.

1. You will write three or more instructional objectives, including conditions, student behavior, and evaluation criteria.
2. You will develop methods of meeting each objective that meet the criteria of concept development discussed in the LAP.
3. You will write or collect appropriate reading material for your LAP and determine its suitabiity for your students' reading levels by testing it for readability level, using Fry's scale or an approved substitute.

4. You will develop a flowchart showing the sequence of activities, write a narrative which follows that sequence, and provide "continuity" through the LAP.

5. You will develop an evaluation procedure for the LAP, including: (1) a pre-assessment or diagnostic procedure; (2) a record-keeping form showing how and where each objective is evaluated; (3) a culminating activity and/or post-test; (4) a form for the student to evaluate his performance and the LAP; (5) a form for the teacher to evaluate the student.

Culminating activity: completion of a LAP and testing of it on at least a few (3–5) students in one of your classes.

I. *BEGINNING TO WRITE A LAP*

In order to write a LAP, you need to know more about LAPs than you know right now. LAPs are known by many different names, but all of these names refer to the same basic instructional tool:

> "An Individualized Learning Pac (ILP) can be linked to an individualized lesson plan guiding the student through a series of learning activities and materials in order to alter the student's behavior or to have him acquire knowledge."—McLean & Killian, p. 1.

Your LAP will emphasize *the integration of reading skills and content material.* In other words, you may write a LAP on many different topics and using many different teaching procedures, but you must include a reading skill component and at least one objective dealing with that reading skill.

II. *DEFINING THE TASK AND WRITING INSTRUCTIONAL OBJECTIVES*

The Task

Your first task is to define your task—the central task to be taught by your LAP. Check that the task will take the appropriate amount of *time.* Aim for a LAP to be completed in *one week.* LAPs which take longer than that run the risk of losing student interest. If you have especially good students or ones that are highly motivated, longer LAPs work well. If your students are easily distracted, perhaps three or four days is long enough. Remember, time is flexible in a LAP, so students will work at their own pace and some will take longer than others.

Check also the *complexity* of the major task. Since you must build the LAP in a careful sequence, the task must be one which can be divided into the necessary learning sequence and still be covered in the time you have chosen.

Write the Major Task for your LAP here:

MAJOR TASK _____

The Sub-tasks

Selecting sub-tasks for this major task involves dividing the task into instructional parts. What would a student need to know in order to succeed in the major task?

For example, in a 7th grade social studies LAP with the major task of understanding Climate in the United States, the sub-tasks included:

1. reading climatic maps;
2. the concept of climate (temperature, precipitation, humidity, wind sunshine);
3. climate's effects on ways of life (shelter, dress, transportation, etc.).

A Science LAP on the same topic would perhaps emphasize some of these factors more than the social studies teacher did, thus the sub-tasks would be different.

List the sub-tasks for your LAP here:

1. _____

2. _____

3. _____

4. _____

INSTRUCTIONAL OBJECTIVES

No doubt you have written instructional objectives for various kinds of teaching pro-cedures —units, lesson plans, etc. The objectives for a LAP are the same sort, but they relate to the sub-tasks you have just listed. Your job is to write at least one objective for each of the sub-tasks.

Since instructional objectives can be written in many formats, no particular form is required in this LAP. You should write objectives that are acceptable in your school system. However, if you have no accepted format, or if you need a review of writing objectives in general, check one of the following sources:

"Instructional Objectives," Chapter 2 of *The Psychology of Learning and Instruction*, by John P. DeCecco (Englewood Cliffs, N.J.: Prentice-Hall, 1969).

Preparing Instructional Objectives by Robert F. Mager (Belmont, Cal.: Fearon Publishers, 1962).

Behavioral Objectives and Instruction by R. O. Kibler, L. L. Barker, and D. T. Miles (Boston: Allyn and Bacon, 1970).

"Preparing Instructional Objectives," Chapter 2 of *Measurement & Evaluation in Teaching*, 3rd Edition, by N. E. Gronlund (New York: Macmillan Publishing Co., Inc., 1976).

As you write instructional objectives for your LAP, keep in mind that you must include at least one objective which deals with a *reading skill*. Broadly stated, that means one objective aimed at the student's competence in vocabulary, comprehension or a study skill. Go back to the descriptions and examples of skills in each of those areas which we have already discussed.

Look at the Major Tasks and sub-tasks of your LAP and answer these questions:

1. What reading skill is most necessary to succeed in these tasks?
2. What reading skill will likely be new to my students? Vocabulary/concept words? A higher level comprehension skill? A specific study skill?
3. What reading skills could I teach along with this content which I know several students are weak in?

Select one or two reading skills which would be the most effective in combination with the content given in the Major Task. Frame an objective or two that fit this skill.

When you are satisfied that you have written appropriate objectives, you are ready for a

CHECKPOINT:

Take the tasks and objectives to your instruc-tor for discussion and approval.

Instructor's initials _____

III. *ACTIVITIES AND RESOURCES*

A. *Activities*

Now you are ready to select the activities that students will carry out to meet each of your objectives. The first concern is with *concept formation*. What concepts will students learn during this LAP? Will they begin with the necessary background to develop these concepts? You will need to check on the important background information in the pre-test you will write later. At the present time, you can concentrate on teaching the concepts in each sub-task. Perhaps you need to review again the principles of concept formation. Any book on educational psychology is a good reference. Or you may read Part I of George Henry's book, *Teaching Reading as Concept Formation* (pp. 1–53) (Newark, Del.: International Reading Association, 1974).

As you select a sequence of activities for each objective, consider whether you have included the following:

1. Presentation of the concept.
2. Examples of it, both positive and negative.
3. Connections between this concept and others students should know.
4. Practice in attaining the concept.
5. Evaluation of student's competence.
6. Additional practice and recycling for a student who fails to meet criterion on the first trial.

These activities should provide some choices for students, where appropriate, and alternative activities to allow for differences in *learning abilities* (fast/slow), *learning styles* (group/individual), *learning modalities* (visual/oral/written), and *learning interests*. No one LAP can provide all these kinds of alternatives, but each LAP should include some choices and alternatives.

The *Reading Skill Objective* will require activities like every other objective. However, the practice and study associated with that objective may use regular content material. It is possible for a student to read one set of material and be developing content concepts and reading skill simultaneously.

B. *Resources*

You need now to find reading materials and other resources for students to use in each activity. Variety is again the key! Even though we are emphasizing reading, be sure one resource includes a *medium besides reading*. Examples: film, filmstrip, audiotape, videotape, overhead transparency, model, lab equipment, any other visual or hands-on materials.

Check each assigned reading resource for readability level—use the Fry graph, SMOG index or another approved formula for this. (Readability formulas are described in detail in Chapter 16.) List resources and reading level for each activity.

Scale Used _____

Title	Readability Data	Reading Level

C. *Construct a Flowchart*

Construct a flowchart of the sequence which the student must follow in completing your LAP. Use the flowchart earlier in this LAP as a model. You may use the symbols and key which are used here, or you may develop your own.

When you have completed your flowchart, you're ready for a . . .

Are you satisfied with your activities?
Your resources?
Your flowchart?

If so, go on to Part IV. If not, check with the instructor.

IV. *WRITE THE NARRATIVE*

Now you are ready to tie all of the activities together, so the student will know where he is going and what he is to do at each activity.

Write directions for each activity that are clear, concise, and appropriate for the reading level of the students. Write them for an individual student; specify what to do, how to answer, what kind of answer, where to answer, where materials are, and how each will be evaluated.

Test all your written material—narrative and directions—for reading level. Use the Fry scale, SMOG or another scale.

Scale Used _____   Grade Level _____

READABILITY DATA

Title	Readability Data	Reading Level

V. *EVALUATION*

Develop an evaluation procedure for the entire LAP, so that each objective, including the reading skill objective, is evaluated somewhere during the LAP. This evaluation can come immediately after the student works on the objective or it can come at the end of the LAP. Work through these steps:

1. Establish an *evaluation procedure* for each objective (quiz, exercise, written or oral statement, project, etc.) Determine which will be self-scored, which teacher-scored. Provide answer keys where necessary. Include all exercises, quizzes or worksheets in the LAP.

2. Establishing a *culminating activity* for the LAP. This can be a post-test, or it can be a project, paper, or other creative effort, or a combination of both. This culmination should provide the student with a sense of closure. Determine the way this activity will be evaluated and by whom.

3. Establish a pre-assessment procedure. This can be a pre-test or any other diagnostic procedure. Include scoring/evaluation directions.

4. Establish checkpoints for teacher-student interaction and mark these in the LAP.

5. Develop a checklist that teacher and student can use to keep track of student progress. Be sure all objectives and checkpoints are included.

6. Develop forms for the student to evaluate the LAP and his own performance. Include

   a. Analysis of his/her own performance.

b. Consideration of how well he/she has met each objective.

c. Evaluation of his/her own product individually and in reference to other products.

7. Develop a teacher evaluation form, including

a. Analysis of student performance (grade, if necessary);

b. Analysis and comment on LAP structure and effectiveness, taking student feedback into account.

VI. *THE FINAL PRODUCT!*

Now you are ready to prepare the finished LAP. Find an attractive way to present the LAP, using space and artistic drawing to vary the typed layout.

Be sure to include your name and content area on the LAP.

FILL OUT THE EVALUATION FORMS FOR THIS LAP!!!!

CHECKPOINT!

Take your activities, resources, flowchart, narrative and evaluation procedure to the instructor for a check.

CHECKLIST

		Date of Completion	1st trial	2nd trial	Comments
	1. Write 3 or more objectives				
	2. Sequence of activities 3. Collection and reading level of material 4. Flowchart				
	5. Level and adequacy of directions and narrative 6. Evaluation procedures				
	Culminating Activity:				
	Final Product				
	LAP completed and approved				

STUDENT EVALUATION FORM

Check the appropriate response for each section of *this* LAP and make comments in the space provided, where necessary. Your comments will lead to improvements in this LAP.

		Needs Improvement, as noted	_Comments_
	_OK, as is_		
1. Stating instructional objectives.			
2. Identifying concepts and designing activities.			
3. Selecting or writing materials and determining reading level.			
4. Developing a flowchart.			
5. Developing evaluation procedures.			
6. General evaluation of the LAP:			
a. structural and procedural strengths, weaknesses:			
b. suggestions for change:			

STUDENT EVALUATION

What is your evaluation of your own performance on this LAP and in your own finished LAP?

How could it be improved?

Grade you think you deserve _____ . Why?

TEACHER EVALUATION FORM

Student performance level:

Objective 1. _____

Objective 2. _____

Objective 3. _____

Objective 4. _____

Objective 5. _____

Culminating activity—final LAP_____

Grade _____

COMMENTS:

LAPs are a valuable means of organizing information for students to use individually or in small groups. The possibilities are limited only by the teacher's imagination. It is possible to develop two to four different LAPs containing the same content objectives but different reading skill instruction or different learning processes or material at different reading levels. LAPs may also be used to free the teacher from direct teaching and allow him/her to work with individual students or groups who need greater direction.

Working independently through a task is a skill often listed as an important outcome of public education. On that basis, using LAPs is direct instruction in this important learning skill. Developing the ability to work independently may be more important in some subject areas, such as science, than in others. However, the development of independence in learning is a responsibility of every teacher.

The LAP, then, has a general value as an independent learning technique. It also has great value in implementing the Decision Model in the classroom, especially in grouping with the classroom (step 3).

The LAP included in Appendix B is aimed at both these purposes. The disadvantaged minority students taught by social studies teacher Harry Dissinger needed the training in independence. They also needed much individual assistance, which Harry was able to provide with the LAP, and much reading instruction built into this LAP and the unit from which it comes.

CONTRACTS

Another technique for providing individualization within the content area classroom is through contracts. The teacher and the student together plan instructional activities based on learning needs. The contracts may be for individuals or groups of students having similar needs. If, for example, the teacher has determined through a criterion-referenced group reading inventory that a certain group of students did not know how to use the glossary in the textbook, a contract could be developed with those students to learn how to use the glossary before proceeding with content learning in which use of the glossary is necessary. The instruction might occur through a LAP, learning center, listening center, or small group instruction with the teacher. Regardless of the vehicle for instruction, the contract is the means of specifying the need for instruction. Completion of the contract demonstrates to both the teacher and the student that specified work has been accomplished. Here is a sample contract that may be adapted for any content area classroom.

Pupil's Name _____ Joe Doe _____ Date of Contract _____ 2/7 _____

Class _____ General Science _____ Period _____ 6 _____

What I need to learn	Materials to use in learning	Target Date for completion	Teacher conference for evaluation	Date Contract is completed
Glossary skills	Learning Center on glossary skills	2/14	Demonstrated with textbook that he could use glossary	2/15

Comments

Joe worked through the learning center during independent study time. He seemed to enjoy working at the center and completing the contract on his own.

Summary

A combination of student-directed and teacher-directed learning is optimal. Either one or the other used exclusively would be chaotic at one extreme and repressive at the other. Ideally, as students improve their reading skills and content background, instruction should move from an emphasis on teacher-directed instruction to more student-directed learning. While students are engaged in independent learning tasks, the teacher is freed to provide extra help to students who are experiencing difficulty. Careful classroom management strategies are needed; lack of planning can lead to chaos in independent learning. While learning is to be independent, it is not to be unstructured. Structured independent learning is valuable in preparing students for self-initiated lifelong learning.

Chapter Activities: Using What You've Read

Learn to Do It!

1. Develop a learning center to go with the unit you developed in Chapter 8. Include at least three skill-building activities. Be sure to include material geared to students reading at independent, instructional and frustration levels. Where possible, include media.

2. Develop a LAP to go with your unit for a duration of at least three class periods. Be sure to include material geared to students reading at each level.

Do It!

1. Have one of your classes work through the learning center. Observe them working in order to see how the center could be more efficient and effective. Be prepared to report on these observations.

2. Have students in one of your classes work through the LAP. Observe their work in the LAP in order to evaluate its effectiveness. Be prepared to report on your conclusions.

References

Dupuis, M. M., and E. N. Askov, *The Content Area Reading Project: An In-service Education Program for Junior High School Teachers and Teachers of Adults.* Final Report of Project 09–6905, Pa. Department of Education. University Park, Pa.: The Pennsylvania State University, 1977.

Greff, Kasper N., and E. Askov, *Learning Centers: An Ideabook for Reading and Language Arts.* Dubuque, Iowa: Kendall/Hunt, 1974.

Chapter 11

Motivating Students:
A Synthesis

Preview

Motivation—why don't students want to learn what I tell them to? What I think they should know? What I want to teach? It's a perplexing but constant problem. Motivating students requires thought and planning by teachers as they build their units. This chapter discusses motivation and suggests techniques for content teachers to use to encourage motivation in their students.

What is Motivation?

The problem of motivation is central to teaching in most content classes. Motivation, usually phrased as "how to motivate students," is discussed frequently in the teachers' lounge or wherever teachers gather.

Motivation is a matter of attitude, an affective concern. Students who are motivated have a desire to learn, to achieve in class. Or they have a desire to succeed in something for which this class is prerequisite. For example, a student is interested in biology, so s/he works hard, learns well, succeeds, achieves in class. Another student isn't particularly interested in biology, but he needs good grades to get into college, so he works hard, learns well, succeeds in that class. The observable result is the same for both students—they succeeded. The motivation was quite different for the two students. Indeed, like other affective concerns, motivation is highly individual, depending for each student on what matters to him/her.

Educational psychology talks about extrinsic and intrinsic motivation. Extrinsic motivation includes motivators outside the student—grades, for example, or prizes, or free time. All sorts of rewards can be used to motivate students extrinsically. Intrinsic motivation includes personal satisfaction at learning something or from working through a long, hard problem. Intrinsic motivation also means a student satisfying his/her curiosity about something that interests him/her. Or gaining a sense of success at mastering a skill or a task that has been difficult.

Teachers usually believe that intrinsic motivation is more lasting and valuable than extrinsic techniques, but grades and other parts of the current educational system are still highly dependent on extrinsic motivation.

Now let's turn specifically to reading and consider motivation to read. In Chapter 6 we said that attitudes toward reading provide increasing problems as students move into secondary school. Students who have difficulty reading will not choose to read voluntarily, just as most people will not choose to do something they don't do well. So we can expect problems in motivating students to read if they don't read well. This attitude toward reading is a problem for any teacher who asks that student to read—in health, math, or social studies, not just in reading class.

Other students, some of them excellent students, can be negatively motivated by reading. Independent level readers like Pam and really gifted students are sometimes turned off because they are not challenged by what they're asked to read. They're bored by low-level reading that doesn't go beyond literal comprehension and minimal cognitive levels. These are students who quickly answer questions of who, what, and when. They want to spend time discussing how and why.

Many students complain about reading that doesn't interest them. Interests are a particular problem with adolescents, because their interests are changing. The list of common adolescent interests, given in Chapter 6, demonstrates that these students may well change interests radically in just a few years.

Another, and related, reason why students are not motivated is that they resent requirements. That is, they may well be willing to read a book or study a topic, but because it is required, because they have no choice, they lose their motivation.

This discussion is but a brief overview of the problems of motivation that teachers face. Our purpose is not to analyze the problem psychologically as much as to present some suggestions for encouraging positive motivation and minimizing negative motivation. We concentrate on intrinsic motivation in this discussion. Extrinsic motivation, like grades and getting into college, are always there. We would encourage teachers to work most seriously with intrinsic motivational techniques.

TECHNIQUES FOR MOTIVATING STUDENTS TO READ IN CONTENT CLASSES

The techniques included here have already been introduced earlier in this book. We believe that effective motivation comes from knowing the students well, planning well, and teaching well. It is surely true that no teacher will successfully motivate all 150 students every day, but s/he can come closest to doing that by using professional judgment to plan appropriate learning experiences for students. This chapter is, then, a synthesis of attitudes and techniques for teachers which have been described more fully earlier in the book.

1. Suit students' reading requirements to their reading levels to promote success. Matching student reading levels to the materials giving content information means that students are much more likely to succeed. And success begets motivation to do it again. Not only will students learn more if the materials are on the right level; they will also want to learn more.

2. Allow students to control their own learning. Whenever possible, allow students to become more independent, more self-directing in their learning. Chapter

10 suggests a number of ways to do this: learning centers, learning packages, independent study, laboratory experiments, practical work in industrial arts or home economics or physical education. Students can organize the time and learning situation to some extent so that they do it themselves.

3. Allow students to make choices. Even if the teacher prescribes the content and the general procedures, if students can choose between two or three things, they will be more motivated than if the teacher prescribes everything. So let them choose the topic for the report from a list the teacher prepares; choose one of two or three novels to read; choose whether to give the report orally or in writing; choose one of three woodshop projects. In many cases, teachers can provide several choices within a unit, in projects, reading, and reporting situations.

4. Provide as many hands-on experiences as possible. Concrete activities tend to be motivating, especially for students who prefer not to read. Growing plants, repairing a lamp, putting up a bulletin board, drawing a poster, making a collage, building a model. . . . The list could go on. If hands-on activities are included as *choices* within a unit, students can opt to do things most attractive to them and, usually, things with which they're more likely to be successful.

5. Cater to student interests. Don't just allow student interests to operate (they will anyway). Aim unit activities at the interests of students. After assessing these interests (as described in Chapter 6), a teacher can develop a list of projects, areas to research, and books to read that reflect them. Many interests are fairly standard; they recur year after year. A student who is a car buff and has little academic motivation must still study world cultures. However, he might be interested in transportation in China, Africa, or wherever. Other interests of more esoteric nature may require the teacher to seek help from the librarian or other resource person.

6. Group students to encourage motivation. Grouping students can help or hinder motivation. Some students work well together. Others get on each other's nerves. If your purpose is motivation to accomplish a task rather than some socialization goal, the groups should be formed to reflect that purpose. Students who are task-oriented and organized may work well together. Students who are creative and thoughtful may work well together. However, pairing a task-oriented student with a creative one, in a problem solving situation, may frustrate both of them. In junior high school especially, the teacher must be alert to what groups work well together. Sometimes allowing friends to work together encourages accomplishment of the task. Other times, groups of friends just giggle and waste time, so that they don't accomplish the task. Some students are threatened by groups and do better if they can work alone. Generally, working in small groups, where everyone shares the task and responsibility for completing it, can help motivation.

7. Relate content reading and learning to students' needs and to the real world. A common complaint from unmotivated students is that school, in reading or any subject, is not relevant to their lives. This complaint may sometimes be overstated. However, we know from learning theory that learning is facilitated when the student can tie it to his/her past experiences or immediate needs. Where can the student see the topic in his/her world? Can s/he use it or see its use? If not in the student's real world, can the teacher show it in action on film or in pictures? This

principle is so basic to learning that we sometimes come to see it as elementary or simplistic, but it remains as important in high-level learning as in the lowest. Our definition of the "real world" can change, though, as our learning becomes more sophisticated. The seventh-grade life science student's real world is the tree from which s/he gets the leaves for his/her leaf collection. By the time s/he gets to advanced biology, s/he can relate the real world to the microorganisms s/he sees under the microscope. It is also true that as the content becomes more complex, it also becomes more abstract and harder to make concrete (consider the binomial theorem, for example). So the problem of relating learning to the real world is complex. Teachers should carefully review both their students' needs and their unit plans to identify the real world connections. Such connections should become a standard part of all teaching.

Planning for Motivation

Motivation is so important that teachers need to plan for it during every unit. The unit begins with a motivational experience, according to Chapter 8. This motivational experience should introduce the topic and provide a preview of what is coming. It should pique the students' interest in the topic, using one of the techniques listed earlier.

In the *Neighbors to the South* model unit, the motivating experience is a set of slides showing the people and culture of Mexico—the unit topic. As the teacher shows the slides, s/he uses an inductive questioning technique to help the students identify the areas to be studied—religion, food, shelter, clothing, history, etc. Comparing Mexico to their own country shows students both similarities and differences. However, the areas are all ones with which the students can identify. If you look again at the objectives and activities in this unit, you'll see the techniques we just talked about—reading materials at students' levels, choices for students, concern for student interests, and the rest. The culminating activity, the fiesta, includes hands-on activities of many kinds.

This emphasis on intrinsic motivation techniques is not meant to exclude extrinsic techniques. Teachers can still give grades. They can still give free reading time to students who finish the assignment early. They can even give gold stars. These techniques will not harm motivation, but they are not sufficient to motivate a student who isn't already fairly well motivated. We believe the more serious motivation problems must be attacked by systematic planning to provide maximum positive motivation in the content and reading instruction which is our major reason for being there.

Summary

Motivation may be either extrinsic or intrinsic. Although grades and other parts of the current educational system are extrinsic, we argue for emphasis on intrinsic motivation in content classes. Students appear to lack motivation to learn for many reasons, but the chief reasons are lack of interest, lack of success, and resentment at the required nature of much schooling.

Techniques for motivating students include: suiting reading to their reading levels to promote success; allowing students to make choices; providing hands-on concrete experiences; catering to student interests; grouping students to encourage motivation; and relating reading and learning to the real world. Motivation should be planned to occur throughout the teaching unit.

Chapter Activities: Using What You've Read

Learn to Do It!

1. This text does not include slides and a fiesta. What kinds of intrinsic motivation did you bring to it? What kinds of extrinsic motivation does this text use to pique your interest in the topic?
2. Look again at your unit: What motivational techniques did you use? Can you improve upon the motivational elements in light of this chapter? Explain your techniques to the class.

Do It!

Try out your motivational techniques in one or more classes. How well did they work?

PART IV
TEACHING SPECIFIC READING SKILLS IN THE CONTENT CLASSROOM

OVERVIEW

Teaching reading skills is what this book is all about. Why have we just now come to it? Reading skills must be taught in the context of the students (identified in Part II) and the curriculum (discussed in Part III). We are now ready to look at specific reading skills and some ways to teach them.

We are using the traditional division of reading into three skill areas: vocabulary (discussed in Chapter 12), comprehension (Chapters 13 and 14); and study skills (Chapter 15). These three areas allow us also to discuss other important and related topics.

Vocabulary skills (Chapter 12) may be described as word attack skills; that is, skills that help readers identify or attack new and unfamiliar words. Building a students' vocabulary is an important goal for any content teacher. However, in many content areas, vocabulary has an added significance. New vocabulary often represent important concepts in the content area. Hence, learning vocabulary is a part of concept development. Sample exercises and activities are included here. Suddenly vocabulary skills are more complex than copying down definitions and using the word in a sentence!

Then there's comprehension. We've said this is the ultimate goal of content reading—understanding or comprehending the text. Chapter 13 deals with comprehension both as *levels*, using Barrett's *Taxonomy,* and as *skills*, such as identifying the main idea. Again, the teaching process requires professional judgment on the approach to comprehension. Sample exercises are included here.

Study Guides and other guided comprehension activities are the topics of Chapter 14.

Finally, study skills. Study skills are aimed at developing independent readers. In searching skills, table and map reading, outlining and notetaking, the reader is learning tools to make him or her an independent learner. Again, sample exercises demonstrate ways to teach them.

Specific reading skill instruction will be a necessary part of any unit. After you finish Part IV, you'll be able to build appropriate activities to teach specific reading skills in your unit.

Chapter 12
Teaching Vocabulary Skills

Preview

Learning new vocabulary is a requirement for students in all content areas. In some courses, learning the vocabulary means learning the content of the course! How can that be? How do readers learn new words and make them part of their useful vocabularies? This chapter describes these learning processes, called *word attack skills*.

Vocabulary sometimes *is* the course. This usually happens when the new words are labels for concepts and the teacher wants to teach for *concept development*. The second part of this chapter deals with teaching vocabulary as concept development. Examples of other types of vocabulary exercises are included, too.

Vocabulary and Meaning

Vocabulary, or mastering the new words in any learning situation, is the most obvious type of reading skill needed by students. Indeed, in many content areas, mastering the new vocabulary in a lesson or unit is equivalent to mastering the content. What we usually mean by *vocabulary* is those words or phrases which label the parts of material to be learned and which are necessary for students to use in talking and writing about it.

Vocabulary represents both reading skill and content background. Vocabulary is *cumulative*. We learn new words all our lives as we learn new things. We need a constantly increasing set of words to talk about what we know. The teaching process assumes that the words we learned last week and last year can be used anytime and that we will understand them. This is true for many people, but our ability to retain those words and their meanings is directly related to several principles of learning:

1. The more frequently we use words, the easier it is to recall and use them again.

2. The more different ways we have used words and seen them used, the easier it is to remember them.

3. The more important or interesting words are to us, the easier it is to remember them.

4. The more we know about the whole subject, the easier it is to remember specific words.

These principles, and teachers' reflection on whether their students are likely to fit them, lead to the conclusion that it is unwise to assume that all students have the same cumulative and easily remembered vocabularies. Teachers need to assess student vocabulary levels frequently.

Another factor in vocabulary development is that students (and all of us) have several different vocabularies. We have a speaking vocabulary, a reading vocabulary, a writing vocabulary, and a listening vocabulary.

Our *listening* vocabulary is the words we understand when we hear them. Our *speaking* vocabulary is the words we can use in our own talking. Our *reading* vocabulary is the words we can understand when we read them, while our *writing* vocabulary is the words we can use in writing. We all develop listening and speaking vocabularies before we can read or write. Indeed, beginning readers are given materials to read with carefully controlled vocabularies, so that they are reading only words which are already in their speaking and listening vocabularies.

Young children, including most elementary grades, and some older students, have larger speaking and listening vocabularies than reading and writing vocabularies. With such students, the Language Experience Approach (LEA) (as discussed in Chapter 9) is useful. The LEA proclaims "What I can say, I can write: what I can write, I can read." The speaking vocabulary is seen as leading the reading and writing vocabulary to higher levels.

Sometime in the intermediate grades or junior high school, most students pass over the threshold into mature reading and writing. In this stage, their reading vocabulary is larger than their speaking vocabulary. These students can read and understand words they have never spoken or heard spoken. They can manipulate written words without first translating them into spoken form.

However, students move from speaking as primary to reading as primary at very different times. Gifted students may do it earlier. Students who are interested in the subject and who have a lot of background knowledge may do it earlier. On the other hand, bilingual and bidialectal students working with standard English texts may do it later; exceptional students, such as Learning Disabled or Educable mentally retarded students, may do it later; students with little interest, motivation to learn, or background knowledge may do it later.

It is recommended, then, that all teachers remember the original primacy of the speaking and listening vocabulary and make much vocabulary study oral in classroom activities. The translation from written to oral and back to written is good practice for most students.

An important skill for teachers is the ability to pick out those vocabulary items necessary for students to understand a particular piece of reading. In identifying words students must know, the teacher can separate them into several groups. The first group is *new words*, those words that the teacher feels the students have never had occasion to deal with before. The new words in a lesson or unit are expected to be problems. After all, if students understood all those words and the concepts they represent, there would be no need to teach them. They would already understand the material! The careful teacher will pretest students on all these new words to be sure they don't know them. This pretest is an on-going diagnosis of students' current stage of knowledge.

The second group of problem vocabulary can simply be labeled *familiar words*. These words have been identified by the teacher as necessary for students to know in order to understand the content. Thus, many of them are content-related. However, the teacher knows that these words have been taught and used in earlier units or previous years. Since vocabulary learning is *cumulative*, these familiar words should be in the students' active vocabularies. The careful teacher does not make that assumption. Instead, s/he pretests the students to be sure that these words are really familiar to them. The pretest has a double purpose: it provides information on who knows which words; it also provides a review and reinforcement for students. Students who have learned the words earlier but haven't used them for some time need to be helped to bring the meanings to their conscious minds.

As the teacher works with the vocabulary for the unit or lesson, s/he should look for a third set of words or phrases—those with *multiple meanings*. Words with multiple meanings may be either new or familiar. The teacher recognizes that the word means different things in different contexts, in different content areas. Thus, a student can be confused.

Consider the word *set*. Math teachers deal with this word frequently. Even a school dictionary such as the paperback Merriam-Webster Dictionary (1974) has nine meanings for *set* as a noun. A math teacher's meaning of set, "a collection of mathematical elements (as numbers or points)" (page 632) is the last on the list in this dictionary. A student meeting *set* for the first time in math class may easily assume that it means the same thing in math as in other areas: stalking game (as "a dog is set"); becoming hard or firm in consistency (as in "the Jello is set"); tendency or direction ("the course is set"); the *set* of a play; the fruit on the apple tree is *set*; a *set* of square dancing; or a *set* in tennis. The list goes on—*set* has many meanings. It serves as a noun, verb or adjective. It fits in many idiomatic expressions (set up, set in, set out, set back). The math teacher dealing with sets wants his/her students to understand the precise meaning of *set* as used in math. Yet s/he must help students fit this meaning of *set* into the meanings they currently have for the word.

In this early planning stage, when the teacher is examining the reading material before building specific activities or exercises, s/he must be alert to words with the potential of multiple meanings and take this into account when planning activities.

Look now at a seventh-grade science teacher's list of words from a unit on "The Biosphere and Its Habitats." We'll use this unit as an example later in the chapter.

CONCEPT WORDS IN "THE BIOSPHERE AND ITS HABITATS"*

A. *New Words*   B. *Familiar Words*

ecosystem	environments	triggers	adaptation
biosphere	abundant	migration	average
moderate	oxygen	presence	suitable
habitat	carbon dioxide	lack	adequate
niche	adapted	constant	unsuitable

*V. Webster, G. S. Fichter, C. R. Coble, and D. R. Rice, *Life Science* (Englewood Cliffs, N.J.: Prentice-Hall, Inc., 1980).

A. *New Words*

moisture	
lichens	
humus	
topsoil	
rodents	
burrowers	
dormant	
plankton	
phytoplankton	
zooplankton	
bioluminescent	
predators	
scavengers	

B. *Familiar Words*

organism	centimeters	context
bacteria	obtain	nutrient-poor
decomposing	extend	enriched
nutrients	determine	decaying
limited	influences	weathered
celsius	anchored	molds
burrow	microscopic	decimeter
polar	microorganisms	calculated
enables	hazards	available
survive	churned	dwellers
processes	varied	dissolved
behavior	sewage	temporary
migrate	organisms	absence

C. *Words with Multiple Meanings*

moderate	polar	triggers	dissolved
niche	behavior	presence	anchored
adapted, adaptation	migrate, migration	constant	

This teacher identified at least one meaning or use for each word in list C which could cause confusion to students. In a great many cases, the words will be used in the Habitat unit with different contexts than in other readings. It is this teacher's judgment that the words listed in C are the ones she must be careful to clarify for students.

USING WORD ATTACK SKILLS
IN CONTENT AREA READING

Students come to content subjects already possessing some skills we call *word attack* skills. That is, these skills are designed to attack new words, to find out what unfamiliar words mean. Our goal as readers, hence as teachers, is to identify necessary words by *sight*. That is, we will immediately recognize a word and attach a meaning to it.

We know that fluent readers do not read every word in a passage. They read only enough to get the meaning from it. The more background knowledge the fluent reader has, the less s/he has to read. The converse is also true, and it explains problems our weak readers have; the less a student knows on the subject, and the less fluent a reader s/he is, the more likely that s/he will have to read every word in order to understand the passage. Word-for-word reading is not only much slower and less efficient; it also makes it harder to develop an overall understanding of the passage, including connections within it. Any time a reader must stop his/her reading to identify a new word, no matter which skill s/he uses, s/he may lose the train of thought. The careful reader must then go back and reestablish the thought pattern before going on.

Thus, our goal as teachers is for students to become familiar with all important words so that they don't need to stop and identify them when they occur. That's what we mean when we say that students recognize certain words by sight. The meanings have become automatic. This is an important step toward the "automaticity" discussed in Chapter 1.

Unfortunately, our students come to us not knowing by sight many words necessary to learn the materials we are teaching. We must ask students to use their word attack skills to identify the new words in their reading. Four major groups of word attack skills are commonly taught in elementary school: (1) use of context clues; (2) use of structural analysis; (3) use of sound patterns; (4) use of outside references. All of those skills are used by fluent readers, often in combination. Teachers need to assess these skills on the IRI or in another way to be sure students can use all of them. Then they need to help students transfer what they know from reading class to the content material.

Uses of Context Clues. The context of an unknown word is the material surrounding it. This context may be a phrase, a sentence, a paragraph or an entire chapter. Context clues are words, phrases or more which help the reader identify—give him/her clues to the meaning of—the unfamiliar word. Context clues are classified in these categories (from McCullough 1958):

CONTEXT CLUES

1. Definition—The descriptive context defines the unknown word. For example, Tom and Dick lived next door. They were __neighbors__ .
2. Experience—Students use past experiences to complete the thought. For example, Jack gave his dog a __bone__ to chew.
3. Comparison with known ideas—The unknown word is compared to something known. For example, you do not have to run, you can __walk__ .
4. Synonym—The preceding context offers a synonym of the unknown word. For example, when the captain gave up, the crew had to __surrender__ too.
5. Familiar expression—Our language is filled with expressions that are meaningful to native speakers but confusing to those learning the language. For example, if he isn't careful he's going to put his foot in his __mouth__ .
6. Summary—An unknown word serves to summarize previous concepts. For example: Down the street came the elephants, clowns, and cages. The __circus__ had come to town.
7. Reflection of a mood or situation—The clouds were black. Scarcely any light came in the window. The house seemed very dark and __mysterious__ .

We can help students learn to use context efficiently by providing practice in identifying and using context clues in reading. The seventh-grade science teacher could help her students in the Habitat unit by looking at the use of context in that book:

A habitat (HAB- ə -tat) is a place where an organism lives. You may think of a habitat as the organism's neighborhood. The habitat of some organisms is very large. The habitat of whales, for example, is the ocean. Other organisms live in small habitats. Ants in an anthill are an example. What type of habitat do you live in?

In this paragraph, *habitat* is defined three times—first, as "a place where an organism lives"; second, as "the organism's neighborhood"; third, as differing by size (ocean large: anthill small). The definition of habitat is central to the unit; therefore the author is defining it by giving various characteristics as well as a simple one-phrase definition (the first) and a synonym (neighborhood). The characteristic, size, is a familiar concept. Thus, in this one paragraph, the context clues for the meaning of habitat include numbers 1, 3 and 4 on the list.

In a broad sense, the author of the unit "The Biosphere and Its Habitats" has used the entire unit to define habitat completely. That is the central topic or concept to be learned. In other situations, where the word is not a central concept but nonetheless a useful term, it is defined in a sentence and left at that: "This decaying material is called *humus*." Under the broader topic of soil, the development of humus is a subtopic that is valuable but not central. Thus, the definition of *humus* as *decaying material* is given once. If a student misses this clue, s/he will not be able to place humus in context successfully.

One way to help students practice using context clues is to provide modified versions of the cloze procedure (given earlier in Chapter 4). The format of the cloze procedure when it is used for practice allows the teacher to delete vocabulary words from a passage as they occur, rather than every fifth word. The student has a list of the words necessary to fill the blanks and s/he need only recognize the clues in the passage which give meaning to the blank. In the example given here, the seventh-grade science teacher has identified the sixteen words she wants students to practice with. The underlined words would be blanks for students to fill in, thirteen in all. A rule of thumb in preparing such cloze exercises is that no more than one word in ten, on the average, should be deleted. This ratio gives students sufficient context to identify the missing word.

CLOZE PROCEDURE AS VOCABULARY PRACTICE

Habitats

The paragraphs below talk about habitats and the animals who live in them.

Use the words listed below to complete the exercise. Each word or phrase can be used once, more than once, or not at all. Fill in each blank with the word or phrase that makes sense in the sentence.

standing	predators	temperature	moving
saltwater	water	scavengers	light
oxygen	constant	freshwater	dormant
air	soil	land	moisture

There are three kinds of habitats in our world: land , water , air .

The largest part of the earth's surface, almost 75% of it, is water . Almost all of this habitat is in the oceans which are the saltwater habitat. Plankton are a common type of organism living near the surface of the oceans. In the deepest parts of the oceans are two types of animals: predators who hunt and eat other animals, and scavengers who feed on dead animals and plants. There are two important features of the ocean habitat. One is light , which helps plants make their own food. The other is temperature , which determines where and at what depths animals can survive.

Freshwater habitats make up only about 3% of the earth's water. Yet we are most familiar with freshwater habitats. They may be springs, streams or rivers (which we call __moving__ water) or ponds, lakes and swamps (which we call __standing__ water). Some of this freshwater is always available, or __constant__ . Other freshwater is only temporary. In temporary freshwater, living organisms sometimes go into __dormant__ , or resting, stages, when the water disappears.

Teacher Information

13 blanks; 186 words; or 1 blank/14+ words

Practice in using context clues can range from filling in blanks in single sentences to full paragraphs, like this example. Teachers can find the material for cloze exercises from the assigned text or from alternative materials. Or they can write the material themselves, as this science teacher did.

This next example is a short cloze exercise developed for an Algebra I class. The math teacher has the same problems as other teachers in using new terminology in context. However, s/he has an additional concern—the use of symbols interchangeably with the words or phrases for which they stand. Kane *et al.* (1974) developed and validated a cloze procedure for use specifically with mathematics materials and other materials with heavy use of symbols, like chemistry and physics. In this example, the text material has been used, with a deletion pattern focusing on the concept of intersection of sets. Underlined words, phrases, and symbols are deleted in the student version.

MATHEMATICS CLOZE EXERCISE

The Arithmetic of Sets: Intersection*

The *intersection* of two sets consists of the elements they have in common. For example, if A = (1,2,3,4,5) and B = (3,4,5,6,7), the intersection of these sets would be (3,4,5), which could be designated set C. The symbol for intersection is __∩__ (read "cap").

In words: The __intersection__ of set A and set B is set C.

In symbols:

$$\underline{A} \quad \cap \quad \underline{B} \quad = \quad \underline{C}$$
$$\text{or } \underline{(1,2,3,4,5)} \cap \underline{(3,4,5,6,7)} = \underline{(3,4,5)}$$

It should be noted that the intersection of two sets is a __subset__ of each set.

Intersection may also be represented pictorially by closed figures called __Venn Diagrams__ . The region within a __Venn Diagram__ is assumed to represent the set being illustrated. Because each of the sets used in the problem is a subset of U, U is called the universe or __universal set__

**From M. P. Dolciani, S. L. Berman, and J. Freilich, *Modern Algebra, Structure and Method, Book I* (Boston: Houghton Mifflin Co., 1962), pp. 30–31.

The following example is an English teacher's exercise from a unit on Mythology.* Each sentence is taken from the reading material within the unit, so that students can return to the larger context of the complete reading, if necessary.

Context Clues   20 points

Goal: to learn to use *context clues* to help you determine an unfamiliar word's meaning.

Explanation: Often you can get a general meaning of a word from other words in the same sentence or paragraph. These words are called Context Clues.

For example: The Indians paid *homage* to many spirits, but most of all, they worshipped the Great Spirit. Here, homage is "defined" by what word? _____

Directions: Underline the word or words which help you to understand the meaning of the underlined word. Then, in the blank, write what you think the word means.

_____ **1.** "You murder me now, and steal my throne—but one of your own sons will dethrone you, for crime <u>begets</u> crime."

_____ **2.** "Her white hands danced among the flax, and she worked so quickly, so <u>deftly</u> , that she seemed to have forgotten the loom."

_____ **3.** "Poseidon smiled to himself because the sky was empty, and he knew that the <u>impulsive</u> Zeus had chosen it because it looked so high."

_____ **4.** "The <u>avaricious</u> king had to have dominion over all of the kingdoms, not only ten."

_____ **5.** "Her body was as <u>pliant</u> as a stem."

_____ **6.** "They <u>curvetted</u> twice in the air, and plunged into the hole again."

_____ **7.** "A great wailing and <u>lamentation</u> arose as the people lifted their faces to Olympus and prayed for Zeus to help them."

_____ **8.** "If any food has passed her lips during her <u>sojourn</u> in Tartarus, then she must remain there."

_____ **9.** "She saw a tree which had been struck by lightning; it was still <u>smoldering</u> ."

_____ **10.** "To his dismay, she was joined by a gaggle of <u>hamadryads</u> , mischievous girls who loved to tell tales."

Use of Structural Analysis. Structural analysis is the process of dividing words into their *roots* and *affixes*. *Affixes* are prefixes, suffixes and infixes. All are common components of words in English, but infixes occur mostly in old words like *man–men*, *sit–sat–set*, in which the differences based on number (singular or plural) or tense (present, past, or participle) are located inside the word. *Prefixes* attach to the beginning of words and *suffixes* attach to the end of words. Prefixes and suffixes are more common in English. They also are the word parts we use in creating new words.

*Prepared by Drucilla C. Weirauch, State College, Pa., Area School District.

Roots are parts of words which carry the base meaning of the full word. Roots may be independent words on their own like the root in spectro*scope*. However, many roots in content subjects are of Latin or Greek derivation and there is no English word using just the root, like *port* in reporter. Such roots' meanings must be determined by use of outside sources or references to similar words.

Affixes have two major purposes. They may be *inflectional* or *derivational*. Inflectional affixes relate to grammatical categories: plurals, verb tense, changing one word class to another. In English, inflectional affixes are either suffixes or infixes, not prefixes. Derivational affixes change the meanings of words and may change the word class to which they belong. Students are likely to have learned inflectional affixes in elementary reading class. They will probably also have learned some basic derivational affixes, like *un-, dis-, -ness,* and *-able*. However, there are higher levels of these affixes which students won't encounter until they begin reading higher-level content materials with wider use of Greek, Latin and other derivatives.

Consider the *inflectional* affixes here:

synthes*is* → synthes*es*

dat*um* → da*ta*

formul*a* → formul*ae*

These singular-to-plural forms must be carefully taught to allow for transfer of the principle of number to these new forms.

There are many more examples of derivational affixes which need study in content fields. Consider the word *spectroscope*, given earlier. It must be seen as related to *spectr*al, *spectr*ometer, and *spectr*um. It must also be seen as related to micro*scope*, tele*scope*, and oscillo*scope*. Each word part is seen, in this analysis, as part of a wider concept: *spectr*—related to light; *scope*—related to seeing through or by.

An additional process students need in order to internalize a new word by structural analysis is how to use it in different contexts:

Spectroscope—noun—an instrument for examining the light spectrum;

Spectroscop*ic*—adjective—made or performed with a spectroscope;

Spectroscop*y*—noun—The study of the spectrum through the use of the spectroscope.

The *-ic* ending transforms spectroscope into an adjective and slightly alters the meaning. The *-y* ending, meaning *study of*, not only changes the meaning but turns the word into a different noun. Spectroscopy should be seen in relation to biology, botany, zoology, history, and other branches of learning.

Practice for students in developing word "families," lists of words with similar parts, is one way of assisting students in seeing the uses of structural analysis.

A Word of Caution.   The usual use of structural analysis is to build the meaning of a word by adding together the meaning of its parts:

reporter =

re = back

port = carry   } one who carries back (information or news)

er = one who

This fairly simplistic process works well when the parts have clear and discrete meanings. Thus, in chemistry, the difference between sulf*ite* and sulf*ate* is clear and important, using this additive process:

sulf = sulfur
+ ite = salt of an acid ending in -ous   sulfite = SO_3 = salt of sulfurous acid
+ ate = salt of an acid ending in -ic   sulfate = SO_4 = salt of sulfuric acid

However, in areas like social studies and literature, in which word parts have multiple meanings or those meanings are less precise, the process of building meaning can be much more difficult. *Amnesty* means a general pardon, while *amnesia* means a loss of memory. The relationship between these two meanings can be explained, but it is not automatically clear to most students. It is interesting that these words both use the Greek prefix *a-*, meaning not, so that the original Greek word is *a + mnesthai* or *not + remember:* the root of both words is the Greek word for remember.

A second caution is about words which look as if they have the same root but don't. A case in point: *indigent* and *indigenous*. Both words are adjectives with Latin roots. *Indigent* comes from the Latin root—*egere*, meaning *need*. With the prefix *in = in*, the meaning is clearly *in need*. However, indigenous comes from a Latin word *(indigena),* and means *native to the country*. Two very different meanings for two words which look alike on the surface.

The conclusion to be drawn here is that identifying a word's meaning by using structural analysis is a useful skill, but that it can't be used simplistically. Students need to see that their judgment about the appropriate meaning of a word in context, and the judicious use of a dictionary, is necessary to avoid the pitfalls of root-affix work. It is also clear that working through word meanings and word families this way is time-consuming. Teachers will not find it appropriate to do this systematically unless the vocabulary items are central to the understanding of the topic or concept.

Think back now to the Learning Center on the "Lost Cities of Mexico" described earlier (Chapter 10). This center is part of the model unit, *Neighbors to the South.* The reading skill taught by the center is structural analysis, the use of roots, prefixes and suffixes. The teacher who developed it calls it "word part analysis." The words used to show the process of taking words apart and putting them back together are all part of the context of the unit. These example words are all part of the lesson on Lost Cities.

The greatest problem for content teachers in structural analysis is to help students transfer the skills learned in reading class to the content situation. In the picture here, Betsy, our frustration level reader, is working with one set of materials to help her transfer the appropriate reading skill: a set of cubes with word parts on them from which she can create new words. Remember that frustration level readers often need more practice than other students; they need more concrete hands-on experiences; they are likely to have more trouble with higher level cognitive work, such as the analysis (taking words apart) and synthesis (putting words together) required here. A learning center is especially useful here, because it allows Betsy to spend the extra time in a highly structured activity, while other students who don't need that much practice are doing something else.

The cubes used in this center are simple for teachers or students to develop. They are color coded (prefixes—gold, roots—green, suffixes—rust). The letters are

Betsy is working with word cubes in the Lost Cities Center, building new words from the prefixes, roots and suffixes on the cubes. *(Photo by Joseph Bodkin)*

press-ons; the posterboard is the kind every school has. Some masking tape, and you're in business. Another hands-on technique in this same center is a flannelboard with velcro strips and a set of word parts on posterboard, with the same color coding. With these word parts, students like Betsy can build new words or take words apart on the flannelboard. Also part of the center are conventional worksheets built on work with word parts; sets of exercises are available on each of the specific skills—roots and prefixes; roots and suffixes; roots with both prefixes and suffixes; and two-root words. The teacher can assign students to all or part of each exercise set, or to only particular sets.

Use of Sound Patterns. The sound of words, or their pronunciation, is important in developing vocabulary. Being able to pronounce new words means being able to use them orally. Thus, the teacher can ensure that students add new vocabulary to their speaking and listening as well as their reading and writing vocabularies by being careful to use the word orally and asking students to use it, too.

Students come to content reading with some understanding of sound patterns. They are likely to be able to use phonics, the relationship of sounds to written symbols, to sound out many words. When they run into an unfamiliar word, they can use these phonic patterns to pronounce the word. So far, so good. Most students can recognize the difference in sound between *kit* and *kite, cap* and *cape, dot* and *dote.* Some can even indicate what the silent *-e* rule is. But using such rules on words like *spectroscope* means applying rules in ways they've never used them. Hence, content teachers must again be concerned with transfer. Simple assessment in the Informal Reading Inventory (IRI) can help teachers know how well students can use the basic phonic rules and how much they can already transfer to words in the appropriate subject.

The application of these phonic rules has several problems for content teachers. The most important is that many new words are longer, with prefixes and suffixes. Let's use *spectroscope* as an example. Most students facing it as a new word will not see that its root, *scope,* follows the final -e rule, but it does. Thus, once the initial break between prefix and root occurs, spectro + scope, the student can apply the phonic patterns s/he learned earlier to attempt pronunciation of the word.

Another part of pronouncing a word is establishing its intonation pattern, or where the accents fall. This is especially troublesome in words of three syllables or more. The skills students need here are (1) breaking words into syllables, roughly a vowel sound and surrounding consonants, and (2) knowing the usual accent patterns in English. Both these skills are used correctly by standard English speakers at an early age, but they may have difficulty articulating the rules they follow. Bilingual and bidialectal students will not necessarily know or follow the same rules. Hence, intonation patterns can be especially troublesome for them.

Look again at our sample words, now including their accent patterns and vowel sounds:

spéc	tro	scōpe	silent	´	= primary stress
spèc	tro	scŏ′	pic	`	= secondary stress
spèc	tró	scə	py		

As we move from *spectroscope* to *spectroscopic,* we drop the -e to add -ic—a familiar rule. This also means the o goes from long o to short o (as in sh*o*t). The accent pattern shifts so that the primary stress goes from the first to the third syllable. In that move to *spectroscopy,* the o is no longer in an accented syllable. Primary stress is on the second syllable and secondary stress remains on the first syllable. We know that, in English, vowels in unaccented syllables almost always have an "uh" sound, the *schwa,* represented by the upside down e— ə . Hence, in these three related words, there are three different accent patterns and three different sounds for the *o* in sc*o*pe. The complexity in these sound pattern changes underscores the problem with vocabulary work in content areas. These word attack skills, often learned in isolation in reading class, must be applied in combination in content classes. Transfer, always difficult to achieve, is even more difficult to develop in these cases. Teachers must teach consciously and carefully in order for their students to grasp the patterns and processes appropriate in a particular subject area.

A Word of Caution. Applying sound patterns is important and useful in content reading. However, some new words are not derived from English and the sound patterns we teach students are useful primarily with English words. Case in point: *epitome.* This Greek word breaks well into prefix + root: epi + tome. *Epi =* on, over, upon. *Tome =* looks like a normal English word, meaning *book,* following the final -e rule: pronounced tōm. Wrong. The meaning of *tome* in *epitome,* while ultimately from the same Greek root, has become generalized, so epitome means a representative example of something: Macbeth is the epitome of the troubled king. The accent patterns and pronunciation do not follow English patterns; they follow Greek patterns—i pit′ ə mē. Teachers must be aware of the language from which vocabulary items derive in order to warn students of words which don't follow the usual English pattern.

Even with this caution, there are several rules of thumb students can use in finding the pronunciation of unfamiliar multi-syllabic words.

1. When there is no other clue in a two-syllable word, the accent is usually on the first syllable: af my

2. In inflected or derived forms of words, the primary accent falls on or within the root word: re poŕ ter

3. If de-, re-, be-, ex-, in-, or a- is the first syllable in a word, it is usually unaccented: re poŕ ter

4. Two vowel letters together in the last syllable of a word may be a clue to an unaccented final syllable.

5. When there are two like consonants within a word, the syllable before the double consonants is usually accented: rub' ble

6. In words of three or more syllables, one of the first two syllables is usually accented: syl' la ble, re por' ter (from Winkley 1966)

Use of Outside References.   The final word attack skill is also a study skill that will be discussed more completely in Chapter 15. When all the other skills fail, students can, in the words of the old saw, "look it up!" This means leaving the context of the reading and the make-up of the word itself to use a glossary, dictionary, or other source of meaning. Students may well have learned to use the dictionary in earlier grades. The important problem in using the dictionary is to be sure that the meaning selected fits the context of the passage. Especially with words like *set*, with multiple meanings, students cannot simply find the first meaning listed and use it. If students don't know the word and also know little about the topic, it can be very difficult for them to identify the correct meaning in the dictionary. For these reasons, using the dictionary is the last resort for identifying a new word.

The glossary of the text or other reading material may be more useful to the students than the dictionary because it will not have so many meanings to confuse the reader. Teachers must be sure students know where the glossary is and how to use it early in the year. Even within this word attack skill, the glossary is preferable to the dictionary as a source of information for students.

Techniques for teaching students how to use the glossary and dictionary are given in Chapter 15. The glossary is included under "How to Use the Book" and the dictionary is included in "Searching Skills."

TEACHING VOCABULARY AS CONCEPT DEVELOPMENT*

Concept development, a cognitive process, is widely given as the goal of content teaching. This is especially true in mathematics, science, social studies, industrial arts, and home economics. It is sufficiently pervasive in contemporary content teaching to spend some time focusing on concept learning and its interaction with vocabulary development.

A concept is known by its characteristics, its components. It is, in Hafner's words, "a class of things or ideas with common elements or characteristics" (1977, p. 27). A concept, such as *chair,* has certain elements which are common to all chairs. Through analysis of the concept *chair,* we can determine what those common elements are. Through a synthesis of its chracteristics, we can develop a composite of "chairness."

---

*Teaching materials in this section were developed jointly with Sandra L. Snyder, now of the University of Tennessee—Chattanooga.

	Chair	_Not Chair_
1.	4 legs	3 legs (stool)
2.	a seat for one person	seats more than 1 (settee, sofa)
3.	a back	no back (stool, bench)

Additional analysis shows some characteristics which a chair *may* have (for example, arms), but which are not necessary for it to be called a chair.

An important point here is that up to this point, we could have done all this analysis without using language. We could use pictures to illustrate the components:

The word *chair* is not the same thing as the object. The word represents, serves as a symbol for, the object. Language, thus, is already an abstract activity, removed from the concrete reality of the object. The concept of a chair, representing not only a concrete object but its essential characteristics, is another step up the abstraction ladder. Remembering learning principles again, students with limited background in the area, students who have limited experience in the topic, students with difficulty learning abstract material, all will have difficulty learning concepts. Add to that list students who have difficulty manipulating the standard English in which concepts are usually presented by teachers, books and other materials. Now the reasons many students fail in concept learning is clearer. However, the need for students to learn concepts is not diminished. What emerges is a need for teachers to plan carefully to avoid or overcome some of the problems identified here.

The first need is for teachers to plan concept teaching to make it as concrete as possible, to provide as much first-hand experience with the actual concepts as possible. Hands-on activities are recommended, along with real-world experience of the concept in action. This includes labs in science, home economics, and shop; and examples of the concept brought to class—an actual chair or spectroscope, if the concept represents an object. If the concept is an idea, as in government, then a field trip may be required—to a city council meeting, a school board meeting, or other government body. A trip to a living pond demonstrates several habitats to the seventh-grade science class. Other more vicarious experiences include movies, slides, videotapes, filmstrips and other pictures. These aren't the same as being there, but they're better than just words.

Just words. As Eliza Doolittle says in *My Fair Lady,* "Words, words, words! I'm so sick of words! Is that all you blighters can do?" Students with the problems discussed earlier often feel this way about concept learning in schools. It seems to be just words, words, words—no pictures, no visual representation of what's going on. Teachers need to plan a teaching strategy that helps students learn the words necessary to work with important concepts and learn to manipulate the words instead of the objects. They can begin, perhaps, by working with the actual chair, but our goal is for them to work, if they can, at the higher abstraction level required to manipulate concepts intellectually by means of language.

Henry (1974) gives a process for conceptualizing which allows teachers to plan effectively. Conceptualizing "means to discover relations and to invent a structure of these relations" (p.14); that is, to analyze the concept into relationships, then to synthesize the components into a whole again. Remembering Bloom's cognitive taxonomy (in Chapter 1), this means that the conceptualizing process is a fairly high-level process, subsuming the three lower levels into the process. For Henry, concept development requires four basic operations:

1) The act of joining (bringing together, comparing, generalizing, classifying). Its logical operator is *and* (moreover, furthermore). Its grammatical form is the co-ordinating conjunction and the connective adverb.

2) The act of excluding (discriminating, negating, rejecting). Its logical operator is *not* (this . . . not that). Its grammatical form *neither . . . nor* (exclusive, dichotomous).

3) The act of selecting (one or the other or both). Its logical operator is *some* (part, few). Its grammatical form is *either . . . or;* quantitative pronouns.

4) The act of implying (if not this . . . then that; cause-effect, result, necessity, proof, condition). Its logical operator is *if . . . then*. Its grammatical form is subordinating connective adverb and the subordinating conjunction. (p. 14–15).

These four operations can help teachers focus on concept development when they plan teaching processes.

Clearly, teaching for concept development requires a great deal of time. Topics taught this way must be central to the subject. Our example of a topic taught by concept development procedure is a seventh-grade life science unit, "The Biosphere and its Habitats." Reading material comes from a standard text.*

Planning for Concept Teaching

Concept teaching begins when the teacher looks at the domain to be taught and chooses those topics and materials which will be his or her focus. All subject areas contain more to learn than can possibly be taught. Choosing what to teach is not easy for teachers. However, the full domain of learning is a jumble of unknown percep-tions to students. Look at the potential topics given in Figure 12–1. This looks like a disorganized mess. The teacher must make sense of it for students by identifying the items to be focused on and the characteristics which make them important. In this set of nine potential topics, a teacher may choose to focus on shape, and have three groups of three (circles, triangles, squares); s/he may focus on the lines and have three groups of three (vertical, horizontal, slanted); or s/he may focus on the small marks superimposed on each item, and have three groups of three (checks, x's or o's). The teacher tells students what is important by helping them focus on important items and *organizing* those items, or showing the relations between them.

One way of helping students make sense of a unit is to provide them with an advance organizer, a process of giving students not only the items to be learned, but also the relationships between them. This process, described by Ausubel (1968), is a critical first step in teaching for concept development. One effective way to provide an advance organizer using the important vocabulary for a unit is the *structured*

---

*V. Webster, G. S. Fichter, C. R. Coble, and D. R. Rice, *Life Science* (Englewood Cliffs, N.J.: Prentice-Hall, Inc., 1980).

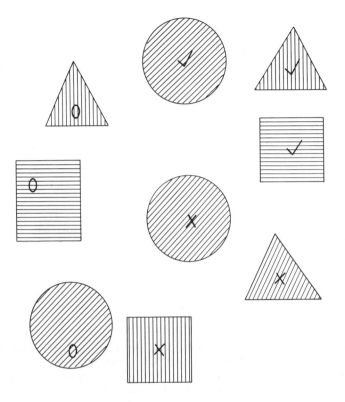

FIGURE 12–1 Concepts—Which Ones to Learn?

overview. Figure 12–2 is a structured overview for the unit on "The Biosphere and Its Habitats" for seventh-grade science. the important vocabulary items here are all *labels* for the concepts which make up the larger concept of *habitat.* Many of these

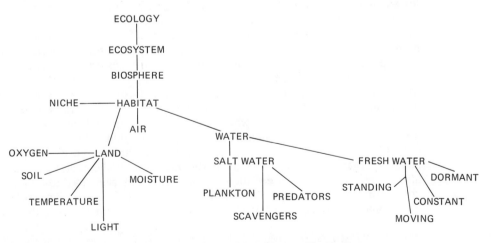

FIGURE 12–2 Structured Overview for the Biosphere and Its Habitats

concepts, such as *oxygen, temperature,* and *light,* are known to students from other units and in other contexts. So these concepts have meanings which can be added to other concepts here, such as *predators, scavengers,* and *plankton,* which will probably have to be developed. The structured overview, given as a motivating and organizing preview for the unit, can help students develop the necessary instructional framework, in Herber's words, or cognitive map. They need such a framework to tie the specifics of each concept together to make the connections necessary to synthesize the concept of *habitat.*

Structured overviews are built in several steps. First, the teacher identifies the concepts and their labels which are central to the unit. Second, the graphic organization is developed. This second step can be done by the teacher and presented whole to the students. Or the connections can be developed with the students in an inquiry lesson or discovery process, using a field trip, movie, or other media to present an introduction and overview of the unit. The results of either approach are the same, however; the students enter the unit study with a sense of where they are going and what they need to learn. The structured overview is an example of the first of Henry's operations, the act of joining.

Vocabulary Study for Concept Development

By now it is clear that vocabulary study is inseparable from concept development. The two are essentially the same thing. Typical exercises for providing practice in learning vocabulary will not necessarily contribute to concept learning. Memorizing the definition of a word, for example, is useful but not enough to guarantee that a student can use it in concept learning. Concept learning emphasizes the four operations Henry listed—joining, excluding, selecting, and implying. Here are some exercises which require that students know the meanings of words but go on to use the meaning in one of these operations.

Joining. Categorizing is one way students can learn that words belong together. The example given here uses the five concepts on the structured overview which are subsumed into *Land Habitats*—Temperature, Light, Moisture, Soil, and Oxygen.

CATEGORIZING

The act of joining

Under the list of words below there are five categories. Place each word in the category to which it belongs (may be listed more than once).

acids	deserts	extreme	nutrient-poor	
air	dim	freezing	polar regions	soak
breath	drink	humus	rain	sun
Celsius	dry	minerals	sand	tropical
clay	energy	moderate	shade	water
cold	enriched	night	snow	

Temperature	*Light*	*Moisture*	*Soil*	*Oxygen*

Students must first put each word under an appropriate category; second, they must explain why they chose that category. Some words may be placed under more than one category (for example, *sun* relates to both light and temperature). The student is encouraged to see that some words relate to more than one concept.

Excluding. An important process in concept development is learning what a concept is *not*, as well as what it is. Remember, the chair is *not* a stool, bench or sofa, although all these words could be subsumed under the larger concept of something to sit on. Frequently, a group of four or five vocabulary words from the same unit can be organized in several ways, depending on the student's cognitive structure. Herber (1978) developed a process of selecting items which have several potential organizations. Below is an example of such an exercise. Here, the student must use his/her knowledge of the unit's content to relate three or four of the words in each list *but* to exclude one. Hence, they *join* the words under a higher level concept, but *exclude* the one unlike word. In III, the excluded word is *oceans*, which contain salt water. All the other choices represent *fresh water habitats*, the general concept which subsumes them all.

DISCRIMINATING

The act of excluding

Choose the one word in each group that does not relate to the others and should be excluded. Write it in the blank labeled "Exclude." In the blank labeled "General Concept" write the concept that describes the remaining words.

I.   oxygen
     carbon dioxide
     temperature
     food
     sun

1. Exclude _____

2. General Concept _____

II. land
     forest
     air
     water

1. Exclude _____

2. General Concept _____

III. oceans
     ponds
     springs
     streams
     lakes

1. Exclude _____

2. General Concept _____

IV. phytoplankton
     zooplankton
     protists
     rodents

1. Exclude _____

2. General Concept _____

This type of exercise can also be varied by placing in each list words which have multiple organizations. Instead of having a single correct answer, as in the exercise above, several correct answers are possible.

A further variation asks the student to look at a group of words and choose the word which subsumes the other four:

assessor
taxation - subsumes the others
customs
import
property

Choosing to exclude words from lists, as with other concept operations, can range from simple, low-cognitive level exercises to high-level exercises requiring both analysis and synthesis.

Selecting. The selection process in concept learning includes, again, making choices and explaining *why*. Selecting suggests that we start with the whole and identify its parts, a form of analysis. One common way of practicing the selection process in vocabulary development is the use of synonym exercises. Figure 12–3 is based again on "The Biosphere and Its Habitats." In this instance, as before, the emphasis is not on finding the one right answer but in choosing several potentially correct answers and judging their worth.

SYNONYM PRACTICE

The act of selecting

Directions: Circle the words under each sentence that could be used in place of the underlined word. Be ready to explain why each is appropriate.

1. Materials and energy needed for life are <u>abundant</u> here.

   scarce   great
   plentiful   negligible
   useful   useless

2. The desert rat <u>adapts</u> to these high temperatures by searching for food at night

   appeals   changes
   adjusts   applies
   adopts   attends

3. These habitats are not always <u>constant</u>.

   there   stable
   pleasant   dormant
   temporary   permanent

In the first example, both *plentiful* and *great* are potentially correct, as are *stable* and *permanent* in the third example. The student's ear for language and his/her sense of the fine differences in meaning will be used in explaining why each is possible and which is better.

Implying. Implication resides in the if-then or cause-effect relationship. The most common form of vocabulary exercise using this higher cognitive level process is the analogy. Analogies ask students to identify the relationship between two words, for example, *in* and *out*, and then to construct such a relationship between another word and an unknown fourth word, for example, *up* and ___?___ . This process requires the use of all three processes (joining, excluding, selecting). For this reason, Gagné (1970) calls this the rule-making process and places it at a higher level than the other three. Henry's organization is based on Piaget's (1957). Both agree that the if-then, hypothesis-making process requires the ability to use the other three and must occur later in the learning process.

Analogies can come in many forms. The student can be given a choice of answers or s/he can be asked to recall the answer from memory. In the analogy above, in: out:: up: ___?___ , the student is asked to recall the answer. Here are some examples of analogies from the Habitat unit which require recognition.

ANALOGY EXERCISE

The act of implying

Underline the word in each grouping which completes the analogy.

1. Niche: habitat as house: country
                              cave
                              neighborhood
                              mansion

2. Extreme: moderate as high: low
                               level
                               top
                               below

3. Plankton: protist as reptile: snake
                                   amphibian
                                   mammal
                                   frog

4. Sewage: water as smoke: food
                            breathing
                            pollution
                            air

5. Ecosystem: forest as government: organization
                                     democracy
                                     politics
                                     legislature

Analogies can be based on a number of relationships—synonyms, antonyms, part-whole, and others. Students need practice in working with the implication process, such as different forms of analogies, so that the thinking process and the format become familiar to them.

Let's turn from science to mathematics. A general math teacher (grades 7 to 8)* developed these concept-oriented vocabulary exercises for use with her students. Here is her explanation.

It is very important for my students to recognize the relationships between the sets of Real Numbers. The term "number" suddenly becomes vague. They need to be specific in their explanations and definitions. This assignment allows them to visualize the structure of the set. In class we would construct the tree diagram starting with Real Numbers. Important to any discussion of sets is the language involved:

Intersection	$\cap$
Union	$\cup$
Empty Set	$\varnothing$

EXERCISE

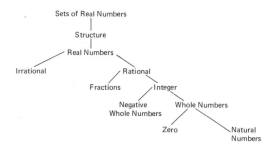

R = Set of Real Numbers
Q = Set of Rational Numbers
I = Set of Irrational Numbers
In = Set of Integers
W = Set of Whole Numbers
N = Set of Natural Numbers

Using the previous diagram, answer the following questions. These questions will show relationships between the sets of Real Numbers:

1. $R \cap Q =$ 6. $N \cap W =$
2. $I \cap R =$ 7. $R \cap N =$
3. $Q \cup I =$ 8. $R \cup W =$
4. $N \cup W =$ 9. $Q \cup I =$
5. $W \cap In =$ 10. $I \cap W =$

ANSWERS

1. Q   3. R   5. W   7. N   9. $\varnothing$
2. I   4. W   6. N   8. R   10. $\varnothing$

*Prepared by Nancy C. Musselman, Penns Valley Junior-Senior High School, Spring Mills, Pa.

This teacher introduces the topic with the structured overview and exercise. She summarizes the year's work with the vocabulary relationships exercise. In this exercise, students connect the concept labels from different units during the year, aiming for synthesis of the material covered throughout the year.

VOCABULARY RELATIONSHIPS EXERCISE *

Directions: If the two words of a pair mean the same or nearly the same, or are otherwise related, write "S" on the line between them. If they mean the opposite or nearly opposite, write "O" between them. if there is no relationship between the words, write "N."

1. approximation	_____	equal
2. add	_____	subtract
3. multiply	_____	divide
4. vertical	_____	horizontal
5. circle	_____	square
6. square	_____	multiply
7. minus	_____	subtract
8. scalene	_____	equilateral
9. right angles	_____	complementary angles
10. even numbers	_____	odd numbers
11. numerator	_____	denominator
12. obtuse	_____	acute
13. ratio	_____	quotient
14. rational	_____	irrational
15. composite	_____	prime
16. complementary angles	_____	supplementary angles

ANSWERS

1. S	2. O	3. O	4. O	5. O	6. S	7. S	8. O
9. S	10. O	11. O	12. O	13. S	14. O	15. O	16. O

The process of concept development is complex and deserves greater discussion than is possible here. Hafner (1977), Henry (1974), and Herber (1978) all give

* Prepared by Nancy C. Musselman, Penns Valley Junior-Senior High School, Spring Mills, Pa.

more detail on concept learning and reading. Books on learning theory and educational psychology, like Ausubel (1968) and Gagné (1970), provide the theoretical base. Consult these sources for discussion in depth.

Effective teachers need to use both word attack skills and concept development at different times during their teaching, depending on the students, topic, and objectives. Therefore, it is important to develop a large repertoire of specific teaching techniques which the teacher can call upon whenever they are useful.

Summary

This chapter has described two different ways of teaching vocabulary skills. First, vocabulary can be taught as word attack skills (skills in identifying unfamiliar words): identifying words by sight, use of context clues, use of structural analysis (roots, prefixes, suffixes), use of sound patterns, and use of outside references.

The second way of viewing vocabulary, and the most common in content teaching, is to teach vocabulary as a means of concept development. Concepts are formed through four processes, the acts of joining, excluding, selecting and implying. Vocabulary study and practice based on these cognitive processes will help students learn how to develop concepts and add to their vocabularies.

Effective teachers choose the vocabulary processes that fit the objectives they have and develop appropriate teaching plans.

Chapter Activities: Using What You've Read

Learn to Do It!

1. For one chapter/unit of your text, develop a list of concept words that (a) are new, (b) are unfamiliar and (c) have multiple meanings. Design a vocabulary exercise to introduce the new words to your students. Use context clues and at least one other word attack skill.

2. For the same chapter/unit, develop a structured overview and vocabulary exercises to develop concepts, using one of Henry's operations--joining, excluding, selecting and implying.

Do It!

Try out the exercises you constructed in one or more classes.

References

AUSUBEL, D., *Educational Psychology: A Cognitive View*. New York: Holt, Rinehart & Winston, 1968.

GAGNÉ, R., *The Conditions of Learning*. New York: Harcourt Brace Jovanovich, 1965.

HAFNER, L. E., *Developmental Reading in Middle and Secondary Schools, Foundations, Strategies and Skills for Teaching*. New York: Macmillan, 1977.

HENRY, G. H., *Teaching Reading as Concept Development: Emphasis on Affective Thinking*. Newark, Del.: International Reading Association, 1974.

HERBER, H. L., *Teaching Reading in Content Areas* (2nd ed.) Englewood Cliffs, N.J.: Prentice-Hall, 1978.

KANE, R. B., M. A. BYRNE, and M. A. HATER, *Helping Children Read Mathematics.* New York: American Book Co., 1974.

McCULLOUGH, C. M., "Context Aids in Reading," *The Reading Teacher*, 11, no. 8 (April 1958), 225–29.

Webster's Seventh New Collegiate Dictionary. Springfield, Mass.: G. C. Merriam, 1974.

WINKLEY, C., "Which Accent Generalizations are Worth Teaching?" *The Reading Teacher*, 20, no. 3 (December 1966), 224.

Chapter 13
Teaching Comprehension Skills

Preview

Recent research in reading comprehension has drawn heavily from schema theory (Otto and White, 1982). What the reader brings to the printed page in terms of prior knowledge and experience is crucial in determining what s/he will comprehend from the reading materials. Previously, less emphasis was placed on characteristics of the reader with greater concern for standard instructional techniques regardless of individual differences in readers' backgrounds in the content area.

According to schema theory, all knowledge is interrelated. When the reader encounters new knowledge through reading, it will be assimilated or comprehended only if s/he has some prior knowledge and experience to which to relate the new knowledge. If not, the new knowledge is either distorted to fit an existing schema or lost.

Similarly, schemata for comprehending different types of text exist. Students need to learn that the schema for reading narrative material differs considerably from that of exposition. Different types of exposition, furthermore, are found in the various content areas.

Since comprehension is the focus of any content study in which reading is used as a vehicle for gaining knowledge, reading comprehension is of utmost concern for any content teacher. Most content teachers rely heavily on assigned reading materials to present new knowledge. Therefore, instruction in reading comprehension as it relates to the content area is essential.

Comprehension Levels and Questioning

Although research has not yet provided definitive answers about the best teaching techniques for encouraging comprehension of reading material, some combination of work on levels of questioning and reading skills seems to be beneficial in helping students understand content materials. Regardless of the teaching strategy selected, the teacher must always insure that students possess adequate background to comprehend new information.

Barrett's *Taxonomy of Reading Comprehension* (1972) has already been presented in Chapter 1 as a convenient way to organize questions with various levels of comprehension.

It has been demonstrated (Guszak 1967) that teachers tend to ask most questions about reading material at the literal level. In other words, the answers to their questions can be found in the reading material itself rather than requiring students to think beyond the material. If students are not required by their teachers' questions to go beyond recalling or recognizing what is in the reading material, it is unlikely that they will perform at other levels of comprehension, for example, inferential or critical reading, on their own (Spache 1976).

To insure that readers understand the types of questions within each level of Barrett's *Taxonomy*, work through the following exercise using "Goldilocks and the Three Bears." Although this story is hardly typical of content area reading materials, it should provide enjoyable practice material in learning to use Barrett's *Taxonomy*. Take out a piece of paper and number it to provide room for questions on all four levels of the *Taxonomy*. Try to create at least three questions within each level. When you have written your questions, compare yours with the ones listed here. Are yours similar?

Comprehension questions for "Goldilocks and the Three Bears":

1.1 *Recognition or Recall of Details.*
What did Goldilocks eat at the three bears' house?

1.3 *Recognition or Recall of Sequence.*
What did Goldilocks do after she sat in the three bears' chairs?

2.4 *Inferring Cause and Effect Relationship.*
Why did Goldilocks enter the three bears' house?

2.7 *Predicting Outcomes.*
Before the students are told the ending of the story, ask the following: What do you think will happen to Goldilocks when the three bears come home?

3.1 *Judgments of Reality or Fantasy.*
Could this story really have taken place? Why or why not?

3.5 *Judgments of Worth, Desirability, or Acceptability.*
Was Goldilocks right to have entered the three bears' house? Why or why not?

4.1 *Identification with Characters and Incidents.*
How did you feel when the three bears found Goldilocks asleep in the little bear's bed?

In using the *Taxonomy* as an assessment tool, the teacher must be careful to distinguish between questions which require convergent thinking—those for which there is one correct answer—and those which require divergent thinking, for which several answers may be appropriate. Literal level questions (for which the answers are stated in the material) and some inferential level questioning (for which answers are not stated directly) require convergent thinking in which there is only one correct answer. Some inferential level questions, plus those at the evaluation and appreciation levels, require divergent thinking, meaning that creative responses may be possible. Test questions, if in multiple choice format, should be of a convergent thinking nature. Open-ended questions are appropriate to assess divergent thinking —if the teacher is willing to accept almost any answer as correct, provided that the student can state a rationale for the answer.

To use the *Taxonomy* most effectively, teachers' questions should be designed ahead of time, not spontaneously during a discussion of a reading assignment. While not all reading material lends itself to questions at all four levels, the teacher should attempt to include questions at all levels at some point during a given unit. A simple record-keeping system to indicate what level of questions were asked during each discussion of assigned reading helps insure that students are asked questions at all levels of comprehension.

Sometimes science and math teachers reject the notion that questions should be asked at all four levels. These teachers express the view that they are concerned only with literal comprehension—that their students simply need to learn the facts. Unfortunately, this type of learning is usually not retained beyond the final examination. Think back to your own high school classes. Do you remember facts and details? Most of us remember very few specifics, but we retained general principles and concepts. Unless new information is linked in some meaningful way to prior background and knowledge, students are unable to remember what they have read except perhaps for immediate recall on a test of factual recall. This type of learning is forgotten all too quickly.

Barrett's *Taxonomy* can help a teacher to plan questions that promote conceptual integration of the new material with prior learning and experiences. The fourth level, Appreciation, is particularly important, regardless of the content area, because it taps the affective domain. Once reading material is integrated with the student's personal concerns, it will not be forgotten. A better label for the fourth level, rather than Appreciation, might be Application to the Student's Life. Application can be practical, such as a better way of keeping a ledger of one's earnings and spendings from an accounting class, as well as personal, such as an emotional response to a short story in English class.

A legitimate question is how can some reading materials, especially from science and math, relate to the affective concerns of students. While no pat answers exist, we urge teachers to find out about the personal concerns of their students through administering interest and attitude surveys, such as those presented in Chapter 6, reading cumulative records, and chatting with students individually before and after class, at basketball games, and so forth. Making content material fit into local and national concerns is another way to relate to the affective domain. For example, in a chemistry class, students might apply their knowledge of chemical elements to discover the contents of locally used pesticides and study the effects of these chemicals on plant and animal life.

TEACHING COMPREHENSION AS READING SKILLS

In addition to asking questions at various levels of comprehension, certain comprehension skills are usually taught. Research (for example, Davis 1944, as well as more recent studies) has demonstrated that although many comprehension skills seem to exist (judging from instructional materials and tests), actually only a few discrete comprehension skills can be identified. One of the most important factors relating to reading comprehension is vocabulary, which is discussed in Chapter 12. We have included for discussion here the comprehension skills that seem most important in content area reading material. It seems logical to teach these skills first at the literal level (using explicitly stated material) and later at the inferential level (where students might have to infer the main idea, for example, rather than locating it in a paragraph). The ensuing discussion of reading comprehension skills assumes this progression from the literal to the inferential level of thinking.

Main Idea

Certainly, being able to state the main idea of what has been read is one of the most important comprehension skills. In the elementary grades students usually learn to identify the topic sentence of a paragraph. They also learn to move beyond the topic sentence in stating the central thought by giving a short selection a title. Finally, they may be asked to identify or create a phrase that states the main idea.

Research (Van Blaricom and White 1976) suggests that the process of picking out the main idea from several choices is easier than requiring a student to state it. Therefore, instruction should initially focus on the identification of the main idea from several choices; after students can perform that task, they can be asked to write a statement of the main idea. Students should also be asked to progress from a main idea that is stated in the selection (literal comprehension) to inferring a main idea which is not stated.

To clarify the difference between a stated (literal comprehension) and implied (inferential comprehension) main idea, consider the following paragraph from a general business textbook (p. 241).

> Society, through law, limits and governs our actions. There are laws against carrying weapons. Tax laws provide money for operating the government. There are laws regulating hunting and fishing and laws requiring licenses for certain businesses.*

In this paragraph, the first sentence is the topic sentence. The main idea concerns how law limits behavior. The main idea is stated in the topic sentence; therefore, asking the students to state the main idea of this paragraph would be a literal comprehension activity. Consider the next paragraph from the same source (p. 245).

> The person accused of a crime is tried (given a trial) in criminal court. If found guilty, the defendant may be fined, imprisoned, or both. For certain crimes the penalty in some states is death (capital punishment). The government acts to apprehend and punish the wrongdoer because crimes not only injure an individual but also are serious offenses against the state—that is, society. Law and order must be maintained. Life, liberty and property must be protected, or society would cease to function; might would make right, and brute force would be in control.†

In this paragraph, no clearly defined topic sentence is present. The main idea, the reasons for punishment for wrongdoing, must be inferred from the paragraph.

---

*L. C. Nanassy and C. M. Fancher, *General Business and Economic Understandings* (Englewood Cliffs, N.J.: Prentice-Hall, Inc., 1973).
†*Ibid.*

Therefore, asking students to state the main idea of this paragraph represents use of the inferential level of thinking.

The following is an example of giving students a choice of response in a junior high school home economics class. Option A involves an exercise in stating the main idea of each section of a pamphlet; Option B presents questions which also require students to understand the main idea of each section in order to answer the questions. Both options require literal as well as inferential thinking. Option A perhaps is more demanding because the student must identify and state the main ideas instead of providing answers to the teacher's questions.

COMPREHENSION EXERCISE: UNDERSTANDING THE MAIN IDEA*

Eighth-grade Home Economics students are studying Child Care for a six-week period. As part of the unit, they are learning about a safe home environment and then about providing a safe environment while babysitting. Students were permitted to select either Noting the Main Idea or Worksheet Questions for their required activity using the booklet, "Sitting Safely" by Metropolitan Life Insurance Company. The activity takes about 45 minutes.

Exercise

REQUIRED ACTIVITY—
Select one of the assignments which will help you understand the pamphlet, "Sitting Safely."

Option A—Noting The Main Idea   Option B—Worksheet Questions

OPTION A—NOTING THE MAIN IDEA

In the space provided, write the main idea for each section in the pamphlet, "Sitting Safely."

1. Suggestions for the baby sitter—
2. Reminder for the Baby to 6 months—
3. Reminder for the Baby 6 to 12 months—
4. Reminder for the Child 12 to 15 months—
5. Reminder for the Child around 2 years—
6. Reminder for the Child around 3 years—
7. Reminder for the Child around 4 years—
8. Reminder for the Child 5 to 7 years—
9. Safe Surroundings—
10. On-The-Job Performance—
11. What to Expect from Parents—

OPTION B—WORKSHEET QUESTIONS

Answer the following questions using the pamphlet, "Sitting Safely" for the information.

*Prepared by Connie Martin, State College, Pa., Area School District.

1. What are two steps you should take if a fire occurs in a home where you are babysitting?
2. How can you gain some experience with children before going out babysitting?
3. Describe how you would feed an infant under 6 months of age.
4. Why is it a good idea for parents of a child 6 to 12 months old to invite a sitter to the home in advance of the babysitting job?
5. What would you do if a one-year-old won't go to bed without his favorite toy?
6. Comment on the following statement, "Two-year-olds are adventurous and independent."
7. How old is a child when he or she is able to listen to a story?
8. List three quiet activities a four-year-old would enjoy.
9. Describe two possible danger areas in the home.
10. Should you accept a babysitting job if you don't enjoy children? Why or why not?
11. What should a babysitter expect from parents regarding transportation to and from the job?

Identifying Important Details

Identification of important details can probably best be taught while teaching students to outline and take notes. The skill of outlining, discussed in Chapter 15, Teaching Study Skills, requires students to identify main ideas and the important details that support each main heading. One of the greatest problems students have in reading content area textbooks is knowing which details should be remembered. The outlining process can help students identify the important details which ought to be remembered.

Determining the Sequence of Events

Students need to be able to determine the sequence of events in a paragraph or selection. Imagine trying to read a recipe and bake a cake without following sequential order! Likewise, performing scientific experiments and understanding historical accounts depend on the students' ability to sequence events.

This skill is perhaps best introduced at an oral level. For example, following an oral report by a class member, guest speaker, or teacher, the students are asked to list the events described in chronological order. Words, such as *first, next, then,* and *finally,* are identified as cues to the sequence of events. Students should then identify chronological sequence in reading a short paragraph as well as in following directions. An exercise in origami, the Japanese art of paper folding, can provide an enjoyable check on each student's ability to follow directions. The exercise is also self-checking by whether or not the desired object has been created.

Study guides, presented in the next chapter, provide another means for checking and developing each student's application of sequencing skills. If the student is able to follow a study guide sequentially through assigned reading material, then s/he may be ready for more independent application of sequencing skills in following directions.

Sequencing can also be reinforced with younger students by means of a "job sheet." Each student is given a list of tasks to be done independently. As the student completes each task, s/he checks off the task on the job sheet. Not only are sequential order and following directions being taught, but independent work habits are also being fostered.

Some learning disabled children who are mainstreamed into content area subjects may have great difficulty with chronological sequence. These students rarely know the time of day and cannot list the months of the year in order. Because of this handicap, these students are usually unable to determine the sequence of events in a paragraph or selection. They also have difficulty following directions independently.

Identifying Cause and Effect

Not all paragraphs or selections are organized sequentially, in chronological order. Another organization that students need to be familiar with involves cause-effect relationships. Key words, such as *therefore, because, since, as a result,* and *so,* should be noted as cues to cause-effect relationships.

Again, as with sequencing, this skill is initially best taught after an oral experience. Movies, filmstrips, television, and records provide additional stimuli for discussion. Causes and effects can be shown visually on a chalkboard or transparency.

Students who come to school from ordered homes in which logic more or less prevails—where certain causes (say, misbehavior) lead to certain effects (that is, punishment or withdrawal of privileges)—should not have difficulty understanding the concept of cause and effect. Those students whose lives are more chaotic may have trouble with cause-effect relationships in reading because they do not see these relationships operating in their lives.

As with other reading skills, students should begin with the application of the cause-effect skill in reading material where the relationship is stated (literal comprehension). Only after students can apply the skill when the relationship is stated should they be asked to infer a cause-effect relationship. Difficulties often occur in reading assignments because teachers assume that students can perform the skill instead of first checking and then teaching as needed.

Developing Critical Reading Skills

We are considering critical reading skills together as a group because they constitute a higher level of thinking than the previously mentioned skills which may be applied at the literal and inferential levels. While the specific questions within level 3.0, Evaluation, of Barrett's *Taxonomy* differ, a commonality exists among these skills. They all require the reader to make judgments, to evaluate what is said against prior knowledge, other sources, or one's own value system. Unless students are required to apply critical reading and thinking skills, they are deprived of the most crucial thinking skills needed today (Herber 1978). While the Peter Sellers character in *Being There* is hardly believable (a character who uncritically does whatever television dictates—and, cynically, becomes President of the United States as a result), many young people uncritically follow the examples of peers as well as television. Critical thinking skills become especially important in helping them think for themselves, whether or not they are using reading materials.

Critical thinking skills can be taught using television as a medium. Television commercials are obvious examples on which to begin application of critical thinking skills. Familiar television programs and specials provide another source. For example, students in an American history class could check a variety of references to discover the accuracy of the portrayal of life in the South as presented in "Roots." Or two views of the same period could be compared, such as *Gone with the Wind* and "Roots."

Newspaper editorials provide another good source of material for teaching critical reading skills. Two editorials, representing different points of view, can be compared to each other and to a third, more objective source.

Perhaps it seems relatively easy to teach critical thinking and reading skills in a social studies or English class, but how can they be taught in such subjects as science, math, or home economics? As long as content study is limited to recall of textbook material, then critical thinking and reading skills will not be used. If, however, the goal is to have the subject matter make some impact on the students' lives, to make learning more than an exercise in memorization, then critical thinking and reading skills do have a place. In one example cited earlier about the chemistry class which explored the ingredients of a locally used pesticide, critical judgments could naturally follow. After the effects on plants and animals are determined, students can judge whether or not the pesticide ought to be used, whether the "price" (in terms of other effects on nature) is too great. Not only are critical thinking and reading skills taught, but the affective domain is also touched as students apply the content study to their lives. (See Herber 1978, for further discussion of reasoning guides in applying critical reading skills.)

Summary

While other reading skills could be identified, we have highlighted the major ones of concern to all content teachers regardless of subject area. Instruction in these comprehension skills will enable students to grasp the content more effectively and efficiently. Next we will consider some techniques for enhancing comprehension of assigned reading material.

Chapter Activities: Using What You've Read

Learn to Do It!

For a chapter/unit in your text, develop one or more exercises to teach the main idea, sequence of events or cause and effect. Be sure to consider both literal and inferential questions. Include at least two questions which develop critical thinking.

Do It!

Try out these comprehensive exercises in one or more classes and evaluate their effectiveness.

References

BARRETT, T. C., "Taxonomy of Reading Comprehension," *Reading 360 Monograph*. Lexington, Mass.: Ginn, 1972.

DAVIS, F. B., "Fundamental Factors of Comprehension in Reading," *Psychometrika*, 1944, no. 9, 185–97.

GUSZAK, F. J., "Teachers' Questions and Levels of Reading Comprehension," in *The Evaluation of Children's Reading Achievement*, ed. T. Barrett. Newark, Del.: International Reading Association, 1967, 97–110.

HERBER, H. L., *Teaching Reading in Content Areas* (2nd ed.) Englewood Cliffs, N.J.: Prentice-Hall, 1978.

OTTO, W. and S. WHITE, eds., *Understanding Expository Material.* New York: Academic Press, 1982.

SPACHE, G. D., *Diagnosing and Correcting Reading Disabilities.* Boston: Allyn & Bacon, 1976.

VANBLARICOM, G. and S. WHITE, "Testing Comprehension of the Central Thought: Selecting Versus Generating Main Idea," in *Reflections and Investigations on Reading.* Twenty-Fifth Yearbook of the National Reading Conference, ed. W. Miller and G. McNinch. Clemson, S.C.: National Reading Conference, 1976, 317–23.

Chapter 14
Guiding Students'
Comprehension

Preview

In Chapter 9 we discussed the Directed Reading Activity (DRA) which is a teacher-directed means of guiding students' reading by introducing new vocabulary and concepts, as well as providing guide questions before reading. After reading, the teacher asks questions at various levels of thinking to insure comprehension of the material (Herber 1978). Skill instruction and enrichment follow. As was mentioned, one option for handling the independent reading portion of the DRA is to provide a study guide.

STUDY GUIDES

Instead of the teacher directly providing the guidance with students, teacher guidance can be provided through study guides. The advantages are as follows:

1. Literal comprehension can be assured through the study guide. The teacher is thus freed to spend time on higher levels of comprehension in class or small group discussions.

2. Study guides can provide for different rates of working. The student who works more quickly can move on to other work while the slower reader can spend the time needed to gain complete comprehension.

3. Different study guides can be provided for readers of different reading levels or adaptations within one guide can be made for the different reading levels. For example, independent readers might be given additional higher-level questions, while frustration level readers might focus strictly on literal comprehension in the study guide (and apply higher-level skills orally in a teacher-directed discussion).

4. Different types of study guides may be used to focus on different types of thinking and reading skills even within the same content area. For example, in a

home economics class, a pattern guide might be appropriate for reading a recipe, while a concept guide might be more appropriate for reading an assignment on nutrition.

5. The teacher may use study guides to teach students independent study techniques. Younger or less able students need more guidance which can be provided by a detailed study guide. As students progress in ability, the study guide can cover longer selections with less guidance. Students can gradually be "weaned" from dependence on study guides and apply the independent study techniques discussed in the next chapter.

The following are samples of guides that have been created by teachers of various subject areas. The guides are intended to be used *after* the new vocabulary and concepts have been introduced by the teacher following the format of the DRA. Unless appropriate background knowledge already exists or has been provided, perhaps by the use of other media, students will not be able to use a study guide effectively. In other words, study guides are *not* a substitute for the teacher's preparation of the students for reading. Study guides, instead, direct the students' reading so that they read purposefully. New vocabulary and concepts should not interfere with comprehension if the teacher has introduced them ahead of time. Sometimes the introduction of new vocabulary and concepts can be done for the unit or a section of textbook material that would constitute several reading assignments. The teacher may, therefore, only need to remind the students of the introductory work done previously before assigning a new study guide.

Discussion should occur following the completion of the study guide. The teacher may lead the discussion, or a group of students may hold a discussion using a set of guide questions. Discussion should focus on higher levels of comprehension (for example, evaluation and appreciation) not covered by the study guide. Again, discussion can occur at the completion of several reading assignments. However, not too much reading material should be covered in one discussion since forgetting will occur unless the major concepts and generalizations are reinforced frequently.

One additional observation is in order before specific types of study guides are presented. Study guide questions and examination questions over the material studied should emphasize the same type of thinking. If the study guide and subsequent discussion and activities emphasize only literal comprehension, it is inappropriate for the teacher to ask inferential, evaluation, and appreciation level questions on an examination. Conversely, if all levels of comprehension are stressed in class, it seems unfair to administer strictly a multiple-choice test of literal comprehension, unless students are informed in advance. Ideally, an examination should have approximately the same proportion of questions at each level as the instruction over the same material.

CONCEPT GUIDES

Concept guides are especially useful in studying literature although they could be used with any subject matter (for example, social studies) where the intent is to present concepts, ideas, and generalizations (Estes and Vaughan 1978). In the following guides, created for the parallel study of *Romeo and Juliet* and *West Side Story,* the emphasis is on not only the concepts found in each story but also the concepts that they share.

Both guides begin with identification of the speakers of key quotations. The purpose is to match the characters with the concepts they represent. The next section of the guide deals with the concept of fate. By matching causes with effects, students are led to see that the characters and their actions in large part caused their destiny rather than their being controlled by fate. The third guide requires students to draw parallels between the two stories by matching characters and events, establishing the commonalities.

CONCEPT GUIDE for *ROMEO AND JULIET* by William Shakespeare (New York: Dell Publishing Co., 1956) *

I. Using the list of characters below, place the name of the character who is speaking each passage in the space following the passage. You may use a name once, more than once, or not at all. Read each quotation carefully.

1. "But soft! What light through yonder window breaks? It is the east, and Juliet is the sun!" (II, 2, 2–3)

   1. _____

2. "What's in a name? That which we call a rose By any other name would smell as sweet." (II, 1, 43–44).

   2. _____

3. "O Romeo, Romeo, wherefore art thou Romeo? Deny thy father and refuse thy name, Or, if thou wilt not, be but sworn my love And I'll no longer be a Capulet." (II, 1, 33–36)

   3. _____

4. "Well, you have made a simple choice. You know not how to choose a man. Romeo? No, not he, though his face be better than any man's yet his leg excels all men's . . ." (II, 5, 38–41)

   4. _____

5. "See what a scourge is laid upon your hate That Heaven finds means to kill your joys with love!" (V, 3, 292–93)

   5. _____

   JULIET   the PRINCE   the NURSE   ROMEO   TYBALT

II. Fate plays a very important part in *Romeo and Juliet*. (Remember that Shakespeare called them the "star-crossed lovers.") In Column A below is a list of "chance happenings." Match each happening with the effect it caused.

COLUMN A	COLUMN B
_____ 1. Romeo meets the illiterate servant.	a. Mercutio gets killed.
_____ 2. Romeo decides not to fight with Tybalt.	b. He goes to the Capulet party and meets Juliet.
_____ 3. Romeo overhears Juliet's soliloquy telling of her love for him.	c. Romeo thinks Juliet is dead, so he commits suicide.
_____ 4. Friar John is released too late from quarantine.	d. He goes to her and asks her to marry him.

* Prepared by Debra McNerlin, Williamsburg, Pa., Community School District

_____ 5. Tybalt encounters Romeo in the street.

    e. Arguments ensue; two men are murdered; Romeo is banished.

_____ 6. Friar Laurence's messenger is quarantined and unable to get to Romeo.

    f. Friar Laurence arrives too late to save Romeo; Juliet commits suicide.

CONCEPT GUIDE for *WEST SIDE STORY* by Arthur Laurents (New York: Dell Publishing Co., 1956)

I. Using the list of characters below, place the name of the speaking character in the space to the right of the quotation. You may use a name once, more than once, or not at all.

RIFF   BERNARDO   TONY   ANITA   MARIA

1. "One month have I been in this country—do I ever even touch excitement? I sew all day, I sit all night. For what did my fine brother bring me here?"   _____

2. "And there's nothing for me but Maria, Every sight that I see is Maria."   _____

3. "What's with you? Four and one-half years I live with a buddy and his family. Four and one-half years I think I know a man's character. Buddy boy, I am a victim of disappointment in you."   _____

4. "More gracious living? Look: I don't go for that pretend crap you all go for in this country. Every one of you hates every one of us, and we hate you right back."   _____

5. "I tried to stop it; I did try. I don't know how it went wrong. . . . I didn't mean to hurt him; I didn't want to; I didn't know I had to. But Riff . . . Riff was like my brother. So when Bernardo killed him— . . ."   _____

6. "WE ALL KILLED HIM; and my brother and Riff, I too. I CAN KILL NOW BECAUSE I HATE NOW."   _____

II. Fate plays a large part in the action of *West Side Story*. In column A is a list of "chance happenings. Match each happening with the effect it caused.

COLUMN A	COLUMN B
_____ 1. Tony goes to the dance.	a. Tony feels obligated to fight with Bernardo.
_____ 2. Tony accidentally kills Bernardo.	b. Tony meets Maria.
_____ 3. Bernardo kills Riff.	c. Chino shoots Tony.
_____ 4. **The police officer detains Maria.**	d. Chino seeks revenge for Bernardo's death.
_____ 5. Anita gets attacked by the Jets.	e. Anita must go tell Tony to wait.
_____ 6. Maria calls out Tony's name at the playground.	f. Anita gets angry and tells them that Maria is dead.

WE HAVE JUST FINISHED A STUDY OF THE TWO PLAYS *ROMEO AND JULIET* AND *WEST SIDE STORY*. As you have noticed by now, much of the play *West Side Story* is similar to Shakespeare's *Romeo and Juliet*.

Read each statement from COLUMN A. These concern *Romeo and Juliet*. Then, read each statement from COLUMN B. These concern *West Side Story*.

Match the letter of the comment or statement from Column B to the item to which it corresponds in Column A. Each letter is used only once. Number one is done for you as an example.

	COLUMN A		COLUMN B
_c_ 1.	The love of Romeo and Juliet.	a.	The Sharks.
___ 2.	The masquerade party at the Capulet home.	b.	The Jets and Sharks are having a gang war.
___ 3.	The Montague family.	c.	The love of Tony and Maria.
___ 4.	The Prince.	d.	The Jets.
___ 5.	Mercutio is slain.	e.	Tony thinks Maria is dead.
___ 6.	Romeo thinks Juliet is dead.	f.	The policemen.
___ 7.	The Capulet family.	g.	Riff is murdered.
___ 8.	Tybalt is slain.	h.	Chino loves Maria.
___ 9.	Romeo and Juliet marry.	i.	The dance in the gym.
___ 10.	Paris loves Juliet.	j.	Bernardo is murdered.
___ 11.	The Capulets and the Montagues hate each other.	k.	Tony and Maria sing their vows.
___ 12.	The nurse.	l.	Anita.
___ 13.	The courtyard in the street.	m.	The fire escape.
___ 14.	The poison.	n.	The playground.
___ 15.	The balcony.	o.	The bullet.

PROBLEM-SOLVING GUIDE

Some subjects lend themselves better to step-by-step reading of material. Reading mathematical verbal problems requires a different type of guide from the concept guide. Instead of reading for concepts, ideas, and generalizations, the task is to solve specific problems. Frequently, however, students have difficulty determining what is being asked in the problem and what details may be relevant to solving it. Using the steps recommended by Earle (1976), the following study guide created by a teacher for a seventh-grade class illustrates the step-by-step process of helping students think logically through a problem.

MATHEMATICS PROBLEM-SOLVING GUIDE*

Directions to students: The following six statements or questions are designed to help you solve the thought problems on this worksheet. Before you read each problem, number your scrap paper from one to six and leave extra room for number one and number five. After you have numbered your paper, come back to this worksheet and read the six questions and follow any directions given. Each thought problem should have the six steps outlined on your scrap paper before you write your answer on the blank beside the problem. Good luck!

1. Read the problem quickly to form a picture in your mind and draw that picture on your paper beside number one.

2. Reread the problem to understand what you are to find out and write what you are to find beside number two. For example, if they want you to find bananas, then write the word "Bananas" beside number two.

3. Reread the problem for a second time to find out exact figures and values and write them beside number three on your paper.

4. Make up a formula to fit the problem and write the formula beside number four on your paper.

5. Solve the problem beside number five on your paper using your formula and the exact values from the problem.

6. Read your answer and the problem again to see if your answer makes sense. If it makes sense, go on to the next problem. If your answer does not make sense then go back and look at each of the steps to see if you can find a mistake. If all else fails, ask me or one of the student helpers for some help.

THOUGHT PROBLEMS

A. What is the speed per hour of a jogger that runs 20 miles in 4 hours? _____

B. At 13 miles an hour how far can Judy run in 23 hours? _____

C. How many hours will it take Sam to go 399 miles if his sailboat travels at the rate of 21 miles

per hour? _____

D. Juan and his mother jogged one week and ran the following number of miles each day: 14 miles, 9 miles, 17 miles, 15 miles, 18 miles, 20 miles and 12 miles. What was the average

number of miles they ran per day? _____

E. Dan Beppu flew 2944 miles in 16 hours to visit his grandfather. What was the average rate

of speed per hour of his plane? _____

F. A health food store manager sold 560 jars of wheat germ at $3 per jar. After paying $892

for a used car, how much money did he have left from his sale of wheat germ? _____

*Prepared by Rodger Smith, Mifflin Co., Pa., School District.

197

Answers to Study Guide

A.

1.

2. speed of the jogger

3. runs 20 miles in 4 hours

4. $\dfrac{\text{miles}}{\text{hours}} = \dfrac{\text{distance}}{\text{time}} = \text{rate/speed}$

5. speed $= \dfrac{20}{4} = 5$ miles per hour

6. yes

B.

1.

2. distance run

3. runs 23 hours at 13 miles an hour

4. $d = rt$

5. $d = 23 \times 13 = 299$ miles

6. yes

C.

1.

2. number of hours

3. 399 miles; 21 miles

4. time $= \dfrac{\text{distance}}{\text{rate}}$

5. time $= \dfrac{399}{21} = 19$ hours

6. yes

D.

1.

2. average miles per day

3. 14, 9, 17, 15, 18, 20, 12 miles; 7 days

4. average miles $= \dfrac{\text{total miles}}{\text{number of days}}$

5. average $= 14 + 9 + 17 + 15 + 18 + 20 + 12 =$
$\dfrac{105}{7} = 5$ miles per day

6. yes

E.

1.

2. average rate of speed per hour

3. 2944 miles; 16 hours

4. rate $= \dfrac{\text{distance}}{\text{time}}$

5. rate $= \dfrac{2944 \text{ miles}}{16 \text{ hours}} = 184$ miles per hour

6. yes

F.

1.

2. how much money is left over?

3. 560 jars at $3 per jar; $892 for a car

4. jars $\times$ price = income
income $-$ car = leftover

5. $560 \times \$3 = \$1680$
$\$1680 - \$892 = \$788$ leftover

6. yes

Another math teacher created the following guide which contains basically the same steps presented in a more visual form for a junior high school class.

MATHEMATICS PROBLEM-SOLVING EXERCISE*

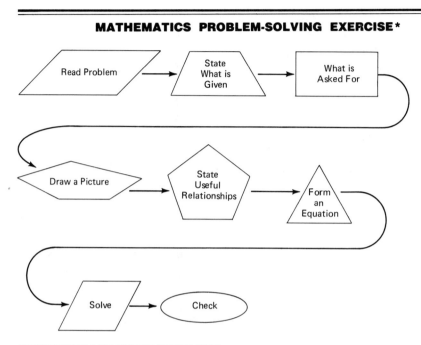

EQUATIONS AND WORD PROBLEMS

EXAMPLE: Miss Clark paid $6.30 for a dinner, including the tip. If the price of the dinner was 6 times the tip, how much was her tip?

1. What unknown quantities are asked for?

   _____ price of dinner   _____ price of dinner and tip

   _____ tip   _____ 6 times the tip

2. What mathematical expressions are useful in this problem?

   _____ X   _____ 6X   _____X + 6X   _____X + $6.30

3. Will a sketch help to make the problem clearer?

4. What mathematical relationships are useful in this problem?

   _____ the tip is 15% of the dinner

   _____ the tip plus price of dinner equals the total bill

   _____ the tip is less than the price of the dinner

   _____ the equation is always balanced

*Prepared by Nancy C. Musselmann, Penns Valley Junior-Senior High School, Spring Mills, Pa.

5. Based on all the above questions, which of the following is correct?

_____ 6X − X = $6.30

_____ 6 + X = $6.30

_____ X + 6X = $6.30

_____ Y + X = $6.30

6. Solve the equation you choose.

7. Check your answer.

Example: The sum of two numbers is 28. One number is 4 more than another. Find the numbers.

1. What is given in the problem?
2. What unknown quantities are asked for?
3. Will a picture help?
4. Formulate an equation.
5. Solve the equation.
6. Check your answer.

A problem-solving activity may be used in any content area. For example, a science lesson might involve written problem-solving activities following a reading assignment in which students are asked to answer questions or perform an experiment (Earle 1976; Thelen 1976).

David, our instructional reader, works on a problem-solving guide for his math class similar to the examples given in this chapter. *(Photo by Joseph Bodkin)*

PATTERN GUIDES

Similar to a problem-solving guide is a pattern guide where the student is guided step by step through a recipe, science experiment, and so forth. Key words are highlighted and each step emphasized so that students carefully follow a set of directions. In fact, a pattern guide can be used to teach sequential comprehension skills wherever chronological order provides the organization of the paragraph or selection. (Estes and Vaughan 1978).

The following pattern guide was created for use at the high school level in a health class. The emphasis is upon helping students see patterns of comparison and contrast.

Pattern Guide
"Signs and Symptoms of Shock"*

The American Red Cross,
First Aid and Personal Safety
(New York: Doubleday and Company, 1973), pp. 60–63.

When someone has been seriously injured, his/her body may react by going into *shock*. This term means that a serious depression of the nervous and circulatory systems occurs. It is important for you to be able to recognize the signs and symptoms of *shock*. Read about *shock* on pages 60, 61, 62 and 63 of your textbook.

Listed below, in *Column A*, are the characteristics or signs of a normal healthy person. Read these. Then list in *Column B* the corresponding characteristics of a person suffering from shock. Number 1 is done for you.

COLUMN A	COLUMN B
1. The skin is warm to touch and normal in color.	1. The skin is cold to touch and pale or bluish.
2. The skin is dry to touch.	2.
3. The person is strong.	3.
4. The pulse is strong and about 70 to 80 beats per minute.	4.
5. The rate of breathing is about 12 to 18 times per minute.	5.
6. The pulse can easily be felt in the wrist.	6.
7. The person will not feel nauseated or sick to his stomach.	7.
8. The eyes are bright with pupils of normal size.	8.
9. The body temperature is normal, about 98.6°.	9.
10. The person is awake and alert.	10.

*Prepared by Linda Merchant, State College, Pa.

Answer sheet for "Signs and Symptoms of Shock"

1. The skin is cold to touch and pale or bluish.
2. The skin may be moist and clammy.
3. The victim is weak.
4. The pulse is usually rapid (over 100) and weak.
5. The rate of breathing is increased. It may be shallow and irregular.
6. It is usually necessary to locate the pulse in the artery at the side of the neck.
7. The victim may feel nauseated and vomit.
8. The victim's eyes are sunken, with a vague expression, and the pupils widely dilated.
9. Body temperature falls.
10. The victim eventually loses consciousness.

PARAGRAPH-BY-PARAGRAPH GUIDE

Some study guides can be incorporated into the reading material, if the reading material is duplicated by the teacher. In "Sandwich Liberation" which follows, two secondary school home economics teachers wrote the instructional material. As they wrote it, they included study guide questions as part of the reading material. Literal comprehension is assured as students answer questions after almost every paragraph. Higher level questions are also included to help students apply what they have read.

INTRODUCING SANDWICH LIBERATION *

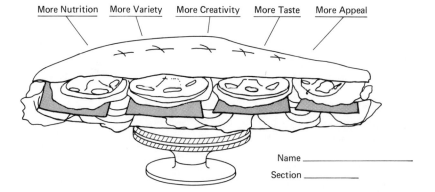

More Nutrition   More Variety   More Creativity   More Taste   More Appeal

Name _____

Section _____

The Earl of Sandwich may have invented the sandwich, but would he recognize it today? The sandwich has been liberated. Layered poor boys, gravy and sauce-covered open facers, lunch box, tea, and party are some of the kinds of sandwiches in America today that put the Earl's model to shame. As you can see from the many types of sandwiches, the popularity of sandwiches has increased, not only in America—the inventor and new home of many

* Prepared by Margaret Campbell and Connie Martin, State College, Pa., Area School District.

sandwiches—but also throughout the world. All this freedom is just what your creative spirit needs. Almost any food is sandwich material, so bone up by following this packet, then give the Earl of Sandwich a little competition of your own.

   1. Who originated the sandwich?

   2. In what country is the sandwich the most popular today?

MORE NUTRITION

From a nutritional standpoint, sandwiches are becoming more and more important in the daily menu. A well-planned sandwich can include many nutrients and be the main part of a meal. Sandwiches are made of bread, which is included in the Daily Food Guide. Enriched or whole-grain bread furnishes carbohydrate, thiamine, riboflavin, niacin, and iron. Butter, margarine, and salad dressing furnish fat. Some fillings include protein foods, such as meat, chicken, fish, eggs, cheese and peanut butter; some fillings include mineral and vitamin foods, such as lettuce, tomatoes, cucumbers, canned salmon, liver and cheese.

    If the sandwich is to be made the main part of a meal, a protein food should be included in the filling. Protein is needed for the growth and repair of body tissues, such as your hair, skin, blood, muscles and nerves. All of your body needs protein. Your heart, liver, lungs, and your brain all need protein to function and stay in good condition.

    You should remember that animal foods are complete proteins. They contain the eight essential amino acids that humans cannot manufacture but other animals can. There are other sources of protein besides animal foods. The Daily Food Guide developed by the U.S.D.A., broken down into four areas—meat, milk, fruits and vegetables, and cereal products—lists plant foods which can be used as meat alternatives. Dried beans, lentils, dried peas, peanuts, and many nuts belong to this list. Since any of the common vegetable protein foods, except peanuts, contain only part of the total set of amino acids, they should be combined with others for you to remain healthy.

    Protein types of fillings combined with enriched or whole-wheat bread, butter or margarine, and lettuce give a satisfying food combination. Your lunch should supply one-third of your daily food requirements.

   3. What are the three basic parts of a sandwich?

   4. The guide developed by the U.S.D.A. to help plan meals with proper nutrition is called _____ .

   5. This guide is broken down into what four areas?

   6. What are the three functions of protein?

   7. Meats are a _____ protein.

   8. Your lunch should supply _____ of your daily food requirements.

   9. How does a sandwich fit into the basic four? (Be specific)

MORE VARIETY

There are a variety of sandwiches for different occasions, such as the lunch and lunch-box sandwiches—the everyday kind, the hearty sandwiches that are meals in themselves, and the dainty sandwiches for parties.

    Sandwiches vary in size from large meal-size sandwiches to tiny, bite-size sandwiches served at parties. There are also smaller sandwiches which are served as an accompaniment to soups or salads at lunch. We usually think of sandwiches as consisting of two slices of bread and filling. Besides two-deckers, we also have one- and three-decker sandwiches.

The hot sandwich is an open-faced one (one bread slice cut rather thick) and topped with hearty foods, such as sliced roast beef or turkey with gravy. A broiled open-face sandwich is made with one bread slice; and small party sandwiches are usually made with one or two thin bread slices. A club sandwich consists of three toasted bread slices and different fillings, such as cold, sliced, cooked chicken or turkey, crisp bacon slices, lettuce, thin slices of tomato, and mayonnaise. Besides, there is the attractive Sandwich Loaf which resembles a frosted loaf cake. The possibilities of sandwiches are endless.

10. Name three times sandwiches can be served.
11. Name two sandwiches for each time in #10.

THE BASE

Sandwiches begin with bread. And what a wide and wonderful variety is available to us today! Everything from pungent rye and pumpernickel to the calorie-counter's very thin sliced white bread . . . and bread developed especially for toasting, petite party breads and homemade style loaves left unsliced. Besides these, there are specialty breads such as oatmeal, cornbread, raisin, banana, nut, French and Italian bread; and soft buns, soft and crisp rolls, and English muffins. Canned date-nut, orange nut, chocolate and brown bread are also available.

Thick slices of bread are very best for hearty sandwiches, such as lunch-box and lunch sandwiches. It is best not to remove the crusts from the lunch-box sandwiches because crusts help keep the sandwich fresh; however, some lunch sandwiches are especially appealing when the crusts are removed. Remove crusts or leave them on, as you wish. The crusts must always be removed from party sandwiches.

For any sandwich, there is a bread to enhance it. Treat yourself to the adventure of trying new breads for sandwich recipes—there are hundreds of variations awaiting your attention and pleasure. The key is your imagination!!!

12. Name two breads, excluding white and wheat.
13. Take one of your examples from #12 and give an example of an unusual sandwich (not peanut butter or cold lunch meat) that could use this bread as a base.

MORE CREATIVITY

Make sandwiches to fit the occasions and conditions under which they will be kept and served. Be sure the choice of sandwich is suitable for the occasion and circumstances under which it must be kept, served, and eaten. Also, consider the likes and dislikes of persons for whom the sandwich is being made. For example, some people prefer mayonnaise to butter; others want both. Some like lots of lettuce, others none at all. There are certain basic principles of sandwich-making that are well worth keeping in mind.

- Before starting to make sandwiches, assemble all the necessary ingredients and equipment needed.
- Have good sharp knives, a wide spreader, and a generous-sized cutting board.
- Many sandwich fillings may be made in advance. Season them well; store in screw-top jars or covered bowls and refrigerate until ready to use. If the filling is made with mayonnaise or salad dressing, use a minimum amount of dressing so that it will not soak into the bread.
- Many prepared fillings, such as meat and cheese spreads in jars and cans, are available in the market.

- Butter or margarine should be softened (not melted) at room temperature; or cream it with a fork until spreadable.
- Use fresh or day-old bread. Take the two slices of bread that lie next to each other in the loaf so that the edges will match. Line up paired bread slices, placing them two by two in rows.
- Using a flexible spatula, spread softened butter or margarine generously and evenly to the edges of one side of each bread slice. Butter or margarine forms the protective covering needed to keep the filling from soaking through the bread—and it also adds flavor.
- If mayonnaise is used, spread in the same way. Ditto for mustard.
- When using fancy cutters, the bread should be cut before it is spread to avoid waste of butter, margarine or filling.
- Be generous with the filling. If it is salad-type filling, place it on the bottom slice and spread it evenly to the edges (but don't let filling ooze over the edges). If a meat or cheese filling is used, distribute the slices evenly to fit the slice of bread. Trim away any pieces that may hang over the edges.
- Add lettuce, relish or slices of tomato to sandwiches if they are to be served immediately. For a lunch box, the lettuce, slices of tomato, and such items should be wrapped separately in foil or clear plastic wrap and added just before eating. This helps prevent transfer of excess moisture and protects the vegetables against becoming limp or wilted.
- Lack of seasoning can break some sandwiches. Proper seasoning can make them.
- Using a cutting board and a very sharp knife, cut the sandwiches into interesting shapes. Use a cutting motion and do not press down too hard to crush the bread and disturb the filling.
- The shapes will depend upon how the sandwiches are to be served——for a lunch box or picnic, the family meal, a snack, or a party. The sandwiches may be cut into squares, sticks, triangles, or rounds. For parties, they may be cut into fancy shapes with cooky cutters.
- Arrange cut sandwiches on plate, add garnish, and serve immediately.
- Have hot sandwiches hot, but never have the cold ones icy cold——it kills the flavor.

14. Name five "good techniques" you should use when making sandwiches.
15. Certain items should not be added to sandwiches until ready to serve. Can you name two and state why?

MORE TASTE

Many times it is necessary to make sandwiches in advance. Sandwiches dry out quickly and therefore require special care to keep them moist. Ingredients for sandwiches (except fresh fruits and vegetables) may be combined a few days before using if they are kept tightly covered and refrigerated to prevent loss of food value. In this way, two or three fillings can be kept on hand to increase variety. Wrap sandwiches individually and securely in wax paper, foil, or plastic sandwich wrap to prevent flavors from mingling. Be sure to label for easy identification at serving time.

Sack lunch sandwiches take special precautions to insure quality.

- Don't remove crusts—that causes drying.
- Wrap lettuce and tomatoes separately to prevent sogginess.
- Butter spread on bread also prevents sogginess and adds flavor.
- Mayonnaise can only be kept safely for four hours. If you don't plan to eat it before then, don't use mayonnaise.

The freezer can be a sandwich's best friend. It lets you do the fussing in advance. Here are a few tips. Breads of all varieties freeze well. Most fillings or completed sandwiches may be frozen and kept in the freezer for three weeks. Wrap individually in wax paper, foil, or cellophane to prevent flavors from mingling. Protein foods for sandwiches freeze successfully except for egg whites, which may become tough. If mayonnaise, jelly, or jam are to be used, they should be added to frozen sandwiches after they have been thawed to prevent sogginess. Salad greens or tomatoes should not be used in any sandwich which is made in advance. Always thaw sandwiches before unwrapping——about two or three hours at room temperature; five or six hours in the refrigerator. The time will depend on the size of the sandwich. And remember, *never* refreeze a thawed sandwich.

16. Name three precautions to keep refrigerated sandwiches moist.
17. Sack lunches take special precautions to insure quality. Can you name them?
18. It is possible to freeze sandwiches, however, certain sandwich ingredients do not freeze well. Can you name three? Why don't they freeze well?
19. Can sandwiches be refrozen? Why or why not?

MORE APPEAL

The way you cut and serve a sandwich is an important part of the sandwich's appeal. Here are some suggestions for cutting and arranging sandwiches to make them as good as they taste. In the open space on the plate, place a salad, cup of soup, or garnish. Suggested garnishes to accompany sandwiches are small bunches of grapes, sweet cherries on stems, cheese cubes on toothpicks, salted nuts, gumdrops, candied orange or grapefruit rind, stuffed fruits, radish roses, and celery hearts.

20. Define garnish. Name five, not listed above, which can be used with sandwiches.

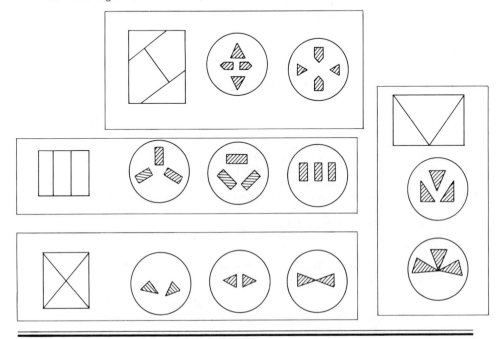

Some frustration level readers, for whom the textbook material is too difficult, may have to rely on a study guide if the material cannot be presented through another medium, such as films, records, or the language experience approach (Thelen 1976). No need exists, however, for them to read every paragraph. And often they understand the material better if they read the last paragraph first. The following is an example of a paragraph-by-paragraph guide intended for frustration level readers. Since the textbook, intended for a twelfth-grade health class, is much too difficult for students reading several levels below grade level expectations, the teacher has provided considerable guidance.

READING GUIDE EXERCISE *

John LaPlace, *Health* (Englewood Cliffs, N.J.:
Prentice-Hall, Inc., 1980) pp. 52–54.

Paragraph 1

a. Read the paragraph.
b. Why is consistent exercise important?
c. Reread Sentence 1. How do you think satisfaction and entertainment relate to consistent exercise?

Paragraph 2

a. Read Sentence 1.
b. Skim the rest of the paragraph to find the one sentence that defines what is meant by variety. Write it.

Paragraph 3

a. Read it.

Paragraph 4

a. Read the paragraph.
b. List three reasons why a warm-up period is essential.

    1. _____

    2. _____

    3. _____

Paragraph 5

a. Read the first two sentences.
    1. Why is it important for beginners not to over-exert themselves?
b. Read the rest of the paragraph.
    1. List the two signs of exhaustion.

        a. _____

        b. _____

* Prepared by Donna J. Dickstein, Mifflin Co., Pa., School District.

Paragraph 6

    a. Read Sentence 2.

    b. Now reread paragraph 5.

    c. How do a. and b. above relate?

Paragraph 7

    a. Read Sentence 1.

        1. Why is toning-down necessary?

    b. Read Sentence 2.

        1. How can you tone down?

    c. Read Sentence 3.

Paragraph 8

    a. Read paragraph 8. It explains how to plan a beneficial exercise program.

    b. Why is regularity a crucial element of an exercise program?

Paragraph 9

    a. Read Sentences 1 and 2.

        1. List three factors which influence ability to recover from physical activity.

           a. _____

           b. _____

           c. _____

    b. Read the rest of the paragraph.

        1. Why is rest important?

Paragraph 10

Read it. This paragraph explains the importance of sleep.

Paragraph 11

    a. Read the paragraph.

    b. What is the best measure of how much sleep you need?

MAINTAINING INTEREST

In selecting an exercise plan or sport, it is important to choose an activity that will provide satisfaction and entertainment. If one selects a program of exercise that is enjoyable, one is more likely to continue the activity over a long period of time. Consistent exercise is the only effective means of maintaining physical fitness, since benefits decline rapidly when activity is stopped.

The best assurance of permanent motivation is variety. If your daily routine is carried on indoors, select an outdoor activity such as jogging or tennis. In the opposite situation, indoor recreation may be more desirable. Group activities provide an atmosphere of companionship and good fellowship to stimulate interest, especially if much of your day is spent alone. Solitary activities are useful, on the other hand, because they do not depend upon the participation of others. Seasonal and local sports in your community or town may also provide diversity. Another approach is to alternate vigorous and moderate, or indoor and outdoor, exercise patterns. We need not limit ourselves to any one choice of activity at any time. The person who jogs two or three times a week might have the time and derive pleasure from tennis or golf or a swim on other days. Many joggers have become ski-touring enthusiasts when conditions permit.

Do not undertake an exercise program without keeping the following principles in mind.

CONDITIONING AND TRAINING

Warm-up. Before starting vigorous exercise, it is essential to engage in a brief warm-up period (several minutes) to limber up the joints and muscles, and to prevent strain on the heart caused by rapidly rising blood pressure. A warm-up period will gradually raise the body temperature to improve the physical work capacity of the large muscles.

Avoidance of Exhaustion. Once the exercise program is under way, it is important to avoid strain and to guard against exhaustion. Overly ambitious beginners generally defeat the long-range goals of exercise by tiring the body excessively, lowering morale. Normal fatigue, however, should not be confused with exhaustion. *Fatigue* occurs when the concentration of lactic acid and carbon dioxide reaches a certain level in the blood, causing a feeling of tiredness. This condition is quite safe and normal, though it must be regarded as a warning signal to the body not to exceed physical limits. Pain in the chest or severe breathlessness are signs that the body is working outside the limits of safety.

Planning and Moderation. A planned progression of exercise will help to avoid the excessive workloads that produce feelings of weakness and strain. By gradually increasing the effort expended in each session, individuals are able to build up their capacity without excess strain. If any step of the plan proves too strenuous, always descend to a previous step until the body is fully conditioned to accept the additional energy output. Exercise is hard work; individuals who are out of condition should practice moderation in the demands made on their systems.

Toning Down. Just as it is necessary first to warm up the body, it is likewise necessary to allow a *toning-down* period in which the body can relax gradually after engaging in exercise. Walking or jogging slowly in place allows the body to readjust to its normal aerobic condition and to a state of relaxation. Failure to observe this rule may result in dizzy spells and faintness.

Regularity and Consistency. A final principle is the maintenance of regularity and consistency in the exercise plan. Random exercise, even if strenuous, will not prove to much advantage, as it will not build up the body to withstand increasing workloads. A beneficial exercise program requires a minimum of three to four activity sessions a week. Fewer sessions may burn up some calories, but they will not increase overall fitness. During long interim periods of inactivity, the body quickly returns to its former state. For this reason, regularity in the program is crucial. The program for each week should be scheduled in advance and should be undertaken at a time that is convenient for exercise. Warm-up and recovery periods should not be afterthoughts, but should be regular parts of the program.

Recovery. Our ability to recover from our last period of physical activity is influenced by the intensity of the activity and our degree of fitness. Age is a factor in that the older we are, the longer it takes to recover. Recovery requires a period of rest. Without adequate rest we are not fully prepared to engage in the next session of physical activity.

The most complete form of rest is sleep. The importance of sleep to physical fitness is becoming better understood as research into its physiological aspects continues. Its role in recuperation from daily tensions and muscular fatigue, in the preparation of an environment for the regeneration of body cells in the restoration of energy, and in the slowing down of such bodily functions as blood pressure, pulse, and temperature is well known.

The amount of sleep needed to maintain optimum fitness is a highly individual matter. Although most adults require from six to eight hours of sleep a night, wide variations exist, influenced by considerations of general health, age, daily activity, emotional state, and sleeping habits. The best measure of whether you are getting enough sleep is the way you feel—you should be rested and ready to face your daily activities within an hour of rising.

GENERAL STUDY GUIDE

When a teacher uses different textbooks and references for students of different reading levels, one general study guide can help students grasp the important ideas from any of the reading material. A seventh-grade teacher devised the following study guide to accompany one of her social studies units. Regardless of the reading materials used, the students were to answer the study guide questions. Note that the questions require thinking at different levels on the *Taxonomy*. The guide helped the students know what was important in the reading materials and gave the unit of study cohesiveness that might be lacking with use of diverse source materials.

STUDY GUIDE: THE WORLD AND ITS PEOPLE*

1. Describe the land of the country under study according to the following:
   a. Climate—(temperate, freezing, torrid)
   b. Topography—(flat, rolling plains, mountainous)
   c. Political Boundaries—(bordering countries or waters)
   d. Identify:
      1. Capital
      2. Important rivers
      3. Mountain ranges
2. Identify three historical or present-day people closely associated with this country.
3. Identify some economic problems that led to the adoption of the new social system in this country.
4. How does their music or art reflect this social system?
5. If you were living in that country at that period of history, would you have supported that social system? Why?
6. Make a chart or graph or drawing that would illustrate one of the above answers. On a later date, your group will present your illustration to the class.

Similarly, another teacher, using the unit *Neighbors to the South* provided in Appendix A, created questions to be used with that material. References, rated by difficulty level, are provided to guide the teacher in matching students with appropriate reading materials. The questions, again as in the previous study guide, enable students who have read different materials to comprehend the main ideas and discuss them with each other. Poor as well as good readers may thus contribute to the class discussion.

* Prepared by Sr. Barbara Zivic, St. Michael's School, Hollidaysburg, Pa.

STUDY GUIDE: THE CULTURE AND PEOPLE OF MEXICO, NEIGHBORS TO THE SOUTH*

1. Where are the two major mountain ranges located?
2. Where is the great plateau?
3. How does the location of these important geographic features affect Mexico's climate?
4. Where do most of the people live?
5. What are serapes and rebozas? Why are they particularly suitable for use throughout Mexico?
6. What three main racial groups make up Mexico's population? What is the approximate proportion of these groups?
7. What was the most powerful Indian group living in Mexico at the time of the Spanish conquest?
8. What effects of the conquest do we still see in Mexico today?
9. Why are so many native languages and customs found in Mexico today?
10. What were some of the changes brought about by the revolution of 1910?
11. What are some of Mexico's main crops?
12. What are Mexico's important natural resources?

KEY TO READABILITY LEVELS

A— average

BA—below average

AR—advanced reader

M— mature theme or sophisticated material

HI— high interest, main characters are junior high school age

SOURCES FOR READING ABOUT THE CULTURE AND PEOPLE OF MEXICO, NEIGHBORS TO THE SOUTH

BA   EPSTEIN, SAM, *The First Book of Mexico*. New York: Watts, 1967.

BA   GARCIA, JOE DELL, *Come Along to Mexico*. Minneapolis: I. S. Denison and Co., Inc., 1965.

A   Illustrated Library of the World and Its People. Vol. 8, *Mexico*. New York: Greystone Press, 1968.

A, AR   "Life World History," *Mexico*. New York: Time, Inc., 1966.

BA   MACGILL, HUGH, *A Mexican Village*. Mankats: Creative Education Society, 1970.

BA   SHANNON, TERRY, *A Trip to Mexico*. Chicago: Children's Press, 1961 (some Spanish text).

A   SUNSET BOOKS, *Mexico*. Sunset Park, Calif.: Lane Magazine and Book Co., 1967.

BA   WOOD, FRANCES E., *Mexico*. Chicago: Children's Press, 1964.

*Prepared by Charlene Chagnon, State College, Pa.

MARGINAL GLOSS

Similar to a study guide is a technique called marginal gloss (Otto, White, and Camperell 1980). Instead of providing a set of questions to be answered as students read an assignment, the teacher provides marginal notes, questions, and commentary to accompany the reading material. Since these notes cannot be written in the margins of every student's textbook, the teacher writes the marginal notes on a separate piece of paper which is duplicated and provided to every student. By means of guide arrows, each student lines up the gloss sheet with the appropriate page. The student, therefore, reads the marginal notes along with the text.

Gloss can be used with all students to teach them how to read a content area textbook actively, attending to key words in boldface print, headings, paragraph transitions, introductory and summary paragraphs, and so forth. In other words, gloss can teach students the "schema" (Otto and White, 1982) of the textbook, such as its organization and paragraph structures. The teacher can gradually decrease the amount of gloss as the students learn to attend to the textbook cues independently.

Frustration level readers can also benefit from the techniques if the gloss provided to them directs them to read certain portions while skipping those parts that are not essential to the content. The teacher may also paraphrase certain portions or add explanatory notes to clarify difficult portions.

As with study guides, marginal gloss does not serve as a substitute for the teacher's introduction to important vocabulary and concepts. It provides the follow-up guidance that many students need while reading. Gloss can encourage students to think about the content as they read by asking higher level questions. It can encourage the transfer of skills learned in an elementary reading program to content materials at any level. Finally, particularly in some subject areas, the teacher may update the content presented by means of marginal gloss. This function is particularly important in content areas in which current information is crucial.

An example of the use of marginal gloss with an American government textbook is provided. The number in the margin refers the student to the commentary on the page. The student uses the arrows to line up the gloss with the column of print in the textbook.

MARGINAL GLOSS*

Local unions were first formed in this country in the 1790s and early 1800s. These early unions were *craft unions,* organized according to the type of job an individual performed. Workers such as bakers, shoemakers, and mechanics banded together in separate groups in order to get fair wages or fair prices. There was nothing known as a national union at this time.

1. How are craft unions different from our present-day unions? Why do you think unions changed?

People in these craft unions wanted many of the same things that unions seek today. High among their demands were increased wages and a shorter working day. (In the early 1800s, many people worked a ten-hour day or more.) To enforce their demands, these unions

2. Note this topic sentence which introduces the paragraph. Why were craft unions formed?

*J. Gillespie and S. Lazarus, *American Government; Comparing Political Experiences* (Englewood Cliffs, N.J.: Prentice-Hall, Inc., 1979), p. 144.

relied largely on strikes. In a *strike,* employees as a group refuse to work.

3. A *strike* as used here is:
   a. a term used in bowling
   b. a term used in baseball
   c. a work stoppage
   d. a stroke of good luck
   e. the act of hitting.

The early unions failed, however, for several reasons. They failed because workers were unorganized, separated by geographic area, and divided by job skills. The unions failed because they lacked money; surely the workers had none to spare. In addition, management clearly had the upper hand. Better organized than the workers, they formed employers' associations. They went to court to stop strikes. Ruling that striking was a form of conspiracy, the courts usually ordered strikers back to work. Unions were banned by law in many places.

4. Again, note this good topic sentence. List at least five of the reasons that early unions failed. (Note that the reasons are continued in the next paragraph.)

The early unions also had to deal with economic conditions. In bad times, many people lost their jobs, and unions lost their power to bargain. In good times, when unions went on strike, management charged "conspiracy" and brought in strikebreakers to replace striking workers.

5. What is a *conspiracy*? If you do not know and cannot tell from context, you need to look it up in a dictionary since it is not included in our glossary.

Summary

Although researchers still do not know all the factors which affect reading comprehension, we have highlighted the instructional practices which seem to help students learn from text materials. Study guides and marginal gloss in particular can provide teacher guidance in comprehension without having the teacher present. The teacher can help individuals or small groups while students are using assigned reading materials in class. Study guides may be individualized to provide for differences in readers, or a study guide may provide cohesiveness when different reading materials are used.

Chapter Activities: Using What You've Read

Learn to Do It!

1. For a chapter/unit, develop a study guide. You may want to write it on the same passage you used for the DRA so it can be used as the independent reading portion. You can develop a concept, problem-solving, pattern or paragraph-by-paragraph guide, depending on the content and your students' abilities.

2. Develop a marginal gloss for a reading passage, using the model in this chapter.

Do It!

1. Try out the study guide with one or more classes.

2. Try out the marginal gloss with one or more classes.

References

EARLE, R. A., *Teaching Reading and Mathematics.* Newark, Del.: International Reading Association, 1976.

ESTES, T. H., and J. L. VAUGHAN, JR., *Reading and Learning in the Content Classroom.* Boston: Allyn and Bacon, 1978.

HERBER, H. L., *Teaching Reading in Content Areas* (2nd ed.). Englewood Cliffs, N.J.: Prentice-Hall, 1978.

OTTO, W., S. WHITE, and K. CAMPERELL, *Text Comprehension Research to Classroom Application: A Progress Report.* Theoretical Paper No. 87. Madison: Wisconsin Research and Development Center for Individualized Schooling, 1980.

OTTO, W., and S. WHITE, eds., *Understanding Expository Material.* New York: Academic Press, 1982.

THELEN, J., *Improving Reading in Science.* Newark, Del.: International Reading Association, 1976.

Chapter 15
Teaching Study Skills

Preview

Most textbooks on reading give only cursory treatment to study skills, yet these are the important skills which enable students to become independent learners. These are the "learning how to learn" skills which are crucial for future out-of-school learning. Learning on one's own is particularly important with the wealth of media sources that make vast quantities of information readily accessible. If students are not to become overwhelmed by these sophisticated and fast-paced communications systems, then they must acquire basic tools which will enable them to cope and keep up with the increased demands.

OVERVIEW

The need for students to learn study skills seems greater than ever before. No longer can it be enough to learn dates and facts about a content area. With knowledge about our world increasing every day, we can learn and remember only a few important facts. We need to learn the skills that make retrieval of dates and facts possible. Today's modern public libraries no longer rely on a card catalog, for example. To locate a particular book, we now can quickly consult a microfiche reader to find out the call numbers of the book. When we want to research a particular topic, we can use a computer search to locate information related to the topic. The ERIC (Educational Resources Information Center) system, for example, has indexed published and nonpublished articles, paper presentations, symposia, and reports by descriptors which enable us to call up these sources, providing bibliographic information as well as abstracts.

With the modern technology available to our students, instruction in the skills of locating and using information from all sources becomes increasingly important. Unfortunately, in the past, content area instruction has tended to focus on memorization of facts which are quickly forgotten after the final exam. Even today, too little attention is being given to instruction in the skills which enable students to retrieve information when it is needed.

Some evidence (Askov, Kamm, and Klumb 1977) exists that teachers themselves have not mastered some of the study skills. Furthermore, students who have not been taught study skills do not seem to pick them up on their own throughout their elementary and secondary school careers (Askov, et al., 1980). If teachers are not familiar with the skills, they either do not teach them or else do a poor job (Kamm, White, and Morrison 1977).

Because study skills include such varied skills, such as reading maps and graphs, locating information in a library, and using specialized references such as an almanac or atlas, it is difficult to give more than cursory treatment to such an important area. One of the authors has written a separate book on this subject, entitled *Study Skills in the Content Areas* (Askov and Kamm 1982). Readers may wish to work through the activities presented in that book—to ensure their own mastery of study skills—in addition to this chapter which focuses only upon the teaching of study skills.

WHAT ARE STUDY SKILLS?

Study skills have been classified in various ways. In fact, some of them, for example outlining, could also be classified as comprehension skills. The classification of skills is not an important issue. What is important is that skills are not overlooked when students need them in content area study.

The following list of study skills (Karlin 1972, p. 187–88) presents the wide variety of skills labeled as study skills. Some of these skills, such as finding the main idea and recognizing significant details, could be considered comprehension skills and are discussed in the previous chapter. The skills listed in parts II and V are considered study skills in most lists.

I. Selection and Evaluation
   a. recognize the significance of the content
   b. recognize important details
   c. identify unrelated details
   d. find the main idea of a paragraph
   e. find the main idea of larger selections
   f. locate topic sentences
   g. locate answers to specific questions
   h. develop independent purposes for reading
   i. realize the author's purpose
   j. determine the accuracy and relevancy of information
II. Organization
   a. take notes
   b. determine relationship between paragraphs
   c. follow time sequences
   d. outline single paragraphs
   e. outline sections of a chapter
   f. outline an entire chapter
   g. summarize single paragraphs
   h. summarize larger units of material

III. Location of Information
   a. find information through a table of contents
   b. locate information through the index
   c. use a library card catalogue to locate materials
   d. use the Reader's Guide to Periodical Literature to locate sources of information
   e. use an almanac to obtain data
   f. understand and use various appendixes
   g. use glossaries
   h. use encyclopedias to locate information
IV. Following Directions
   a. see the relation between the purposes and the directions
   b. follow one-step directions
   c. follow steps in sequence
 V. Specialized Skills
   a. understand the significance of pictorial aids
   b. read and interpret graphs
   c. read and interpret tables
   d. read and interpret charts
   e. read and interpret maps
   f. read and interpret cartoons
   g. read and interpret diagrams
   h. read and interpret pictures

One diagnostic-prescriptive system of study skills, the Study Skills element of the *Wisconsin Design for Reading Skill Development* (Chester, Askov, and Otto 1973), divides study skills into three general areas—maps, tables and graphs, and reference skills. These categories are not totally inclusive; however, they represent the most common study skills.

At Level A, or kindergarten, only map skills are taught, the three strands being (1) representation, the symbol system used in maps to represent objects in the environment; (2) orientation, which includes both the directional system and the grid system to enable students to locate points and to describe the location of points on maps, globes, and in the environment; and (3) measurement, use of a scale bar or verbal equivalent to express distances on a map. These skills are reintroduced at Level B, first grade, in a slightly more difficult form along with the first exposure to reference skills (book skills and alphabetizing). At Level D, end of third grade, the skill of organizing and evaluating information is introduced as well as an evaluation skill (fact and opinion) which could also be classified as a comprehension skill. In Levels E, F, and G (fourth, fifth, and sixth grades) no new strands are introduced, but the skills are reapplied and refined with more difficult and complex materials. In summary, the strands within each area area as follows:

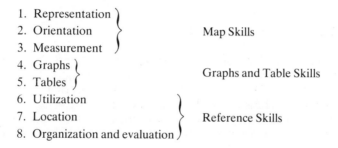

1. Representation ⎫
2. Orientation   ⎬   Map Skills
3. Measurement ⎭
4. Graphs ⎫
5. Tables ⎬   Graphs and Table Skills
6. Utilization   ⎫
7. Location   ⎬   Reference Skills
8. Organization and evaluation ⎭

Consider, for example, one strand of study skills within map skills—orientation—and follow it through the levels. A spiraling effect can be seen as the skill becomes more complex at each difficulty level. At level A kindergarten students begin learning orientation skills in map reading, not by reading a map, but by learning directional terms in the environment and in pictures. Knowledge of these terms prepares students for later use of directional labels. At Level B (first grade), students first use the concept of a grid to locate objects or to describe the location of objects. Instead of labeling the grid with letters and numbers, the grid is labeled with familiar pictures (such as animals on one axis and vegetables on the other). The purpose is to acquaint students with the notion of a grid system which is applied with increasingly greater sophistication. At Level C (second grade), students use a simple number-letter grid similar to a state or city map. At Level D (third grade), grid is not taught, but the directions that students learn in Level A (kindergarten) are brought to the sophistication necessary for map reading as students study the cardinal directions (north, south, east, west) on a globe. (Students first learn directions on a globe because it is a more accurate representation of the earth than a map is.) At Level E (fourth grade), students learn intermediate directions, such as northeast or southwest, in the environment and on both globes and maps. Again the task is both to locate a point and to describe the location of a point. At Level F (fifth grade), the grid system is reintroduced and combined with the directional system as students must use degrees of latitude and longitude, as well as cardinal directions, to locate the same point on various map projections. The important concept is that north is not always at the top of the map as it is in the familiar Mercator projection. Finally at Level G (sixth grade or junior high), students locate points on any projection using latitude and longitude (the grid and directional systems) as well as using latitude and longitude to determine directions on any projection.

Please note that in study skills, the emphasis is on *reading* maps, graphs and tables, not on creating them. Constructing a table as part of a science laboratory experiment, for example, is an excellent way to introduce table reading skills—if the exercise does not end with simply creating the table. The teacher must also present opportunities for students to *read* tables which they have not constructed and teach table-reading skills. Although two processes are opposite sides of the same coin, a teacher cannot assume that students can read graphic materials simply because they have had some experience creating them. They need to learn the specialized reading skills necessary to read and interpret graphic materials.

As mentioned earlier, the list of study skills in the *Design* is not totally inclusive of all the study skills that one might include. Some other skills which might be added, for example, include adjusting reading rate to the purpose and difficulty of the reading task and independent study habits.

INDEPENDENT STUDY TECHNIQUES

One set of skills not included in the *Design* but frequently included among other lists of study skills is instruction in independent study techniques. While study guides, presented in Chapter 14, are an excellent means of insuring comprehension of a reading assignment, students need to learn how to study material independently. The teacher cannot always provide guidance for every bit of reading that must be done in studying in a content area. Students may read different materials, for example, in preparing independent reports or projects. The teacher cannot possibly anticipate all reading needs with a study guide at all times. Besides, the goal is for students to become independent learners. As mentioned in the previous chapter, study guides should gradually wean students from much teacher guidance to greater independence in reading. The goal is for students to read content materials independently with good comprehension as they will ultimately have to do with out-of-school learning. Instruction in the use of independent study techniques can help them accomplish that goal.

The earliest and probably most widely known technique for independent study is SQ3R (Robinson 1961). Others, such as PQRST (Spache 1963), are variations on the original SQ3R. The initials are relatively unimportant: what is important is teaching students the process which can be used on a short selection or a whole book. The gist of SQ3R is as follows:

S—Survey: Quickly read through the major headings as well as the introductory and summary paragraphs to get an overview of the selection. In a book, survey involves reading the Table of Contents and prefatory material that explains what the intent and audience of the book are. In this step the material may be deemed acceptable or rejected as inappropriate for the reader's intended purpose. This survey process is essentially the same as skimming.

Q—Question: Based on the survey, the reader formulates questions that s/he expects will be answered in the reading material. Questions may be created by converting headings or chapter titles into a question format. Initially, questions should be written down with space for answers. As students become sophisticated in applying independent study techniques, the question phase becomes internalized, with no need to put the questions in writing.

R—Read: Now the student is able to read purposefully because of the questions set forth. It is easier to grasp the main ideas and see the relative importance of supporting details.

R—Recite: The student now answers the questions that were set down in the second step. Answering the questions in writing provides a permanent record of notes. Other important details are also jotted down under the questions. If the questions have identified the main ideas of a selection, then in essence answering them becomes similar to the process of outlining. These notes should be written in the student's own words to insure that they are meaningful.

R—Review: At a later point the student should review his/her notes to recall the main ideas and important details. Because the student has gone through the process of actively reading the material—by formulating and answering questions—the student's notes should be meaningful. In fact, rereading notes should be more meaningful than rereading the material itself.

Teaching students to use independent study techniques fits the view of the reading process presented in Chapter 1. The preparation and background that a reader brings to the reading material is considered crucial in determining how much will be comprehended. With the use of the Directed Reading Activity and study guides, the teacher is guiding students through the material and helping them identify important points. Through the use of independent study techniques such as the SQ3R, the reader guides him/herself through the task of reading. By anticipating what will be said, the reader becomes actively involved in the reading task. The reader who is comprehending is not passively processing what the writer has set forth, but s/he is actively engaged in the problem-solving task of trying to answer anticipated questions.

Students usually do not readily accept the extra work involved in using independent study techniques. They prefer to read and reread material passively rather than actively trying to anticipate what the author is saying. Because this "lazy" approach is somewhat understandable, the teacher must require students to formulate and answer questions. These must be checked, as one would a study guide, until the independent study process becomes truly independent. Effective independent study habits may indeed be the most important learning that students can take away from content area study.

One caution in using SQ3R is in order. Sometimes a student's questions tend to be trivial if the textbook headings do not adequately state the main idea of the section. For example, if a heading in a social studies textbook were labeled "The Louisiana Purchase," a student might convert that heading to "What was the Louisiana Purchase?" While an answer which contains the date and extent of territory purchased for a given amount of money might be appropriate in some instances, the important point may actually be the impact that the Louisiana Purchase had on the eventual development of the United States. Therefore, students should be aware that a heading may not always form the best question if the material presented goes beyond the scope suggested by the heading.

Because independent study techniques are so important, they should be taught and reinforced by all teachers at all levels. Teachers in a department, grade, or school should agree on one format, such as SQ3R, so that students do not become confused by variations on the same general idea. Instruction in the other study skills, such as those included in the *Wisconsin Design for Reading Skill Development,* also requires careful teacher planning, as presented in the next section.

INSTRUCTION IN STUDY SKILLS

Ideally, teachers of a given content area, such as social studies or home economics, at the elementary, junior, and senior high school levels should work together to plan study skills instruction. A list of skills can be used as a starting point to survey the array of study skills in determining what skills are important in a given content area. The important skills that students need in order to study the particular content area should be identified. If another content area, such as English, is already teaching a given skill such as outlining, the same format ought to be used, with transfer of the skill in a new content area, such as social studies, being emphasized. A brief review may be necessary. We cannot assume that students will automatically apply a skill in a new content area simply because it was previously taught in another content area.

The next step, after the crucial skills are identified, is to determine appropriate grade levels for initial teaching and review for each of the skills selected. Thus, teachers of a given content area can create a scope and sequence chart of study skills showing what skills will be taught and reviewed at each grade level. Teachers cannot rely on a textbook series to make these important decisions. In fact, one elementary social studies textbook series surveyed in depth (Askov and Kamm 1974) introduced complex study skills at levels where the children lacked the conceptual background to apply them. Some textbooks also do not provide adequate instruction in the skills but expect students to apply them in content study.

David and a classmate are trying to peel an orange without tearing the skin—one way to show the relationship between a globe and a flat map. *(Photo by Joseph Bodkin)*

Study skills exercises, to be most effective, should be integrated into content area studies. A skill can be taught as it is needed in the content, or ahead of time with a brief review at the time of application of the skill.

Consider again the difference between maps and globes, referred to earlier. David, our instructional level reader, is shown trying to peel the skin of an orange without tearing it. If he flattens the skin, as the "skin" of the globe is flattened in making a map, he will inevitably tear the skin near the stems. Similarly, distortion occurs at the poles when reality on a globe is presented in the flattened form of a map. This point may be vividly demonstrated to students by having them compare the size of Greenland on a globe and map. Due to distortion at the poles, Greenland appears much larger on a map than on the truer representation of the globe. Study skills thus become meaningful as students have to use them in their content subjects. Reading graphic materials, such as maps, tables, and diagrams, poses a particular problem since students will probably ignore such materials unless particularly directed to them and taught how to read them.

A sample exercise follows in which a chemistry teacher developed an activity on reading a graph as applied in her chemistry class. Notice that the instructional activity precedes reading the textbook and follows a scientific demonstration. Skill application is guaranteed to have meaning!

STUDY SKILLS EXERCISE: READING A GRAPH *

The purpose of this exercise is to show the pressure-temperature relationships of a gas, and to introduce the absolute temperature scale. The activity starts with a demonstration dealing with the effect of temperature on pressure of a gas. This activity allows the student to collect experimental data and see it arranged in a chart and to represent the same data as in a graph.

This activity is to take place prior to Section 4–3, 4 in Chapter 4 of the text. At the end of the activity, the student should be able to state the effect of temperature on the pressure of a gas.

Today's demonstration deals with the relationship between temperature and pressure. The bulb of "John's Law Apparatus" will be filled with a given amount of air and then submerged in three different temperature baths: (1) boiling water; (2) ice-water mixture; and (3) dry ice-amyl alcohol mixture. The pressure will be read for each temperature bath. You are to record the following data during the demonstration.

Room temperature   : Gauge Pressure =

Temperature of boiling water   : Gauge Pressure =

Temperature of ice water mixture   : Gauge Pressure =

Temperature of dry ice-amyl alcohol : Gauge Pressure =

1. Plot the data with temperature along the abscissa and gauge pressure along the ordinate. The origin should be at $T = 300°C$ and $P = 0$ PSI (Pounds per square inch). Draw the best straight line through these points.
2. Extrapolate the line formed by the four points to the line $P = 0$.
3. Answer the following questions:

   _____ a. Is the relationship between temperature and pressure direct or indirect?

   _____ b. As temperature decreases, pressure _____ .

   _____ c. We earlier defined temperature as a measurement of Kinetic Energy. Does the centigrade scale accurately measure Kinetic Energy? Explain your answer.

*Prepared by Deborah Fineberg, Penns Valley Junior-Senior High School, Spring Mills, Pa.

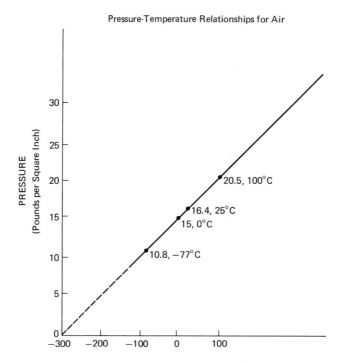

Pressure-Temperature Relationships for Air

ANSWERS

    a. There is a direct relationship between pressure and temperature.

    b. As temperature decreases, pressure decreases.

    c. Kinetic Energy is energy of motion. If gas molecules are moving they would exert a pressure. If they are not moving, there should be no pressure. This graph shows that the centigrade scale does not accurately measure Kinetic Energy because at 0°C, there is a pressure of 15 PSI. Therefore, 0°C does not mean 0 Kinetic Energy.

A very different type of graph, yet basically the same skill, was taught by a middle school home economics teacher in preparation for sewing a pattern.

STUDY SKILL EXERCISE: READING A CHART *

Teacher's Preface: When I teach clothing, I use this sheet to teach students how to read the pattern graph on the back of the pattern envelope. This teaches them how to find the amount of material needed to make a specific garment. If they can read the sample, they should be able to read any pattern back.

    You read pattern envelope backs like a graph. To do this correctly, you must know:

* Prepared by Brenda Nye Maddy, Harrisburg, Pa., Middle School.

1. Width of material (35 inches, 44 inches, 54 inches, or 60 inches).
2. The size you take, according to *your* measurements.
3. The view number you wish to make *or* which part of the pattern (blouse, pants, skirt, jacket).

EXAMPLE: Look at pattern "A" at the top of your sheet. It is marked for 44- or 45-inch wide material. The size is a 12. The view number is View 1, or the pants.

Find the section of pattern "A" for pants. Now find the material width of 44-inch or 45-inch wide.

Find size 12 at top.

Come down the 12 column and across the 44-inch or 45-inch line for pants. Where the two meet is how much material you need for pants of that pattern (#6165).

You would need 2¼ yards if you were making that pattern.

Now, follow the same procedure to answer any questions on how much material you will need for any given garment. There are many things found on pattern envelope backs. All answers will be found on envelope back "A" (#6165) or on envelope back "B" (#5864).

1. The pattern number for pattern "A" is _____ . For pattern "B" it is _____ .
2. You are making pattern "A," size 10, view 1 or 2—pants, and the material is 44

   inches wide. How much material will you need to make these pants? _____
3. Pattern "B," size 14, short skirt, material is 36 inches wide. How much material will

   you need to make the skirt? _____
4. Every pattern has suggested fabrics to use for that particular pattern. List the first three suggested fabrics for pattern "A."

   _____   _____   _____
5. Each pattern also lists sewing notions needed. List all of the notions needed for pattern "B."
6. Pattern pieces are lettered. Pattern envelope backs tell you which letters are needed for what you are making. Look at pattern "A." What letters would you use to make pants—View 1 and 2? _____
7. Pattern "B"—jumper or tunic. Which pattern pieces will you use?

   Letters   _____ _____ _____ _____ _____
8. Pattern "B"—How much elastic do you need for the tunic or jumper?

   Size 10 _____   Size 12 _____   Size 16 _____
9. How many pattern pieces are given for pattern "A"? _____
10. Pattern "A"—size 14, view 3—shorts, material is 60 inches wide. How much

    material should you buy for shorts? _____
11. Pattern "B"—size 8, short skirt, material is 54 inches wide. How much do you

    need? _____
12. What is the pattern number for pattern "A"? _____
13. Pattern "A"—List notions needed (on back of sheet).

14. From either envelope back, list the standard body measurements for a:

	Size 10	Size 12	Size 16
Bust	_____	_____	_____
Waist	_____	_____	_____
Hip	_____	_____	_____
Back	_____	_____	_____

15. Extra _____ is needed to match plaids, stripes, or one-way designs.

16. What are lightweight wool, wool flannel, tweed, gabardine, double knit, canvas,

chino, poplin, linen, challis? _____ What pattern number has these fabrics under suggested fabrics?

17. Pattern "B"—What is the width of the lower edge of the short skirt?

Size 8 _____   Size 12 _____   Size 16_____

18. Pattern "A"—Size 8, view 2 or 3—top, 45 inch wide material. How much material is

needed for contrasting cuffs and facings? _____

If you got these right, you can answer any questions from *any* envelope back you are given.

An industrial arts teacher found that chart reading was an important skill in his content area. Step-by-step instructions precede the chart so that students can use it.

STUDY SKILLS EXERCISE: READING A CHART *

Many times it is necessary to put threads on or in a piece of metal. This is done by a tap or a die. The tap is used to make internal threads and the die is used to make the external threads such as on a bolt. These tap and die sets make an American National thread that is the most common type used in the United States. The two common series are:

1. National Coarse (NC) has fewer threads per inch for the same diameter than the other series (NF). It is used for general purpose work.
2. National Fine (NF) has more threads per inch and is used in precision assemblies.

The chart is read in the following way:

a. Determine the size of the threads and the number   SEE FOLLOWING CHART
of threads per inch to be used. (size of tap)
b. Find that tap on the chart.
c. Look to the right of this size for the threads per inch.

*Prepared by John Kubalak, Penns Valley Junior-Senior High School, Spring Mills, Pa.

   d. To the right of the threads per inch is the size of drill that is used so the hole may be threaded with the proper tap.

1/4–20–NC

The above is an example of the proper way a threaded hole would be on a drawing. The 1/4 would describe the diameter of the bolt, the 20 would tell that there are 20 threads per inch of bolt and the NC stands for National Coarse which is the series.

National Screw Threads Commission—Standard *

American National Fine (NF)			American National Coarse (NC)		
Size of Tap	Threads per in.	Tap Drill	Size of Tap	Threads per in.	Tap Drill
#4	48	43	#4	40	No. 43
#5	44	37	#5	40	No. 38
#6	40	33	#6	32	No. 36
#8	36	29	#8	32	No. 29
#10	32	21	#10	24	No. 25
#12	28	14	#12	24	No. 16
$\frac{1}{4}$	28	3	$\frac{1}{4}$	20	No. 7
$\frac{5}{16}$	24	1	$\frac{5}{16}$	18	F
$\frac{3}{8}$	24	Q	$\frac{3}{8}$	16	$\frac{5}{16}$
$\frac{7}{16}$	20	$\frac{25}{64}$	$\frac{7}{16}$	14	U
$\frac{1}{2}$	20	$\frac{29}{64}$	$\frac{1}{2}$	13	$\frac{27}{64}$
$\frac{9}{16}$	18	$\frac{33}{64}$	$\frac{9}{16}$	12	$\frac{31}{64}$
$\frac{5}{8}$	18	$\frac{37}{64}$	$\frac{5}{8}$	11	$\frac{17}{32}$
$\frac{3}{4}$	16	$\frac{11}{16}$	$\frac{3}{4}$	10	$\frac{21}{32}$
$\frac{7}{8}$	14	$\frac{13}{16}$	$\frac{7}{8}$	9	$\frac{49}{64}$
1	14	$\frac{15}{16}$	1	8	$\frac{7}{8}$

* Based on 75 percent full thread.

In the following exercise on outlining using a passage from an English class, junior high students are provided with the outline structure. Additional help could be provided by the teacher by filling in some of the main headings or details. As discussed in Chapter 14, outlining is a good technique for teaching students to pick out the main ideas and important details. A well-organized passage, such as the one below, is a good choice for outlining instruction.

STUDY SKILLS EXERCISE: OUTLINING *

Directions—Following is a theme written with a carefully planned outline. You are to read the theme carefully, then *reconstruct the outline* used by the writer. Use the ruled outline following the theme. The number of the topics and their relationship are correctly indicated by the blanks in the outline.

Though I happened to get my first white mouse by chance, I now can think of three good reasons for having mice.

The first reason is the pleasure you can get from owning and observing a small animal. I never get tired of watching my mice scurry around, eat, and play.

My next reason is probably a more serious one, although it didn't at first occur to me. Owning small animals such as mice, rabbits, or guinea pigs is educational. You learn a lot about small animals and what they must have to be healthy and happy through owning and observing them.

Too, there's a financial profit to be made from raising pets, especially if they reproduce as quickly as mice do. My third reason, therefore, is the fact that sometimes you can make money, or at least try to. I wouldn't want to emphasize this, because I've never managed to make much of a profit myself. In fact, I always plow my profits back into the business, and I never have any money to buy pet food when I run out—which is often.

If you're going to raise mice, you need the proper equipment. A guinea pig will live happily in any cardboard box, but a mouse would climb out in five seconds. The most important piece of equipment you need is a mouseproof cage. Fortunately for me, my father had some old window screens and made me a wire cage with steel wire on all six sides. Once I had this, I didn't need to worry about my mouse running away, but I did discover that only a cage isn't enough.

The cage needs three additional kinds of equipment. Since mice spend much of their time eating, you need to have food and water dishes. This is easy; any type of dish or container will do. The second thing a mouse cage needs is a nest of some sort. Mice like to build themselves a nest where they can sleep and raise their young. This can be a little cardboard box. Of course the mice will eventually chew it to pieces, but it is easy to replace. Lastly, because mice quickly start smelling "mousy," they need fresh litter in their cage. Shredded newspaper will do, and it costs nothing.

Once you have your mice, your cage, and the rest of your equipment, you have to learn how to take care of your pets. These are two things my parents always insisted upon. I have to give my mice food and water every day, and I have to keep the cage clean.

Feeding mice isn't any trouble. Mice eat almost anything, but they especially like a mixture of seeds, which can be bought at any pet store. They also like bits of fresh vegetables and bread. There always should be water for them.

I didn't realize how important keeping the cage clean is until I'd had my first mouse about a week. I hadn't changed the litter, and as a result, our basement began to smell "mousy." When I changed the litter, the smell went away.

You can expect happy, healthy, fat mice if you feed them properly, give them a neat box and plenty of water, and always keep their cages clean.

I.

    A.

    B.

    C.

* Prepared by Christine Kolasa, State College, Pa., Area School District.

227

II.
    A.
    B.
        1.
        2.
        3.
III.
    A.
    B.

ANSWERS

   I. Reasons for having mice—A. Pleasure   B. Educational   C. Profit
  II. Raising mice—A. Mice   B. Cage   1. Dish   2. Nest   3. Litter
 III. Caring for mice—A. Food   B. Sanitary conditions

While research has tried to establish which study techniques, such as outlining, notetaking, and underlining, seem to produce the best learning, it is now recognized that the particular technique applied is not as important as the "depth of processing" required (Anderson and Armbruster 1982). In other words, students tend to retain

Pam is beginning some independent research for her English class. The librarian is showing her how to use the filmstrip projector, while her English teacher looks on. *(Photo by Joseph Bodkin)*

what they have said in their own words through notetaking because paraphrasing requires a greater depth of processing than, say, underlining. Material in which the interrelationship among ideas is crucial can best be studied through outlining. Material, such as dates and facts, which is to be learned only at a literal level, can be underlined to highlight the points to be remembered. Just as important as teaching these study techniques to students is teaching them flexibility. The teacher must at first guide them in analyzing the demands of the reading task to decide what study strategy is most appropriate.

Pam, our independent level reader, is shown doing independent research for her English class. She is gathering information in preparation for constructing a model of the Elizabethan stage. Since at this point she is interested only in literal comprehension of facts, she is making a list of the important characteristics of the early stages stated in the material. It would be a waste of Pam's time, and less accurate with this material, to require that she state everything in her own words. On the other hand, an interpretation of a scene from a Shakespearean play would involve Pam in restating the ideas in the play. A verbatim transcription would clearly be inappropriate.

One final caution is in order. Frequently teachers ask students to apply study techniques, such as outlining and notetaking, without providing instruction in the skills. If the teacher also does not check the product of such efforts, difficulties in applying the study techniques may not be recognized. David, for example, when required to take notes from his science textbook, which is appropriate for his reading level, at first said that, of course, he knew how to take notes. When pressed for specifics, he blurted out, "What is notetaking anyway? Don't I just copy what the book says?" The resulting notes would undoubtedly contain unimportant as well as important information mixed together in a verbatim transcription of the textbook.

Summary

By teaching study skills teachers are giving students the means to continue learning throughout their lives after their formal schooling has been completed. The goals of instruction in study skills are twofold: (1) The students will learn the skills that will help them better understand the content areas being studied; and (2) they will develop a positive attitude toward applying those skills. The first goal is obviously important to content area teachers. The second goal is equally important in teaching students to use library resources and read graphic materials *independently* instead of relying on others or ignoring them. The essence of study skills is independent learning, the goal of all education.

Chapter Activities: Using What You've Read

Learn to Do It!

1. Familiarize yourself with SQ3R (again?) by using the technique to enhance comprehension of Chapter 16.
2. For a chapter/unit of your text, develop a study skills exercise. Use skills listed in parts II and V of Karlin's list on pp. 216–17.
3. "Depth of processing" is important in enabling efficient learning (p. 228). Develop a lesson to teach paraphrasing skills to students in your content area.

Do It!

Try out the exercise or lesson you just constructed on one or more classes. How well did it work?

References

ANDERSON, T. H., and B. B. ARMBRUSTER, "Reader and Text—Studying Strategies." In W. Otto and S. White (eds.), *Reading Expository Material.* New York: Academic Press, 1982.

ASKOV, E. N., and K. KAMM, "Map Skills in the Elementary School," *Elementary School Journal*, 75, no. 2 (November 1974), 112–21.

————, *Study Skills in the Content Areas.* Boston: Allyn and Bacon, 1982.

ASKOV, E. N., K. KAMM, and R. KLUMB, "Study Skill Mastery Among Elementary School Teachers," *The Reading Teacher*, 30, no. 5 (February 1977), 485–88.

ASKOV, E. N. and others, "Study Skills Mastery: Comparisons between Teachers and Students on Selected Skills," *Perspectives in Reading Research and Instruction, Twenty-Ninth Yearbook of the National Reading Conference* (Michael L. Kamil, ed.). Washington, D.C.: The National Reading Conference, 1980, pp. 207–12.

CHESTER, R. D., E. N. ASKOV, and W. OTTO, *The Wisconsin Design for Reading Skill Development; Teacher's Planning Guide: Study Skills.* Minneapolis: National Computer Systems, 1973

KAMM, K., S. WHITE, and B. MORRISON, "A Report of Procedures Used in the Implementation of an Objective-Based Reading Program in 15 Schools." Working Paper 246. Madison, Wis.: The Wisconsin Research and Development Center for Cognitive Learning, 1977.

KARLIN, R., *Teaching Reading in High School*, (2nd ed.) New York: Bobbs-Merrill, 1972.

ROBINSON, F. P., *Effective Study* (revised ed.) New York: Harper & Row, 1961.

SPACHE, G., *Toward Better Reading.* Champaign, Ill.: Garrard, 1963.

PART V
SELECTING MATERIALS
FOR THE CONTENT CLASSROOM

OVERVIEW

Selecting materials is an important responsibility for content teachers. Selection includes identifying and evaluating textbooks for adoption by the department, school, or district. Selection also includes finding and evaluating supplementary and alternative materials for use in the classroom. Selection is Step 5 on the Decision Model, completed only after the students are known, the objectives and grouping patterns identified, and the teacher strategies and student activities identified. This part of the book looks at the different levels of selection which a teacher goes through. First, the teacher seeks out materials at the time the unit is planned, when the general type and level of student is known but before the specific students have arrived. Second, the teacher chooses from the available materials as s/he is teaching the unit, to provide appropriate learning materials for the actual students in his or her classes.

A selection procedure is suggested in Chapter 17 which can become a standard procedure for evaluating all the materials content teachers use. Developing a file of materials evaluations provides teachers with evidence that they have reviewed many materials and made professional judgments about their appropriateness. Such a wide choice of materials makes specific selection easier for particular students.

An important consideration in selecting reading materials is their reading level, or readability, discussed in Chapter 16. The overall goal of content teachers is matching students' reading level to appropriate reading materials. That is, reading materials they can read. Consider the possibility of having students similar to Betsy, David, and Pam in a single class. How can a teacher provide reading on the right topic for independent, instructional, and frustration level readers in the same class? Assessing texts and other reading materials for their difficulty level is a useful tool for content teachers.

A third component in materials selection, discussed in Chapter 18, is the use of media other than the written word in content classes. Finding and evaluating media is an additional task for content teachers. Films, cassettes, slides, lab materials, hands-on and simulation materials; all of these have potential value as teaching aids. Finding these materials and integrating them into the unit plan and teaching procedures requires different resources from reading the text.

By the end of Part V, you'll be ready to develop a list of materials useful in your own unit and evaluate each of them.

Chapter 16
Readability and
How to Use It

Preview

Assessing the difficulty level of reading materials is a problem for content teachers. How can teachers measure the reading level of a text? How reliable are publishers' estimates? What factors determine the difficulty of a text? This chapter suggests the most common ways of assessing readability levels and identifies the problems that remain in using these procedures. The goal of the chapter is developing teachers' professional judgment in assessing the reading difficulty of texts in their content areas.

What Is Readability?

Readability is a much-discussed problem in content area reading. Most teachers have experienced the problem of student readers for whom the text is too hard, with the result that these readers do not succeed in reading the material. Recently, there has been discussion of the other side of the problem: the gifted or independent reader who will not read the material because it is too simple or simplistic. A continuing problem (discussed in Chapter 6) is the reader who can read but won't, no matter what kind or level his/her reading skills. When we talk about readability, we are dealing with selecting reading materials for students, Step 5 on the Decision Model.

Broadly stated, readability is concerned with matching reader and text. A more complete definition is this one given by Dale and Chall (1948):

> In the broadest sense, readability is the sum total (including interactions) of all those elements within a given piece of printed material that affects the success which a group of readers have with it. The success is the extent to which they understand it, read it at optimum speed and find it interesting.

This definition suggests that the matching process is fairly complex and should be applied individually to each piece of reading. The four major components of readability are:

1. Linguistic factors in the text.
2. The reader's background information on the subject.
3. The reader's interest in the subject.
4. The aids to reading found in the text.

Linguistic factors are most commonly measured by readability formulas, which we will discuss later.

The reader's background knowledge and interest should be known to the teacher through the diagnosis carried out in Steps 1 and 2 of the Decision Model. Generally speaking, the more knowledge the student already has about the topic *and* the higher his/her interest is, the easier the material will be to comprehend. For most students, generating interest (or motivation) is important in the teacher's planning. So, too, is it important to *plan* to tie together material from previous learning to the material about to be read and learned. This principle is at the heart of advance organizers and pre-reading activities. The conclusion to be drawn is that teachers can overcome or compensate for problems with background and interest by careful diagnosis and planning for instruction.

More and more, careful text selection can help in the solution to readability problems related to component 4. Texts can be found which provide aids to reading for the students using them. Chapter 17 goes into this in greater detail. In general, these reading aids include: definitions of terms in context or set off in the text, *good* comprehension questions, the use of sideheads and other sectioning within chapters, effective use of pictures and graphics, and other techniques to make the reading easier to comprehend.

Linguistic Factors in Readability

When the word "readability" occurs in most discussions, however, the definition is limited to linguistic factors. All the widely used formulas for estimating readability levels focus on this component. Reiter (1973) has identified the following linguistic factors in readability:

1. Vocabulary—how long are the words? How familiar are they to the reader? The longer or less familiar the words, the harder the reading.
2. Sentence Structure—the longer and more syntactically complex the sentences, the harder they are to read.
3. Relationships—connections between words, sentences or parts of sentences; these usually mean relations between concepts or ideas. The more relationships required, the harder the reading.
4. Levels of Abstraction—content reading becomes more abstract, less concrete. The reader must connect concrete and abstract. The more abstract the reading, the harder it is to read.

These evaluations of what makes something harder to read should remind you of the word attack principles given in Chapter 12 and the discussion of cognitive and comprehension levels and concept load. English teachers may call this "style." Everyone knows a writer whose prose is more complex and difficult to understand, or another writer who assumes the reader has a great deal of background and therefore doesn't provide explanations or connections.

One way of describing these cognitive or concept or background factors is by their *density*. Speaking now about how these factors occur in words, density refers to the number of words or phrases in a passage which relate to the topic under discussion. That is, words or phrases which may be unfamiliar to the reader. (Remember that, frequently, knowing the terms is the same as understanding the concept or topic, because the terms are labels.) Here is a dense passage:

> How a *Transformer* Works. In our explanation of *electromagnetism* it was pointed out that a *coil* of *wire carrying* a *current* has a *magnetic field set up* about it. When another *coil* of *wire* is brought close to it, the *magnetic field* is *cut* and a *current* is caused *to flow* in the *second coil*. We say that a *current* is *induced* in the *second coil*. There must be an actual *cutting* of the *lines of force*. Remember that *alternating current* changes direction frequently. Because it does, the *coil* does not have to *move through* the *magnetic field*. The *ebbing* and *flowing* of the *current* takes care of the *cutting* and causes the *field* to *build up* and then *collapse*. This provides the necessary *cutting* of the *field* by the *wire*.*

The words and phrases in italics are all part of the terminology necessary to understand basic electronic technology. However, the density of this passage is roughly one content term in each three words.

Now check out the following word problem from a seventh-grade math book:

> A *1.3m* stick *casts* a *shadow 5.4m long. How high* is a *goalpost* which at the same time *casts* a *shadow 27m long?*†

This passage not only contains content terms, it also uses symbols instead of words for some of them. Further, it assumes knowledge of "shadow casting" in addition to mathematics.

Word problems in mathematics are often dense. So is poetry. These two types of writing cause students difficulty because of their density. In the math problem, almost every word is necessary to solve the problem. The words are either quantities or concepts or processes. In poetry, the density reflects multiple layers of meaning, so that the reader must consider several different meanings for the same set of words.

Abstraction levels may be involved in dense writing. Consider this selection from a social studies text on the federal government:

> DIVISION OF POWERS. The Constitution outlines a federal division of powers. Certain powers are *delegated*, or assigned, to the national government. Other powers are *reserved*, or kept, by the state governments. And some powers are *concurrent* or shared; that is, the powers are exercised by both the national and the state governments. Finally,

---

*D. W. Olson, *Industrial Arts for the General Shop* (Englewood Cliffs, N.J.: Prentice-Hall, Inc., 1973), p. 199.

†From Haber-Schaim, Skvarcius, and Hatch, *Mathematics 1* (Englewood Cliffs, N.J.: Prentice-Hall, Inc., 1980), p. 303.

certain powers are *denied* to the national government and certain powers are denied to state governments.*

This paragraph is full of terms related to the topic. In contrast to the industrial arts text quoted earlier, this passage does not contain concrete references. It discusses *powers*, their delegation and reservation, all remaining on an abstract level. A student reading this passage can experience great difficulty making connections between this material and anything s/he already knows.

By and large, density is not quantifiable. Teachers can assess the relationships, abstraction and syntactic complexity levels involved in a piece of reading, but so far, no well-established process for developing grade levels or scores has been developed.

Syntactic complexity is currently receiving more attention. At least two formulas for measuring syntactic complexity or density have been published (Botel and Granowsky 1972; Golub 1975). However, neither has yet been put to wide use in assessing textbooks. Both formulas are based on generative and transformational grammar and demand that the person assessing the text have a reasonably thorough understanding of that grammar. The three syntactic features which occur in more traditional readability formulas are also important in the complexity formulas: length of sentences, frequency of subordinate (or dependent) clauses and frequency of prepositional phrases.

Readability Formulas in Wide Use

The linguistic factors most commonly used in readability formulas are those which seem to be the easiest to count: word length, sentence length, word familiarity, and sentence complexity (defined as number of subordinate clauses and/or prepositional phrases).

The Dale-Chall formula (1948) probably has the greatest reputation for validity today. This formula works with two variables: average sentence length and word familiarity. Familiarity is judged by matching the words in the passage with the Dale list of 3,000 familiar words. While this formula is widely used, it has one great problem for content reading: every word *not* on the Dale list increases the reading difficulty, as measured by this formula. In many content texts, a high percentage of the words will not appear on the Dale list; hence the reading level score is high. However, if students have been adequately prepared, some of these words are not *really* unfamiliar. Hence, the reading level may be artificially inflated. The same problem can occur with any formula using word familiarity as a factor, based on a general word list.

One attempt to counter this is the work of Kane, Byrne, and Hater (1974). Their formula for assessing the difficulty of mathematics books uses a word list of mathematics terms familiar to students at the seventh-grade level, the eighth-grade level, and so on. Their lists show that students' vocabularies tend to grow, to accrue more terms related to the subject, as they study those areas. (That's also what we said in Chapter 12.) Thus, to use word familiarity as a factor, a teacher may need to give his/her own pretest of key terms which students should know on entering the course. Generally, the more specific the word list is—to subject area (math) and to specific course (Algebra I)—the more useful it is to you as a teacher.

*J. Gillespie, and S. Lazarus, *American Government, Comparing Political Experiences* (Englewood Cliffs, N.J.: Prentice-Hall, Inc., 1979, p. 194).

A second widely used readability formula, the *Fry Graph for Estimating Readability* (1968, 1977), uses only sentence length (in words) and word length (in syllables) to measure reading difficulty. Figure 16–1 shows the Graph and instructions for using it. This formula may be the most widely used formula today, because it avoids the "familiarity" pitfall and doesn't get into syntactic issues. It is based on sampling principles, as the others are, so that a random selection of three 100-word samples is used for estimating a book. Fry recommends that if the results within the three samples differ markedly, more samples should be used. Many books will be shown to have uneven readability because of uneven writing, difference in content discussed, or multiple writers. It is not safe to assume that reading level in a book goes from easier to hard, or that the level is fairly constant. Recent research (Fitzgerald 1980) suggests that the three-sample recommendation may be unreliable, although previous research (Vaughan 1976) shows high correlations between the Fry, Dale-Chall, and SMOG scales. Even if the Fry estimate is reliable, its validity is open to question because it deals with only two variables affecting readability (Marshall 1979). However, the Fry graph seems to be as reliable and valid as other formulas, and it is undeniably easy to use. Hence its wide use by publishers, reading specialists, and teachers.

A third formula, the *Raygor Readability Estimate* (1979), is growing in popularity. It is similar to the Fry in its strengths and weaknesses. It uses the same sampling procedure and the same two variables. However, it defines word length not in number of syllables, but in number of letters. Words with six or more letters are counted as hard words and figured into the formula (Baldwin and Kaufman 1979). Figure 16–2 shows this graph and its instructions.

In both these formulas, which are based on computer analysis of large amounts of text, the graph identifying reading levels shows large "gray areas" where the analysis is considered invalid. The logic of these areas is clear—to fall in them a passage either has very long sentences and very short words or the reverse. The analysis on which the graphs are based suggests that published writers (that is, *anything* published) will not write that way. Hence, an analysis which shows such a set of data either has found a highly unusual writer or has been done incorrectly.

Another point to make about these formulas is that they are designed to be used with prose, rather than poetry or other formats. As the text format moves away from straight prose, the formulas may not accurately reflect reading difficulty (Smith 1969; Brown 1965). Math, science, industrial arts, and music texts are most likely to face this problem, but many others will find it occasionally. Kane, Byrne, and Hater (1974), working with readability of math texts, identified some of the reasons why: (1) students who were required to move from word to symbol and back (since $d = rt$, the distance = 20 mph × 4 hours) had more trouble reading; (2) when the reading did not move smoothly from left to right, as you are doing now, but instead moved up, down, and sideways, readers had more trouble reading $\left(\overrightarrow{r} = \frac{d}{t} \downarrow \right)$; (3) formulas and other symbols generally add to the density of the writing. That is, it takes many more words and more space to say something in words than is necessary when symbols are used:

$$X_1 = 4 \pm \sqrt{y - 6}$$

X sub one equals four plus or minus the square root of y minus six.

GRAPH FOR ESTIMATING READABILITY—EXTENDED

by Edward Fry, Rutgers University Reading Center, New Brunswick, N.J.

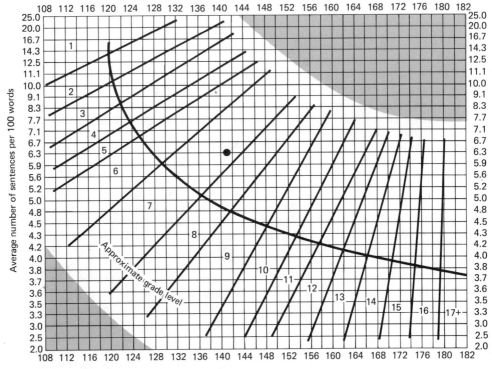

Average number of syllables per 100 words

Randomly select 3 one-hundred-word passages from a book or an article. Plot average number of syllables and average number of sentences per 100 words on graph to determine the grade level of the material. Choose more passages per book if great variability is observed and conclude that the book has uneven readability. Few books will fall into gray area, but when they do, grade level scores are invalid.

Count proper nouns, numerals and initializations as words. Count a syllable for each symbol. For example, "1945" is one word and 4 syllables and "IRA" is 1 word and 3 syllables.

EXAMPLE:	SYLLABLES	SENTENCES
1st Hundred Words	124	6.6
2nd Hundred Words	141	5.5
3rd Hundred Words	158	6.8
AVERAGE	141	6.3

READABILITY 7th GRADE (see dot plotted on graph)

EXPANDED DIRECTIONS FOR WORKING READABILITY GRAPH

1. Randomly select three (3) sample passages and count out exactly 100 words beginning with the beginning of a sentence. Do not count proper nouns, initializations, and numerals.

2. Count the number of sentences in the hundred words estimating length of the fraction of the last sentence to the nearest 1/10th.

3. Count the total number of syllables in the 100-word passage. If you don't have a hand counter available, an easy way is to simply put a mark above every syllable over one in each word, then when you get to the end of the passage, count the number of marks and add 100. Small calculators can also be used as counters by pushing numeral "1", then push the "+" sign for each word or syllable when counting.

4. Enter graph with average sentence length and average number of syllables; plot dot where the two lines intersect. Area where dot is plotted will give you approximate grade level.

5. If a great deal of variability is found in syllable count or sentence count, putting more samples into the average is desirable.

6. A word is defined as a group of symbols with a space on either side; thus, "Joe," "IRA," "1945," and "&" are each one word.

7. A syllable is defined as a phonetic syllable. Generally, there are as many syllables as vowel sounds. For example, "stopped" is one syllable and "wanted" is two syllables. When counting syllables for numerals and initializations, count one syllable for each symbol. For example, "1945" is 4 syllables and "IRA" is three syllables and "&" is 1 syllable.

NOTE: This "extended graph" does not outmode or render the earlier (1968) version inoperative or inaccurate; it is an extension.

FIGURE 16–2 The Raygor Readability Estimate. Alton L. Raygor—University of Minnesota

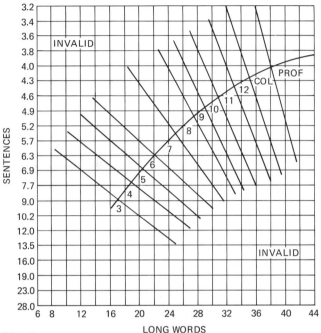

Directions:

Count out three 100-word passages at the beginning, middle, and end of a selection or book. Count proper nouns, but not numerals.

1. Count sentences in each passage, estimating to nearest tenth.
2. Count words with six or more letters.
3. Average the sentence length and word length over the three samples and plot the average on the graph.

Example:

		Sentences	6 + Words
Note mark on graph.	A	6.0	15
Grade level is about 5.	B	6.8	19
	C	6.4	17
	Total	19.2	51
	Average	6.4	17

While these problems are not neatly quantifiable, they can be assessed generally by the teacher. The more symbols and formulas given in a text, the less likely that a standard readability rating (for example, using the Fry graph) will be an accurate estimate of reading difficulty.

What can we conclude about the use of readability formulas on content materials? First, we always want to know which formula was used and what variables were assessed. Second, we always consider the teacher's own evaluation of the materials and his/her knowledge of student background and interest more important than readability estimates. Third, used judiciously and with knowledge of their strengths and weaknesses, readability estimates can be useful in providing a wide range of materials for students to use.

Summary

Four factors are of importance in assessing reading difficulty in content materials: linguistic factors, the reader's background information, the reader's interest, and the aids to reading found in the text. Teachers should assess all four factors in determining the readability of a text.

Readability formulas are widely used to estimate reading level, but they deal primarily with linguistic factors only. The Fry and Raygor Readability Estimates are suggested as reasonably valid, reliable, and easy to use. Developing teachers' professional judgment in assessing the difficulty level of reading materials is the goal of this chapter.

Chapter Activities: Using What You've Read

Learn to Do It!

Choose one of your texts and assess its readability using both the Fry and Raygor formulas. You may want to check whether you are handling the graphs accurately. Comment on the density of cognitive factors and the passage's syntactic complexity. Remember to use three 100-word passages. Compare your results with the grade level the publisher claimed the book was written for.

References

BALDWIN, R. S., and R. K. KAUFMAN, "A Concurrent Validity Study of The Raygor Readability Estimate," *Journal of Reading,* 23, no. 2 (November 1979), 148–53.

BOTEL, M., and A. GRANOWSKY, "A Formula for Measuring Syntactic Complexity: A Directional Effort," *Elementary English*, April 1972, 513–16.

BROWN, W. R., "Science Textbook Selection and the Dale-Chall Formula," *School Science and Mathematics,* 65 (February 1965), 164–67.

DALE, E., and J. CHALL, "A Formula for Predicting Readability," *Educational Research Bulletin,* 27, nos. 1 and 2 (January-February 1948), 11–20, 37–54.

FITZGERALD, G. G., "Reliability of the Fry Sampling Procedure," *Reading Research Quarterly*, 15, no. 4 (1980), 489–503.

FRY, E., "A Readability Formula That Saves Time," *Journal of Reading*, 11, no. 7 (1968), 514–15.

———, "Fry's Readability Graph: Clarifications, Validity and Extension to Level 17," *Journal of Reading*, 21, no. 3 (1977), 242–43.

GOLUB, L. S., "Syntactic Density Score," *Measures for Research and Evaluation in the English Language Arts,* ed. W. T. Fagan, C. R. Cooper, and J. M. Jensen. Urbana, Ill.: National Council of Teachers of English, 1975.

KANE, R., M. A. BYRNE, and M. A. HATER, *Helping Children Read Mathematics.* New York: American Book Co., 1974.

LAMB, P., "The Measurement of Readability: Review of Literature." Paper presented at the Annual Conference, American Educational Research Association, 1973.

McLAUGHLIN, G. H., "SMOG Grading: A New Readability Formula," *Journal of Reading,* 12:8 (May 1969), 639–46.

MARSHALL, N., "Research: Readability and Comprehensibility," *Journal of Reading,* 22:6 March 1979, 542–44.

MAXWELL, M., "Readability: Have We Gone Too Far?" *Journal of Reading,* 21:6, March, 1978, 525–30.

NELSON, J., "Readability: Some Cautions for the Content Teacher," *Journal of Reading,* 21:7 (April 1978), 620–25.

RAYGOR, A. L., "The Raygor Readability Estimate: A Quick and Easy Way to Determine Difficulty," *Reading: Theory, Research and Practice.* In 26th Yearbook of the National Reading Conference, ed. P. D. Pearson. Clemson, S.C.: National Reading Conference, Inc., 1977, 259–63.

REITER, I., *The Reading Line.* New York: Cambridge Book Co., 1973.

SMITH, F., "Readability of Junior High School Mathematics Textbooks," *Mathematics Teacher,* 62 (April 1969), 289–91.

STENDAL, T. C., "How to Use Readability Formulas More Effectively," *Social Education,* 45:3 (March 1981), 183–86.

VAUGHAN, J. L., JR., "Interpreting Readability Assessments," *Journal of Reading,* 19:8 (May 1976), 635–39.

Chapter 17
The Selection of Texts and Alternative Reading Materials

Preview

This chapter concerns Step 5 on the Decision Model, who selects the materials you use in teaching and how these materials should be selected. *Five principles* useful as a base for selecting materials will be discussed. Following that, we present a procedure for evaluating materials that you can use for a course, unit, or lesson.

THE SELECTION PROCESS

Materials in our discussion is a generic term covering all the concrete things a teacher may use to help students learn what they need to learn. *Materials* include textbooks, of course, but they also include paperback books, magazines and newspapers, reference books, library sources, and any and all reading sources available in the world at large. In addition, materials include media of all kinds, not just print media. This list includes films, filmstrips, slides, audio- and videotapes, maps, globes, transparencies and an ever-increasing variety of media. Other kinds of materials are the hands-on materials used in many classes, from science lab equipment to woodshop equipment to the kitchen equipment in cooking class. Some classes use a great amount of hands-on equipment. Others use very little. The choice of materials from all these types depends largely on the students' needs and on the content objectives to be learned.

Who selects materials? In the final analysis, each teacher selects the materials appropriate for particular students in a particular lesson. This is the message of the Decision Model. Teachers make their professional decision to use specific materials after they know what the students' needs are (Step 1) and what their objectives for teaching are (Step 2). They have *also* decided how they will present the learning situation in groups to students (Step 3) and what instructional strategy and management processes will be followed (Step 4). Before this chapter is finished, we will talk specifically about materials selection for specific units and lessons.

Before we can talk about units, however, we need to go back to a more basic issue in materials selection—how are materials selected in advance to ensure that teachers have a wide variety to choose from when they're planning a unit or lesson. In many places, this process begins with *textbook adoption.*

Textbook adoption generally means a school or school district choosing a text for use in particular classes. For example, the school or district needs to adopt an Algebra I text, a basic biology text, or an American literature text. Adopting a text usually means that the district, through some selection process, selects a text and the school board approves that selection. Then enough texts are purchased so that each student in that class will have one to use. Think how many books that can be—from 20 copies of an advanced French or calculus text in a small high school to thousands of copies of a book every seventh grader must use in social studies or English, for example.

Textbook adoption policies differ widely across the United States. Some states, like Texas, adopt a few texts statewide for a particular course. In other states, districts may choose texts widely, but must provide the state with a rationale for the use of any text. Ultimately, the selection of texts is generally accepted to be a function of the state as it regulates education within its boundaries (English 1980). Wherever teachers teach, it is important to know what the state says about materials for use in their classrooms.

In many districts, textbook adoption is an ongoing process, as we believe it should be. Even though the legal requirements may be to adopt texts officially every three or five years, these districts encourage teachers to be continually aware of new materials and to plan for changes in texts, if these changes would support the teaching and learning process more effectively. In such districts, a committee of teachers and administrators frequently considers texts which might be appropriate for a given course. From that committee, the selection recommendation goes through a department head or coordinator, the building principal, the curriculum director or assistant superintendent to the superintendent. When the superintendent approves, the school board must usually consider the recommendation and officially adopt the text. School board adoption may be pro forma or it may be fraught with controversy. Community groups are becoming more and more involved in responding to professional text selections. Indeed, the community's concerns about issues such as language, religious beliefs, and politics, as well as differing views of the purposes of education, play a large role here. Your analysis of the community, as suggested in Chapter 5, will help to anticipate issues which may affect the selection of textbooks and other materials. All teachers, however, must be concerned with textbook adoptions in their school and district. The first step is to find out what that process is.

We are dealing here, then, with a long-term process, the adoption of particular texts for use in particular courses. The adoption is for an extended period, three to five years. The adoption is a formal and legal matter, a part of the state's legal concern for schools and a matter for the School Board to act upon. We are also dealing here with the immediate, short-term process of a teacher selecting the reading and other materials necessary for a group of students to master an objective. An inescapable conclusion is that materials selection is a large and important process, with implications for every teacher. Despite its placement on the Decision Model, aspects of materials selection go on at many levels and in many ways.

PRINCIPLES OF SELECTION

Certain principles underlie materials selection. These principles apply to school and district-wide adoption processes as well as the teacher's decision on materials to use today.

1. If students should be active in their learning, a fundamental principle of learning theory, then *materials should encourage active learning* by the students who use them. Active learning, as opposed to passive learning, means that the student's mind is engaged in figuring out what is happening, in answering questions, in providing alternatives to situations. Texts and other materials which lend themselves to higher level learning (on Bloom's taxonomy) or to higher comprehension levels (on Barrett's taxonomy) will encourage more active learning. Texts that encourage rote memorization of names, dates, and formulas will not encourage this kind of active learning. Active learning does *not* mean, necessarily, that a student must be physically active. Books can engage the mind most actively. However, younger students (middle and junior high school) and some types of exceptional students will respond better to concrete materials and to physical activity. All this means, for example, that doing a science lab experiment is better than merely reading about it, but students must read about it first. Making a cake is better than reading about it, but students must read the recipe to do it. Reading a novel is sometimes better than, or perhaps different from, seeing the movie. Active learning will often include reading. Such reading may well be coupled with activity. Hence, the best reading material will make the connection with the activity.

2. Teachers should select materials to *suit the needs of individual students*. If the Decision Model is followed, teachers will match appropriate materials to groups of students, based on objectives to be met. Materials within a unit or lesson need to take into account specific types of students. Gifted students and/or independent level readers need to have enrichment reading and materials for further learning—extra lab experiences, challenging math problems, and the like. Frustration level readers need alternative materials which match their reading level. Reading which has a low reading level but high interest level is appropriate for them. Students with particular exceptionalities may require specific readings and materials. Blind and partially sighted students may need to use braille materials or audiotapes of required readings. Bilingual students need materials based on their level of English proficiency. All these groups of learners will be described more completely, including their needs for materials, in Part VI.

An example of a unit in eighth-grade social studies underlies the need for multiple reading levels. Even without diagnostic information, the average eighth-grade class, grouped heterogeneously, can be expected to contain students reading at fourth- to twelfth-grade levels. This range is based upon a simple formula:

$$\text{Reading Range} \approx \text{grade level} \pm \frac{\text{grade level} + 1}{2}$$

(Estes & Vaughan, 1978)

An 8th grade social studies teacher,* knowing this wide range was possible, collected American history books for three different reading levels.

> *The American Nation*
>
> *Liberty and Union*
>
> *The Free and the Brave*

When he gathered diagnostic data on students, he discovered that his students had standardized test reading scores *(California Test of Basic Skills)* of nearly non-reader to adult (percentile scores of 10–99). He therefore developed a basic reading system of three groups:

Group	Reading Level	Basic Text
I	Grade Level 0–5	*The American Nation*
II	Grade Level 6–8	*Liberty and Union*
III	Grade Level 9 & up	*The Free and the Brave*

In addition, he provided study guides with each reading assignment and learning centers incorporating slides, filmstrips and additional reading activities.

3. The third principle is that the materials should *reflect student interests* whenever possible. This principle speaks to the areas of interest which students tend to go through as they pass from childhood through adolescence to adulthood. Adolescence, especially, is a time of exploration. The stages and areas of interest (from Carlsen) given in Chapter 6 are useful here. As teachers plan courses and units, they can select supplemental enrichment reading geared to the interests of the age group they are teaching and the specific interests of their students, identified on interest questionnaires.

Don Neely provided for interest areas in his eighth-grade American history class. He used *Books for You*, mentioned in Chapter 6, to identify fiction and non-fiction about American history which might suit his students. He was especially aware of adolescents' interests in biography, autobiography and historical fiction. He was also careful to include books by and about minority groups in the period being studied: blacks, Indians, immigrants of various origins. Finally, he made sure each list included some easy reading and some advanced reading, so students of all levels would find appropriate reading materials. As an added help to students, he asked not only the school library, but also the public library and the local bookstore, to cooperate in making the books on his list available to students.

Interest-oriented materials are much more likely to attract and hold student attention. Materials that are career-oriented or pre-vocational can be used in this way, as can materials designed to encourage continued leisure use of topics. Students interested in biological careers will enjoy reading about the DNA researchers or contemporary biologists as well as about Leeuwenhoek or, for chemistry enthusiasts, Madame Curie and Joseph Priestley. The argument over whether the world is round

---

*Donald Neely, Hollidaysburg, Pa, Area School District

or flat comes to life in considering Columbus and other explorers. The risk-taking involved in exploration can be connected to contemporary exploration undersea and in space. The potential for vocational and avocational applications of content objectives should be explored as a highly interest-oriented activity. Reading about these possibilities is feasible for both students and teachers. Such reading is optional, for those students who are interested. Teachers can handle the logistics of the readings because these are preplanned, independent activities.

4. The fourth principle of materials selection is that the materials *suit the curriculum in the school or district and are sensitive to the needs and attitudes of the community*. This principle is discussed in Chapter 5. Its application to materials selection means that the teacher can explain his/her rationale for selecting materials, as well as content, in a way that the community will accept. No teacher or school can please all of its constituents. However, the teacher should feel confident that s/he has the support of the community.

One application of this principle is that all minorities, including women, should be included in the reading and visual materials used in a course, balanced out over time. Texts should be chosen to reflect the different ethnic groups in American society, as well as the particular state and community in which we teach. The way in which we involve minorities depends on the makeup of the community. Dealing with literature by and about blacks is appropriate in any English classroom. However, the choice of literature and the way it is presented may differ depending on whether blacks are members of the community or not. If students have no firsthand experience with black people, they will read about black experiences as an exploration of such questions as how similar or different their lives are or how similar their interests and concerns are. Students in classes including both black and white students, reading the same selection, can compare firsthand their responses to the reading.

5. The fifth principle in materials selection is that *specific materials are selected in the appropriate order* as steps on the Decision Model. The adopted textbook is *not* the curriculum. Teachers choose the materials that are necessary to teach the students they have and the objectives they have set. On a practical basis, this often means supplementing the adopted textbook in several ways. First, teachers can use *alternative texts*, as Don Neely did. Alternative texts may differ in reading level, approach or content. Neely chose three texts, his adopted text and two alternative texts, so that he could meet his students' needs in reading level. The content of the three texts is essentially the same.

Second, the teacher can supplement, or add to, the adopted text using media of all kinds. Third, s/he can supplement the text with other reading materials (for example, magazines and newspapers, or reference materials) for information or enrichment. Fourth, s/he can supplement the text with any number of hands-on or concrete materials and experiences (labs, field trips, and the like). All of these decisions on specific materials for the lesson or unit are made *only* after the decisions required in Steps 1 through 4 on the Decision Model have been made.

These basic principles for materials selection are a synthesis of issues raised throughout this book. The principles themselves have been discussed earlier and are here applied to the process of selecting materials. Now we can look at a basic procedure for evaluation of materials and a procedure for collecting information on a wide variety of texts and alternative and supplemental materials.

EVALUATION OF TEXTS AND PRINT MATERIALS

Selecting and Adopting in Advance

When the principles given here are followed, print materials evaluation is a procedure that all teachers do. The evaluation procedure may involve a single teacher or an entire department or grade level. We recommend a committee to evaluate specific texts. Each teacher will have input, but a representative committee can undertake the formal evaluation and comparison of the materials available for adoption. Kuykendall (1980) synthesizes the evaluation procedure into five basic questions.

1. Does the material do what it says it does?
2. Is the material supported by a solid rationale?
3. Is the content of the material sound and well-balanced?
4. Is the material designed for learning as well as for teaching?
5. Is the material geared to the abilities and interests of the students intended to use it?

A committee dealing with textbook adoption, in advance of the time it will be used, could do well to answer these five questions on each potential text and then compare the answers.

However, these general questions, while important, do not cover all the concerns generally expressed by the various levels of professionals who deal with text adoptions. Administrators need to know about items like durability and cost. A thorough analysis for presentation to the school board would need to include this information.

A second concern is for quantification of the results. Comparison between texts is often easier if the analysis can be given a numerical value. The text analysis procedure which follows provides one way to make such a comparison. Each characteristic is given a rating, using a Likert-type scale, from 0 to 6. The sum of these ratings provides a total score for the text. A committee can rate several texts, develop an average score for each one and report to the faculty their joint evaluation by giving a set of comparison scores.

A third consideration is that a single text frequently cannot be evaluated or adopted in isolation. Math, grammar, reading, and foreign language texts are usually adopted by series. The series may range from two years (such as Algebra I and Algebra II) to four years (such as grammar books, grades 9 to 12) to the full reading series K through 8. When teachers are evaluating texts which are part of a larger program, they must look at evaluations of all books in the series. A numerical rating scale makes these comparisons more useful.

A final consideration is that many texts and series now published are accompanied by audio-visual materials, a testing program, workbooks, and other materials in addition to the basic text. These materials are important in evaluating the full impact of the text or series. When the committee compares such programs, it must have some way of looking at the full range of materials available.

The Program-Series-Text Analysis Outline given here is one way to meet the multiple demands for text evaluation and adoption.

PROGRAM-SERIES-TEXT ANALYSIS OUTLINE

Name of analyst _____

Name of program or text to be analyzed _____

Author(s) of program or text to be analyzed _____

Publisher of program or text to be analyzed _____

Date of publication _____ Edition _____

Grade level(s) for which the program or text is primarily intended _____
** Under *Explanation*, give examples or short comments in response to the item.

Product Characteristics

1. What does the author consider the most appropriate length of time in weeks or years for use of the whole set of materials?

   _____ Weeks   _____ Years

   Check which of the following items are covered in this analysis. If any listed in a. through f. are unavailable, list as such and why they are unavailable.

	Present Cost		*Present Cost*
a. Student text	_____	e. Workbook	_____
b. Teacher's guide	_____	f. Rationale	_____
c. Audio-visual materials	_____	g. Other (explain)	_____
d. Testing program	_____		

2. Check which of the following are included in the program or text:

a. Complete table of contents	_____	d. Useful references of additional reading	_____
b. Full index	_____	e. Appropriate print size	_____
c. Complete glossary	_____	f. Emphasis in bold print, color, etc.	_____

Content

3. What is your general overall judgment of the physical and technical (not substantive) durability of *all* materials in the program or text?

0	1	2	3	4	5	6
Inadequate			Adequate			More than adequate

Explanation:

4. To what extent are pictorial sources, maps, graphs, charts, tables, and other illustrative material integrated and utilized with textual narrative and questions?

0	1	2	3	4	5	6
Not at all			To a mod- erate extent			To a great extent

Explanation:

5. To what extent are key terms and concepts defined for the student in student materials?

0	1	2	3	4	5	6
Not at all			To a mod- erate extent			To a great extent

Explanation:

6. To what extent are adequate data readily available in the student materials to answer questions asked of students?

0	1	2	3	4	5	6
Not at all			To a mod- erate extent			To a great extent

Explanation:

7. Using questions asked of students, identify which levels of comprehension (using Barrett's *Taxonomy*) are required to answer. Give at least *one* example of each level available.

8. In general, how accurate do the factual data and interpretations of the data seem to be in all parts of the program?

0	1	2	3	4	5	6
Very unsound			Moder- ately sound			Very sound

Explanation:

9. To what extent is a multi-ethnic approach integrated in the student materials?

0	1	2	3	4	5	6
Not at all			To a mod- erate extent			To a great extent

Explanation:

10. List the ethnic groups included in the materials:

Explanation:

Is the multi-ethnic approach presented in the materials sensitive or suitable to the needs of ethnic groups within your school population? Answer "yes" or "no." ___

Explanation:

11. How is the role of women portrayed in the student materials?

Is that portrayal sensitive or suitable to the needs of females within your school population? Answer "yes" or "no." _____

Explanation:

12. Indicate the disciplines most prominent in the program. Mark them "1," "2," or "3" in order of prominence. If they cannot be distinguished, mark them all "1." If more than three disciplines are prominent, mark them "interdisciplinary."

Social Studies:				*English:*	
Anthropology	_____	Psychology	_____	Grammar	_____
Economics	_____	Sociology	_____	Composition	_____
Geography	_____	Social Psychology	_____	Literature	_____
History	_____	Other (explain)	_____	Other (explain)	_____
Political Science	_____				

Science:		*Mathematics:*			
Biology	_____	Algebra I	_____	Solid Geometry	_____
Chemistry	_____	Algebra II	_____	Calculus	_____
Physics	_____	General Math	_____	Computer Science	_____
Earth & Space Science	_____	Plane Geometry	_____	Other (explain)	_____
General Science	_____	Pre-algebra Math	_____	*Elementary:* Social studies	_____
Other (explain)	_____	Trigonometry	_____	Science	_____
				Math	_____
				Other (explain)	_____
				Grade	_____

Explanation:

The Cognitive Domain

13. The acquisition of knowledge which includes concept formation (the many meanings which can apply to one word such as "horse," "war," or "revolution") and the development of basic study skills (such as those listed in a. through l. in question 14) and critical or analytical thinking skills (such as those listed in m. through q. in question 14) are generally referred to as cognitive processes. In general, how clearly does the author state and define his cognitive objectives in behavioral terms (expected student performances) in the teacher's manual?

0	1	2	3	4	5	6
Not at all			Fairly clearly			Very clearly

Explanation:

14. To what extent do the student materials and suggestions in the teacher's guide include cognitive learning processes which focus development on the following?

   a. Observing or perceiving (If it occurs, list in which item(s) of the program or text it is suggested or asked of the students)

0	1	2	3	4	5	6
No emphasis			Moderate emphasis			Much emphasis

Explanation:

   b. Listening (list where)

0	1	2	3	4	5	6
No emphasis			Moderate emphasis			Much emphasis

Explanation:

   c. Discussing (list where)

0	1	2	3	4	5	6
No emphasis			Moderate emphasis			Much emphasis

Explanation:

   d. Defining and expanding the meanings of key terms or concepts (list where)

0	1	2	3	4	5	6
No emphasis			Moderate emphasis			Much emphasis

Explanation:

e. Reading (list where)

0	1	2	3	4	5	6
No emphasis			Moderate emphasis			Much emphasis

Explanation:

f. Writing (list where)

0	1	2	3	4	5	6
No emphasis			Moderate emphasis			Much emphasis

Explanation:

g. Contrasting and comparing for the purpose of noting similarities and differences (list where)

0	1	2	3	4	5	6
No emphasis			Moderate emphasis			Much emphasis

Explanation:

h. Locating, gathering and classifying information relative to a particular study in progress (list where)

0	1	2	3	4	5	6
No emphasis			Moderate emphasis			Much emphasis

Explanation:

i. Interpreting globes, maps, or other types of map projections (list where)

0	1	2	3	4	5	6
No emphasis			Moderate emphasis			Much emphasis

Explanation:

j. Making maps (list where)

0	1	2	3	4	5	6
No emphasis			Moderate emphasis			Much emphasis

Explanation:

k. Interpreting tables, graphs, or charts (list where)

0	1	2	3	4	5	6
No emphasis			Moderate emphasis			Much emphasis

Explanation:

l. Making tables, graphs, or charts (list where)

0	1	2	3	4	5	6
No emphasis			Moderate emphasis			Much emphasis

Explanation:

m. Recognizing a problem for further inquiry (list where)

0	1	2	3	4	5	6
No emphasis			Moderate emphasis			Much emphasis

Explanation:

n. Drawing inferences, making tentative conclusions, or stating hypotheses (list where)

0	1	2	3	4	5	6
No emphasis			Moderate emphasis			Much emphasis

Explanation:

o. Testing the validity of hypotheses (list where)

0	1	2	3	4	5	6
No emphasis			Moderate emphasis			Much emphasis

Explanation:

p. Forming generalizations (list where)

0	1	2	3	4	5	6
No emphasis			Moderate emphasis			Much emphasis

Explanation:

q. Synthesizing information from a variety of sources and experiences (list where)

0	1	2	3	4	5	6
No emphasis			Moderate emphasis			Much emphasis

Explanation:

15. In all the materials, then, what is the author's emphasis on memorization of data as opposed to critical or analytical thinking such as the steps noted in m. through q. in question 14?

0	1	2	3	4	5	6
Much memory work (recall)			Some of each			Much critical or analytical thinking

Explanation:

16. To what extent does the teacher's manual include specific teaching strategies and additional lessons within the cognitive domain for use of the materials with the following kinds of students?

a. Slow students

0	1	2	3	4	5	6
Not at all			To a moderate extent			To a great extent

Explanation:

b. Average students

0	1	2	3	4	5	6
Not at all			To a moderate extent			To a great extent

Explanation:

c. Gifted students

0	1	2	3	4	5	6
Not at all			To a moderate extent			To a great extent

Explanation:

The Affective Domain

17. Learning concerned with a closer look at one's attitudes, value clarification, empathizing, and any behavior which causes a student to be *willing* to perform as a responsible person both inside and outside the classroom (social participation) is part of the affective domain. In general, how clearly does the author state and define his affective objectives in behavioral terms (expected student performance) in the teacher's manual?

0	1	2	3	4	5	6
Not at all			Fairly clearly			Very clearly

Explanation:

18. To what extent do the student materials or suggestions in the teacher's guide encourage students to explore, clarify, and act:

a. On their own values?

0	1	2	3	4	5	6
Not at all			Moderate emphasis			Much emphasis

Explanation:

b. On values held by others?

0	1	2	3	4	5	6
Not at all			Moderate emphasis			Much emphasis

Explanation:

c. On the presentation of alternative and conflicting points of view?

0	1	2	3	4	5	6
Not at all			Moderate emphasis			Much emphasis

Explanation:

19. How are values and attitudes presented in the student materials by the author?

0	1	2	3	4	5	6
Imposed values by the author			Balanced			Free of imposed values by the author

Explanation:

20. To what extent does the teacher's manual include specific teaching strategies and additional lessons within the affective domain for use of the materials with the following kinds of students?

a. Slow students

0	1	2	3	4	5	6
Not at all			To a moderate extent			To a great extent

Explanation:

b. Average students

0	1	2	3	4	5	6
Not at all			To a moderate extent			To a great extent

Explanation:

c. Gifted students

0	1	2	3	4	5	6
Not at all			To a moderate extent			To a great extent

Explanation:

The Testing Program

21. To what extent does the testing program or other evaluation processes provided with the program test the students for factual recall?

0	1	2	3	4	5	6
Not at all			To a moderate extent			To a great extent

Explanation:

22. To what extent does the testing program test for basic skill development such as that listed in a. through l. in question 14?

0	1	2	3	4	5	6
Not at all			To a moderate extent			To a great extent

Explanation:

23. To what extent does the testing program test for critical or analytical thinking skill development such as that listed in m. through q. in question 14?

0	1	2	3	4	5	6
Not at all			To a moderate extent			To a great extent

Explanation:

24. To what extent does the testing program test for continued development of concept formation?

0	1	2	3	4	5	6
Not at all			To a moderate extent			To a great extent

Explanation:

25. To what extent does the testing program test for value clarification such as that noted in question 18?

0	1	2	3	4	5	6
Not at all			To a moderate extent			To a great extent

Explanation:

26. To what extent does the testing program take into account the learning abilities and capacity for learning of the slow students?

0	1	2	3	4	5	6
Not at all			To a moderate extent			To a great extent

Explanation:

27. To what extent does the testing program take into account the learning abilities and capacity for learning of the average student?

0	1	2	3	4	5	6
Not at all			To a moderate extent			To a great extent

Explanation:

28. To what extent does the testing program take into account the learning abilities and capacity for learning of the gifted student?

0	1	2	3	4	5	6
Not at all			To a moderate extent			To a great extent

Explanation:

The Author's Rationale

29. How much evidence is there that the development of the program or text was guided by a clear rationale? In essence, can the author's rationale be found explicitly in all materials of the program or text?

0	1	2	3	4	5	6
No evidence			Moderate amount			To a great extent

Explanation:

30. To what extent do you, the analyst, agree with the author's rationale?

0	1	2	3	4	5	6
Not at all			To a moderate extent			To a great extent

Explanation:

Summary

31. Suppose the following types of students were to be in the grade level for which this program or text is intended. Imagine, too, that these students asked: "What good's spending a year on this program or text gonna do me?" What do you think would be her or his answer?

    a. A slow learner or a student with reading problems.

0	1	2	3	4	5	6
It would be of little if any benefit to me.			It would be of some benefit.			It would greatly benefit my needs.

Explanation:

    b. An average student who reads at the grade level for which the program or text was intended.

0	1	2	3	4	5	6
It would **be of little if** any benefit to me.			It would be of some benefit.			It would greatly benefit my needs.

Explanation:

c. A gifted student who reads above the grade level for which the program or text is intended.

0	1	2	3	4	5	6
It would be of little if any benefit to me.			It would be of some benefit.			It would greatly benefit my needs.

Explanation:

32. Considering the grade level for which this program or text is primarily intended, how *relevant* do *you* think this program or text would be in meeting the needs of the following kinds of students in your school?

a. Slow students

0	1	2	3	4	5	6
Unsuitable			Suitable to a moderate extent			Very suitable

Explanation:

b. Average students

0	1	2	3	4	5	6
Unsuitable			Suitable to a moderate extent			Very suitable

Explanation:

c. Gifted students

0	1	2	3	4	5	6
Unsuitable			Suitable to a moderate extent			Very suitable

Explanation:

d. Other types of students, including exceptional students. Explain.

33. Considering the entire program or text, what type of teacher do you think would be most effective in using these materials?

34. In general, to what degree would you recommend that these materials be used for the designated level(s)?

0	1	2	3	4	5	6
Not recommended			Recommended with qualifications			Highly recommended

Explanation:

35. How adequately does the analyst think her or his analysis represents the materials analyzed?

0	1	2	3	4	.5	6
Very inade-quately			Somewhat adequately			Very adequately

Explanation:

36. Develop a *readability review* of the program or text by using these three readability procedures to analyze it:

    1. The Fry Graph for Estimating Readability (graph and instructions given in Chapter 16).
    2. The Raygor Readability Estimate (graph and instructions given in Chapter 16).
    3. The SMOG formula (McLaughlin 1969):
        a. Choose three sets of ten sentences from places throughout the book.
        b. Count the number of words with *three or more syllables* (polysyllabic words) in each set of ten sentences.
        c. Add the three numbers of polysyllabic words.
        d. Develop a grade level using this formula:
           SMOG grade level = 3 + square root of polysyllabic word count

    Interpret the readability data in a short explanation. Remember, the Fry level predicts a student reading at this level will read this material at 50–70% accuracy in comprehension while the SMOG formula predicts 90–100% accuracy in comprehension. The Fry is roughly the frustration level; the SMOG is roughly the independent level.

37. Write a one- to two-paragraph conclusion in which you summarize the strengths and weaknesses of the program or text and your judgment about with what kinds of students and in what kinds of situations you would use the book.

Selecting Materials for Lessons or Units

As we stated earlier, each teacher is responsible for selecting materials for use in the classroom at a specified time. The final selection may well take into account the text, program, or series adopted for use in the course. However, the teacher makes the final decisions as to what is useful in the adopted text and what alternative and supplemental materials should be used.

The areas for consideration in planning a unit or lesson are the same ones given in the Decision Model: the *content* to be covered; the specific *needs* of the students in the class, especially *reading levels;* the *grouping* patterns planned for the unit; and the *teaching strategies* planned for the unit.

The unit plan given in Chapter 9 asks that each unit contain a list of materials and equipment needed and a list of reading assignments. We recommend that teachers planning and teaching units develop an annotated bibliography of potential materials for the unit. This bibliography should include the following information: (1) Title, author(s); (2) Publisher, place of publication; (3) Edition, copyright date; (4) Media available (text, primary source, filmstrip, lab manual, workbook, slides, etc.); (5)

Grade level of student designed for; (6) Readability level and formula used, if applicable; and/or (7) Annotation (one to two paragraphs), describing strengths and weaknesses, unique features, special instructional or reading help for students, other comments relevant to the use of the material. This bibliography can be put on 5 × 7 cards or in another format that is easy to keep and easy to find whenever it is necessary to use it.

Summary

Selecting materials involves a long-term process of evaluating texts for three- to five-year adoption by the school and a short-term process of selecting materials for a unit or specific lesson. Both procedures are described in this chapter. The five selection principles discussed include: (1) materials should encourage active learning; (2) materials should suit the needs of individual students; (3) materials should reflect student interests; (4) materials should suit the curriculum and be sensitive to the community; and (5) materials should be selected in appropriate order, given the Decision Model—after other important decisions have been made.

Chapter Activities: Using What You've Learned

Learn to Do It!

Use the Program/Series/Text Analysis Outline beginning on p. 249 to study a text or a series (if the text is part of one). It may be advantageous to use the text you used for the Readability Study to give you future insights on any discrepancies between your grade level and the level the publisher recommended for it.

Do It!

Estes and Vaughan (1978) devised the formula

$$\text{Reading Range} \approx \text{grade level} \pm \frac{\text{grade level} + 1}{2}$$

What is the expected reading range in your grade level? Using available data on standardized tests, assess the actual range of reading in one class.

References

ENGLISH, R., "The Politics of Textbook Adoption," *Phi Delta Kappan*, 62, no. 4 (December 1980), 275–78.

ESTES, T. A., and J. L. VAUGHAN, Jr., *Reading and Learning in the Content Classroom.* Boston: Allyn & Bacon, 1978.

KUYKENDALL, C., "What's New in Teaching Materials," *English Journal*, 69, no. 5 (May 1980), 77–78.

McLAUGHLIN, G. H., "SMOG Grading: A New Readability Formula," *Journal of Reading*, 12:8 (May 1969), 639–46.

Chapter 18

Using Reading and Media
To Teach Content

Preview

Media other than reading can be valuable sources of learning. Throughout this book, materials other than print materials have been discussed and demonstrated as part of well-structured learning experiences. This chapter summarizes the principles in using *all* media, print and non-print, and reinforces the value of variety in learning materials.

Throughout this book, we have encouraged teachers to use a wide variety of materials in their teaching. This chapter recaps our position and provides additional principles for selecting media beyond reading materials.

As a beginning, consider Dale's "Cone of Experience" (1969) as a basis for selecting media for teaching. This cone moves from materials with the broadest application and the widest use, but the least personal involvement, to materials with the most immediate personal application, but the narrowest and least efficient use of teacher and student time. Figure 18–1 gives this cone.

Reading fits at the top of the Cone, under verbal symbols. Verbal symbols are abstractions and tend to be the least personal of all the media available to the teacher. Reading is also efficient in many ways—it is low-cost and efficient in time, and it allows the student to go back and study material over again. At the other end, direct experience is a great teacher with enormous potential for student motivation. However, it is costly and relatively inefficient in use of time. Generally, one chance is all you get, so students who are absent or who forget have no chance to repeat the experience. The teacher also has limited control over what happens during the experience.

As an example, consider the study of government. A teacher may use any medium to present the concepts and information. If s/he uses reading, s/he can be sure that all relevant information is covered. However, students may well feel that the material is impersonal. They may have difficulty relating the abstract principles of government to their own lives. At the other end of the scale, a field trip to see

FIGURE 18–1 Dale's Cone of Experience*

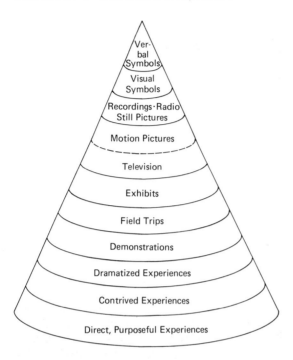

government in action may be very useful—a trip to Congress, the state legislature, the city council or school board. However, the teacher can't be sure anything will go on during the students' visit that will demonstrate the principles neatly. It would take many hours of watching, for example, to see a bill move through Congress to become a law. At one extreme on this scale, the teacher would form a government and have the students play roles (simulate) in various situations or actually govern themselves, as in student government. The problem, again, is efficiency in time and resources and control over the content learned.

The conclusion, then, is our message from the beginning. To provide the best coverage of content within reasonable time and resources, the teacher's best choice is a variety of media which contribute to student learning. This choice is based on the diagnosed needs of the students (Step 1 on the Decision Model), the Objectives (Step 2), the Grouping Patterns (Step 3), and the teaching strategies (Step 4). All of these professional decisions have been made by the teacher earlier in the planning process.

As a general guide to making appropriate choices, the matrix given in Table 18–1 can be useful. One axis represents common types of instructional media. The other axis represents common types of objectives. High, medium, and low levels relate to the effectiveness of the media type in helping students with particular kinds of learning.

*From *Audiovisual Methods in Teaching,* Third Edition, by Edgar Dale. Copyright 1946, 1954 © 1969 by Holt, Rinehart and Winston, Inc. Reprinted by permission of Holt, Rinehart and Winston, Inc.

TABLE 18–1 The Relationship of Instructional Media Selection to Learning Objectives

INSTRUCTIONAL MEDIA TYPE:	TYPES OF LEARNING OBJECTIVES					
	Learning Factual Information	Learning Visual Identifications	Learning Principles, Concepts, and Rules	Learning Procedures	Performing Skilled Perceptual-Motor Acts	Developing Desirable Attitudes, Opinions, and Motivations
Still Pictures	Medium	HIGH	Medium	Medium	low	low
Motion Pictures	Medium	HIGH	HIGH	HIGH	Medium	Medium
Television	Medium	Medium	HIGH	Medium	low	Medium
3-D Objects	low	HIGH	low	low	low	low
Audio Recordings	Medium	low	low	Medium	low	Medium
Programmed Instruction	Medium	Medium	Medium	HIGH	low	Medium
Demonstration	low	Medium	low	HIGH	Medium	Medium
Printed Textbooks	Medium	low	Medium	Medium	low	Medium
Oral Presentation	Medium	low	Medium	Medium	low	Medium

(Source: W. H. Allen, "Media Stimulus and Types of Learning," *Audiovisual Instruction*, 12, no. 1, 1967). Reprinted by permission of Association for Educational Communications and Technology.

One final note on the process of choosing media and reading. Many types of media besides texts and supplementary readings require students to read. Programmed instruction, by computer or any other form, requires a great deal of reading. Many filmstrips, slides, and other forms of still pictures have accompanying study guides, worksheets, or other reading materials. Therefore, the teacher who is carefully matching materials to students needs to look at the amount and kind of reading required by the medium. Generally speaking, materials with more visuals (still or motion pictures, TV, charts, graphs, maps) are easier to comprehend than those with mostly words. Concrete objects and experiences are easier to comprehend than more abstract activities.

The choice of teaching materials is a complex and important activity for teachers. Even though this choice comes late in the professional planning process, it remains critical in its effect on student learning. The wise teacher provides multiple materials for students to use in mastering important objectives, so that individual assignments are possible.

Sources of Media

All sorts of media materials for teaching, like print materials, are being produced at a rapid rate. Keeping up with what is available is a formidable task for any teacher. To be sure they have considered all possible materials in building a unit, teachers should check with their librarian and audiovisual specialist. Catalogs from publishing companies and media sources, plus reviews in professional journals (*The Mathematics Teacher, The Science Teacher, The English Journal*, etc.), are good sources of information on media. Check state and regional, as well as local, school agencies for rentals of films and other media. It is important to order new materials early enough to preview them before they are used in class.

Summary

The choice of media and reading materials is a professional decision that teachers make after they know the shape of the instruction they're planning. A wide variety of materials, both print and non-print, is the best resource for meeting the needs of a variety of learners. Teachers should analyze their materials choices using Dale's "Cone of Experience" to provide appropriate content and high interest for students.

Chapter Activities: Using What You've Read

Learn to Do It!

Develop a list of at least five media materials to augment your unit. Check the table on p. 265 to see whether you can diversify the types of media you have chosen. Where possible, avoid any cells designated as *low*.

References

ALLEN, W. H., "Media Stimulus and Types of Learning," *Audiovisual Instruction,* 12:1, 1967.

DALE, EDGAR, *Audiovisual Methods in Teaching,* 3rd ed. New York: Holt, Rinehart and Winston, 1969.

WELLIVER, P. W., ed. *Orientation to Instructional Media,* 2nd ed. University Park, Pa.: Pennsylvania State University, 1980.

PART VI
READING AND EXCEPTIONAL LEARNERS IN THE CONTENT CLASSROOM

OVERVIEW

The heart of individualizing instruction in the content classroom is to provide instruction that is appropriate to the special needs of each student. A great many students can be taught in similar fashion, because their needs are similar. These are the instructional level students. Most content instruction is geared to them, the "average" or grade level students. In this part of the book, we focus instead on four groups of special learners: frustration level readers, independent level readers, exceptional students, and bilingual students, as they appear in content classes. The adjustments that teachers make to meet these students' needs are the essence of individualizing instruction.

Frustration level readers read below the level needed to use regular course textbooks successfully. They need alternative materials, a slower pace, and more teacher assistance, in order to make it possible for them to succeed.

Independent level readers read so well that the regular course textbook is often not challenging to them. They may become bored or uninterested in class. Teachers need to challenge them with alternative and supplementary materials, higher level assignments, and more critical reading tasks.

Exceptional students come to the content classroom with an IEP, an Individualized Educational Program. Content teachers need to know what an IEP is and other important components of PL 94–142. They must understand the various exceptionalities which students might bring to their classes. Our special concern here is the wide variety of reading problems that these students may bring with them.

Finally, the needs and problems of bilingual students are discussed. Bilingual students, primarily Hispanic but including many other cultures and languages, bring with them another wide variety of problems. However, these problems are different from the other special students we've discussed. Their reading problems need special assessment and special instruction.

All four of these special groups could be discussed in a full book—and most of them have been. We provide a brief look at their problems, especially in reading, and refer content teachers to other, more complete discussions of the topic.

Chapter 19
Techniques for Teaching
Frustration Level Readers

Preview

We have labeled students for whom the instructional material in the content area is too difficult as frustration level readers. Even if they can manage to pronounce most of the words, they do not adequately comprehend the reading material. The teacher is faced with the choice of adapting the text or finding alternative ways of presenting the content. Our discussion of how to deal with this type of learner follows the steps in the Decision Model for Diagnostic Teaching for Grouping.

Identify Relevant Characteristics of Each Student

The reading teacher identifies the frustration level readers—those for whom the content area textbook is too difficult—by administering the criterion-referenced group reading inventory and/or a cloze test. These informal tests, however, tell us only that a student cannot adequately comprehend material from the textbook. They do not tell us at what level a student does read.

Teachers have access to standardized reading test scores that provide some indication of reading level. Some students, however, do not perform as well as they can on such tests because they are not motivated by a standardized test, they may work too slowly to achieve within the time limits of the test, or they may not understand the directions if English is not their native language.

If the frustration level students are included in a special reading program, the teacher can probably provide information on the reading level of each student; or if the students are mainstreamed from a learning disabilities or special education room, their reading levels should be included on the IEP. On the other hand, without input from a specialist, how can a content teacher know at what level materials should be given to those students who cannot read the textbook? Probably the easiest solution is to create a cloze test for the less-difficult alternative materials. In this manner, the content teacher has some estimate of reading level for those students who can't comprehend information from a textbook.

Other characteristics of frustration level readers are important. Do they have prior knowledge or experience related to the content area? If so, they have an advantage because they can draw on a strong conceptual background in relating new material to what is already known. Unfortunately, poor readers often do not have a strong knowledge base because their limited reading skills have hindered them in learning. Usually they have gained what knowledge they have through listening, television, or firsthand experiences.

The interest and motivation level of these students is also important. Unfortunately, most of them have experienced frustration in learning when instruction has

Betsy and her Jersey heifer, Rosemarie, practice for the show. Betsy spends over three hours a day with her animals, milking, feeding, and caring for them. *(Photo by Joseph Bodkin)*

not been adapted to their level. They have been forced to read what they cannot understand, and they have been ridiculed or harassed when they have failed to complete assignments correctly. A few frustration level readers feel good about themselves because of their achievements in sports, hobbies, scouts, and the like. For others, strong family support maintains their motivation and interest even though they meet constant failure and frustration.

Many frustration level readers, however, do not feel good about themselves as learners. By the time the content area teacher has them in class, they have already determined how they will meet frustration. A few, of course, who do have healthy self-concepts in spite of frustration, attempt to do the assigned work, seeking help from friends, parents, and the teacher. Many students, however, have given up and decided that they can't do the work; they may become disruptive out of sheer boredom and frustration, or they may withdraw.

The picture of the frustration level reader is by and large not a rosy one. S/he is not easy to teach, nor is s/he always responsive to a teacher's attempt to help. Teachers must constantly remind themselves that learning to read or learning from reading has not been easy for this student. It takes time to build a trusting relationship with a teacher.

The content teacher needs to find out what frustration level readers can do. In Betsy's case, a teacher's interest in her dairy cattle is important in establishing a good relationship. A teacher who does not take her efforts seriously, or who makes fun of her, would very likely produce "turn off" behavior in Betsy. On the other hand, if the content study could be related to Betsy's concerns, such as calculating in math class the cost of raising a dairy cow, Betsy's interest in the content area would be aroused. Her attitude toward the subject, teacher, and school in general could substantially improve. The secret is, of course, finding out what does interest Betsy and showing an interest in it and respect for her.

Specify Teaching Goals for Each Student

Once the reading level and extent of background knowledge in the content area are known, the teacher can specify realistic goals for each student. Content objectives as well as reading and study skill objectives need to be considered. The criterion-referenced group reading inventory helps identify those students who have particular skill weaknesses in reading and study skills. To produce the best learning, it is important for the teacher to communicate these goals to all students. Frustration level readers particularly need to know what they are expected to learn.

Group by Interest, Need, Ability, Etc.

Because content teachers deal with large numbers of students, it is only practical to group students and to plan instruction in terms of the group. Grouping by reading level is necessary, especially if alternative reading materials are used for frustration level readers instead of the content area textbook. While the teacher may think of those frustration level readers as a group in creating a study guide or planning use of alternative materials, the students should not perceive themselves as an unchanging group. If the teacher also groups for skill needs, interests, prior experience, and so forth, then the group established by reading levels won't become stereotyped. The particular concern, of course, is that the frustration level readers not become labeled as the class "dummies."

Select Instructional Strategy—
Management Procedure for Each Group

Because using the content area textbook, even with the support of the Directed Reading Activity, is inappropriate for frustration level readers, the teacher must find some other means of presenting the content. Other than alternative materials at a lower reading level, which we discuss in the next step of the model, what can a content teacher do? Some suggestions have been presented throughout this book; these are summarized here.

If the teacher does not have access—or chooses not to use—alternative reading materials, s/he must adapt the textbook in some form so that frustration level readers can comprehend the content. The methods discussed are ordered by the extent to which the textbook is actually modified for these students. The key to successful instruction, however, is variety. One method, if used exclusively, would prove tedious. One strategy is to tape-record the textbook. While others are reading, frustration level readers are following along in their textbook at a listening center. The tape can furthermore point out the importance of certain headings, charts, maps, and so forth. While the task of taping an entire textbook is overwhelming, it is possible to place only essential parts of it on tape. Often community volunteer groups are willing to make tapes to accommodate disabled readers as well as visually handicapped students. After listening to the tape recording, students may respond to study guide questions and/or participate in a class discussion of the material. The frustration level readers receive the same preparation for and follow-up after reading as the instructional level readers. The only difference is that they listen to the material rather than read it silently. The teacher is freed to circulate around the room to help individuals or to work with the independent readers.

Another strategy, which gives the teacher less flexibility than the listening center, is direct teacher supervision. When the instructional group begins reading silently, the teacher works with frustration level readers. S/he calls attention to the main ideas as found in the headings and introductory-summary paragraphs. The unessential information is omitted; because the teacher knows what the learning goals are for the assigned reading material, attention is focused on the important aspects of the reading material. Tangential information is eliminated.

The teacher can accomplish the same goals through a highly structured study guide created for frustration level readers. The study guide acts as a surrogate teacher, directing them to read only certain portions of the assigned material. The advanatages are that the teacher is freed to help individuals during study time, and that students may do the assigned work at home. The only problem is that frustration level readers may have more difficulty following a study guide independently. Perhaps use of study guides should occur only after students have worked directly with the teacher for several months.

Another technique is rewriting the textbook in a simpler form. Independent level readers who might be ahead of the rest of the class in assigned readings could paraphrase the material as a check on their comprehension. Their paraphrased versions could be used as rewritten forms of the textbook content. If greater control is considered necessary, the teacher can rewrite essential portions, controlling vocabulary as well as sentence length and complexity. Again, unessential portions are eliminated.

Finally, the language experience approach can be used. In this strategy, the content area concepts have to be presented through another medium such as films, filmstrips, videotapes, audiotapes, and records, or through direct or vicarious experience, such as a field trip or a presentation by a guest speaker. Afterwards, the students discuss the content as presented. This discussion is recorded by the teacher or an independent level group member. This transcription becomes the rewritten textbook for the frustration level reader. Since they have written it, they have no difficulty reading or comprehending it. Because it is written in language that they speak, other frustration level readers in future classes may use the dictated material as a textbook.

Regardless of what instructional strategies are selected, variety is important. Reading experiences are also important for frustration level readers. If they are never required to read, they will not improve the reading skills that they do have. Therefore, alternative reading materials are considered next.

Select Instructional Materials for Each Group

Use of alternative reading material fits most easily in a unit approach to instruction. All students are studying the same aspect of the content area, such as the westward movement in social studies, but they are using different reading materials to learn the content. The frustration level readers can share with readers of all abilities what they have learned because they alone have read a particular set of reading materials.

Lists of alternative reading materials are sometimes provided in the content area textbook. Librarians and reading teachers are also useful resource people in helping content teachers find less difficult materials. Films and other media can also be considered as alternative learning materials for those who cannot comprehend from the textbook.

The teacher may use learning centers and learning activity packets (LAPs) as alternative methods of presenting content. If the intent of these is to present content in a simplified form for frustration level readers, then the learning center and LAPs would not be used by all students. Some learning centers and LAPs, on the other hand, might offer skill instruction to those who need it or enrichment and extension to all students regardless of reading level.

Try Out Strategies and Materials with Each Group

The teacher needs to be a careful observer, particularly with frustration level readers. Because they have experienced frustration and failure in the past, they may not respond positively at first to the teacher's efforts to individualize. Do not be discouraged or give up! Unfortunately, some teachers, after one attempt, say, "See, I told you grouping students wouldn't work!" Teacher and students have to learn together about accommodating their needs in the content classroom.

Whenever an activity is successful, try to analyze why it worked. Instead of using exactly the same activity again and again, try to build on the elements that made it work. For example, use of manipulative materials in lieu of worksheets might be the key to success. Manipulative activities can be included in future plans, but the precise activity will be different.

Evaluate Each Student's Performance and Appropriateness of Goals

While it is useful to think of the frustration level readers as a group, the teacher must evaluate each student's performance individually. Not all students respond equally well to basically the same instruction. For students who are unsuccessful, analysis of the learning situation is particularly important. The teacher needs to determine whether the problem lay in the instructional materials, teaching strategy, interactions within the grouping pattern chosen, motivation, language difficulties, or other areas. Once the problem is determined, modifications can be made.

Often students fail to meet a teacher's expectations because the criterion (test) doesn't match the goals and instructional activities. Typically, poor readers learn only the main ideas from a reading assignment. In other words, they learn only what the teacher has directed them to learn. They do not tend to pick up incidental information as do more skilled readers (Rothkopf 1982). Therefore, they are most vulnerable when the teacher does not test what s/he has indicated is important in the material. If the teacher has stressed main ideas, then the test ought not to stress factual recall. Similarly, if the teacher has emphasized thinking about reading material at all four levels of Barrett's *Taxonomy* (1972), then the test ought to include some open-ended questions for which no one right answer exists. If the teacher intends to assess only the literal comprehension level but stimulate thinking at other levels in class discussions, s/he should tell this to students.

Often students can identify the problem themselves. A brief conference may reveal problems that the teacher can compensate for in the classroom if s/he is aware of them. Close communication with parents is important, especially at the elementary school level. Parents of high school age students need to be informed also, although problems can often be resolved more effectively at school. Teenagers, of course, are very aware of their newly found independence and often resent their parents' involvement in school.

Special Techniques

Some students have difficulty learning words in the usual methods followed in school. Most instruction is largely dependent on the visual and auditory learning modalities. Some students, however, need reinforcement through the tactile modality, or the sense of touch. Unfortunately, the sand table which is typically found in the kindergarten room is not used when children are beginning to learn to read. Most modern reading instructional programs are heavily dependent on phonics in teaching word recognition skills. But some students seem to be unable to learn through the auditory modality, or phonics. As a result, they fall behind in reading.

When these students face the task of learning new vocabulary in content area reading, they need vocabulary instruction prior to reading as do all students. Some of them, however, may need to have tactile reinforcement of new words in order to remember them. Presentation through only the visual and auditory modalities may be inadequate. Some students may need to trace words written in crayon with their finger while they say the words, followed by writing the words with a pencil. The words may be written on index cards and kept in their own file of new and known words.

Frequent review of content vocabulary is necessary. The teacher should not assume that words, once learned, will be remembered if they are not reviewed. The important words should be presented in a different context. If a student does not recognize a word that was once learned, then s/he should go back to tracing the word while saying it aloud.

Frustration level readers also are often those students who benefit from manipulative materials. For example, in the vocabulary learning center described in

Chapter 10, students manipulate cubes to form new words containing roots and affixes. Because they can physically manipulate the word parts, they can get a better grasp of word parts and how they affect meaning. Some students, most often frustration level readers, need physical involvement in learning.

Frustration level readers also benefit from frequent writing experiences in the content classroom. After reading assigned material, they should be asked to state in their own words what they have learned. Not only does this procedure help them identify the important ideas in assigned reading, but it also provides practice in using the new vocabulary. It is a good check on what each student is learning, providing the teacher with a technique by which to monitor instructional progress. Needless to say, the more opportunities that the student has to express him/herself in writing, the easier written expression becomes for the student. Increased facility in writing probably has positive effects on reading abilities as well.

A final note: Frustration level readers may have vast experiences to draw on, but these experiences may be unrelated to school learning. Because of limited reading abilities, they have not had access to concepts ordinarily gained through incidental reading. Therefore, the content area teacher must be especially careful not to assume a conceptual background that is not present.

As teachers, we usually function with a middle-class set of values and assumptions. Our frustration level students, however, may not be operating with the same frame of reference if they come from less advantaged homes. As teachers, then, we must be careful not to assume that we share a common set of background experiences with our students—unless the teacher has grown up in the community in which s/he teaches. Differences in values and experiences become particularly important in subject areas such as English and social studies, and especially in developing the higher levels of thinking on Barrett's *Taxonomy*. We are safer to provide conceptual background for new learning rather than to assume that frustration level readers already have that background.

Summary

Using the Decision Model for Diagnostic Teaching by Grouping, we have considered each step in terms of frustration level readers, those students for whom the textbook is too difficult. The teacher faces the decision of either adapting the textbook so that this group can use it or selecting alternative reading materials that are less difficult. Some special teaching techniques can also help frustration level readers learn the content study.

Chapter Activities: Using What You've Read

Learn to Do It!

1. Find a text dealing with your unit or other content you wish to teach with a lower readability than the assigned or regular text. Using either the Fry or Raygor formula, find the readability of this text. Develop a cloze test from it.

2. You earlier developed vocabulary exercises to teach concepts to regular students (Chapter 13). Adapt these exercises for frustration level readers or develop a new exercise that will consider the characteristics of poorer readers.

Do It!

Use the cloze test with your students who are poor readers. Compare their results on this easier material with cloze results on the regular text.

References

Barrett, T. C., "Taxonomy of Reading Comprehension," *Ginn 360 Monograph.* Lexington, Mass.: Ginn, 1972.

Rothkopf, E. Z., "Adjunct Aids, and the Control of Mathemagenic Activities During Purposeful Reading." In W. Otto and S. White, eds., *Reading Expository Material.* New York: Academic Press, 1982.

Chapter 20
Techniques for Teaching Independent Level Readers

Preview

Independent level readers read grade level materials with ease. How can teachers provide challenging work for them in class? Careful diagnosis and analysis of these readers' needs is important. This chapter focuses on independent readers and specific techniques for working with them.

Characteristics of Independent Level Readers

Independent level readers have been defined in earlier chapters as students who read grade level materials easily, students who need to be challenged by materials which go beyond the grade-level text. These students are not necessarily "gifted" in the sense that they are exceptional. They do not have Individualized Educational Programs (IEPs). However, these independent level students have specific needs which teachers should be prepared to meet.

Pam, our independent level reader, provides an example of specific needs. Pam is a shy, non-assertive student, but an excellent and avid reader. She needs several kinds of special activities in different subject areas.

As an eleventh-grade student, Pam is taking English, social studies, advanced math, and chemistry. She has elected to continue studying a foreign language and is currently in French IV. She is also active in choir and band.

Pam's English teacher can respond to her needs by encouraging her to read additional materials in the areas that interest her. She prefers novels to short stories, so when her class read Crane's *The Red Badge of Courage*, her teacher encouraged her to read other novels about the Civil War, such as *Roots, Cowslip, Gone With the Wind,* and *Jubilee.* Her American History teacher introduced her to Bruce Catton's *A Stillness at Appomattox.*

Pam's chemistry teacher finds that her independent reading level makes it possible for her to read the text *Chemistry: Experimental Foundations* (Prentice-

Pam is working here on independent reading materials on Shakespearean England, preparing to report to her English class. *(Photo by Joseph Bodkin)*

Hall), which has a reading level of 10, according to Fry. Since she is less interested in chemistry than in history, Pam chooses not to concentrate on additional reading in chemistry. Her alert chemistry teacher has found her several books about chemistry and famous chemists, such as *Men and Molecules* and *The Double Helix*. Pam has chosen one to read and report on orally to the class.

Like other students, Pam does many things besides reading. Her activities in music in and outside of school take time. Her parents encourage these social group activities, because Pam is relatively shy. Her total development as a person requires that she grow socially as well as intellectually. Her teachers must also take into account her needs beyond academic activities. Independent readers like Pam challenge content teachers to identify and meet their unique needs.

TEACHING TECHNIQUES BASED ON THE STEPS
OF THE DECISION MODEL

Think back now to the steps of the Decision Model, originally given in Chapter 2. At each step in the model, the content teacher can make adjustments to fit specific needs of special students.

An independent level reader like Pam must be identified in Step 1, Identifying Learner Characteristics. Content teachers will identify the independent readers in their classes by using diagnostic tools like the criterion-referenced group reading inventory and cloze. Teachers must beware of taking advice from tests or other teachers on which students are independent readers. Many students test as independent readers in one or two subjects but not in others. Pam is not reading at an independent level in her math class, although she is at this level in history, English, and science. The conclusion is clear: each content teacher must make an independent assessment of reading level.

A second area of assessment is in motivation. Many students will have different levels of interest in different subject areas. As discussed in Chapter 6, the diagnosis of independent or high level reading does not mean that the student has high interest in the subject. Think back to Pam. She has high interest in English and history but less interest in chemistry. Yet she reads in all three classes at the independent level. The same difference can exist in students' self-direction.

Alternative Objectives, Step 2 on the Decision Model, can be identified for independent level readers. These objectives may take the form of options in which the independent readers read more challenging material than instructional readers do. In one tenth-grade English class, the independent readers read *Lord of the Flies* as an example of the novel, while other levels read *Alas Babylon*. In a seventh-grade social studies class, the independent readers read and produced *Antigone* while they studied ancient Greece, while the other students read about the Greek theatre and watched the performance.

Grouping patterns (Step 3) can reflect independent readers in different ways. Independent readers can be grouped together to allow them to work on alternative activities. In groups of three or four, these readers can undertake additional lab activities in science, read and discuss additional literature in English class, or do library or field research in social studies.

Another way of grouping would form groups that include the independent reader with other level readers. In these groups, the independent reader could assist the other readers in working through activities. For example, in a group activity based on a three-level study guide, the independent level reader can help the others work upward through the evaluation level questions. Following Barrett's *Taxonomy*, a study guide can contain questions which begin at the literal level, move upward through inferential questions, and culminate in evaluation and appreciation questions. Herber (1978) suggests a similar format. Such study guides can be designed for small group work. The plan for involving independent readers with those on the frustration and/or instructional levels would work like this:

1. All students read the assigned material as well as they can and answer literal questions. This can be an in-class activity or homework assignment.

2. In class, the small group discusses the answers to the literal questions. After they have agreed on these answers, they move up to inferential and evaluation questions. At these levels, the independent reader can exercise leadership and act as a peer tutor to the others, as necessary.

The independent reader who is self-directed can profit from highly independent learning activities in groups of one or two, such as

reading a book and writing a review of it

identifying an issue and interviewing several people about it

searching in the library for the history of a phenomenon and reporting on it to the class

The reward for these independent activities may be in creating a model or conducting extra labs or reading different materials. Some students will enjoy reporting orally to the class; others will find that threatening. The teacher must determine what the objective is and which form of evaluation is better for the student in question.

Step 4 on the model asks for a decision on Organizing for Instruction. The teaching strategies for independent learners will emphasize their ability to move quickly through the lower comprehension levels and up to the evaluation and appreciation levels. Such strategies will include group activities, student-directed activities like LAPs, learning centers, and independent contracts.

Selection of appropriate materials (Step 5) is another important way to meet the needs of independent readers. Alternative materials that will challenge these readers should be identified when units are planned. If several texts are available, reading selections for independent readers can allow for broader or deeper coverage of the material. Trade books on the topic are often useful. A classroom library on the unit, built of books and other reading materials from the school library, can allow for wide reading under the teacher's guidance.

The Try It! step (6) is always important to verify that the teacher's analysis is accurate. It is possible that informal diagnosis can be in error and the student identified as independent is really reading at a lower level. Such a misdiagnosis can be frustrating to student and teacher. Especially early in the year, the teacher should be extremely careful in following the diagnosis with verification in class. Following the tryout comes the Evaluation step (7). The independent reader can be expected to respond positively to higher level questions—essay questions, application activities, problem-solving situations. However, like all students, independent readers must learn how to complete these activities. While they may learn more quickly, they must still receive well-organized instruction on the material to be learned.

A constant problem with independent readers is motivation, especially at the junior high level. Many good students are reluctant to be seen as different from their peers. They prefer to be "one of the crowd." Psychologically it is more important for them, at this stage in their adolescence, to be accepted by their peers than to be challenged intellectually or academically. It becomes a challenge to the teacher to provide incentives for students to do anything different from the rest of the class.

The teacher's role needs to be that of providing alternatives that are interesting and motivating to these independent readers. Rather than simply adding *more* reading to the assignments given other students, the teacher would be better advised to provide similar amounts of reading which are more challenging. For example, the English teacher who wants an independent reader to read an additional novel and write a paper comparing it to the novel the whole class read should be prepared to excuse that student from some other classroom assignment—vocabulary testing, grammar drill, etc. The health teacher who wants independent readers to read beyond the basic text might ask them to read a more challenging text *instead* of the regular text. Indeed, such a health teacher could have a small group of independent readers leave the class for the two or three days when the regular reading is discussed and have them spend the time reading from several sources in the library and preparing an oral report for the whole class on material beyond the text. The emphasis should be not on piling on additional work, but on providing challenging alternatives for independent level students.

Summary

Independent level readers deserve special attention from their teachers. These readers should be assured that they will be continually challenged by appropriate materials and, at the same time, that they will be carefully taught the skills and knowledge they need.

Chapter Activities: Using What You've Read

Learn to Do It!

1. If any of your colleagues have developed assessments of student reading skills and have scores on the same students as you have, compare scores. Is there validity in the statement "Many students test as independent/instructional/frustration level readers in one or two classes but not in others" (p. 279)?

2. Develop a strand in your unit for independent readers. Include a list of five additional resources (texts at a higher readability, novels, biographies, media, etc.) useful for independent readers.

3. Develop a teaching strategy to augment the concept development exercise developed in Chapter 13, designed for independent readers.

4. Develop a study guide to go with a chapter/unit of a text with a higher reading level.

Do It!

Work through one or more of these activities with independent readers in your class(es).

Chapter 21
The Exceptional Student
in the Content Classroom

Preview

The new requirements of PL 94–142 make content teachers responsible for dealing with a wide variety of exceptional students in their classrooms. What problems arise? How can these students be accommodated and taught? How is reading related to the exceptional student? This chapter discusses some ways of dealing with exceptional students and gives special attention to their potential reading problems.

Since 1975, when PL 94–142 became law, content teachers have been involved with the entire educational system in finding ways to provide instruction to growing numbers of exceptional children. The number of these students is growing in two ways. First, under the law's assessment provisions, more students with special needs are being identified. Second, more exceptional students are being returned to the regular classroom for part or all of their instruction.

Content teachers are now faced with the need to understand the various handicapping conditions, to develop positive attitudes toward their exceptional students, and to feel confident that they know how to work successfully with exceptional children in their classroom. We will briefly discuss these three issues in this chapter. However, each of them could easily require a complete book in its own right. Our discussion will be limited to key elements, with references to additional reading for greater depth.

UNDERSTANDING HANDICAPPING CONDITIONS

PL 94–142 states its purpose this way:

> It is the purpose of the Act to assure that all handicapped children have available to them, within the time periods specified, a free appropriate public education which emphasizes special education and related services designed to meet their unique needs. (PL 94–142, 1975, section 3c.)

This law has made it a federal mandate to provide an "appropriate public education" to all students identified as exceptional. In addition, this education is to be available from age three to twenty-one for such an exceptional student.

These two features of the law have special significance for secondary teachers. For many years, special education classes have been common in elementary schools. They have been less common at the secondary level. In the years before PL 94–142, by the time exceptional students reached high school age they either had dropped out, transferred to special private institutions or vocational schools, or been assimilated into the lower tracks of high school classes. Those of us who have taught for several years can recollect that we had a few "slow learners"—a few students who just couldn't seem to learn to read, a few who were seriously maladjusted—but these students were not made visible. We put up with them, pitied them, sometimes really taught them.

PL 94–142 no longer allows us this attitude. Because the age limit has been raised to 21, any exceptional student's parents may request that we keep that student in our school until that age. As we identify more and more students with special needs, we find that most teachers at all levels have several students in their classes who are identified as exceptional. Our challenge is to understand these students and develop empathy for them.

We are speaking only of those students for whom an *Individualized Educational Program* (IEP) has been developed. The IEP, required by law, defines the student's special needs and sets forth objectives for the student to master during a given school year. The IEP may indicate specific content areas for emphasis, or it may deal with skills. On the basis of the IEP, the student is placed in an educational situation which meets his/her special needs. The IEP will determine what situation is, for that student, the *Least Restrictive Environment* (LRE). LRE is an important concept with PL 94–142. LRE says, basically, that handicapped children must be educated as much like their non-handicapped peers as possible, unless it can be shown that the student will benefit more from an alternative service. LRE includes a wide range of alternatives and educational services to an exceptional student:

Regular class

Regular class in a regular school with supporting services

Special education program in a regular school

Special education in a special facility

An approved private school program

A state school program

At-home instruction

This list moves from least restrictive (regular classroom) to most restrictive (a state school or at-home instruction). The IEP team determines for each student what the LRE is. The IEP team usually consists of the teacher, a school representative (often a counselor or school psychologist), the parents, and, with older students, frequently the student. You may be asked to serve on such a team, either for students in your homeroom or as a result of parent or counselor request.

It is possible for students to be in regular classes (mainstreamed) for part of the day but not all of it, or for a few subjects but not all of them. The decision is based on the student's needs.

DEFINITIONS OF HANDICAPPING CONDITIONS

Even though mainstreaming is only one facet of least restrictive environment, content teachers are more involved in mainstreamed cases than any other section of PL 94–142. In order to refer a child for special services and to educate the exceptional child properly, it is necessary to understand the various exceptionalities. The following definitions are for explanatory purposes only. No one child should be considered to exhibit any particular description. Cartwright, Cartwright and Ward (1981) are an excellent source for further discussion of these conditions.

The exceptional student is difficult to define because s/he represents many different medical and psychological groups of students. An exceptional student is one who deviates intellectually, physically, socially or emotionally from what is considered to be normal growth and development. This deviation must be so great that the student cannot receive maximum benefit from a regular school program and requires a special class or supplementary instruction and services.

1. The Intellectually Exceptional Student—This phrase encompasses two large groups. At one extreme are students who are characterized by high mental ability (gifted); at the other extreme are students who are referred to as mentally retarded.
   A. The Gifted Student: These students have measured intelligence which exceeds an intelligence quotient of 130. Such students constitute about 3 percent of the population. Definitions of giftedness differ widely. Some broaden the areas of giftedness to the gifted and talented, including:
      1. general intellectual ability
      2. specific academic aptitude
      3. creative or productive thinking
      4. leadership ability
      5. visual and performing arts
      6. psychomotor ability (Gallagher 1975, p. 10).
      The PL 94–142 definition generally used in schools emphasizes high intelligence as primary.
   B. The Educable Mentally Retarded (E.M.R.): These students have intelligence quotients between 55 and 80.
   C. The Trainable Mentally Retarded (T.M.R.): These students have intelligence quotients between 30 and 55.
   D. Severe and Profoundly Mentally Retarded (S.P.M.R.): Individuals with an intelligence quotient lower than 30. They must also be evaluated by a physician prior to any placement.
2. Learning Disabled Student (L.D.)—A deficiency in the acquisition of basic learning skills, including, but not limited to, the ability to reason, think, read, write, spell, or do mathematical calculations, as identified by an educational and psychological evaluation. A student is assigned to a program for the learning disabled when the evaluation clearly indicates that s/he can demonstrate average or above-average intellectual functioning on an appropriate intelligence measure.
3. Brain Damaged (B.D.)—A moderate to severe injury to the brain, as identified by a neurological examination, resulting in severe behavior and learning disorders.
4. Hearing Impaired (H.I.)—A hearing loss ranging from mild (hard of hearing) to profound (deaf), as identified by an audiologist and otologist, which interferes with the development of the communication process and results in failure to achieve full educational potential.
5. Blindness—Those students in whom there is visual acuity of 20/200 or less in the better eye with correcting glasses or peripheral vision so limited that the widest diameter the student can see includes an angle no greater than 20 degrees. (A student with 20/200 vision is not totally blind.)

6. Speech and Language Impaired—Communications disorders or impaired language, voice, fluency or articulation to such a degree that academic achievement is affected and the condition is significantly handicapping to the affected person. This is determined by a speech clinician.

7. Socially and Emotionally Disturbed (S.E.D.)—A condition exhibiting one or more of the following characteristics over a long period of time and to a marked degree: an inability to build or maintain satisfactory interpersonal relationships with peers and teachers; inappropriate types of behaviors or feelings; a general and pervasive mood of unhappiness or depression; or a tendency to develop physical symptoms, pains, or fears associated with personal or school problems. Such a student must be identified in writing by a board-certified or approved psychiatrist. No person shall be assigned to a program (S.E.D.) for disciplinary reasons alone.

8. Physically Handicapped (P.H.)—Orthopedic and/or other health impairments of sufficient magnitude to limit a student's classroom accommodation and educational performance. Physically handicapping conditions include cerebral palsy, muscular dystrophy, spina bifida and other spinal defects, and impaired motor ability as a result of accidents or other disease.

TEACHER ATTITUDE AND EXCEPTIONAL CHILDREN

Teacher attitudes toward exceptional children are formed through years of involvement in the society at large. Teachers are people too, and the attitude of many people has been that exceptional people, handicapped people, should be separated from the rest of us. In order to comply with PL 94–142, and to provide for more humane acceptance of exceptional students in our classes, teachers must consider their own attitudes toward these students. It may be understandable that we have some negative attitudes, but it is no longer acceptable.

Our first task is to identify our own attitudes toward particular handicaps and toward the students who bring them to our classes. Test yourself in the following exercise.

Attitudes Toward Exceptional Children*

You are teaching a ninth-grade class in your subject area. This morning, Clare, the school psychologist, came to see you and told you that there are six exceptional children who might possibly be candidates for mainstreaming in your content area class. She said that she has come to you rather than some of the other teachers since she felt that you might be more sensitive to the needs of these exceptional students. She believes that mainstreaming these students into your class would really be to the students' benefit, and she wants to know how you feel about the idea. She left the following list of six names with you and asked you to indicate your feelings about each one. Please indicate your feelings by ranking the students in order, beginning with the one you would most like to have mainstreamed (place a 1 before that student's name) and ending with the one you would least like to see mainstreamed (place a 6 before that student's name).

_____ Rachel—who is physically handicapped. She had both legs amputated after an automobile accident and also has some facial disfiguration. She is average in ability.

* Prepared by James Nolan, West Branch School District, Kylertown, Pa.

_____ JoAnn—who is socially-emotionally disturbed. She is prone to periods of severe depression, is normally very withdrawn, and has exhibited aggressive behavior on a few occasions.

_____ Mark—who is educable mentally retarded. He is shy, lacks social skills and has great difficulty reading. He is seventeen years old and is determined to get a diploma.

_____ Rick—who has a mild to moderate hearing loss, and a severe speech impediment which makes it extremely difficult to understand him. He is above average in ability.

_____ Lori—who is a gifted student. She has failed at least three subjects each year and only seems to use her intelligence to challenge the teacher.

_____ Todd—who suffers from muscular dystrophy. He is in a wheelchair, has control only of gross motor movements, some speech slurring, but he is very bright and likes school very much.

When you have finished this exercise, ask yourself why you ranked the students as you did. Are you more concerned about students' cognitive ability? If so, you may be challenged by Lori, the gifted student but less willing to work with Mark, the mentally retarded student. Are you fearful of JoAnn's potentially aggressive behavior? Are you repelled by Rachel's physical appearance or Todd's lack of motor control? We all have feelings like this, but we must learn to control them. What we need most as teachers are understanding, patience, and faith in these students' ability to learn, even though it may be in a different way at a different pace from other students.

WHERE DOES READING FIT IN?

Content teachers, especially at the secondary level, face many students whose reading ability is lower than average. Not all of these students are handicapped, as defined in PL 94–142. We are talking here *only* about students who have an IEP, providing legal evidence to the teacher that they need individualized instruction. In addition, some students with IEPs, especially gifted students, may well have superior reading ability and need enrichment rather than remediation.

Reading fits in to instruction of mainstreamed students, then, as you might expect: each student's needs must be evaluated individually. It is highly likely that an IEP will speak specifically to the student's needs in reading, however, as well as other basic skills. Especially for those students who are functioning at a lower level, emphasis on their acquiring reasonable competence in reading is of primary concern to both parents and school. The IEP will determine how reading is treated in an individual student's program. It is dangerous to generalize about groups of students, regardless of their exceptionality. However, here are a few broad guidelines which may help shape the content teacher's planning. The categories are those given earlier in this chapter.

1. The Intellectually Exceptional Student
   A. *The gifted child* may have very good reading skills, but s/he may also read on grade level or below. On the continuum of reading levels, the gifted student may be anywhere; hence careful diagnosis is important. A gifted student who reads well can be treated like the independent reader (Chapter 20). The gifted child who reads on grade level is still

reading below his/her capacity. The gifted child who reads poorly needs attention to motivation and general attitude problems. S/he may have poor reading skills but high creativity; s/he may need challenge and a high level of personal attention. Check the self-direction levels of gifted students before assigning independent activities, since gifted students are not automatically self-directed.

B. *Educable Mentally Retarded.* These students will have limited educational goals in secondary content subjects. That is, they will not aspire to algebra, to chemistry or physics, to literature like *Moby Dick* and *Hamlet*, or to a study of Russian political structure. However, these students will become, with help, productive members of our society. They have reason to learn how to do basic arithmetic; to understand consumer and life science; to read short stories, poetry, newspaper and magazine articles; and to understand government and take part as a citizen in democratic processes. The reading level of EMR students is likely to be limited. They are likely to need alternative reading materials with controlled reading levels, as described in Chapter 19 on Frustration Level Readers.

C. *Trainable Mentally Retarded.* These students are unlikely to be mainstreamed into content classrooms, especially at secondary level. If a content teacher has a TMR student, s/he should contact the counselor and special education resource teacher immediately for guidance.

D. *Severe and Profoundly Mentally Retarded.* These students are unlikely to be placed in a regular classroom.

2. The Learning Disabled Student.

Many of the mainstreamed students in content classes are LD students. Their average or above average intelligence suggests that they have the capacity to learn in content classes. However, their problems with symbol systems make it likely that reading will be a problem for them. LD students show a wide variety of problems. This means that the individual students' IEPs must be the content teacher's guide to their strengths and weaknesses in reading and other skills. LD students may need to learn through sources other than reading, through concrete and hands-on experiences, and through carefully structured activity.

3. Brain Damage.

Teaching a brain-damaged student requires careful consultation with the school psychologist, counselor, and other resource teachers. Brain damage is likely to result in serious problems with learning, frequently including reading. Brain-damaged students may decode reasonably well, but have great difficulty in comprehending. Few brain-damaged students will be found in content classes, especially at the secondary level.

4. Hearing Impaired.

These students may well be placed in content classes throughout the school. There is no necessary connection between hearing loss and reading. However, many students with impaired hearing do not have the language development expected of children their age. Students may need to sit in front of the room, near the teacher's voice, or to have a fellow student help explain oral assignments. Teachers can be alert to face hearing-impaired students when speaking if those students can lip-read. Again, it is important for content teachers to consult with the school's specialists and resource teachers to determine the student's potential for reading.

5. Blindness.

Students with visual problems will clearly have difficulty with reading. However, that difficulty may result less from inability to comprehend what is read than from inability to see the text. Since vision problems have a wide range, content teachers must be careful to determine the student's specific problem. A student whose vision is corrected with glasses may need larger print books. S/he may need more time to read if reading causes his/her eyes to tire. But s/he may be able to complete much of the reading necessary for the class. Such students may profit from sitting closer to visual materials—the chalk board, wall maps, etc. On the other hand, a student who is legally blind will need to learn through sources other than texts—Braille texts or audio sources, for example.

6. Speech and Language Impaired.

Because oral speech precedes reading in the development of the language skills, it is common for students who have speech problems to also have reading problems. However, this is by no means an automatic connection. Content teachers must, again, look at the specific provisions of each student's IEP. If reading is a problem for these students, it is likely that the content teacher will need to use alternative or rewritten materials with controlled reading levels to provide the student with information. The teacher must also work to build tolerance in the other class members for the speaking problems of such students. As difficult as it may be, these speech-impaired students need opportunities to speak to their peers as any other student might. Part of the teacher's responsibility is to create a classroom climate in which these students feel comfortable speaking, in small groups or within a wider classroom discussion.

7. Social and Emotionally Disturbed.

Students with emotional problems severe enough to warrant identification and the resulting IEP will need individualized teaching in content classes. These students will vary widely in their interests, attitudes toward school, and attitudes toward particular classes. However, there is no necessary reason to think that they have problems with reading. Emotionally disturbed students may refuse to read or take part in classroom activities, but these problems may be more attitudinal and emotional than skill related. Over a period of time, perhaps years, a student with emotional problems can miss a large amount of skill instruction. Thus, in later years the emotionally disturbed student may be below the expected reading level in content classes. As a result, the careful teacher will look at all aspects of the students' background and current skill levels before designing instruction for them. Close coordination with the school psychologist and counselor is necessary in making appropriate assignments.

8. Physically Handicapped.

Students who are identified as physically handicapped may suffer from any number of limitations. By definition, these physical handicaps are not necessarily connected to intellectual functioning. However, multiple handicaps are fairly common, especially with cerebral palsy. The connection between physical handicapping and reading is also cloudy. Some handicaps, like cerebral palsy, may well suggest problems with reading because students have difficulty with the required coordination. Some students who can read will not be able to handle the texts and physically manipulate the materials. However, handicaps from accidents or progressive diseases like muscular dystrophy will not necessarily impair reading ability.

It is important for teachers to encourage physically handicapped students to become or remain as independent as possible. Teachers can assign another student to serve as a helper in class for a physically handicapped student. Such a helper may assist in holding or manipulating materials, from turning pages to handling laboratory equipment. The helper may also assist the student's mobility, such as moving a wheelchair or setting up materials so the student can handle them on his/her own.

Summary

The last few pages have suggested the wide range of problems faced by exceptional students. Content teachers will be wise to identify their students with IEPs and work carefully with the counselor or special education resource teacher to identify the reading levels and strengths of these students. Specific student learning problems and the implementation of the specific objectives given in IEPs provide the content teacher with direction in working with exceptional students. An individualized approach is not only a legal mandate, it is the only professionally appropriate way to work with exceptional students. Content teachers with such students in their classes will need to learn more about specific exceptionalities. The reference list at the end of this chapter is a modest beginning to such reading.

Chapter Activities: Using What You've Read

Learn to Do It!

Choose one category of exceptionality, either found in a student in your school or one that you are particularly interested in, and study their particular needs, especially in the area of reading. Use the reference list given here for resources. Be prepared to make a presentation to the class on your findings.

Do It!

Add to the above any anecdotal or observational data you have gathered from a student(s) in your class/school.

References

ALLEY, G., and D. DESHLER, *Teaching the Learning Disabled Adolescent: Strategies & Methods,* Chapter 3. Denver: Love, 1979.

CARTWRIGHT, G. P., C. E. CARTWRIGHT, and M. E. WARD, *Educating Special Learners.* Belmont, Calif.: Wadsworth, 1981.

GALLAGHER, J. J., *Teaching the Gifted Child* (2nd ed.) Boston: Allyn & Bacon, 1975.

GILLESPIE-SILVER, P., *Teaching Reading to Children with Special Needs.* Columbus, Ohio: Merrill, 1979.

KALUGER, G., and C. KOLSON, *Reading & Learning Disabilities* (2nd ed.) Columbus, Ohio: Merrill, 1978.

KIRK, S., J. M. KLIEBHAN, and J. W. LERNER, *Teaching Reading to Slow and Disabled Learners.* Boston: Houghton Mifflin, 1978.

SAVAGE, J. F., and J. F. MOONEY, *Teaching Reading to Children with Special Needs.* Boston: Allyn & Bacon, 1979.

Chapter 22
Teaching Reading
to Bilingual Students
in the Content Classroom *

By Joseph Prewitt Díaz*

Preview

The purpose of this chapter is to explain how to diagnose the language proficiency of the limited English proficiency (LEP) student. It will provide some strategies for assessing these students. It will conclude with suggestions for implementation of a program to assist these students to increase their proficiency in English within the content classroom and at the same time master content material. This chapter is by no means a handbook on how to deal with limited English proficiency (LEP) students, and concludes by suggesting that ultimately, the teacher must decide the appropriate program for LEP students in the content classroom. It is important to keep in mind that in the majority of cases, by the time LEP students are assigned to the subject matter classroom they will have been exposed to English as a Second Language (ESL) for at least one semester. It is also important to note that there are approximately three million LEP students in the United States.

What Is Bilingual Education?

Bilingual education is the provision of content area and developmental reading instruction in their dominant language to limited English-proficiency (LEP) students, along with a comprehensive English as a second language (ESL) program, until such time as the student can transfer his/her reading skills into English and understand academic instruction in English (Cohen 1979). The primary concern of bilingual educators is LEP students who must be taught in their dominant, or native, tongue.

As many as three million students in the United States speak, read, and write a language other than English; about 85 percent of these students are Hispanic. Bilingual education is designed to teach these students to understand, speak, read,

*Dr. Prewitt Díaz, a native of Puerto Rico, is Assistant Professor of Education and Bilingual Education and Puerto Rican Studies, Pennsylvania State University.

and write English and to teach them subject matter in their native language, so that they can progress through school and successfully complete a standard high school education as prescribed by their local school districts.

Bilingual education programs are hard to describe because no two programs are the same. Golub (1980) indicates that, generally, bilingual education programs can be characterized as follows, depending upon the socioeconomic and political function of the program:

1. *Mixed classes—assimilation.* This is the transition to English model; it is not aimed at dual-language skills. LEP students are immersed in monolingual, English-speaking classrooms. Some instruction in English as a second language is provided.

2. *Separate classes—assimilation.* This is a modified transitional model in which LEP students are in separate bilingual education classes for their academic course work, English language, mathematics, social studies, and science. Although the teacher, and if possible the aide, are bilingual, the main emphasis is on learning to understand, speak, read, and write in English and to learn subject matter using both the English language and the students' native language. This model is characteristic of large urban schools where students stay in the bilingual education classes until they can be placed into the monolingual English, regular school program.

3. *Mixed classes—pluralism.* This is a low-keyed maintenance model. It is most often considered to be the predominant model of bilingual education, even though the guidelines for federal funding require the transitional model. LEP students are supposed to be placed in mixed classes, although this rarely happens. Students are given instruction in the English language and their native language, as well as subject matter instruction in both languages, until they are ready to transfer to the monolingual English, regular school program.

4. *Separate classes—pluralism.* This is the most radical maintenance model which can be found when the ethnic language and culture are used exclusively for instruction. English is supplemental.

In all of the models listed above except the last, an LEP student is expected to make the transition into the regular monolingual English program within a short time. For most elementary school children, the transition occurs in two years; for most secondary school students, in three years.

How Is the Limited English Proficiency (LEP) Student Identified?

The task of accurately assessing the language proficiency of LEP students is especially challenging since data regarding specific language assessment procedures are limited. The task involves seeking an instrument which will measure listening, speaking, reading, and writing. Each of the skills possesses the three characteristics of language: meaning (semantics), arrangement and grammar (syntax and morphology), and sound (phonology). The best assessment of any of the language skills will encompass all three characteristics.

An instrument which was designed to assess reading, writing, listening comprehension, and speaking in English and Spanish is the Language Assessment Battery (LAB). The LAB (English and Spanish) has three levels. Each level consists of four tests: Test 1—Listening; Test 2—Reading; Test 3—Writing; and Test 4—Speaking.

Level II of the LAB covers grades 7 through 12, and has a total of 92 items. Tests 1, 2, 3 are group administered; Test 4 is individually administered.

It is important for the content area teacher to become aware of the score LEP students have obtained on instruments such as the LAB for several reasons. In the first place, the teacher will gain some indication of the language proficiency of the students from the LAB scores. This will enable the teacher to adjust the materials to meet the linguistic needs of these students. Secondly, the content area teacher will be able to compare the students' progress using the LAB scores as the basis. Finally, s/he will be able to use the LAB in order to determine when the LEP students should be transferred into mainstream courses.

Transferring Reading Skills from Spanish to English

The research on reading and the bilingual student (Cohen 1980; Garcia 1977; Golub 1977; and Prewitt Diaz 1980) has indicated that a student will transfer reading skills from the native language to the second language. These researchers warn that in order to decide the language in which to emphasize reading, the teacher must determine in what language the student is now cognitively stronger.

In a discussion of entry criteria into a reading program, Cohen (1980) indicates that if the student is inappropriately selected for dominant language reading in Spanish, the transference will be from a language of weakness and therefore ineffective. In other words, students who are placed in Spanish reading groups for developmental reading should be cognitively stronger in Spanish and thus able to build stronger reading foundations in Spanish.

This single issue, the placing of children into Spanish reading classes in order that they first acquire their reading skills in their stronger language, is the most significant goal of bilingual education. In this sense, bilingual education is a form of individualized instruction because it gives the teacher an opportunity to capitalize on students' strengths.

There are several common errors in identifying bilingual students' reading skills which might affect the content area teacher (Cohen 1980). The first error occurs when students who are partially proficient bilingual students, or students with English language proficiencies that are weak but significantly stronger than their Spanish skills, are inappropriately selected for instruction in Spanish. This might occur when a district uses English-only tests.

A second error occurs most often as a result of the inadvertent exclusion of non- or limited English proficiency (LEP) students. This can occur when students score very low on both parts of a test that measures proficiencies in both languages. Whereas the previous remedial situation needs English remedial reading, this situation needs remediation in the native language as a form of basic instruction.

A third error occurs when limited English proficiency students are appropriately placed in the program but are mainstreamed too quickly, a process that is unfortunately observed to a greater degree with each passing year because of the politics and misunderstandings attached to the transition process.

Language of Instruction

The teacher can ask: In which language will this student best learn? To answer this question, cognition must be measured in both languages. Instruction must be offered in Spanish until the student's cognitive abilities in English are strong enough to process newly presented academic information. With the LEP student, the content area teacher will probably receive a measure of cognitive development. If the teacher does not receive one, it is suggested one be administered. Using a cognitively based approach to the identification of dominant language, whether a standardized approach or a teacher-made approach, will result in better implementation of the transfer. The transfer is more likely to be successful because students will be acquiring reading skills and transferring skills from their cognitively stronger language.

One of the most misunderstood aspects of bilingual education is the degree to which English as a second language (ESL) is a key to the eventual academic success of participating students. Too often ESL activities are linked to dominant language instruction. They can have even more impact under the umbrella of bilingual education than when they are conducted in the traditional manner, in which the students are isolated from the district's academic curricula. The most important role of ESL in bilingual education is that it provokes an easier transferability of developmental reading skills by introducing English vocabulary words that can be used to promote the transfer of phonics skills from Spanish to English (Cohen 1980; Golub *et al*. 1980).

When do reading skills transfer from Spanish to English? Spanish reading skills

Joito reads to his younger sister, Maria. The book is written both in Spanish and in English. *(Photo by Joseph Bodkin)*

at various levels of difficulty can be transferred into English almost immediately. As suggested earlier, Spanish phonic skills, a majority of which are directly transferable into English, can be transferred into English as they are acquired in Spanish if the students have receptive English vocabulary skills for use as examples. On a more sophisticated level, reading comprehension skills can be transferred into English in almost all instances.

The teaching of reading involving the LEP student is the responsibility of the content area teacher as well as the reading teacher. The teaching of reading to LEP students depends on the strategies used by the teacher. Some teachers introduce English reading skills on a skill-by-skill basis as they are mastered in Spanish. Others introduce the English reading skills in clusters, requiring mastery of a group of similar Spanish reading skills before promoting a transference of skills into English. The content teacher should become familiar with the strategies being used with his/her students in the specific situation.

For years, monolingual English reading programs have used linguistic, cognitive, and other hierarchies in arranging the presentation and sequencing of reading skills. However, none of the bilingual reading programs have arranged both languages into a hierarchical system that would promote parallel development and transference on a skill-by-skill basis for every reading skill.

Techniques for Teaching LEP Students

There are a number of suggestions to provide guidance to content teachers who teach LEP students.

1. Present new content area concepts either visually or verbally in their first language as they are introduced in English.
2. Promote discussion and interest and concept development in the first language, as well as in English.
3. Promote reading activities which incorporate content concepts in the first language.
4. Promote writing activities in the first language, as well as in English. Start with short, structured writing exercises (like answering direct questions) and move gradually to longer, more creative writing (like paragraphs, themes, or reports).
5. Only *after* the students understand vocabulary and concepts in the first language can the vocabulary be introduced in English.
6. Follow with the same concepts in written form in the second language.
7. Early writing activities in the second language should be simple, even to copying from the chalkboard into a notebook.
8. Move on to more advanced reading and writing activities which include other sources of information; include also higher levels of reading and writing, such as critical and evaluative thinking. These suggestions follow the principles of the Language Experience Approach discussed in Chapter 9.
9. In general, use as much concrete, hands-on activity as possible.
10. Visual aids which incorporate the oral element, such as a movie or a filmstrip with tape, provide excellent practice in listening comprehension and stimulate class discussion.

These techniques for teaching LEP students are easier to incorporate in some content areas than in others. In science, the emphasis on concrete, hands-on activities can be readily accomplished. Experiments, demonstrations, models, and many visuals are useful. Reading and writing can be used to supplement concepts already introduced orally and visually.

In social studies, skits and simulation exercises force LEP students to use their English. A great many cross-cultural activities are possible. The teacher can pair an Anglo student with an LEP student to study a third culture. Guest speakers provide important practice in listening comprehension. As always, keeping a journal provides writing practice.

The mathematics class provides a number of opportunities for language activities. The use of the metric system, common to Central and South America and much of the world, can be discussed, and the two systems (English and metric) compared in both languages. The use of games encourages oral language development and practice with English. Concepts can be reinforced with word problems and logic, requiring more language.

The content teacher in any class can find useful and challenging activities for the LEP student which contribute to content knowledge and also provide practice in various language skills.

Content teachers should look for help to the ESL teacher and the reading specialist. These two resource people should create a type of IEP for each LEP student. This program will indicate the student's level of proficiency in various content areas. Students' proficiency levels in both the native language and English should be available. In addition, these teachers should know the school district's resources for working with LEP students—dual-language books, for example. Questions about LEP students and materials to work with them can ultimately be referred to the National Clearinghouse for Bilingual Education, Arlington, Va.

Summary

The type of reading program to be implemented for LEP students is dependent upon the students' cognitive development as expressed through the native language and then in the second language. The goals of the reading program for LEP students should come from the teacher's ability to diagnose the students' cognitive development in the native language and the students' readiness to translate that cognitive development into reading in English.

Chapter Activities: Using What You've Read

Learn to Do It!

Identify teaching materials for use with LEP students in your unit. Add them to your annotated bibliography. Are there topics in your content area in which few materials are available?

Do It!

Identify an LEP student in your school. Interview him/her about his/her experiences in English language classes. Develop a case study of his/her problems in reading and content area classes.

References

COHEN, B. "Model and Methods for Bilingual Education." Boston: Teaching Resources Corporation, October, 1979.

————, "Issues Related to Transferring Reading Skills from Spanish to English." *Bilingual Education Paper Series,* 3, no. 9 (April 1980).

GARCIA, R. L., "Language and Reading Development of Bilinguals in the United States." The University of Oklahoma, 1977, EDRS 145–499.

GOLUB, L., "Evaluation Design and Implementation of a Bilingual Education Program, Grades 1–12, Spanish/English," *Education and Urban Society* 10, no. 3 (1977), 363–84.

————, "Literacy Development of Bilingual Children." Paper presented at the National Council of Teachers of English/National Conference on Research in English, Cincinnati, O., November 1980.

————, "Language Assessment Battery." Lombard, Ill.: Riverside, 1976.

PREWITT DIAZ, J. O., "Choosing the Language for Initial Reading Instruction in Bilingual Education," *Education*, Department de Instruccion Publica de Puerto Rico, 47 (May 1980), 55–59.

SCHUMANN, J. H., "Social and Psychological Factors in Second Language Acquisition, "*Understanding Second and Foreign Language Learning,* ed. Jack C. Richards. Rowley, Mass.: Newbury House, 1978.

THOMAS, Sister Marie, "Puerto Rican Culture." Paper read at the New York State Bar Association, Family Hour Section, January 29, 1969.

PART VII
EVALUATION OF READING AND TEACHING IN THE CONTENT CLASSROOM

OVERVIEW

Evaluation is Step 7 on the Decision Model for Diagnostic Teaching by Grouping. As a part of any teaching situation, evaluation is central to determining how much students have learned and how effective the teacher's planning was. Both aspects are dealt with here in a brief overview. Appropriate references for more complete discussions of evaluation are included.

Chapter 23
Evaluation of Student Progress and Teacher Effectiveness

Preview

We are considering both types of evaluation—that is, of student mastery and teacher effectiveness—together in this chapter because they are necessarily related to each other. If students are not making satisfactory progress, this reflects negatively on a teacher's effectiveness in presenting the content material. On the other hand, satisfactory progress on the part of students is one validation of the teaching strategies selected.

What Is Evaluation?

Evaluation, as presented as part of the Decision Model for Diagnostic Teaching (see Chapter 2), is logically related to diagnosis and organization for instruction. We view evaluation as a process rather than solely as a culminating experience. Perhaps some of the reader's teacher preparation experiences have included a similar concept of evaluation. For example, evaluation in a teaching methods course may have included more than a paper-and-pencil midterm and a final examination. Perhaps the professor has also evaluated process variables, such as correct English usage in oral and written forms, ability to work cooperatively in small groups, and communication of ideas orally in front of a group.

If evaluation is seen in this more complete form, much more useful information can be gained in helping students acquire content knowledge. If a student is doing poorly on examinations, it is useful to be able to examine his/her performance on the process variables. The student who is also not participating in class discussions and activities has more serious and pervasive problems than one who has made progress in process variables but has fallen down on paper-and-pencil tests. It is likely that these two hypothetical students have very different problems associated with their poor performances on written examinations. In this case, then, evaluation is closely related to diagnosis.

Evaluation as a process variable also enables the teacher to modify instruction as it is carried out. In other words, evaluation is also closely related to organization for instruction. For example, the teacher may have designed a learning center as a means for accomplishing a particular objective. Observation of the students working at the learning center reveals that they are encountering difficulties with a particular activity. As students' questions arise, the teacher soon realizes that the directions are ambiguous, or perhaps s/he realizes that this particular activity is too difficult for students to do independently at a learning center. In either case, the teacher would have to alter organizational plans given the feedback from the evaluation process.

DESIGNING EVALUATION PROCEDURES TO ASSESS STUDENT LEARNING

In planning evaluation procedures to accompany unit plans, for example, the initial focus should be on the terminal, behavioral, or performance objectives. The objectives should state the behaviors to be expected at the end of the teaching activity: what the teacher expects his/her students to be able to do after instruction in a particular skill. These behaviors serve as indicators which let the teacher know whether or not learning has taken place, and the degree and direction of that learning.

The other type of performance objectives describe the processes taking place during the learning tasks. These objectives, sometimes called *enabling* objectives, state the desired behaviors during the learning process before assessment of mastery of the terminal objectives (Gronlund 1981).

The evaluation component can be viewed as a criterion-referenced assessment of mastery of the performance objectives. The nature of the evaluation is specified in the objectives. For example, if the performance objective states that the student should be able to locate cities on maps using the lines of latitude and longitude with 90 percent accuracy, the best evaluation would be to have students actually locate cities on maps using this grid system. To attain mastery, the student would have to locate the correct point nine out of ten times. This may be accomplished through a paper-and-pencil test or through teacher observation of performance.

Choosing indicators of skill mastery requires a professional decision as to which might be the most useful, the least encumbered, and the most efficient criteria for assessing learning. Note that the indicators chosen should be the most useful ones, not necessarily the most easily observed. Both terminal and enabling objectives are used in the sample unit plan, *Neighbors to the South* (Appendix A). An example of a terminal objective is X: "Given a written evaluation based upon . . . , students will complete the objective part of the final evaluation with 90 percent accuracy." Another example within Objective X is "Students will write one paragraph describing five essential facts they have learned concerning the culture and people of Mexico. This will be based upon . . . ." The nature of the evaluation is clearly described in the terminal performance objective.

On the other hand, an enabling objective is found in D: "Given teacher-assigned group placement, students will select a topic for group research from the list compiled in Objective A, or submit an alternate proposal for teacher approval." Instructional strategies focus on creating the situation described in Specific Learning Outcome D. The evaluation component is described as follows: "Students will meet this objective when, in small groups, they demonstrate that they (1) have decided on a process by which they will select a topic; (2) assign leadership roles; and (3) choose a topic from the list or submit an alternative proposal." As can be seen from this example, evaluation does not necessarily have to involve a paper-and-pencil test, but it can rely on teacher observations made during instructional activities.

While the emphasis is on systematic evaluation, inherent in this entire evaluation design process is the notion that any evaluation design is only as effective as a teacher's ability to make professional decisions regarding which indicators are most appropriate. These indicators determine whether or not an instructional objective has been met, as well as the adequacy of the overall planning. The indicators may take on a great variety of forms, and therefore often preclude the evaluation of design involving paper-and-pencil tests. Teachers should explore a variety of strategies in designing evaluation procedures to pick the most appropriate indicators of student learning.

Systematic classroom observations of pupil behavior are useful, especially in the evaluating enabling or process objectives. The teacher must first formulate a list of behavioral indicators that would show that a curriculum objective is being met. This "sign or symptom system" of systematic classroom observation (Mitzel 1963) involves a detailed checklist of pupil behaviors that would be observed at regular intervals. These behaviors should be stated in objective, non-evaluative terms. For example, if pupil's safe use of machinery in an industrial arts class is an objective, then one behavioral indicator that a student is following safety practices is that s/he puts on protective glasses while using welding equipment. Since it is difficult for the teacher to make such observations while actively conducting a lesson, checklists are useful primarily during students' independent or group work on an assigned task. The behavioral indicators may be listed across the top of the page with the students' names in a column on the left side. When a student is observed exhibiting a particular behavior, it may be checked as an indication of success in relation to the objective.

Let's consider an example of what happens when a teacher selects inappropriate indicators. Let's say a science teacher is teaching a unit on evolution. Her objectives include the reading of some material outside the textbook. In assigning this material, however, she neglects to tell students what her objective is in reading the material—to think about the main ideas and relate them to the material in the textbook. Since the students have received no guidance, because they do not know the teacher's objective, they read the material in the same way they read their textbook. Since the teacher usually gives multiple choice tests of factual recall, they study with this type of evaluation in mind. When the teacher gives them an essay test which requires them to relate the ideas in the supplementary reading to the textbook, most students are unable to complete the evaluation satisfactorily because of inadequate preparation. Not only does the teacher need to select appropriate indicators of mastery, but s/he also needs to communicate the nature of these to students.

Another type of criterion-referenced measurement may involve attitudinal variables. Although objectives for student attitudes may not lend themselves to behavioral statements, they may be evaluated by looking for behavioral indicators. For example, if one objective is to improve students' attitudes toward the study of mathematics, the teacher might decide that the following are indicators of an improved attitude: completion of homework assignments, completion of optional extra problems, expressed interest or curiosity about a particular type of problem or activity, sharing of an application of the problem procedures in another class or at home, reading of books related to mathematics, and so forth. If the teacher notes an increase in these behavioral indicators in a student, s/he may assume that the student has become more positive in his/her attitude toward mathematics.

If a teacher thinks of student evaluation only in terms of norm-referenced tests in which students' performance is compared to age and grade peers in a national norming sample, teaching can be very discouraging indeed, especially if one teaches students from lower socioeconomic level neighborhoods. Achievement on norm-referenced measures is so closely related to family background that it simply does not reflect specific learning gained in a particular class (Mayeske 1973). In order to evaluate student learning in a particular class, criterion-referenced measurement makes more sense, so that the teacher can determine which students have and have not mastered the objectives set forth. S/he can pull together the students who are having difficulty with a particular objective in a small group for intensive instruction for a short period of time. In our example above, with students locating cities on maps using lines of latitude and longitude, a group of students who had not mastered this skill could be given extra instruction so that they would be able to carry out the other content objectives in which the use of this skill was assumed.

DESIGNING EVALUATION PROCEDURES TO ASSESS TEACHER EFFECTIVENESS

Evaluation of student learning naturally gives indications of teacher effectiveness. If none or very few of the students masters a particular objective, the instructional strategies for teaching that objective to students must be examined. It is possible that the strategies were not at fault but that some other factor, such as lack of readiness on the part of the students to engage in that objective, interfered with student learning. Again referring to our example of students learning to use lines of latitude and longitude, students who had not learned the concept of the grid system in determining directions would be unable to apply the skill of using intersecting lines in locating particular cities on a map. The teacher, in this instance, had not done an adequate job of assessing student readiness for the objective, or perhaps had overestimated the student readiness level based on reported experiences in prior grades.

Criterion-referenced measurement of instructional objectives, so helpful in knowing which students have and have not mastered the objectives set forth, puts the teacher on the line. If objectives are consistently not mastered by students, the teacher must question his/her effectiveness. On the other hand, the concrete evidence (through criterion-referenced measurement) that students are learning can bolster teacher morale as well as demonstrate effectiveness to administrators.

Evaluation, as we said earlier, is an ongoing process. A teacher ought to be constantly tinkering with the instructional system used in the classroom. The adage seems true: some teachers teach for twenty years, while others teach for one year twenty times. We hope that our readers will strive to be like the former type of teacher, regardless of how long they teach. Evaluation is the ongoing feedback system which enables teachers to know what needs to be modified and what proves effective. Well-seasoned and effective teachers set goals for themselves each year to make teaching a vital rather than a stagnant process. Active participation in professional societies can help keep teachers up to date in a field. As new information becomes available, teachers can evaluate their present activities in light of what is currently being recommended. Most professional journals welcome articles by teachers who can share their insights with others. Constant self-evaluation nurtures the desire for improvement and keeps teaching a vital process.

Thus far, we have spoken only of self-evaluation. The word *evaluation* also implies judgments made by others. In the supervisory model currently being recommended, called *clinical supervision* (Cogan 1973), the teacher participates in his/her own evaluation, setting forth certain objectives for improvement on which s/he wants to work. The supervisor's classroom observations and feedback are oriented toward whether or not the teacher is accomplishing his/her goals. Feedback unrelated to those goals is not supposed to be offered until a later point, when the teacher sets a related goal. The clinical supervision model is based on the assumption that teacher participation in the evaluation process is more likely to bring about lasting change in a positive direction.

Summary

Evaluation, seen in this light, is not something to be dreaded. It reflects how close a match the teacher has made between instruction and evaluation. If the teacher is teaching or emphasizing one aspect of a content area in instruction but testing another, the evaluation should indicate a problem. Evaluation may also reveal if the teacher is not communicating the goals and expectations of content study to the students. Open statements of objectives for learning are only fair and ultimately help the student set these for him/herself.

Classroom visitations by supervisors can be viewed positively as another source of information in the evaluation process. The teacher also has a right to know how s/he is being evaluated. Evaluation, whether by oneself or others, is the process that encourages teacher growth and professional behavior.

Chapter Activities: Using What You've Read

Learn to Do It!

1. Develop evaluation procedures for your unit. Be sure each objective is evaluated. Aim for a variety of evaluation procedures during the unit.
2. Develop a procedure to evaluate your unit. How will you gather student reactions to it? How will you record your reactions as you teach it?

Do It!

1. Give one or more of your evaluation procedures to a class. Record the results and your reaction to the results.
2. Conduct an evaluation of your unit while you're teaching it and after you finish teaching it. What changes would you make before teaching it again? What are its strengths and weaknesses?

References

COGAN, M. L., *Clinical Supervision*. Boston: Houghton Mifflin, 1973.

GRONLUND, N. E., *Measurement and Evaluation in Teaching* (4th ed.). New York: Macmillan, 1981.

MAYESKE, G. W., et al., *A Study of the Achievement of Our Nation's Students.* Washington, D. C.: U.S. Government Printing Office, 1973.

MITZEL, H. E., "The Place of Systematic Observation in Classroom Research." Paper presented to the Conference on Research Design and the Teaching of English at the Annual Meeting of the National Council of Teachers of English, San Francisco, 1963.

PART VIII
CONTENT AREA READING IN THE TOTAL SCHOOL PROGRAM

OVERVIEW

Where does content reading fit into the rest of the school program? How can a content teacher help other practicing teachers become effective content area reading teachers? These two topics are explained in this part.

The complete school reading program has three components—developmental, content, and remedial. What they are and how they fit together is part of the discussion. The chapter then goes on to describe the resources available in a complete reading program to support the content teacher.

Changing other teachers' behavior, the final chapter, provides a brief overview of change processes so necessary in schools today. Some suggestions for starting the change process, as well as continuing it, are included.

Chapter 24
The Complete Reading Program

Preview

The work of the content teacher is enormous! How can one teacher do all that this book suggests? Only slowly, over a period of time, says this chapter. In addition, the complete reading program includes a large number of resource people who can support the work of the content teacher. Look for a list of these people and the help they can give the content teacher in the chapter that follows.

Components of a Complete School Reading Program

The content teachers reading this book may well feel that the task of teaching reading in their content classes is enormous, even overwhelming. This feeling is perfectly normal, in our view. The task is large and important. It should not be minimized. Practicing teachers who have worked through the unit planning, selection of alternative reading materials, and the rest of the techniques suggested here report that it has taken them three years to convert a full year's course into this format. After all, teachers who are teaching every day have a limited amount of time to spend in planning. Therefore, preservice teachers who feel overwhelmed by the amount of work described here should take things a little at a time. Plan one unit and try it out. Then tackle another unit, and so on. Planning and using these teaching techniques becomes easier as teachers gain more practice with them. Practice also helps teachers identify which techniques fit their specific content area or particular students better —the basis for the professional judgments that we have been discussing.

Another important feature of content teachers' work with reading is that YOU ARE NOT ALONE! There are a number of other people in the school who are there to help students read better and help you teach them better in content classes. This chapter will discuss the various components of a complete school reading program and the personnel in these components.

A complete school reading program has three major components: the *devel-*

opmental reading program, the *content* reading program, and the *remedial* reading program (Hill 1979). These three components should be present at all levels of schooling, from K through 12, but their relative emphasis will differ as grade levels increase. Figure 24–1 gives a graphic version of the changing emphasis on the three components at different grade levels. The figure is suggestive rather than exact, to give an approximation of the emphasis in good school reading programs.

A number of important points are involved here. First, developmental reading is a continuing need from kindergarten through senior high school. Developmental reading involves teaching students how to read—the basic processes of reading and their use in students' developing lifestyles. Developmental reading in primary grades is easy to identify—the process of beginning reading and the need for students to be taught and to practice reading in order to become fluent readers. By intermediate grades, developmental concerns shift to advancing students' word attack skills and their use of higher levels of comprehension. In junior high school, students need instruction in how to work with expository writing, with searching skills, and with multiple sources. They also need to work with critical reading skills. In senior high school, developmental tasks may be more vocationally oriented, or oriented to higher-level study skills for college bound students. The emphasis on developing new reading skills gradually diminishes as instructional and independent level readers move to higher skill levels. However, the need for a developmental component in the total reading program is never completely gone.

A second point related to Figure 24–1 is that content reading is also present throughout the school cycle. Students begin reading materials in math, science, and social studies in the earliest grades. Not much emphasis is placed on content reading in the primary grades, but the base is there. Content reading gradually becomes the central emphasis of the reading program by junior high school. In essence, content reading is the application of developmental reading skills to the situations in which adults use reading—to gain information, to learn about people, and all the purposes discussed in Part I of this book.

A third point is that the need for an effective remedial component is present throughout the school reading program. This represents a philosophical position that

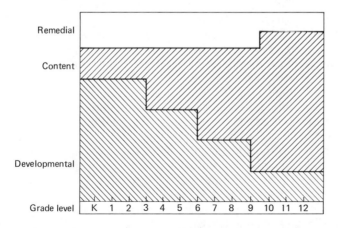

FIGURE 24–1   Changing Emphasis on the Components of the Reading Program

the school, and indirectly the society supporting the school, owes its young people a continuing opportunity to master this most basic of skills, reading. As a country and as a profession, we have accepted the proposition that literacy is important, indeed fundamental, to a democratic society. Thus, we need to provide support for those students who do not maintain the increasing reading levels of their peers and are classified as needing remedial help.

Defining remedial reading is not simple, because different sources use different definitions. However, the most common definition of remedial students is those reading two or more grade levels below grade placement at the intermediate level (grades 4–8) and three or more grade levels below at the secondary level (grades 9–12), as measured by a standardized reading achievement test (Spache 1976). These students are not necessarily exceptional, as defined by PL 94–142, although they may be; students needing remedial help include Betsy, our frustration level reader. They may also be bilingual or bidialectal. These distinctions are important, however. A student is judged to need remedial help in reading *solely* on his/her diagnosed needs in reading, *not* because s/he has a label like "learning disabled" or "bilingual." Not all exceptional, bilingual, or bidialectal students need remedial help in reading. It is important for teachers, students, and society at large not to stereotype students in this way.

Another facet of remedial reading for content teachers to remember is that, for the most part, students receiving remedial help in reading will still remain in their content classes. Even though Betsy is receiving remedial reading instruction two times a week, she remains in science, social studies, English, and math along with all the other students.

The Organization of the School Reading Program

Many school districts support an organized reading program, from K through 12, usually supervised by a reading supervisor or coordinator. This professional position requires not only teaching experience but experience as a reading teacher or specialist. The reading supervisor oversees the complete reading program, selects reading teachers, orders materials, and organizes inservice programs on reading for the entire faculty.

Frequently, the reading supervisor is also the school district's director of the supplementary federally funded reading program. Title I, a part of the federal educational programs included in the Elementary and Secondary Education Act (ESEA), has been an important support for the complete reading program described here since its inception in the 1960s. Title I, designed to provide intensive remedial education for students from disadvantaged or poverty level homes, has been replaced by Chapter I of the Education Consolidation and Improvement Act of 1981. The federal government provides grants to the states, which set up their own system of eligibility and funding within the federal guidelines. In many parts of the country, a large proportion of the remedial reading instruction provided in schools is supported by federal money. In these programs, students receive instruction in reading skills after careful diagnosis and with small pupil-teacher ratios (one to five in elementary schools, one to ten in secondary schools). Parent involvement is also encouraged in these programs.

Title I teachers, that is, teachers supported by federal funds, are reading specialists or people hired to serve specifically in reading instruction. In some states, these teachers serve also as resource teachers for content teachers at the intermediate grade and secondary level.

Resource teachers in reading are an important part of the complete school reading program. The reading resource teacher should be a reading specialist. In many states, this is a certification level beyond initial teacher certification requiring graduate work in reading and teaching experience. The reading resource teacher may provide some remedial instruction and may be supported by federal funds. However, his/her important function, for our purposes, is to work with content teachers in developing the materials and plans described in this book. The reading resource teacher is an excellent source for alternative reading materials, especially materials written at lower reading levels. S/he is also a resource for teaching techniques—new ways to teach vocabulary or study skills or critical reading. The reading resource teacher is usually responsible for testing students' reading level. S/he is the person to whom content teachers refer students who exhibit great difficulty in reading content material but who have not already undergone diagnostic testing in reading (student permanent record files are the source for results of previous diagnostic testing). It is important for content teachers to seek out the reading resource teacher in their school to discuss what services s/he is providing and how they can become part of his/her work.

Other personnel within the school play lesser roles in the complete reading program. The school *librarian* is an important resource for identifying and ordering materials for specific classes. S/he is also a source of instruction in research processes and library procedures. Content teachers should use the librarian's expertise in developing reading lists for units and lists of research topics, and in building classroom libraries for specific units. These resources include periodicals and reference materials, as well as books.

Another resource person is the *audiovisual specialist*. The audiovisual specialist is an excellent source of media materials for particular units—films, filmstrips, slides, etc. S/he is also an important resource when teachers develop their own media—videotapes, audiotapes, slides, transparencies, and the like. The AV specialist knows what is available and how to get it. S/he also knows the district's resources in materials and equipment for building new AV materials.

A further resource person for content teachers is the *special education resource teacher*. This teacher, who is certified to deal with exceptional children, may teach a self-contained class of special students or s/he may operate a special education resource room. In the resource room, exceptional students who are mainstreamed in some subjects receive separate instruction for other subjects. The special education resource teacher is an excellent source for information on specific handicaps, for materials for specific instruction of exceptional children, for advice on implementing IEPs, and for general support in working with exceptional students. S/he is also a key to the vast array of specialists available for specific handicapping conditions, such as speech clinicians, and for the more general needs served by the school psychologist (Cartwright, Cartwright and Ward 1981).

A final resource person for the content teacher is the *school counselor*. Counselors serve a wide variety of needs within schools, from running the school-wide testing programs to student scheduling to their favorite task, counseling individual students. Counselors are often involved in the IEP process, as well as in helping students and their parents decide what program and what specific courses to take. Content teachers will find that counselors maintain the permanent records of students in most instances. Thus, when the content teacher needs information on past experiences and performance of a student, his/her first source is the counselor and the permanent records. The counselor is also a source of information on a student's immediate problems, like a divorce or illness in the family, or on recurrent school problems like truancy and disciplinary problems. Serious and continuing reading problems, often coupled with other personal problems, can be identified in a short visit with the counselor to go over a student's records.

The resources (both people and material) of a school with a complete reading program are many and varied. A program like the one described here provides all sorts of support mechanisms for content teachers who seek them out. By and large, these resources will not come to the teacher; the teacher must go to them. One mark of a professional is his/her knowledge of the resources available and willingness to use the expertise of others in solving his/her problems.

It must be said, unfortunately, that not all schools have the complete reading program described here, nor are all the professional employees in the roles described uniformly willing to work with content teachers. It becomes important for content teachers to seek the resources available in the teaching situation in which they find themselves. Then they must use the available resources to help themselves and the students they teach.

Summary

Content teachers need to understand the three components of the complete reading program—the developmental, content, and remedial components. The resources available within these components are important for content teachers to understand and use: the reading resource teacher, often a Title I teacher; the reading supervisor or coordinator; the librarian, the audiovisual specialist, the special education resource teacher, and the counselor. The content teacher receives support from many sources, if s/he will seek them and use them appropriately.

Chapter Activities: Using What You've Read

Do It!

Discover the resources offered by your school and school district (or the school and school district in which you may teach in the future). Include in your report:

1. Information on any ongoing developmental reading program your students are or could be involved in.

2. Opportunities for students with reading problems to be given remedial reading. How often? One-on-one or large group? Are any of your students part of such a program?

3. Remedial reading teachers—what services do they provide? Are your students involved?

4. Reading resource teachers—what services will they provide—material production, classroom instruction, testing, etc.

5. Librarian/audiovisual specialist/special education resource teacher/school counselor—what services do they provide, especially those that would be useful to you as a content area reading teacher?

References

CARTWRIGHT, G. P., C. C. CARTWRIGHT, and M. E. WARD., *Educating Special Learners.* Belmont, Calif.: Wadsworth, 1981.

HILL, W. R., *Secondary School Reading: Process, Program, Procedure.* Boston: Allyn & Bacon, 1979.

SPACHE, G. D. *Diagnosing and Correcting Reading Disabilities.* Boston: Allyn & Bacon, 1976.

Chapter 25
Changing Other Teachers' Behavior

WHY CHANGE?

Changing instruction through staff development has often been a stepchild of American education. Why change a good thing—an institution, a tradition? In the fall of 1957, after Sputnik was launched, Americans began to ask why the Russians had been the first people in space, and many focused their attention on the educational system. Early in the 1960s, critics at the federal, state, and local levels began to look at schools; the press probed education, and lowered national standardized test scores also indicted American education. This led to the educational revolution of the mid-1960s, with the introduction of terms like "relevance," "flexibility," "innovation," and "affective education." If the child failed, it was the fault of the system that was unable to teach its teachers to cope with the varied and complex problems of educating all the pupils of the nation's public schools. It was emphasized that each child was a distinct individual with individual needs, feelings, and goals. Thus, in the late 1960s, we heard such terms as "self-worth," "humanism," and "individuality."

Change as a way of life for the American school system was just beginning to take hold when the 1970s arrived with faint sounds of "accountability" from disgruntled parents, politicians, and taxpayers. These groups began talking of holding educators accountable for their output; that is, for the achievement of children in their care (Dillion 1976). The accountability concept came together with such problems as a declining birth rate and resultant decline in teacher turnover, public dissatisfaction with achievement scores, and general societal pressures upon the school system.

Just who is to take the most important role in making sure that schools are accountable is not clear. What is clear is the recognition on the part of many people that schools can be helped by improving the people who work in them. Many groups are vying for the opportunity to participate in developing a policy for, or to take control of, change. Local school districts are providing more leadership for change, even using members of the active teaching staff to instruct or assist their colleagues. Institutions of higher learning continue their influence through graduate programs with formal degrees. School boards, administrators, state Departments of Education, regional units, professional education associations, legislation, and court decisions make change an integral part of the American school system.

Thus, it would seem safer to say not "why change," but "how" and "who"? The rest of this chapter will discuss the importance of change agents, what their role should be, the barriers to change they will find in their school systems, and some of the factors they can use in order to minimize barriers that may arise.

WHY A CHANGE AGENT?

Now that we know that change is going to occur, who should do the changing? While we should not discount the various agencies, organizations, and systems that can help bring about change, ultimately it comes down to the role of one person: the change agent. Who is this person? Lippitt, Watson, and Westley made available the first conception of the social "change agent," a person who had the skills necessary to help a client work out problems in an integrated step-by-step sequence (Havelock 1975). Much behavioral and social research on the consultation process, human relations, organizational development, and group dynamics shows how such a change agent might be effective in working with individuals and groups.

Another notion of the "change agent" was put forth by Everett Roger. His concept was rooted in the "county agent" in the Department of Agriculture's Extension Service. The county agent is not only a counselor and diagnostician to individual farmers, but also a conveyor of new facts and practices based on agricultural research and experimentation. By the late 1960s, Havelock and others were proposing a fusion of these two traditions in a new concept of the change agent as process helper and knowledge linker (Havelock 1975). Certain skills, such as interpersonal and inter-group relations, consultation, need definition, diagnosis, problem solving, and the acquisition, dissemination, and use of resources, are needed by the educators of the future at various levels and in various role categories.

It is important for the change agent to have some basic knowledge concerning "open systems," individual personality factors which help or hinder the use of knowledge and the concept of group relationships. Without this knowledge, change agents will not be able to encourage change.

Schools are open systems; people are open systems. In other words, there are variables in each system which act with and upon one another to bring about a sort of balance in the system. These systems receive messages (or input) from inside and outside the system and usually deal with them in some way by producing various types of output. A school system has internal variables, such as the structure of the organization, which send messages. It also receives messages from the outside, from society as a whole or from the school board in particular. All of these messages, both inside and outside the system, color how its output will be achieved (Havelock 1969). Remember such words as "flexibility," "relevance," and "accountability" from earlier in this chapter? These were messages (or input) from outside the system that influenced educational change.

Likewise, people receive messages (or input) from their internal systems and from the world as a whole. Their internal needs, values, personality, and satisfaction are very important to them. This, coupled with messages from outside their own system, provides individuals with situational and interpersonal influences that lead to certain kinds of behavior. These internal and external inputs can help the individual to develop certain expectancies about his/her own behavior. If the change agent has no concept of what affects a person or of what is important to that individual, then s/he has little hope of any change taking place. Change must be attached to an individual's motivational base, i.e., what is important to him/her. It is paramount, then, that the change agent understand what is important to his/her colleague, from the standpoint of both his/her internal motivations and external influences.

It is not enough to have some grasp of societal and organizational systems as well as knowledge about individuals; inter-group relations are also a factor in getting a change accepted. While it is true that the change agent is a most important person, s/he does not work alone. The agent must persuade people. S/he usually is trying to persuade them in a group. There are those group influences that are direct; for example, interpersonal processes that directly affect the change adoption process. Indirect influences are factors which predispose individuals to be or not to be susceptible to change as a result of interests or forces not connected with the change process. Direct interpersonal influences concern such things as the credibility of the change agent, the legitimacy of his or her strategies and leadership role. Indirect interpersonal and group influences include the participation level of the group, acceptance by the group of each other and the change agent, group cohesiveness, and the similarity between the adopter and the others with whom s/he interacts.

Teachers as Change Agents

While discussing this topic, it is likely that the new teacher or change agent will ask: "Why me? All I want to do is to introduce a program into my school that will help students learn! I am not a social scientist, or psychologist, or group manipulator." In essence, however, teachers are all of these. Daily contacts within a classroom give them experiences and knowledge about people and groups and organizations. This knowledge, combined with subject expertise, makes a teacher what is called an *internal* change agent—one who is employed by the organization to which s/he is consulting (Cubbon 1978). The literature does not suggest that teachers can be better change agents than external change agents, but they do have some advantages (Havelock 1973):

1. Teachers know the system—they know where the power is; can identify opinion leaders; know where the leverage points are.
2. Teachers speak the language—literally and figuratively; they know the special way in which their colleagues discuss things and refer to things, their tone and style.
3. Teachers understand the norms (the commonly held beliefs, attitudes, and behavior) and probably believe in them, too.
4. Teachers can identify with the system's needs and aspirations—since many of the system's needs are theirs, they have a personal incentive for helping.
5. Teachers are familiar figures, a known quantity—most of what they will do is understandable and predictable; they aren't new and "unfamiliar" and do not pose a threat.

Teachers do, of course, have some disadvantages, such as lack of power and no independence of movement due to other obligations; they may have to redefine their relationships with other members of the system. These are pitfalls which are not to be ignored; however, teachers should concentrate on what they will take back to their school and their colleagues—and, most importantly, their students.

BARRIERS TO CHANGE

So now, armed with this expertise, knowledge about people, groups, and organizations, teachers are ready to go back and implement. Back home, however, teachers may find resistance to their changes, both from those who have authority in the school and from those who do not have authority but will be affected by the proposed change—both administrators and teachers. There are internal and external variables at work, and a discussion of some potential objections that may not be expressed verbally, but are there nevertheless, is a valuable activity. It is important for the change agent to realize that some things can be done in order for the change to become more acceptable to those involved.

Minimizing Resistance to Change

Havelock (1973) presents several common reasons why people resist change, whether they have power or not. Here are some common causes of resistance to change on the part of persons having a veto power over the proposal, that is, the authority to accept or reject a proposal. Such a person, usually an administrator or supervisor, may reject it for any one or more of the following reasons:

1. Inertia. A desire to retain the status quo even where the present situation is obviously inferior. There is the tendency to want to do things in the accustomed manner. For example, a person ordinarily wants to sit in the same seat he sat in during the first day of class, even though that seat was originally a random choice. (In fact, many a student has become disturbed to find someone in "his" seat.) Resistance is aroused mostly because a new method is a change, which has no relation to the specific proposal. Thus a supervisor, for example, may oppose the new method merely because it is different from what s/he is accustomed to doing.

2. Uncertainty. Regardless of how inferior the existing method may be, at least it is known how well it functions. However, how well a proposed change will function is a matter of prediction that is sometimes grossly in error. Any deviation from the current procedure involves a risk; there is no guarantee that the new method will bring better results after the cost and trouble of installation have been incurred. The feeling that many have is: "Why should we create a potential source of trouble by introducing a new system when the existing one works?" In this case, the person is unwilling to trade inferiority of which s/he is certain for superiority of which s/he is uncertain.

3. Failure of the person who needs to change to see the need for the proposed change.

4. The change proposal may not be understood by the person rejecting it. Even though this person is not directly affected by the proposal, a failure to understand the nature and functioning of the new system may well arouse over-cautiousness and a feeling of inferiority and resentment.

5. The fear of obsolescence. A person who has invested years of experience to build up a high level of skill, knowledge, and judgment in administering a certain system stands to have these fruits of experience made obsolete by adoption of a new procedure. When a new system is proposed, a fear of the inability to become equally proficient under the new system may well cause any person to be apprehensive as to his/her future value and security in that job. Under such circumstances, resistance to the proposal is likely.

6. Loss of job content. A change may reduce the skill required, scope, importance, or responsibility offered by a person's job. For example, a proposed change may reduce the size of the work force supervised by the person objecting. Such effects are commonly referred to as *job dilution*. This usually reduces the prestige value of the job and the value of the job holder to the organization, and therefore may well arouse resistance.

7. Desire to retain favor of the work group. If a change is unpopular with his subordinates, a supervisor is likely to resist the proposal.

8. A personality conflict between the change agent and person to be changed.

9. Resentment of outside help. The implication is that the person cannot handle his own problems.

10. Resentment of criticism. This might well occur if the person to whom the proposal is aimed originated the present method. Noncritical statements are often *construed* as criticism; so beware not only of critical statements, but of ones that might be taken as such.

11. Lack of participation in development of the proposed change. Embarrassment at not having conceived of an idea which on hindsight appears obvious will probably cause resentment. There might well be a feeling of this kind if some or all of the ideas are somebody else's, giving rise to some sort of face-saving reaction.

12. Tactless approach on the part of the proposer. *Sometimes a few words can make the difference.* Remember those famous last words: "That's no way to do it...."

13. Lack of confidence in the ability of the person proposing the idea. This situation is commonly encountered by inexperienced people.

14. Inopportune timing. Rejection may have been received only because the proposal was made when the person rejecting it was emotionally or physically upset, or when he was unusually busy, or when teacher relations were strained.

Sometimes there is resistance to change on the part of persons directly affected by a proposed change, usually teachers. Some common causes of resistance to change on the part of persons having no direct voice in the matter of acceptance or rejection of the proposal, but directly affected by it, include the following:

1. Inertia, especially when the change is sudden or radical.

2. Uncertainty as to just what a change will bring. Even though the current situation may not be satisfactory to the teacher, s/he may not care to risk the possibility of a poorer situation.

3. Ignorance of the need for or purpose of the change. Only too often changes are made with little or no explanation to the teachers, sometimes with the feeling that it is none of their business.

4. Failure to understand the new method or policy may arouse suspicion or an insecure feeling.

5. A loss of job content. A change that means a reduction in skill required, or of importance, or of responsibility, may readily arouse resistance.

6. Pressure of the work group. Each member of the work group often reacts so as not to offend the others, even though as an individual he does not feel as strongly as his actions would indicate. Every work group has certain ingrained policies, some expressed and others implied, that constitute a "code of behavior" and that help to govern the actions and reactions of its members. A person's reaction to a change is usually influenced by what he knows or anticipates the group wants, even to the point of sacrificing personal gain for continued approval of his co-workers. And this is important: older members, who are the most frequent and stubborn resistors, are often the most influential persons in the work group.

7. Fear of economic insecurity. A change may result in displacement of the employee or a reduction in his earnings. The latter may arise especially if there is an inability to master the new method, or at least to reach the level of proficiency that the person had attained under the replaced method. This is particularly true of older people.

8. Alteration of social relationships, or fear of that, such as the breakup of a closely-knit work group.

9. An antagonistic attitude toward the person introducing the change or what s/he represents. It may be personal antagonism toward his/her function, or toward management in general. The latter, an attitude that is often hostile, causes individuals and groups to resist almost any change, in fact almost everything but the paycheck that comes from the direction of management. This might be called "resistance on general principles." The attitude underlying it is common.

10. Origination or introduction by an "outsider." Superintendents and/or principals are usually considered as external to the teachers' economic and social group; in fact, they are frequently quite unpopular. Resentment and resistance are quite likely if such persons introduce or are known to have originated a change.

11. No participation in development of the new method or policy. It appears to teachers that changes are often adopted without their best interests in mind. They want an opportunity to express and protect these interests, to have a part in deciding what they must do and how.

12. A tactless approach on the part of the person introducing the change.

13. Inopportune timing. Resistance may have been received only because the change was introduced when feeling was running high between the work group and management, or because the change was made with little or no advance notice.

Suggested Methods for Minimizing Resistance to Change

The following recommendations should be considered in planning the introduction of an idea and in modifying the idea to make it more saleable and palatable.

1. Convincingly *explain the need* for the change. Don't overlook the teacher in this respect.
2. Thoroughly *explain the nature* of the change. Use straightforward, clear, well-organized language to assure that persons understand the method or policy. Do not overlook the importance of this understanding. Tailor your written and oral reports to suit the particular audience. For example, policy-makers in general should be given a condensed description of the proposal, emphasizing the overall picture and making liberal use of charts, graphs, and other visual aids. Reports to persons who must administer the new procedure should include a thorough and easily understandable description of how the procedure is to function.
3. Encourage participation, or at least the *feeling of participation*, in the development of the proposed method. In general, people are concerned about making their own ideas and recommendations succeed, whereas in general they have a neutral or negative attitude toward the ideas of others. The feeling of participation may be imparted in several ways.
    a. *Consult;* ask for information, opinions, suggestions. Show a real interest in what these people have to say. Seek advice even if you think you do not need it, and you may benefit in more ways than one. The mere opportunity to express him/herself, the mere request to contribute, may well give a person a feeling of participation in developing a new method, even though none of his/her ideas have actually been included in the new setup.
    b. Of course, whenever possible, *include the worthwhile suggestions of others* in your final proposal and give credit to the appropriate individuals.
    c. In some instances it may be advisable, or even necessary, to incorporate a person's idea that is inferior to that which you would otherwise use in order to get him/her into the act. This "sugaring up" or compromising of proposals in order to get them accepted and to minimize adverse reactions will probably make the difference between success and failure on many occasions.
4. Use a *tactful* approach in introducing your proposal. Watch your wording and mannerisms, and above all, avoid criticism or anything that may be construed as such.
5. Watch your timing.
    a. In attempting to gain adoption of an idea, avoid making your proposal when the recipient is upset, busy, etc. Allow sufficient time for him/her to think it over; don't rush the matter. Who knows; sometime later s/he may concede, or may even propose the ideas as his/her own.
    b. In introducing a new method or policy to colleagues, provide ample advance notice. Avoid introducing certain changes when relations are abnormally strained.
6. In the case of major changes, if possible, introduce the change in stages. The mere magnitude of some proposals sometimes frightens people and arouses objection.
7. In attempting to gain acceptance, capitalize on the features that provide the most personal benefit to the person(s) you are trying to sell.
8. If possible, by appropriate questioning, maneuver a prospective rejector into "thinking" of the idea himself. This procedure of "planting" the idea in his mind is usually effective if it can be worked. The difficulty is that this is not easily accomplished, nor are we generally so noble that we make a habit of letting others get the credit for our ideas.
9. Show a personal interest in the welfare of the person directly affected by the change by:
    a. paying particular attention to older persons, close social relationships, individual differences, etc.
    b. providing thorough training in the new procedure.
10. Whenever possible, have changes announced and introduced by the immediate supervisors of those affected.
11. Keep a log of contacts with teachers and other personnel as a record of involvement.

The foregoing measures, concerning minimizing resistance to a *specific* change, are no substitute for a long-term "conditioning" for change. These measures should be supplemented by a long-term effort to prepare teachers for, and harden them to, change in general. This conditioning process, involving both a technical and a psychological preparation, should provide the following:

1. Adequate training, so that the people affected will be capable of mastering new methods and techniques.
2. Psychological conditioning of people for change, by:
    a. educating them to the importance of change to the welfare of the students. The inevitability of change, the consequences of stagnation, and so forth, should be emphasized.
    b. keeping appropriate people informed of trends and expected developments in practice, policy, and technology so that they can anticipate changes and be psychologically and technically prepared.
    c. maintaining a policy of, and reputation for, fair treatment of those affected by change, on matters of retraining, job content, etc.

Not to be undersold as an effective long-term measure in minimizing resistance to change is awareness of the phenomenon itself. If a person is aware of the causes, manifestations, and frequency of this reaction, he will be less inclined to resist change. Thus, a worthwhile countermeasure is to install this awareness in the minds of all personnel, especially supervisors.

Probably the most important recommendation is to *plan the introduction of the idea and modify it when necessary*. In applying the principles of change given here to content area reading, the following might be helpful:

1. Demonstrate the need for the change. Create a group reading inventory and/or a cloze test, give it to several classes, and report the results.

2. Thoroughly explain the nature of the change using language teachers will understand and examples from the local situation.

3. Encourage participation; people will work if they feel their ideas are considered important. Consult, include their suggestions; compromise when needed.

4. Be tactful; avoid criticism.

5. Watch your timing. Let people think it over; give advance notice if possible or applicable; introduce change in stages. Start with simple techniques that are easier to accept, then gradually move into more complex topics.

6. Try to show where the changes will help them the most. Help content teachers restructure their courses to accommodate different reading levels.

7. Show a personal interest in the welfare of the people affected by the change.

8. Work with a few well-respected people first (perhaps one from each content area) asking them to try out some techniques. Others will observe them and follow if they are successful.

Summary

It should be apparent by now that change is not something of which we must be afraid. Each individual grows and changes, systems grow and change, the world is growing and changing. It is the special responsibility of education to allow for this growth and change; to provide for this growth and change; to facilitate this growth and change. This is why we educate; that is what we should educate toward. We do not accept stagnation in our classrooms; we should not accept it from ourselves.

Chapter Activities: Using What You've Read

Do It!

1. In Chapter 24 you developed a list of the resources that your school/school district offered to you as a teacher who wished to improve the reading skills of your students. If the resources in your school district are inadequate, what measures could you use to obtain the kind of professional support and expertise you feel you need?

    You can identify with the system's needs and aspirations, but you will also run into all of the resistance to change Havelock described. Be prepared to demonstrate the need for change. Consider both administrators and teachers in your school as you plan whom you would contact.

2. The chapter you have just read deals with changing attitudes. Look back at the pre-test you took before you worked through this book. Look, too, at your notes at the end of Chapter 1. Have your attitudes toward content area reading changed? If so, how did this book affect those changes? Reread the section on Minimizing Resistance to Change. The answer to how your own attitudes changed may help you to change others' attitudes.

References

BISHOP, L. J., *Staff Development and Instructional Improvement.* Boston: Allyn & Bacon, 1976.

CUBBON, S., "Historical Review and Statement of Current State of Educational Linking." Unpublished Report, Central Susquehanna Intermediate Unit. Lewisburg, Pa., 1978.

DILLION, E. A., "Staff Development: Bright Hope or Empty Promise?" *Educational Leadership*, December, 1976.

DRABA, R. E., "Guidelines for Viable Inservice Education," *Journal of Reading,* 18:5. February, 1975.

HAVELOCK, R. G., et al., *Planning for Innovation.* Center for Research on Utilization of Scientific Knowledge. Ann Arbor, Mich., 1969.

HAVELOCK, R. G., *The Change Agent's Guide to Innovation in Education.* Englewood Cliffs, N.J.: Educational Technology Publications, 1973.

HAVELOCK, R. G., and M. C. HAVELOCK, "Training for Change Agents," Center for Research on Utilization of Scientific Knowledge. Ann Arbor, Mich., 1975.

KRALIK, D. J., "Creative Educational Leadership." Tacoma, Wash.: Intermediate Unit, Office of Education, Pierce County, 1970.

LIPPITT, R., et al., *The Dynamics of Planned Change.* New York: Harcourt, Brace and World, 1958.

NATIONAL SCHOOL PUBLIC RELATIONS ASSOCIATION, "Inservice Education: Current Trends in School Policies and Programs." Arlington, Va., 1975.

OLIVERO, J., "Helping Teachers Grow Professionally," *Educational Leadership,* December, 1976.

Conclusion
Putting It All Together

Now that you have completed the full course in content area reading and individualized instruction, you're ready to implement it in your everyday teaching. Before you do that, complete the posttest of the self-assessment you took at the beginning of the book. Look back at the *Knowledge of Content Area Reading Test* and the *Statement Survey: Attitude Assessment* beginning on p. 000. Take these tests and score them as you did before (refer to the answers on page ____ for the Knowledge Test; score the attitude assessment as on p. 000). Now enter your scores here:

	Pretest	*Posttest*
Knowledge of Reading Test	_____	_____
Statement Survey:	_____	_____

We hope you see improvement in both scores. The most important result of this study, we believe, is your increased confidence in your ability to help your students read and learn successfully in your content classroom.

Appendix A

TITLE: Neighbors to the South

TARGET AUDIENCE: This unit is designed for students in Grades 7, 8, and 9. Students should be identified according to performance levels (below average, average, and above average) and according to lingual experience (English-speaking, English- and Spanish-speaking) for grouping purposes.

TIME ALLOTMENT: Approximately six weeks (five 45-minute class periods per week); may be expanded to a double period per day, with teaming of Social Studies and English or Reading teachers, to allow for in-depth coverage of both content material and accompanying reading and study skills.

INTRODUCTION: The unit has been designed to provide teachers with a flexible framework which can be utilized to teach any topic to students at any grade or competency level, integrating reading and study skills with mastery of content. Although this unit has been designed around content material on Mexico, actual content area objectives have been excluded to allow heavier emphasis to be placed on reading and study skills. It is presumed that teachers will incorporate and develop actual content material into the unit. The curriculum is student-centered and multitextual. Students are identified according to performance levels (below average, average, and above average) and according to lingual experience (English-speaking, English- and Spanish-speaking) and grouped heterogeneously so peer teaching will result. Students will be evaluated both as a group and individually. Points are assigned to each requirement and students falling below expectations may contract to do additional work for extra credit. Individual conferences are held to discuss grade scale and develop contracts.

1

Prepared by Dr. Anne Mallery, currently of Millersville, Pa., State College and Dr. Andrea Lee, currently of Marygrove College, Detroit, Mich.

GRADE SCALE—   0– 70 points—F
71–140 points—D
141–220 points—C
221–290 points—B
291–350 points—A

OBJECTIVE	*MAXIMUM POINTS*
B—(sentences)	5
E—(library worksheet)	10
G—(notetaking exercise)	20
I—(commercial videotape)	15
J—(oral report)	50
K—(text writing)	40
N—(mural)	10
O—(vocabulary exercise)	20
P—(learning centers)	15
Q—(student vocabulary activity)	20
R—(fiesta)	20
S—(recreational reading)	15
T—(vocabulary evaluation)	20
U—(options)	40
X—(final written evaluation)	50
	350 points

UNIT DESIGN: Activities in an activity packet are leveled and may be used to supplement the grade of the less able student. Learning centers should be designed to reinforce reading skill deficiencies identified through subject evaluation and performance of unit requirements. Points should also be affixed to each center and be added to the students' score upon successful completion of the activity.

Example of Learning Centers and Activities:

Center I   Reading Comprehension—Students are instructed to read supplementary materials (handouts, brochures, magazines) and complete a sheet of questions. Questions should include examples of main idea, detail, inference, sequence, and conclusion.

Center II   Listening Comprehension—Students listen to teacher-made cassettes. Tapes should provide students with the main idea of the selection and set purpose for listening. Upon completion of the dialogue, students should be instructed to write a synopsis of the selection with illustrations. Evaluation should include attention to main ideas, details, and sequence.

Center III   Visual Discrimination, Visual Perception—Students complete jigsaw puzzle.

Center IV   Creative Writing—Students select a picture from among a group of selections and are instructed to identify people, place, time, and activity, then write a short story about what preceded and followed the picture.

Center V   Reasoning, Critical Thinking—A set of questions are provided to students as a film preview. Students read questions to set purpose and then watch the film strip. (Previews are usually available through library services.) Questions are then completed. Questions should be constructed to require students to use information presented in the film.

Center VI   Following Directions—An art center should be set up providing materials for an art activity but requiring students to read and follow directions to complete the project.

Center VII   Oral Composition—A tape center is set up with easy-to-read biographical books and a tape recorder. Students read a book and complete a sheet listing information.

Center VIII   Famous People—Background (birth, family life, education); contribution; impact on Mexican life. The student then assumes the character of a famous person and prepares a cassette telling how this person's life contributed to Mexican culture.

TERMINAL GOAL: This unit will have as its purpose the integration of content material on the people, geography, and culture of Mexico with those reading and study skills necessary to absorb this content.

General Learning Outcomes

1. (affective domain) Students will demonstrate interest in the people, geography, and cultural diversity of Mexico.
2. (cognitive domain) Students will develop research topics for oral reports, given teacher-designed instruction and multiple resources.
3. (cognitive domain) Students will demonstrate reading and study skills, given teacher instruction.
4. (affective domain) Students will demonstrate ability to interact with a group, assign leadership roles, and delegate responsibility.
5. (psychomotor domain) Students will demonstrate creative ability by selecting a project option from a teacher-made list or submit a proposal for an optional project for teacher approval; and by participating in fiesta and mural-painting activities.

Specific Learning Outcomes (Enabling Objectives)

N.B. Numbers in parentheses following each objective refer to the General Learning Outcome(s) to which the specific objective is related. Numbers are listed in descending order according to the primary emphasis which a particular lesson is designed to develop: e.g. (2, 4) would indicate that the primary emphasis is to attain the General Learning Outcome of oral research reports, while a secondary emphasis would be that of developing group interaction skills. Circled objectives will be counted for point accumulation and grading purposes.

A. Given a slide presentation on Mexico with accompanying teacher commentary, students will participate in a guided large-group discussion and compile a list of topics which will serve as possible research ideas. This objective will have been met if the class names the following topical areas after viewing the slides and hearing the teacher commentary:

       climate
       geography

8

2

industry
population
cultural problems
transportation
trade
education
art forms
exploration   (1,2)

(B.) While viewing the slide presentation for a second time, with Mexican music as a background, students will write a one-sentence observation which can be discerned from the media presentation, related to the topics listed above.   (2, 3)

C. Given teacher guidelines for establishing groups (food; decorations; music and dance; costumes; and guests) students will volunteer to join a planning group for the unit's culminating activity, a Mexican fiesta.   (4, 1, 5)

D. Given teacher-assigned group placement, students will select a topic for group research from the list compiled in Objective A, or submit an alternate proposal for teacher approval.   (4, 2)

(E.) Given a library tour conducted by appropriate personnel, students will demonstrate knowledge of research procedures by individually completing a teacher-made worksheet covering card catalog, Dewey decimal system, reference materials, vertical file, media usage, etc., with 90 percent accuracy.   (2, 3)

F. In groups, students will locate research materials on various reading levels and bring them to the classroom for the construction of a classroom library. Compiled materials will be available to all groups.   (3, 1, 2, 4)

(G.) Given a lecture demonstration on listening and a common method of notetaking, stu- 10 dents will demonstrate skill in notetaking by using the method to capsulize one live teacher lecture, one chapter chosen from the reading resource books, and one taped lecture on Mexico. Criteria will consist of comparing student notes to teacher-prepared sets.   (3, 2)

H. Students will demonstrate ability to pursue research topics individually and in groups, using available resources, by using assigned time profitably, as determined by teacher observation.   (2, 3, 4)

(I.) Given a teacher lecture on effective speaking techniques, students will practice the skills 9 outlined by writing and delivering a one-minute commercial designed to sell a Mexican product. These will be videotaped and evaluated by classmates and teacher according to these criteria: adherence to outline; presentation; logical sequence of ideas; and originality.   (3, 1, 2, 5)

(J.) Having prepared research presentations, small groups will give oral reports, while remainder of class takes notes.   (2, 4, 1)

(K.) Given a guided discovery lesson on effective writing techniques, small groups of students will utilize notes taken during oral reports to write specific chapters for a student-made text on Mexico. Text will be typed and distributed. Evaluation will be according to the instrument for determining writing effectiveness included in this unit.   (3, 4)

L. In small groups, students will plan a section of a Mexican mural to be painted in class, 9 deciding how their particular topic can be visually portrayed.   (4, 5, 1)

M. Students will complete a rough sketch for a section of a mural dealing with a particular 10 topic, and transfer the sketch onto the wall mural with carbon paper.   (5, 1, 4)

(N.) Students will plan the painting of the mural, allocating responsibilities to various group 9
members, and paint their section of the mural. Each group will explain their section of the
mural in both a one-page written commentary to be affixed to the mural and recorded on   2
a cassette tape.   (5, 4, 3)

(O.) Given a lecture presentation on vocabulary development, students will select four words
from a teacher-assigned book and apply the Frontier Vocabulary System to each
word.   (3)

(P.) Given teacher-designed learning centers with vocabulary activities, to accompany the 9
videotape presentation on "Lost Cities" (theme vocabulary: emphasis on roots and
affixes) students will select at least two activities to be completed during the class period,
placing completed work in appropriate envelopes. Students completing learning center
activities will select a book from the recreational reading table.   (3, 1)

(Q.) Given materials and working in pairs, students will create a vocabulary game or activity 9
based on vocabulary words selected for the class glossary on day 20. (Selection of
words may be from the entire class list, e.g., four (4) words × thirty (30) students = 120
words.)   (3, 5, 4)

(R.) Students will divide into groups as determined in Objective C, assign leadership, and
delegate responsibility for fiesta day to be held on day 30. Students will draw up and
submit a plan for their area of concern to teacher by day 19. Teacher will approve plan by
initialling it.   (5, 4)

(S.) Given books for recreational reading (various reading levels), students will choose a 10
book with teacher assistance, and upon completion will complete a guidesheet for
reporting on recreational reading. Students will be required to complete and report on at
least fifty pages (may be completed in or out of class).

(T.) Students will complete a written test based upon vocabulary contracts with 100 percent
accuracy.   (3)

(U.) Students will select options from the activity packet totaling at least forty points (points are
listed on each option). Options which are student-designed will be submitted to the
teacher and assigned a point value.   (5, 1, 3)

V. Students will check their completed activities against the unit activity list, determine
which activities they have not yet completed, secure necessary materials, and complete
activity to attain objective. Student work must be completed by day 30 in order to count
for credit.

W. Given a teacher-led review, students will fill in the review outline as teacher works it on the
overhead projector to prepare for the final written evaluation.

7   (X.) Given a written evaluation based upon objectives E, G, H, I, K, O, P, Q, T, students will
complete the objective part of the final evaluation with 90 percent accuracy.   (3)

Given several open-ended sentences based upon Objectives C, D, F, J, L, R, students
will evaluate unit, according to their perceptions on the effectiveness of grouped activities.   (4)

Students will write one paragraph describing five essential facts they have learned
concerning the culture and people of Mexico. This will be based upon Objectives A, B, M,
N, S, U.   (1)

Students will sign up for a five-minute private conference with teacher (can be scheduled
anytime within next week) to discuss performance as to Objectives J, M, N, V, W. (2, 5)

Y. Students will participate in culminating activity by voluntarily taking part in various
activities on fiesta day.   (5, 4, 1)

SUGGESTED TIME ALLOTMENT FOR MEETING OBJECTIVES
AND LEARNING OUTCOMES

Day	Objective	Description
1	A	motivation; research ideas
	C	fiesta grouping
2	B	motivation; discerning
	D	selecting research topics
3	E	library tour
4	F	1/2 class secure research materials
	G	1/2 class lecture on notetaking
5	F	reverse groups from day #4
	G	
6	G	notetaking activity
	H	individual and group research
7	G	notetaking activity
	H	individual and group research
8	H	individual and group research
9	I	presentation on speaking techniques
		begin work on commercials
10	H	research
	I	commercials
11	H	research
	I	commercials
12	J	oral reports (3)
13	J	oral reports (2)
	L	mural planning
14	J	oral reports (2)
	K	text writing
15	K	1/2 group—text writing
	M	1/2 group—draw
16	K	reverse groups from day #15
	M	
17	N	two groups paint
	R	three groups plan fiesta
18	N	switch groups
	R	

8 ⌈ (days 1–2)
  ⌊

3
+
4

Day	Objective	Description
19	N R	switch groups
20	O	vocabulary lecture and activity
21	P S	teacher-made vocabulary activities recreational reading
22	Q	students design vocabulary games, puzzles
23	T	sharing ideas—vocabulary evaluation
24	U	options
25	U R	options plan fiesta
26	R S	plan fiesta recreational reading
27	R V	plan fiesta complete unfinished activities
28	W	review
29	X	unit evaluation
30	Y	fiesta

3
+
4

7

STRATEGIES:

Day 1—Objective A, C (guided discovery mode—convergent)

8

1. Have bulletin boards or posters up to create atmosphere.
2. Introduce unit with slide presentation and teacher commentary.
3. Guided discussion—a. this unit is about Mexico.
          b. some topics we might want to consider are. . . .
4. Write student suggestions on board.
5. Use questioning strategy to arrive at desired list of topics.
6. Discuss culminating activity with students (Mexican fiesta).
7. List various preparation groups (food, music and dance, etc.) See objective.
8. Discuss responsibilities of each group.
9. Allow students to volunteer for groups, guiding choices so each group has adequate representation.

Day 2—Objective B, D (guided discovery to inquiry mode—convergent to divergent)

1. Distribute worksheets with list of topics from Objective A.
2. Instruct students to watch slides and write a one-sentence observation from each topical area.

3. Show slides with music background. Repeat if necessary.
4. Assign students to groups.
5. Allow groups to select a research topic from the list.
6. Provide for adequate coverage of topics by entire class.
7. Tell students that alternative proposals may be submitted for teacher approval.
8. Distribute objective checklist to students with points and grading criteria. Explain.

$$3 + 4$$

Day 3—Objective E (lecture-recitation—convergent)

1. Plan library tour with appropriate personnel.
2. Distribute teacher-made worksheets.
3. Take students to library.
4. Assist library personnel.
5. Allow students to complete worksheet in library.

Day 4—Objective F, G (lecture-recitation—convergent)

1. Split class into two groups.
2. 1/2 group to library to secure research materials for oral report.
3. Make sure the "library group" can split into their respective research groups to look for materials.
4. Present lecture on listening and notetaking. (Use handout as content guide.)
5. Distribute handout to students and begin practice for assignment.

Day 5—Objective F, G

1. Switch groups and proceed as on Day 4.

Day 6—Objective G, H (includes convergent and divergent activities)

1. Split classes into research teams.
2. Three groups work on research projects, using any available materials.
3. Three groups work on notetaking activity.
   a. Ten-minute live teacher lecture on Mexican music. (Students take notes.)
   b. Listening station—10-minute taped lecture on Mexican art. (Students take notes.)
   c. Duplicated article on Mexican dance or theatre. (Students take notes.)
4. Switch notetaking groups at given intervals.

Day 7—Objective G, H

1. Switch groups and proceed as on Day 6.

Day 8—Objective H (divergent)

1. Split classes into research teams.
2. Allow students to work on research projects.
3. Set up viewing stations for filmstrips, etc.
4. Provide access to library.
5. Call individual students to check on notetaking activity.
6. Provide assistance to students as requested. (Research.)

Day 9—Objective I (guided discovery to divergent activity)

1. Begin lesson by giving a short (30-second) speech in three different ways (e.g., dull, normal, enthusiastic).
2. Discuss which version students enjoyed best and why.
3. Work into presentation on effective speaking techniques.
4. Use "effective speaking handout" as a guide to cover main points.
5. Distribute handout and discuss how TV commercials are set up; how they follow this format.
6. Show several videotaped commercials if possible; if not, allow students to relate TV commercials with which they are familiar.
7. Give students assignment to write and deliver a one-minute commercial to sell a Mexican product.
8. Display examples or pictures of Mexican products.
9. Students make choices and begin to structure commercials.

3
+
4

Day 10—Objective H, I (divergent—inquiry activity)

1. Students work on research or commercials.
2. Set up videotape recorder to film commercials as they are ready.

Day 11—Objective H, I

1. Continue as on Day 10.
2. Allow students to operate videotape recorder if regulations permit.

Day 12—Objective J (student reports)

1. Instruct students to take notes while oral reports are being given.
2. **Quickly review notetaking techniques.**
3. Two or three 10-to-15 minute reports.

Day 13—Objective J, L (student reports)

1. Continue procedure for oral reports. (Two groups.)
2. Explain wall mural idea to students. (Different sections of the mural will reflect various research topics.)
3. Develop notion of the purpose for a mural.
4. Allow groups to discuss how they might visually portray their topic.
5. Distribute newsprint for initial sketching of ideas.

Day 14—Objective J, K (guided discovery—convergent)

1. Continue procedure for oral reports. (One group.)
2. Conduct guided discovery lesson writing techniques.
3. Use several written examples to show different ways to express ideas verbally.
4. Use questioning strategy to develop concepts on handout.
5. Distribute handout and assign groups the task of writing a chapter to be included in student-written text on Mexico.
6. Finished chapter will be submitted to teacher for approval.
7. Allow students to type text on dittoes. (Illustration of chapter may be chosen as an activity for Objective U for a total of thirty points.)

Day 15—Objective K, M (divergent)

1. Divide class into two sections.
2. 1/2 class continues text writing.
3. 1/2 class begins to draw mural.
4. Provide newsprint (large sheets).
5. When drawings are complete, submit to the teacher.
6. Give large sheet of carbon paper, and show how to transfer to wall mural paper.

3
+
4

Day 16—Objective K, M

1. Switch groups and proceed as on Day 15.

Day 17—Objective N, R (small group work)

1. Divide class into "fiesta planning" groups.
2. Have paints, brushes, water, etc., ready before class.
3. Assign a student to monitor time.
4. Allow at least 10 minutes to clean up and set up for next class.
5. Other groups develop concrete plans for fiesta (to be submitted by Day 19).

N.B. Each group will plan on one day and paint on the two days allotted for this activity.

Day 18—Objective N, R

1. Switch groups and proceed as on Day 17.

Day 19—Objective N, R

1. Switch groups and proceed as on Day 17.
2. Collect fiesta plans for teacher approval and initials.

Day 20—Objective O (lecture recitation)

1. Begin lesson by asking students to imagine what it would be like to live in a world without words.
2. Discuss notion of specific vocabularies for specific areas; e.g. sports, medicine, music.
3. Ask for examples.
4. Develop notion that class can develop a Mexican glossary.
5. Ask students what they might "do" with the words in a glossary.
6. Use questions to secure answers—spell them, define them, etc.
7. Present Frontier system using overhead projector and transparencies.
8. Allow students to choose a book from the Mexico library shelf which they may be reading or would like to read.
9. Distribute dictionaries and index cards.
10. Ask students to choose four words which they do not know.
11. Select one word to use as a class example, e.g. "hemp." Take students through the Frontier system.

12. Allow students to complete other words similarly.
13. Collect cards to make master list for distribution tomorrow.

3
+
4

Day 21—Objective P, S (guided discovery)

1. Redistribute cards and master list.
2. Distribute contracts. Students contract for a minimum of five and a maximum of twenty words from the master list (spell, define, use in a "context" sentence).
3. Show videotape.
4. Have learning centers set up ahead of time.
5. Give group instructions as to numbers allowed, time allottment, etc.
6. Point out recreational reading table and guidesheets.
7. Students to complete at least two centers, then move to recreational reading table or study vocabulary.

Day 22—Objective Q (inquiry—divergent)

1. Provide materials for students.
2. Have several examples of vocabulary activities, puzzles, games around room.
3. Students may choose words for their game from the master list.
4. Students instructed to design simple game, puzzle, etc., using several glossary words.
5. Extra time should be spent in preparing for vocabulary evaluation.

Day 23—Objective T (convergent)

1. Teacher administers written vocabulary evaluation.
2. Students select those sections which are appropriate to their vocabulary contract.
3. Remaining time used for sharing of games designed yesterday.

N.B. Vocabulary evaluation is competency-based. Students may submit plan for demonstrating skill if scores are not acceptable.

Day 24—Objective U (divergent—guided discovery)

1. Provide multiple sets of option cards.
2. Make sure all necessary materials are available.
3. Instruct students that they will have two class days (and outside time) to complete forty option points (minimum). Any combination of activities will suffice (activities are multi-leveled).
4. Spare time may be spent in playing student-made vocabulary games, etc.

Day 25—Objective U, R

1. Continue work on options.
2. Spare time to be spent in vocabulary work or recreational reading.
3. Take last 15 minutes of class time for groups to make final plans for the fiesta.

Day 26—Objective R, V (small group work)

1. Allow groups to work for 20 minutes on planning fiesta.
2. Groups not needing time may work on vocabulary or options.
3. Remind students that recreational reading activity must be completed by Day 30.
4. Have students check on Objective Sheet for unit to list incomplete assignments.

3
+
4

Day 27—Objective R, V (individualized)

1. Students to work on incomplete activities.
2. Have all materials ready for easy access to students.
3. Groups needing to plan further for fiesta may request that time.

Day 28—Objective W (guided discussion)

1. Distribute a review outline to students.
2. Teacher conducts guided discussion using overhead to prepare for written evaluation.
3. Explain parts, relationship to objectives sheet, etc.

Day 29—Objective X (convergent)

7

1. Written unit evaluation:

objective section	15 minutes	20 points
open-ended sentences	10 minutes	10 points
content essay	20 minutes	20 points
		50 points

2. Have sign-up sheet ready. Students sign up for a five-minute private conference with teacher to discuss overall performance on unit.
3. Check final preparations for fiesta.

Day 30—Objective Y (student-centered activity)

1. Culminating activity for unit.
2. Set up equipment.
3. Coordinate time and assign responsibilities for clean-up, set-up, etc.
4. Go over ground rules for behavior.
5. Wrap up unit by highlighting main concepts and activities covered during last six weeks.

LIST OF MATERIALS NEEDED FOR EACH DAY

Day 1— Slide projector
Screen
Slides on Mexico
Blackboard
Paper and pencils for students

5

8

Day 2— Slide projector
Screen
Record player or tape recorder

8

	Mexican record or tape
	Slides on Mexico
	Worksheet with list of research topics

5

Day 3— Arrangements for library usage
Worksheet to accompany library presentation

Day 4— Teacher-procured materials (public library, embassies,etc.)
School library
Handout on the Cornell method of notetaking

Day 5— Same as Day 4

Day 6— Ten minute cassette lecture for notetaking exercise (teacher-made)
Cassette recorder and earphones for listening station
Classroom library resources

Day 7— Same as Day 6

Day 8— Classroom library resources
School library
Projector, filmstrip viewer, etc., for previewing media

Day 9— Handout on effective speaking techniques
Magazine pictures depicting Mexican "products"

Day 10—Magazine pictures from Day 9
Research resources
Videotape equipment

Day 11—Same as Day 10

Day 12—Lecture or table for a "panel" discussion (hardware as requested by student presenters)
Paper and pencil

Day 13—Same as Day 12
Large sheets of newsprint for planning mural

Day 14—Same as Day 12
Handout on effective writing techniques
Typewriter

Day 15—Handout on effective writing techniques
Typewriter
Paper
Large sheets of newsprint
Large sheets of carbon paper
Paper taped to wall—24′ × 3′

Day 16—Same as Day 15

Day 17—Newsprint for recording ideas for fiesta
Tempera paint
Small containers (three for each color)
Water

Paint brushes (one for each small container)
Paper towels
Sponges

5

Day 18—Same as Day 17

Day 19—Same as Day 17

Day 20—Handout on vocabulary development (overhead projector and transparencies)
Classroom library books
3″ × 5″ file cards
Dictionaries (preferably one for each student)
Contracts

Day 21—Four learning centers (teacher-made vocabulary activities)
Crossword puzzle
Board game
Peg board
Magazines to cut up
Paste
Scissors (each center to be self-contained)
Table with books selected for recreational reading
Guidesheet for reporting on recreational reading
Videotape equipment

Day 22—Materials for students to design vocabulary activities
Old game boards
Posterboards
Scissors
Rubber cement or glue
Masking tape
Marking pens
Colored paper
Graph paper
Typewriter
Cassette tapes and recorder
Blank transparencies
Overhead projector

Day 23—Worksheet to evaluate two vocabulary activities other than the student's own
Paper for vocabulary evaluation (whole group) on contracts

Day 24—Activity packet (materials needed to complete options included in packet)

Day 25—Same as Day 24
Newsprint to finalize planning for fiesta

Day 26—Fiesta planning
Art materials for decorations group
Record player, etc., for music and dance group
Materials for food group to make menus
Table with books selected for recreational reading
Guidesheets for reporting on recreational reading
Materials for fiesta costume groups

Day 27—Same as Day 26
    Materials available for all unfinished activities (check with students ahead of time)

5

Day 28—Review outline for students
    Overhead projector
    Transparencies

Day 29—Teacher-made test
    Open-ended evaluation sheet

7   Point tally sheets

Day 30—Fiesta
    Record player, records
    Projector for slides or film (if students request)
    Tables for food
    Students will request additional materials as needed by each group

EVALUATION OF OBJECTIVES:

N.B. Objectives which have not been circled may be presumed to have been met   6
    satisfactorily unless the teacher specifies something to the contrary to an
    individual student. Group activities require participation by all members.

OBJECTIVE:

A. Students will meet this objective when they participate in the teacher-led discussion
    (target is 75 percent of class participating) and name the topical areas outlined in the
8   objective.

(B.) Students will meet this objective when they complete a worksheet so that it includes a
    one-sentence observation on each of the topics listed in Objective A. Teacher will assign
    a point total from 1 to 5 based upon: relatedness to slides; sentence structure; spelling
    and punctuation. Students will have the opportunity to provide a rationale for their
    sentences in terms of relatedness to the slides.

C. Students will meet this objective when they volunteer to participate in one of five "fiesta
    day" groups. Teacher will question students who choose not to volunteer.

D. Students will meet this objective when, in small groups, they demonstrate that they have
    (1) decided on a process by which they will select a topic; (2) assigned leadership roles;
    and (3) chosen a topic from the list or submitted an alternative proposal.

(E.) Students will meet this objective when they complete a teacher-made worksheet with 90
    percent accuracy.

F. Students will meet this objective when they have participated in a group search for
    materials. This will be evaluated by teacher and library personnel and rated as satisfac-
    tory or unsatisfactory.

(G.) Students will meet this objective when they complete the notetaking activity by using a
    common method to capsulize the three lecture segments. Evaluation will be based upon
    individual comparison of student notes to teacher-made sets to check for 90 percent of
    main points covered in lectures and perfect adherence to the notetaking method.

H. Students will meet this objective when, as determined by teacher observation, they
    demonstrate ability to pursue research topics independently and in groups. Teacher will

note time management, respect for other students, group participation, etc., and advise students if performance is less than satisfactory.

6

I. Students will meet this objective when they have attended the lecture and completed the "commercial" activity. Commercials will be videotaped and evaluated both by students and teacher according to these criteria:

adherence to outline	5 points
presentation	5 points
logical sequence of ideas	3 points
originality	2 points

Teacher will randomly select four students' evaluations and average them, then average that score with his/her score and determine the point total.

J. Students will meet this objective when they present a 10-to-15 minute oral report on their particular topic. Students not presenting reports will take notes using a common method, as teacher observes both presentations and notetaking. Teacher evaluation of oral reports will include the following aspects:

content	25 points
presentation	10 points
media and visual aids	5 points
logical progression of ideas	5 points
introduction and summary	5 points

K. Students will meet this objective when they complete the textwriting assignment. Evaluation will be according to the instrument for determining writing effectiveness which is included in this unit.

L. Students will meet this objective when they use time provided to plan their section of the mural. Evaluation will be by teacher observation.

M. Students will meet this objective when, in groups, they draw their section of the mural, present it to the teacher, and transfer it onto the wallpaper using carbon paper.

N. Students will meet this objective when they decide as a group how they will delegate responsibility for mural painting activity, paint the mural, and complete the commentaries. Evaluation will be according to these criteria:

group process	3 points
painting	4 points
mechanics (clean-up, organization)	1 point
commentaries	2 points

O. Students will meet this objective when they attend the lecture presentation, participate in the discussion, and complete the Frontier vocabulary activity with 100 percent accuracy. (5 points each card)

P. Students will meet this objective when they have viewed the videotape and completed with 100 percent accuracy a minimum of two learning centers. (5 points each center, including recreational reading)

(Q.) Students will meet this objective when, working pairs, they design and complete a vocabulary game or puzzle based upon the master vocabulary list. Evaluation will be based on the following criteria:

6

use of vocabulary words	10 points
group process	3 points
design of game, etc.	4 points
writing of game directions	3 points

(R.) Students will meet this objective when they have, in groups, submitted a plan for their "fiesta" responsibility area. This activity will be evaluated by teacher judgment on:

group process	3 points
feasibility of plan	2 points
clarity of plan	5 points
operationalizing plan	10 points

(S.) Students will meet this objective when they have completed a guidesheet on recreational reading material which will reflect knowledge of:

content	8 points
main idea	4 points
student comment	3 points

(T.) Students will meet this objective when they complete a written test on vocabulary contracts with 100 percent accuracy. Students not achieving perfect scores may submit alternative plans for demonstrating vocabulary competency.

(U.) Students will meet this objective when they select and complete options in activity packet, with a maximum total of 40 points. Options will be evaluated by individual conferences between teacher and student to agree upon a point total.

V. Students will meet this objective when they check their unit objective sheet, note activities to be completed, and compare their findings with teacher records. Students and teacher will confer concerning any discrepancies.

W. Students will meet this objective when they attend the review session and complete the review outline worksheet as directed by teacher. Teacher observation will be the method of observation.

(X.) Students will meet this objective when they have finished a written evaluation based upon the unit. Objective section (20 points, content and reading skills) to be completed with 90 percent accuracy; open-ended sections (10 points, group process, affective objectives) will be satisfied if each sentence is completed; essay response (content, 20 points) will be rated according to the following criteria:

7

mastery of content	15 points
paragraph structure	3 points
clarity of ideas	2 points

Y. Students will meet this objective when they put fiesta plans into operation, attend the class, and voluntarily participate in all scheduled activities. Evaluation will be by teacher observation.

WRITING EVALUATION FOR OBJECTIVE K

Name _____

Group _____ 6

Topic _____

Date _____

	Excellent 8 points	Good 6 points	Average 5 points	Needs Improvement 3 points	Poor 2 points
Content					
Organization					
Language Usage					
Neatness					
Supporting Details					

COMMENTS:

Bibliography
Books

BUSONI, R., *Mexico and the Inca Lands.* Mexico: Holiday House, 1942.

CALDWELL, J. C., *Let's Visit Mexico.* New York: John Day, 1965.

CALVIN, G., *The Lands and Peoples of Central America.* New York: Macmillan, 1961.

CASTILLO, C., *Mexico.* Chicago: Wheeler, 1939.

EISEMAN, A., *Mañana Is Now.* New York: Atheneum, 1974.

EPSTEIN, S. and EPSTEIN, B., *The First Book of Mexico.* New York: Franklin Watts, 1955.

FRANCK, H. A., *Mexico and Central America.* Dansville, New York: F. A. Owen, 1927.

GOMEZ, B., *Getting to Know Mexico.* New York: Coward-McCann, 1959.

JOHNSON, W. W., *Mexico.* New York: Time, Inc., 1966.

KAREN, R., *The Land and People of Central America.* Philadelphia: J. B. Lippincott, 1972.

MARX, M. R., *About Mexico Children.* Chicago: Melmont Publishers, 1959.

MOLNAR, J., *Graciela*. New York: Franklin Watts, 1972.

NEWLON, C., *Famous Mexican-Americans*. New York: Dodd, Mead, 1972.

PAUK, W., *How to Study in College*. Boston: Houghton Mifflin, 1974.

PINCHOT, J., *The Mexicans*. Minneapolis, Minn.: Lerner, 1973.

QUINN, V., *Picture Map Geography of Mexico, Central America and the West Indies*. Philadelphia: J. B. Lippincott, 1943.

ROSS, P. F., *Mexico*. Grand Rapids, Mich.: Fideler, 1955.

WITTON, D., *Our World Mexico*. New York: Julian Messner, 1969.

Published Materials

Mexico, the Cities. *Picture—Story Study Print Set*. Chicago: Society for Visual Education.

Mexico, the Countryside. *Picture—Story Study Print Set*. Chicago: Society for Visual Education.

Mexico, Crafts and Industries. *Picture—Story Study Print Set*. Chicago: Society for Visual Education.

Poetry in Translation

BENSON, R., ed., *Nine Latin American Poets*. New York: Las Americas, 1968.

BODET, J. T., *Selected Poems of Jaime Torres Bodet*. Bloomington: Indiana University Press, 1964.

COPEN, J. M., ed., *The Penguin Book of Spanish Verse*. Baltimore, Md.: Penguin, 1956.

CRAIG, G. D., compiler, *The Modernist Trend in Spanish American Poetry*. Berkeley: University of California Press, 1934.

FITTS, D., ed., *An Anthology of Contemporary Latin American Poetry*. Norfolk: New Directions, 1942.

FLAKOLL, D. J. and C. ALEGRIA, ed., *New Voices of Hispanic America; An Anthology*. Boston: Beacon Press, 1962.

FLORES, A., ed., *An Anthology of Spanish Poetry from Garcilaso to Garcia Larca*. Garden City, N.Y.: Anchor Books, 1961.

GOLDBERG, I., ed., *Mexican Poetry: An Anthology*. Girard, N.Y.: Holdeman-Julius, 1925.

———, *Some Spanish Poets*. New York: Greenwood Press, 1968.

GOROSTIZA, J., *Death Without End*. Austin: University of Texas Press, 1969.

HAYS, H. R., ed., *Twelve Spanish American Poets: An Anthology*. New Haven, Conn.: Yale University Press, 1943.

NERVO, A., *Plenitude*. Los Angeles: J. R. Miller, 1928.

Novo, S., *Nueva Amor*. Portland, Ore.: Mosher Press, 1935.

Paz, O., ed., *Anthology of Mexican Poetry*. Bloomington: Indiana University Press, 1965.

Torri, J., *Julio Torri: Essays and Poems*. New York: Publications of French Studies, 1938.

Underwood, E. W., *Anthology of Mexican Poets: From Earliest Times to Present Day*. Portland, Ore.: Mosher Press, 1932.

Literature

Azuela, M., *The Underdogs*. New York: New American Library, Inc., 1962.

Blue, R., *I Am Here, Yo Estoy Aqui*. New York: Watts, 1971.

DeGerez, T., *2 Rabit 7 Wind: Poems From Ancient Mexico*. New York: Viking, 1971.

Faderman, L., and B. Bradshaw, ed., *Speaking for Ourselves: Contemporary Ethnic Writing*. Palo Alto, Calif.: Scott Foresman, 1979.

Newlon, C., *Famous Mexican-Americans*. New York: Dodd, 1972.

Thomas, P., *Down These Mean Streets*. New York: Knopf, 1967.

Vasquez, R., *Chicano*. New York: Doubleday, 1970.

Short Stories in Translation

Arreola, J. J., *Confabulario and Other Inventions*. Austin, Tex.: University of Texas Press, 1964.

Cohen, J. M., ed., *Latin American Writing Today*. Baltimore, Md.: Penguin Books, 1967.

Donoso, J. and W. Henkin, eds., *The Triquarterly Anthology of Contemporary Latin American Literature*. New York: Dutton, 1969.

Flores, A., and D. Poore, *Fiesta in November: Stories from Latin America*. Boston, Mass.: Houghton Mifflin, 1942.

Jones, W. K., ed., *Spanish American Literature in Translation,* Vols. 1 and 2. New York: Frederick Ungar, 1888.

Martinez, Caceres, and Arturo, In Memoriam: Mexican Short Stories. New York: Vantage Press, 1967.

Onis, H. de, ed., *Spanish Stories and Tales*. New York: Knopf, 1954.

Pietri, A. U., ed., *Prize Stories from Latin America*. New York: Doubleday, 1964.

Rulfo, J., *The Burning Plain and Other Stories*. Austin, Tex.: University of Texas Press, 1967.

Torres-Rioseco, A., *Short Stories of Latin America*. New York: Las Americas, 1963.

Appendix B

LEARNING **A**CTIVITY **P**ACKET

EARLY PEOPLES OF AFRICA

CIVILIZATION IN THE NILE VALLEY—THE ANCIENT EGYPTIANS

Student's full name _____

Section   _____

Content Area   Social Studies _____

                          Mr. Harry B. Dissinger
Instructor   Harrisburg, Pa., School District

LAP on Early People of Africa—THE ANCIENT EGYPTIANS

This is a *Learning Activity Package* (LAP). It was written to help you learn about the Egyptian Civilization.

You will study the *history* of the people who lived in the Nile River Valley. You will also see how *geography* influenced the way in which these people lived.

The *Study Guide* (Objective 4) will help you in your reading about the different roles that the Egyptians played in history. The Egyptians produced great inventors, farmers, writers, builders, embalmers (undertakers), teachers, scientists, and rulers.

You will *learn by doing!*

By making a model of the Great Pyramid you will learn how the Egyptians did it.

By constructing a *Time Line* you will learn the important events that helped to shape the history of ancient Egypt.

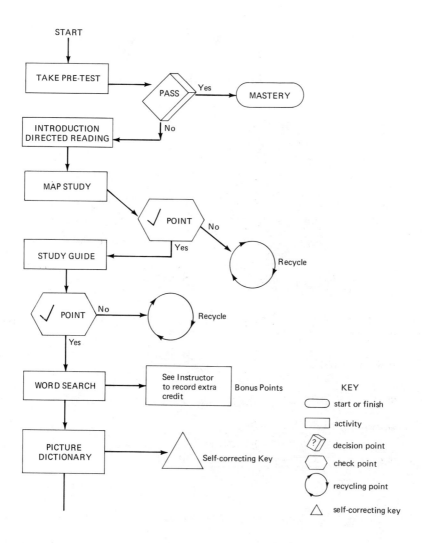

KEY

start or finish

activity

decision point

check point

recycling point

self-correcting key

You will have the opportunity to do a little *creative writing*.

By making a *Dictionary* complete with illustrations you will build your word power.

Finally, you will take a *Post-test* ("post-" means after—so you will take this test *after* you complete objectives 1 through 11) to see how much you have learned by doing these things.

Now you will learn how to read a *flowchart!!*

Then—you will take a *Pre-test* ("pre-" means before) to find out how much you already know about the Egyptians.

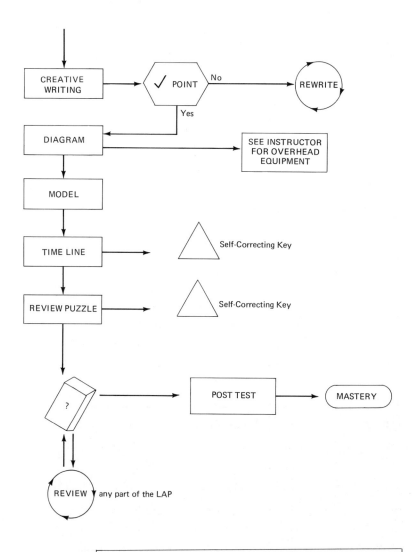

The multi-media learning kit, *Ancient Civilization: Egypt,* #2112, from which parts of this LAP are reprinted may be ordered from the publisher, Instructo/McGraw Hill, Cedar Hollow Road, Paoli, Pennsylvania 19301.

CHECKLIST OF STUDENT ACTIVITIES

Instructions: The objectives for this LAP are listed below. They are numbered from 1 to 12. As you complete each objective check it off and record the date.

_____ Objective #1—Pre-test

_____ Objective #2—Directed Reading—Egypt: Land of the Nile

_____ Objective #3—Map Study—Ancient Egypt

_____ Objective #4—Study Guide—Chapter 4—Early Peoples of Africa

_____ Objective #5—Word Search

_____ Objective #6—Making a Picture Dictionary of Ancient Egypt

_____ Objective #7—Creative Writing—The Building of a Pyramid

_____ Objective #8—Diagram—A cross-sectional view of the Great Pyramid

_____ Objective #9—Constructing a cross-sectional Model of the Great Pyramid

_____ Objective #10—Making a Time Line of Ancient Egyptian History

_____ Objective #11—Pyramid Puzzle—a review

_____ Objective #12—Post-test

Objective Number	Date of Completion	Instructor's initials
#1	_____	_____
#2	_____	_____
#3	_____	_____
#4	_____	_____
#5	_____	_____
#6	_____	_____
#7	_____	_____
#8	_____	_____
#9	_____	_____
#10	_____	_____
#11	_____	_____
#12	_____	_____

Student's Name _____ Section _____

Listed below are the competency levels required for satisfactory completion of each objective in the LAP on ancient Egypt:

OBJECTIVE 1—You will take a pre-test to determine your present level of understanding about the geography and culture of the ancient Egyptians.

Anyone receiving a 15 to a 16 will have the *option to omit* Objectives 2, 5, 8, 9, and 11. Anyone scoring less than 14 on the pre-assessment will be *required* to complete all 12 objectives.

OBJECTIVE 2—Directed Reading—Egypt: Land of the Nile

To complete this objective satisfactorily, you must be able to recognize and underline 85 percent of the vocabulary words upon reading the selection.

OBJECTIVE 3—Map Study: Ancient Egypt

Satisfactory completion of this objective requires that you will be able to:

1. color the Nile Valley and Nile Delta green
2. color the region controlled by ancient Egypt red
3. draw the symbol for the great Pyramid at the city of Gizeh
4. draw a black arrow to indicate the direction in which the Nile River flows
5. color the blocks in the key accurately so that anyone can interpret his or her map
6. locate and label the following: Mediterranean Sea, Nile River, Red Sea, Memphis, Luxor, Aswan, Thebes, Napata, Sinai Peninsula, Gizeh, Nubia
7. use the scale of miles to calculate the distance between the ancient cities Memphis and Napata
8. demonstrate to the instructor accurate use of the four cardinal points of direction

(You must complete the 8 requirements in this objective with 85 percent accuracy.)

OBJECTIVE 4—Study Guide

The Study Guide has been included in the LAP to guide you in your reading of the text, *Old World Backgrounds*, pp. 49–63.

Satisfactory completion of this objective requires that you complete all eleven pages of the Study guide with 85 percent accuracy.

OBJECTIVE 5—Word Search (Vocabulary Recognition Exercise (VRE))

This activity is designed to see how well you recognize the vocabulary of ancient Egypt upon completion of Objective 4 (Study Guide).

This objective is an *extra credit option*—you will be awarded one (1) point for each word that you find in the puzzle.

OBJECTIVE 6—Making a Picture Dictionary of Ancient Egypt

Satisfactory completion of this objective requires that you will be able to:

1. use a dictionary to locate and write the phonetic spelling for each word in the picture dictionary

2. use texts and reference books to write a complete definition for each entry word
3. cut out the correct illustration for each entry word and paste it in the appropriate space

OBJECTIVE 7—Creative Writing: Building of the Pyramids

You will be asked to describe what the workmen are doing in each of three pictures. You will be asked to identify each tool or simple machine being used and tell how it made the work easier.

Satisfactory completion of Objective 7 requires that you:

1. give an accurate and detailed description of each of the three pictures, using a minimum of three complete sentences per picture
2. use sentence structure that is syntactically correct
3. follow rules of punctuation and spelling
4. write legibly

OBJECTIVE 8—Cross-sectional Diagram of the Great Pyramid of Khufu

This objective is a prerequisite to Objective 9 (Model of the Pyramid). You will use a transparency to correctly label the cross-section of the tomb. You will place the correct terms on the appropriate lines.

OBJECTIVE 9—Model of the Great Pyramid

Satisfactory completion of this objective requires that you will be able to:

1. read and follow the instructions given for assembling the model
2. label the following items before assembly process begins: Pharaoh's chamber, queen's chamber, Great Hallway, Entrance, underground passageway

(Anyone who can successfully assemble the model will have fulfilled this requirement.)

OBJECTIVE 10—Time Line of Ancient Egyptian History

Satisfactory completion of this objective requires that you will be able to:

1. write each key date in the correct date block on the time line
2. cut out each picture block and paste it in the correct place corresponding to the event.

OBJECTIVE 11—Pyramid Puzzle

This objective is designed to reinforce your retention of vocabulary utilized in Objective 6 (Picture Dictionary).

You must use the LAP to complete the puzzle with 90 percent accuracy.

OBJECTIVE 12—The Post-Test

Upon completion of Objectives 1–11 you will be given a Post-test.

You must receive an 80 percent or better to pass this objective. Anyone who receives a 79 percent or less will be required to take a re-test—after he/she has reviewed all parts of the LAP indicated by the instructor.

PRE-TEST

Directions: Complete the following statements about the ancient Egyptians by filling in the blanks with the words listed below.

SCRIBE	MUMMY	4236
PAPYRUS	NILE RIVER	HIEROGLYPHICS
3100	MENES	KHUFU
PYRAMID	SHADOOF	ARCHAEOLOGIST
PHARAOH	2600	AFRICA
		1400

Name: _____ Section: _____ Date: _____

1. Egypt is located on the northeastern part of what continent? AFRICA
2. The ancient Egyptians invented a form of picture writing called   HIEROGLYPHICS
3. The Egyptians wrote on   PAPYRUS   which they made from a tall water plant.
4. In ancient Egypt a person whose occupation (job) was writing hieroglyphics was called a SCRIBE .
5. The Egyptians could travel up and down the length of the country using the   NILE   RIVER   as a "highway."
6. A   MUMMY   was a dead body that Egyptians embalmers preserved from decay.
7. An   ARCHAEOLOGIST   is a scientist who studies people, customs, and life of ancient times.
8.   PHARAOH   was the title of the ruler of ancient Egypt.
9. A PYRAMID   was a huge ancient Egyptian tomb with a square base and sloping sides which meet at a point at the top.
10. Egyptian farmers used a device called a   SHADOOF   to irrigate their fields. It was a long pole with a bucket at one end and a weight on the other.

Key Dates and Events in Ancient Egyptian History

11. In   4236   B.C. the Egyptians invented a 365-day solar calendar.
12. In 3100 B.C. Pharaoh   MENES   united upper and lower Egypt into one Kingdom.
13. In   3100   B.C. Egyptians invented a form of "picture writing" called hieroglyphics.
14. In   2600   B.C. the Pharaoh   KHUFU   built the Great Pyramid at Gizeh.
15. In   1400   B.C. Egyptian power reached its peak during the rule of Amenhotep III.

Pre-assessment Score _____

Note—If you scored *less than* 14 on the Pre-test go on to OBJECTIVE #2 in the LAP, and complete the entire packet. If you scored between 15 and 16 you may *omit* Objectives 2, 5, 8, 9, and 11.

EGYPT: LAND OF THE NILE—Objective #2—Directed Reading

Directions: As you read the selection *underline* the following words and phrases:

In paragraph #1—*underline*—Egypt is located/Africa/Mediterranean Sea/Red Sea
In paragraph #2—*underline*—ancient/Egyptians/Nile River/"highway"

In paragraph #3—*underline*—Nile/longest river in the world—4,160 miles long/flow north-
ward/delta/fanshaped piece of land/mouth of a river/soil/
good for growing crops

In paragraph #4—*underline*—desert/little land/for farming/yearly average rainfall/less than
ten inches/summer temperature/over 100°F./winter temper-
ature/seldom below 40°F.

NOTE—See Instructor for Transparency on Ancient Egypt when you are ready to do map
exercise.

You will also need a *red* and a *green* color pencil.

Reminder—labels in all capital letters—use PENCIL ONLY!!

Take DIRECTED READING (Objective #2) and MAP STUDY (Objective #3) to your teacher
for discussion and approval!

Instructor's initials: _____

NOTE—Check your *flowchart* to see where you are now, and where you are going next!!

Text, *World Background for American History*. Authors: Eigling, King, Harlow, James.
Publisher: Laidlaw Brothers. recommended reading level: Middle School 6–8.

STUDY GUIDE—Early Peoples of Africa

CIVILIZATION IN THE NILE VALLEY—Chapter 4
****

On Page 49 you will begin to study the civilization that developed in the Nile Valley.

A Good Place to Live

1. Describe conditions in the Nile Valley that attracted New Stone Age settlers:

   A. climate _____

   B. clothes material _____

   C. food _____ and _____ : _____ and _____

The Gift of the Nile

2. What happened in the Nile Valley every summer? (sentence) _____

   _____

3. One early historian called Egypt the "_____" because it gave water and rich
   soil.

EGYPT: LAND OF THE NILE

Egypt is located in the northeastern part of Africa. The Mediterranean Sea lies north of it and the Red Sea lies to the east.

In ancient times Egypt was a long and narrow country. Egyptians could travel up and down the length of the country using the Nile River as a "highway"

The Nile is the longest river in the world — 4,160 miles long. The waters of the Nile flow northward from the highlands of central Africa to the Mediterranean Sea. At its Mediterranean end the Nile has formed a large delta. A delta is a fan-shaped piece of land at the mouth of a river. The Nile Delta is made up of mud and sand that is carried down the river. The soil of the delta is good for growing crops.

Most of Egypt is a dry, desert land. Except for the fertile Nile Valley and Delta, there is little land that can be used for farming. The yearly average rainfall is less than ten inches. The summer temperature is often over 100° F. in the shade. In the winter the days are sunny and the temperature seldom falls below 40° F.

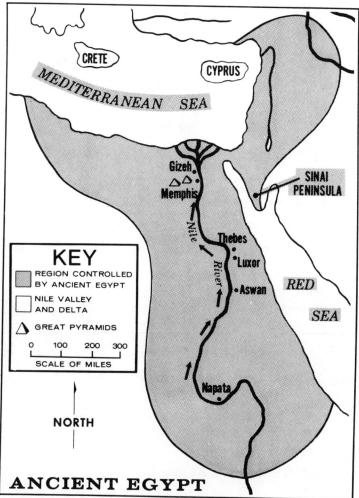

Directions:

1. Color the Nile Valley and Nile Delta green.

2. Color the region of ancient Egypt red.

3. Draw the symbol for the Great Pyramid at the city of Gizeh.

4. Draw a black arrow to indicate the direction in which the Nile River flows.

5. Locate and label the following:
   Mediterranean Sea
   Nile River
   Red Sea
   Memphis
   Luxor
   Aswan
   Thebes
   Napata
   Sinai Peninsula

6. Make sure you color the blocks in the key so that others can read your map.

4. On Page 50 you are told *two ways* that the Nile river could be *treacherous*.

   A. If not enough rain came, how did it affect the people? (sentence) _____

   _____

   B. If too much rain came, what happened? (sentence) _____

   _____

The World's First Calendar

1. What was the name of the star that guided the Egyptians in making a calendar?

   _____ , sometimes called the _____ _____ .

2. The Egyptian Calendar

   A. How many moons? _____

   B. What marked the beginning of the Egyptian new year? _____

   C. How many days in their month? _____

   D. This made a total of how many days in the year? _____

   E. How many feast days were there? _____

   F. With feast days, how many days in an Egyptian year? _____

   G. Egyptian calendar was inaccurate (incorrect) because _____

   _____

On Page 51—*Egyptian Farmers Learn to Irrigate*

1. Farmers *diverted* flood waters into _____ and _____ .

2. The Egyptians invented a machine called _____ to lift water into their canals.

   EXTRA CREDIT—Trace the cartoon drawing on Page 51—write the caption underneath the picture and color the water blue.

3. Turn to the glossary on Page 417, write the definition of *"civilization"*

   civilization _____

   _____

Nobles, Freemen, Slaves

1. Tell about the nobles. (sentences) _____

   _____

   _____

2. What did the *slaves* do? (1 sentence) _____

   _____

3. The _____ farmers were very important to Egypt. The _____ they

grew in the Nile Valley was Egypt's main source of _____ . Eventually, the Mediterranean countries grew so much grain that Egypt became known as the

" _____ ." (top of Page 52)

4. List other groups of freemen in Egypt, whose skilled hands made them craftsmen.

_____   _____   _____

_____   _____   _____

One King Rules Egypt—Page 52

5. What King (or *pharaoh* as Egyptian rulers were called) brought all of Egypt under

his control? _____ Pronounced (mē - n$\overline{e}$z)

On *Page 53* you will learn about Egyptian rule.

1. What is a dynasty? _____

_____

2. Egypt had _____ such dynasties in all, and they ruled for a total of nearly

_____ years.

The Government of Egypt

3. In Egypt the kings and _____ were thought to be _____ . The king's

word was _____ . Every _____ , _____ and _____

paid _____ in the form of _____ or _____ because Egypt did

not have _____ until 300 B.C.

4. The king (or pharaoh) could not govern the whole country alone. He appointed

_____ to help him. His most important assistants were the _____ ,

the _____ , the chief _____ and the _____ of _____ .

5. The country was divided into provinces called _____ . Each nome had a

_____ appointed by the _____ . Each town in the nome had a

_____ who was responsible to the _____ _____ .

A Land of Many Gods

1. Because the _____ was thought to be a god-king, _____ and

_____ were closely related.

2. Who was the most important of the Egyptian gods? _____

Pronounced (ra). He was the god of the _____ .

3. The Egyptians thought gods sometimes took the form of _____ .

4. What animals are mentioned as being sacred (religious)?

   _____   _____   _____

5. One ruler, King _____ (ä′ kë - nä t′ n), did away with all the gods except one.

6. (see caption under picture—Page 53)
   Unlike previous rulers of Egypt, Akhenaten believed that only _____

   _____ , _____ (ā′ tōn) existed.

On Page 54 we begin to look into the Egyptian's feelings about death.

Preserving the Dead—Page 54

1. In what two things did the Egyptians believe strongly? (sentences)

   A.   _____

   B.   _____

2. Tell how Egyptian *embalmers* preserved the body? (sentences)

   They treated it . . . . _____

   _____

3. What was the treated dead body called? _____

Tombs and Pyramids—Page 54

1. Many kings were buried in _____ _____ carved out of solid rock in a

   place near Thebes called _____ _____ _____ _____ .

2. About _____ kings built _____ which were towering, four-sided stone tombs that came to a point on top.

3. Check the *glossary* on page 421 for a definition of *pyramid*.

   Pyramid _____

   _____

4. What fact is incredible (amazing) about the building of the pyramids? (sentence)

   They were built . . . . _____

   _____

5. What simple machines were used to construct (build) the pyramids? (See caption above the picture.)—Page 54

   _____   _____   _____

6. Labor that went into the building of the pyramids was supplied by _____

   _____ (two words) and _____ . (Page 55)

7. Craftsmen made fine _____ , _____ , or _____ for the tombs of kings.

8. The most famous pyramid is one near the city of _____ . It is called the

_____ _____ (two words) because of its huge size. One early historian

recorded that it took _____ men more than _____ years to build it.

Preparing for the Afterlife—Pages 55–56

1. Egyptians believed that the _____ of a dead person (called the Ka) would use the same things that the person had used in life. They placed such things

as _____ , _____ , _____ , _____ , _____ ,

_____ , _____ , _____ , and _____ in the tombs.

2. _____ even found a _____ - _____ boat in a secret room under one pyramid.

3. Because the *climate* of Egypt was _____ many things were preserved for thousands of years.

4. Look at the picture at the top of page 56. What are the Egyptians doing in the picture? (refer to caption underneath the picture) (two sentences)

The Egyptians are . . . . _____

_____

_____

Why do you think that two of the Egyptians have shaved their heads bald?

_____

Egyptian Writing—Pages 56–57

1. The Egyptians invented a form of picture writing called _____ . Each

_____ stood for a number of things in the language.

2. Eventually the Egyptians developed a system called _____ . (p. 57) This system

was based on *hieroglyphics*, but the symbols were written with _____ on soft materials.

A Better Writing Material—Page 57

1. At first Egyptians probably used _____ as a writing surface.
2. Then someone discovered that a better writing material could be made from

_____ , a reed that grew wild along the _____ .

3. Explain how paper was made in ancient Egypt. (sentences)

Workmen split the . . . . _____

_____

_____

_____

_____

4. The Egyptians made ink from _____ .

5. They made pens by _____ .

6. The world's first books were called _____ . They were made by rolling long

_____ on _____ _____ .

The next activity in your LAP is called _Ancient Writing._ Below the _sub-title:_ "Information for the Amateur Archaeologist," are three paragraphs. As you read these paragraphs _underline_ the following words and phrases:

In paragraph #1—_underline_—Egyptian writing/3100 B.C./hieroglyphics/"sacred carvings."

In paragraph #2—_underline_—first/they used/a picture to represent a word/They changed their writing system/one symbol/to represent one sound/ pictures to represent/whole words

In paragraph #3—_underline_—Hieroglyphics/carved into/Egyptian temples/tombs/trans- lating/archaeologists/discover

Children Go to School—Page 58

1. Why was there a great need for keeping records in Egypt? (sentence)

   There was a great need . . . . _____

2. What were writers (before printing) called? _____

3. A _____ had to learn to use about _____ symbols.

4. When you were in the second or third grade you learned that our alphabet had

   _____ letters. (Think of all the hours of practice your teachers have given you in writing 26 letters. Imagine how long it would have taken you to learn all the symbols in Egyptian writing!!)

5. Do you think an Egyptian school would be _harder_ or _easier_ than yours? Why? ____

   _____

6. What were Egyptian boys taught in school? _____

   _____

7. What about girls? _____ . Do you think this

   was fair? Why? _____

8. Do you think that boys and girls should be given an equal chance to learn? Why?

   _____

ANCIENT WRITING

INFORMATION FOR THE AMATEUR ARCHEOLOGIST

The earliest examples of Egyptian writing date back to 3100 B.C. This form of writing, which was called hieroglyphics, was based on pictures. Hieroglyphics means "sacred carvings."

When Egyptians first began to write they used a picture to represent a word. The pictures had to be drawn very carefully so that they could be understood. As time passed the Egyptians found that they needed too many pictures to tell their stories. They changed their writing system, trying to make it easier to use. Finally, they decided to write one symbol to represent one sound in the language, keeping certain pictures to represent certain whole words.

Hieroglyphics have been found carved into the walls and pillars of Egyptian temples. They have also been found in the great tombs. By translating hieroglyphics, archeologists have been able to discover much about ancient Egyptian life.

DIRECTIONS
1. Below is a make-believe message that was found on an imaginary archeological expedition. It was found in a tomb of a great pharaoh. Use the decoding key to decode the message.
2. On the back of this page write a paragraph describing the pharaoh.

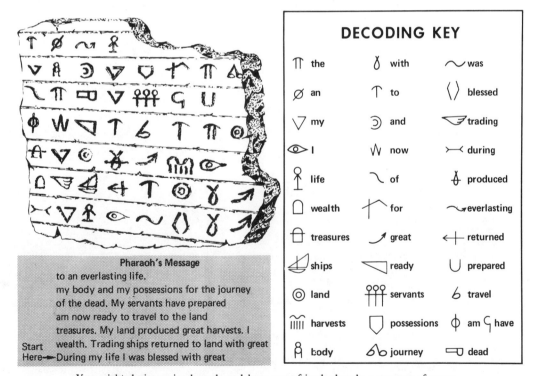

Pharaoh's Message

to an everlasting life.
my body and my possessions for the journey
of the dead. My servants have prepared
am now ready to travel to the land
treasures. My land produced great harvests. I
wealth. Trading ships returned to land with great
Start Here→ During my life I was blessed with great

DECODING KEY

⑪ the	⑧ with	～ was
∅ an	⑦ to	⟨⟩ blessed
▽ my	⤳ and	⪦ trading
◉ I	⩗ now	⤝ during
⑂ life	⤵ of	⑃ produced
⏏ wealth	⤙ for	～↗ everlasting
⊟ treasures	⤴ great	←+ returned
⛴ ships	◿ ready	∪ prepared
◎ land	⦀ servants	⑥ travel
⏜ harvests	⏝ possessions	φ am ⑀ have
⑃ body	⑥⊙ journey	⫿ dead

You might devise a simple code and have your friends decode a message of yours.

Unlocking the Past—Page 58

1. In 1799, a French visitor to Egypt made an important discovery near what city?

   _____ . He found a broken piece of stone. It is called the _____

   _____ .

** (refer to picture at top of page 58 and captions below and to the right of the picture to answer the next two questions)

2. The message on the Rosetta Stone was written in what three languages?

   _____   _____   _____

3. The _____ inscription on this stone provided a _____ to ancient

   _____ _____ .

Other Accomplishments—Page 59

1. List the three courses taught in Egyptian universities.

   studied diseases _____

   studied the stars _____

   learned to measure distances for boundary lines to property _____

   _____

(see caption above picture)—Page 59

2. Egyptians gave the world the beginnings of _____ when they learned to

   _____ land in order to re-establish _____ that had been eliminated during

   the annual _____ of the Nile.

Egypt is Invaded—Page 59

1. Egyptians found two natural separations from other people. In a sentence tell what

   they were. Vast deserts . . . . _____

   _____

2. In 1730 B.C. Egypt was invaded by fierce tribes called the _____ . They came

   from _____ . pronounced (hĭk′ šōs)

3. These warriors fought from war _____ pulled by _____ .

A Period of Turmoil—Page 60

1. How long did the Hyksos rule? _____ (years)

2. Egypt was unable to obtain a lasting peace because Egyptian kings became

   involved in wars for _____ . In the next _____ years, Egypt built and

   lost three _____ .

3. By 525 B.C. Egypt lost its _____ for good. In that year the _____ took
   over Egypt.

OTHER CIVILIZATIONS IN AFRICA

The Kingdom of Kush—Page 60

(Read the caption above the picture to answer the next two questions)

1. From the picture at the bottom (Page 60) what do you notice about the skin color of
   the fighters?

   Their skin color is: _____ , which means that Kush was
   probably the world's first Black Kingdom.

2. From the picture's caption (Page 60) what four things can you tell about the
   Kushites?

   A. _____

   B. _____

   C. _____

   D. _____

**Look at the picture on Page 61 and read the last paragraph on the left side of the
   page.

1. Kush lost Egypt to another _____ , but retained her own _____ .

   Meroe (Mĕr′ ō ē) became the _____ and center of the _____

   industry in _____ (continent).

2. Much of the story of ancient Kush is yet to be learned. No one has been able to fully

   _____ the Kushite _____ . The ruins of Meroe hold many _____
   of Kushite life.

3. _____ was the religious center of Kush. (nā pă′ tā)

The Phoenician Colony of Carthage—Page 61

1. One other _____ developed in North Africa in ancient times.

2. In 814 B.C. a trading colony called _____ (Kär′ thĭj) was established by
   Phoenician traders.

3. This colony became one of the most powerful countries around the _____
   Sea.

Africa South of the Sahara—Page 62

1. Early _____ tribes had not developed a _____ _____ (two words) in ancient times in _____ south of the _____ (desert).

2. Examine the picture on page 62 to describe the homes of the early African blacks. Early African blacks lived in . . . . _____

   _____

3. When did permanent settlements begin to develop in early Africa?

   (sentence) _____

CHECKPOINT—Objective #4

Take the Study Guide to your Teacher for discussion and approval

***** Extra Credit Report ***** Instructor's Initials _____

Directions: Using the Resource book, *A Glorious Age in Africa,* choose to read a story about *one* of the three great African empires. Your choices are: Ghana (pp. 13–50); Mali (pp. 51–78); or Songhay (pp. 79–112).

1. As you read the selection
2. Write *fifteen to twenty* facts about the story that interested you.
3. Trace the map of the kingdom which you reported on.
4. Paper for the report and the map are included in the LAP.

NOTE—Your report and map will be handed in separately when you have completed all of the objectives in the LAP.

Reading Reaction

1. Did you find the reading in *A Glorious Age in Africa easy* or *hard* to understand?

   _____

2. Was the story you read interesting? _____ Yes _____ No (Check one)

3. Do you like the idea of reporting on what you have read? _____ Yes _____ No

4. Did you understand exactly what to do after you read the directions? _____ Yes _____ No

5. Was it hard for you to find fifteen interesting facts in the story you read? _____ Yes _____ No

EGYPTIAN *WORD SEARCH*—Objective #5

Nile	hieroglyphics	papyrus	gods	king
flax	waterfowl	scrolls	cat	Africa
fish	calendar	reed	cow	huts
clay	Egyptians	irrigate	mummy	read
stone	landowners	shadoof	Kushites	write
flood	geometry	nobles	Sahara	dry
soil	craftsmen	freeman	Mali	desert
land	crocodile	slaves	Negro	death
tax	dynasty	farm	Sudan	lever
river	pyramids	valley	rule	ramp

S	I	S	D	I	M	A	R	Y	P	G	O	D	S	K
A	P	E	L	A	N	D	O	W	N	E	R	S	O	U
H	T	A	E	D	S	H	A	D	O	O	F	I	C	S
I	R	R	I	G	A	T	E	A	T	M	L	N	A	H
S	Y	N	I	L	E	L	L	A	T	E	O	G	L	I
R	D	A	E	R	V	G	C	P	S	T	O	N	E	T
U	S	E	F	I	S	H	Y	A	U	R	D	A	N	E
L	O	O	X	S	O	I	L	P	S	Y	P	O	D	S
E	W	A	O	R	G	E	N	Y	T	K	C	U	A	M
L	T	R	E	V	I	R	L	R	U	I	R	S	R	U
I	T	Y	R	D	O	O	E	U	H	N	A	A	I	M
D	T	O	P	Y	D	G	T	S	X	G	F	N	M	M
O	R	A	D	N	E	L	A	C	O	W	T	O	S	Y
C	E	D	Y	A	E	Y	R	R	A	R	S	B	M	P
O	S	D	E	S	R	P	A	O	F	I	M	L	A	M
R	E	N	L	T	E	H	H	L	R	T	E	E	L	A
C	D	A	L	Y	V	I	A	L	I	E	N	S	I	R
S	F	L	A	X	E	C	S	S	C	L	Y	A	L	C
A	S	E	V	A	L	S	O	N	A	M	E	E	R	F

Directions: *Circle* the words hidden in the puzzle. You may read up, down, forward, backward, or diagonally.

Dictionary of Terms—Ancient Egypt (to be used with Objective #6)

1. *archaeologist* (är′ kē äl′ ə jist)—A scientist who studies people, customs, and life of ancient times.
2. *delta* (del′ tə)—The deposit of earth and sand that collects at the mouth of a river.
3. *desert* (dez′ ərt)—Dry, sandy region; land too dry to grow many plants.
4. *flail* (flāl)—An instrument used for threshing grain by hand; symbol of the pharaoh's power as ruler of Egypt.
5. *funeral barge* (fyōō′ nər əl bärj)—Boat used to carry the coffin of a dead pharaoh across the Nile River to his pyramid.
6. *hieroglyphics* (hī′ər ə glif′ iks)—Writing system invented by the ancient Egyptians. Means "sacred carvings."
7. *mummy* (mum′ ē)—Body of a dead animal or human being preserved from decay by ancient Egyptian embalmers.
8. *oasis* (ō ā′ sis)—A fertile spot in the desert where there is water.
9. *obelisk* (ō′ bə lisk)—Ancient Egyptian monument; a four-sided shaft with top shaped like a pyramid.
10. *papyrus* (pə pī′ rəs)—A tall water plant used to make "Egyptian paper."
11. *pharaoh* (fer′o)—Title of the ruler of ancient Egypt—ex. Khufu.
12. *pottery* (pöt′ər ē)—Clay pots, dishes, or vases made by potters and hardened by heat.
13. *pyramid* (pir′ ə mid)—Huge, ancient Egyptian tomb with a square base and sloping sides meeting at a point at the top.
14. *scribe* (skrīb)—In ancient Egypt, a person whose occupation was writing hieroglyphics.
15. *shadoof* (shä dōōf)—Device used by Egyptian farmers to irrigate their fields. A long pole with a bucket at one end and a weight on the other end.
16. *valley* (val′ ē)—Lowland area between two hills or mountains—ex. Nile Valley.

MAKING A PICTURE DICTIONARY OF ANCIENT EGYPT

1. Cut out the correct picture for each entry word and paste it in place. Pictures for each entry word can be found on page 11 or page 12.
2. Use texts and reference books to write a complete definition for each entry word. Write the phonetic spelling for each entry word in the parentheses following the word. A dictionary may be helpful.
3. After completing the work above make a booklet. Cut along top lines of booklet as indicated. Fold along dashed line in center of each page. Paste the back of booklet page 2 to the back of booklet page 3. Make a suitable, colorful cover for your picture dictionary.

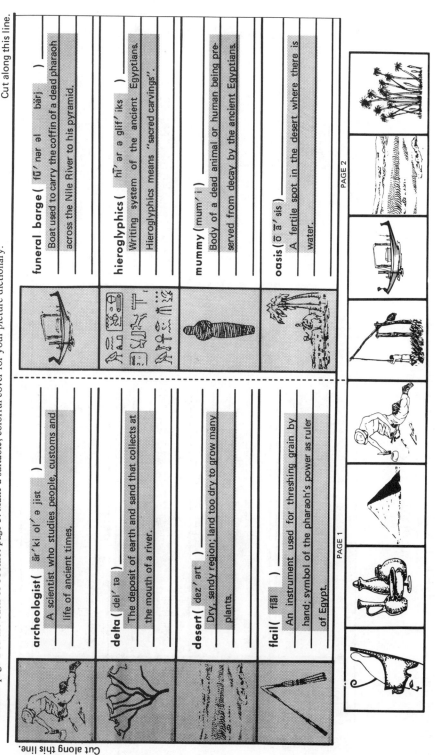

funeral barge (fū′ nər əl   bärj   )
Boat used to carry the coffin of a dead pharaoh across the Nile River to his pyramid.

hieroglyphics (hī′ ər ə glif′ iks   )
Writing system of the ancient Egyptians. Hieroglyphics means "sacred carvings".

mummy (mum′ i)
Body of a dead animal or human being preserved from decay by the ancient Egyptians.

oasis (ō ā′ sis)
A fertile spot in the desert where there is water.

PAGE 2

Cut along this line.

archeologist (är′ ki ol′ ə jist   )
A scientist who studies people, customs and life of ancient times.

delta (del′ tə)
The deposit of earth and sand that collects at the mouth of a river.

desert (dez′ ərt)
Dry, sandy region; land too dry to grow many plants.

flail (flāl   )
An instrument used for threshing grain by hand; symbol of the pharaoh's power as ruler of Egypt.

PAGE 1

363

MAKING A PICTURE DICTIONARY OF ANCIENT EGYPT

(CONTINUED)

Cut along this line.

pyramid (pĭr′ ə mĭd **)**
Huge, ancient Egyptian tomb with square base and sloping sides meeting at a point at the top.

scribe (skrīb **)**
In ancient Egypt a person whose occupation was writing hieroglyphics.

shadoof (shä düf′ **)**
A long pole with a bucket at one end and a weight on the other. Device used by Egyptian farmers to irrigate their fields.

valley (văl′ ĭ **)**
Lowland area between hills or mountains.

PAGE 4

obelisk (ŏb′ ə lĭsk **)**
Ancient Egyptian monument; four-sided shaft of stone with top shaped like a pyramid.

papyrus (pə pī′ rəs **)**
A tall water plant used to make "Egyptian paper".

pharaoh (fâr′ ō **)**
Title for the ruler of ancient Egypt.

pottery (pŏt′ ər ĭ **)**
Clay pots, dishes or vases made by potters and hardened by heat.

PAGE 3

Cut along this line.

364

THE BUILDING OF A PYRAMID

On the lines provided describe what the workers are doing in each picture.
Identify each tool being used and tell how it makes the work easier.

Cutting the Stone

At the stone quarry workmen cut huge blocks of granite for the pyramid of an Egyptian pharaoh. Copper chisels and dolerite (coarse-grained basalt rock) hammers are used to chip away the rough spots on the stone.

Moving the Stone

Quarry workmen load granite blocks weighing several tons onto a wooden sledge. Workmen use log rollers and sledges to move the rough cut blocks to barges waiting along the banks of the Nile.

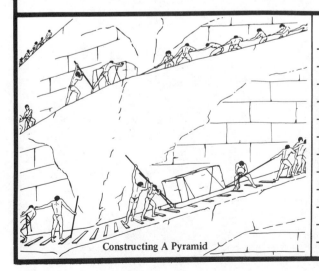

Constructing A Pyramid

Ramps are built along the four sides of the pyramid. Workmen use sledges and levers to haul heavy stone blocks up the ramp. Logs are placed under the sledges to reduce friction. One layer of blocks is placed atop another until the pyramid is completed.

TAKE PICTURE DICTIONARY (Objective #6) and CREATIVE WRITING (Objective #7) to your instructor for discussion and approval!!

Instructor's initials: _____

COMMENTS:

NOTE—Check your *flowchart* again to see where you are now, and where you are going next!

THE GREAT PYRAMID OF PHARAOH KHUFU

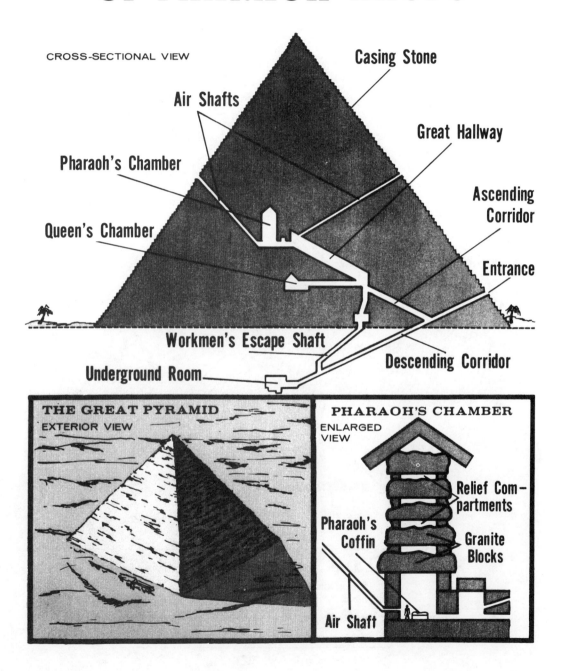

CROSS-SECTIONAL VIEW

Casing Stone

Air Shafts

Great Hallway

Pharaoh's Chamber

Ascending Corridor

Queen's Chamber

Entrance

Workmen's Escape Shaft

Descending Corridor

Underground Room

THE GREAT PYRAMID
EXTERIOR VIEW

PHARAOH'S CHAMBER
ENLARGED VIEW

Relief Compartments

Pharaoh's Coffin

Granite Blocks

Air Shaft

CONSTRUCTING A CROSS-SECTIONAL MODEL OF THE GREAT PYRAMID

1. Use the terms listed below to correctly label the cross section of the tomb. Place each on the appropriate line.

   Pharaoh's Chamber

   Queen's Chamber

   Great Hallway

   Entrance

   Underground Passage

2. Cut out along outside edges of pyramid on solid lines.

3. Fold on solid lines where arrows indicate.

4. Paste flap under side A.

Your pyramid should look like this:

Try putting two models together to make a whole pyramid.

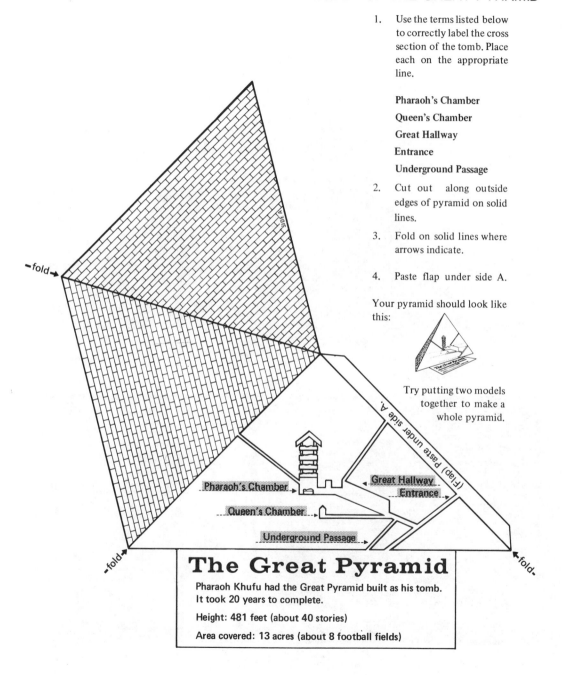

fold

side A

(Flap) paste under side A.

Pharaoh's Chamber

Great Hallway

Entrance

Queen's Chamber

Underground Passage

fold

fold

The Great Pyramid

Pharaoh Khufu had the Great Pyramid built as his tomb. It took 20 years to complete.

Height: 481 feet (about 40 stories)

Area covered: 13 acres (about 8 football fields)

MAKING A TIME LINE
ANCIENT EGYPTIAN HISTORY

Name _____

Key Dates in Ancient Egyptian History

4236 BC	The Egyptians invent a 365-day solar calendar.
3100 BC	Pharaoh Menes unites Upper and Lower Egypt into one kingdom.
3100 BC	The Egyptians invent a form of picture writing called hieroglyphics.
2600 BC	Pharaoh Khufu builds the Great Pyramid at Gizeh.
1400 BC	Egyptian power reaches its peak during the rule of Amenhotep III.

DIRECTIONS

1. Cut along heavy solid line.
2. Write each key date in the correct date block on the time line.
3. Cut out each picture block and paste it in place.

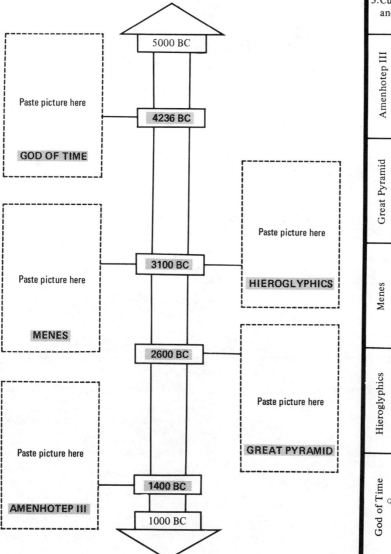

Paste picture here

GOD OF TIME

Paste picture here

MENES

Paste picture here

AMENHOTEP III

5000 BC

4236 BC

3100 BC

2600 BC

1400 BC

1000 BC

Paste picture here

HIEROGLYPHICS

Paste picture here

GREAT PYRAMID

Amenhotep III

Great Pyramid

Menes

Hieroglyphics

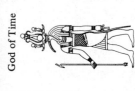
God of Time

369

PYRAMID PUZZLE

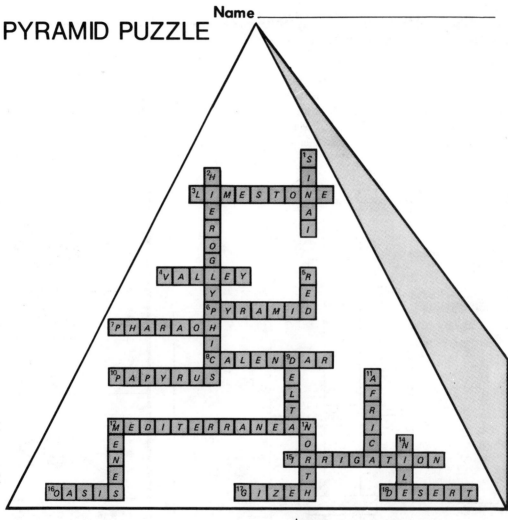

Complete the crossword puzzle in the pyramid.

Across

3. A kind of stone used by Egyptians in building tombs
4. Lowland area between hills or mountains
6. Huge tomb with square base and sloping sides meeting at the top
7. Title for ruler of ancient Egypt
8. Table used for dividing time into days, weeks, years
10. Plant used to make "Egyptian paper"
12. Large sea located north of Egypt
15. Method of supplying water from a main source by means of canals and ditches
16. A fertile spot in the desert where there is water
17. Site of the Great Pyramid
18. Dry, sandy region; land too dry to grow many plants

Down

1. Peninsula of ancient Egypt lying north of Red Sea
2. Writing system of the ancient Egyptians
5. Sea located east of Egypt
9. Earth and sand deposited at the mouth of a river
11. Continent on which Egypt is located
12. Pharaoh who united Upper Egypt and Lower Egypt
13. The Nile River flows in this direction
14. World's longest river

Student Evaluation

How do you feel about the work you have done in this LAP?

Did the LAP help you improve your reading?

Grade you think you deserve _____ . Why?

Teacher Evaluation Form

Student performance level: OBJECTIVE 1: _____

OBJECTIVE 2: _____

OBJECTIVE 3: _____

OBJECTIVE 4: _____

OBJECTIVE 5: _____

OBJECTIVE 6: _____

OBJECTIVE 7: _____

OBJECTIVE 8: _____

OBJECTIVE 9: _____

OBJECTIVE 10: _____

OBJECTIVE 11: _____

OBJECTIVE 12: _____

Culminating activity—final LAP _____

Grade _____

COMMENTS:

Student's Name _____ Section _____

Appendix C

1. a		18. c
2. d		19. d
3. b		20. a
4. c		21. c
5. a		22. d
6. a		23. c
7. d		24. d
8. a		25. a
9. c		26. d
10. d		27. c
11. b		28. b
12. a		29. a
13. b		30. c
14. c		31. c
15. d		32. d
16. a		33. b
17. b		34. c

Index

Index

47706

Dupuis, Mary M.

LB
1050.45   Content area
D86   reading
1982